Operating System Basics and Practice

Jiasheng Hao • Yindong Xiao •
Wenjian Zhou • Peicheng Wang •
Huawei Technologies Co., Ltd.

Operating System Basics and Practice

A Hands-on Approach with openEuler

Springer

Jiasheng Hao
School of Automation
University of Electronic Science and
Technology of China
Chengdu, Sichuan, China

Yindong Xiao
School of Automation
University of Electronic Science and
Technology of China
Chengdu, Sichuan, China

Wenjian Zhou
School of Automation
University of Electronic Science and
Technology of China
Chengdu, Sichuan, China

Peicheng Wang
School of Automation
University of Electronic Science and
Technology of China
Chengdu, Sichuan, China

Huawei Technologies Co., Ltd.
Shenzhen, China

ISBN 978-981-95-2184-5   ISBN 978-981-95-2185-2   (eBook)
https://doi.org/10.1007/978-981-95-2185-2

Jointly published with Posts & Telecom Press.
The print edition is not for sale in Mainland China. Customers from Mainland China please order the print book from: Posts & Telecom Press.

This work was supported by Huawei Technologies Co., Ltd..

© Posts & Telecom Press Co., Ltd 2026. This book is an open access publication.

Open Access This book is licensed under the terms of the Creative Commons Attribution-NonCommercial-NoDerivatives 4.0 International License (http://creativecommons.org/licenses/by-nc-nd/4.0/), which permits any noncommercial use, sharing, distribution and reproduction in any medium or format, as long as you give appropriate credit to the original author(s) and the source, provide a link to the Creative Commons license and indicate if you modified the licensed material. You do not have permission under this license to share adapted material derived from this book or parts of it.

The images or other third party material in this book are included in the book's Creative Commons license, unless indicated otherwise in a credit line to the material. If material is not included in the book's Creative Commons license and your intended use is not permitted by statutory regulation or exceeds the permitted use, you will need to obtain permission directly from the copyright holder.

This work is subject to copyright. All commercial rights are reserved by the author(s), whether the whole or part of the material is concerned, specifically the rights of translation, reprinting, reuse of illustrations, recitation, broadcasting, reproduction on microfilms or in any other physical way, and transmission or information storage and retrieval, electronic adaptation, computer software, or by similar or dissimilar methodology now known or hereafter developed. Regarding these commercial rights a non-exclusive license has been granted to the publisher.

The use of general descriptive names, registered names, trademarks, service marks, etc. in this publication does not imply, even in the absence of a specific statement, that such names are exempt from the relevant protective laws and regulations and therefore free for general use.

The publishers, the authors, and the editors are safe to assume that the advice and information in this book are believed to be true and accurate at the date of publication. Neither the publishers nor the authors or the editors give a warranty, express or implied, with respect to the material contained herein or for any errors or omissions that may have been made. The publishers remain neutral with regard to jurisdictional claims in published maps and institutional affiliations.

This Springer imprint is published by the registered company Springer Nature Singapore Pte Ltd.
The registered company address is: 152 Beach Road, #21-01/04 Gateway East, Singapore 189721, Singapore

If disposing of this product, please recycle the paper.

Foreword

Digital Growth Through Base Software Expertise

The technological landscape has shifted due to changes in cloud computing and artificial intelligence (AI), particularly through the rapid rise of large language models that transform how humans engage with machines. These emerging technologies are redefining modes of production and daily human interactions. At the core of these advancements lies base software, a core technology essential to the future of the information industry and the digital economy.

Base software is a robust platform and a backbone for essential functions like data processing, network communication, and system security. There is a strong demand for reliable and efficient base software due to its importance in the entire information technology ecosystem, paving the way for groundbreaking innovations.

Huawei has collaborated with global partners to establish cutting-edge digital infrastructure, which is backed by a vibrant software ecosystem composed of Kunpeng, Ascend, openEuler, CANN, MindSpore, and more, that lays a computing foundation for the digital world. Huawei is a brand built on the principles of inclusivity, fairness, openness, collaboration, and sustainability. In its position as a global communications and solutions provider, Huawei is ideally positioned to support a vibrant open-source community in a shared industry ecosystem.

Behind any innovation is a team of talented personnel, and as such, talent remains the most critical resource for high-tech industries. Given its importance as an underlying technology, base software blends universal and specialist areas, requiring experts with in-depth operating system (OS) knowledge and the ability to drive independent innovation.

With over three decades of experience in the information and communication technology (ICT) sector, Huawei has gained extensive knowledge in honing the skills of renowned professionals. By collaborating with educational authorities, universities, institutions, and industry partners, Huawei has formed its own talent cultivation strategies. The company has further formed strategic partnerships that have produced global talent benchmarks and fostered a dynamic and sustainable ICT ecosystem, which has catalyzed major innovations, growth, and societal progress.

Huawei's partnership with academia dates back to 2013 when Huawei partnered with international universities to launch Huawei ICT Academy, which provides specialized curricula, online learning platforms, advanced tools, and faculty training programs. The Academy aims to produce industry-ready professionals who are capable of solving real-world challenges, showcasing an effective model of education-enterprise collaboration. To further strengthen this ecosystem, Huawei regularly publishes ICT talent ecosystem white papers, holds global ICT competitions, and hosts talent recruitment fairs, creating a self-sustaining cycle of skill development and opportunity.

Textbooks are essential in transferring cutting-edge knowledge, which is why Huawei works with universities and other bodies to modernize educational practices tailored to ICT talent growth. The Huawei ICT Academy textbook series—developed jointly by Huawei engineers and university experts—publishes the latest advances in base software in key areas, covering OpenHarmony, openEuler, openGauss, MindSpore, and Ascend C.

This series aims to provide greater clarity and completeness, emphasizing theoretical and practical work to reflect real-world applications and connect classroom learning with industry practices. Supplementary resources such as source code, lab guides, online courses, and exams further hone technical and hands-on skills.

In the age of intelligence, there will be challenges and opportunities, requiring aspiring professionals to invest time and resources into the base software field. Expanding your expertise with practical skills and software proficiencies will help aspiring students thrive in an ever-changing field and provide an ideal platform for a long-term career.

Huawei extends an invitation to join its mission of fortifying OS foundations and nurturing vibrant open-source communities. Together, we can redefine the frontiers of base software technology, ignite fresh waves of innovation, and accelerate the growth of the digital economy.

Huawei ICT Strategy and Business Development Department   Honghua Peng
Shenzhen, China

Preface

This book aims to lay out the argument for more strategic development and investment in operating systems (OSs), owing to their role in industry transformations. As information and communication technology (ICT) and cloud-edge-device models evolve, collaboration between industry and academia is essential. This book equips readers with the modern OS fundamentals and the practical skills needed to apply this knowledge holistically and comprehensively.

Written to express a systematic decomposition approach, we clarify complicated theoretical concepts by presenting curated practical cases. In nine chapters, we cover a broad spectrum of topics, including the evolution of OSs, openEuler development environment, embedded OS development, and open-source innovation within openEuler.

To ground these topics in practicality, the book provides hands-on cases for file system operations, shell scripting, virtual local area networks (VLANs), firewalld, and WordPress. Each case relates to the next, underpinning the principles and design principles behind practical solutions.

A major theme of this book is the influence of openEuler as a next-generation evolution of Linux. Positioned as an innovative open-source OS, openEuler provides an enhanced Linux kernel that addresses evolving ICT needs, particularly in cloud-edge-device collaboration, as an advanced support for digital infrastructure. It ensures seamless compatibility with other Linux distributions while expanding its existing ecosystem to cover servers, cloud computing, edge devices, and embedded systems. Through the support for diversified computing, openEuler offers a perfect platform for technological innovation, playing a vital role in nurturing the next generation of talented personnel in cutting-edge fields like artificial intelligence (AI) and the Internet of Things (IoT).

This book features two core attributes that make it an indispensable resource for mastering Linux and openEuler.

It emphasizes foundational OS theory with practical work, providing a detailed exploration of Linux. Based on the "divide and conquer" methodology—echoing the UNIX philosophy of "do one thing and do it well"—we explore mainstream tools like **wc**, **sort**, **find**, **vim**, **grep**, **sed**, **gawk**, pipes, and redirection, as well as maintenance topics such as log management.

This knowledge is then compounded through extensive, hands-on experience rooted in openEuler. The book covers an array of practical scenarios that aim to help readers gain a deeper understanding of the Linux OS. These topics include daily system operations, text streams, application development, embedded Linux projects, networking, and system security.

The authors comprise educators and practitioners who boast rich experience in engineering and UNIX-style OS development. They have contributed to cutting-edge projects in robotics, virtual instruments, embedded applications, and collaborations with the Ministry of Education and Huawei. Despite our best efforts, we acknowledge that there may be errors or unintentional omissions in this book. We encourage and appreciate feedback and suggestions for improvements from our readers to ensure that our content is accurate and up to date.

Our sincere gratitude to Huawei for supplying high-quality industry-education integration resources that formed much of the basis of this content. A special thanks to Huawei engineers, Zhao Xiaohu, Yang Lei, and Li Yang, who provided key technical expertise and valuable insights throughout the writing process, and to Zhang Tianli, Ma Lei, Wang Yang and Bingli Ye for their meticulous work on chart design and content proofreading.

We hope that this book can guide you on your journey to mastering the openEuler OS. May it inspire you to innovate, excel, and lead in evolving ICT and cloud-edge ecosystems.

Chengdu, Sichuan, China Jiasheng Hao
August 2025 Yindong Xiao
  Wenjian Zhou
  Peicheng Wang

Official Textbooks for Huawei ICT Academy

Expert Committee

Director
Lyu Weifeng, Vice President, Beihang University

Deputy Directors
Ma Dianfu, Professor, School of Computer Science and Engineering, Beihang University
He Qinming, Professor, College of Computer Science and Technology, Zhejiang University
He Yanxiang, Professor, School of Computer Science, Wuhan University
Honghua Peng, President, ICT Strategy and Business Development Department, Huawei
Tang Xiaoguang, Director, China Region Strategy & Marketing Department, Huawei
Sun Hu, Huawei Service Fellow and Chief Project Management Expert
Sun Gang, Director, ICT Talent Partner Development Department, Huawei

Committee Members (in Alphabetical Order)
Fan Ju, Professor, School of Information, Renmin University of China
Fang Juan, Vice Dean, School of Computer Science, Beijing University of Technology
Guo Yao, Vice Dean, School of Computer Science, Peking University
Liu Yaolin, Education-Enterprise Cooperation Director, ICT Talent Partner Development Department, Huawei
Su Tonghua, Vice Dean, School of Software, Harbin Institute of Technology
Sun Hailong, Professor, School of Software, Beihang University
Wang Han, Vice Dean, Ye Peida School of Innovation and Entrepreneurship, Beijing University of Posts and Telecommunications

Wang Jingquan, Director, Base Software and Talent Development Department, Huawei

Wang Xin, Director, China Talent Ecosystem Development, Huawei

Wei Biao, ICT Academy Solution Architect, Huawei

Zhou Xuan, Vice Dean, School of Data Science and Engineering, East China Normal University

Contents

1	**Overview**		1
	1.1 OSs and the ICT Era		1
	1.2 Origin of OSs		2
		1.2.1 The Multics Project	2
		1.2.2 Birth of UNIX	2
	1.3 Evolution of OSs		4
		1.3.1 Evolution of UNIX: From Academic Freedom to Copyright Battles	4
		1.3.2 Rise of Desktop OSs	6
		1.3.3 Open Source Innovation of GNU/Linux	8
		1.3.4 OSs in the ICT Era	9
	1.4 openEuler's New Ecosystem		12
		1.4.1 openEuler Overview	12
		1.4.2 openEuler Community	13
		1.4.3 openEuler Software Ecosystem	14
	1.5 Summary		15
2	**Introduction to Operating Systems**		17
	2.1 Basic Components of OSs		17
		2.1.1 Typical Architecture	18
		2.1.2 Kernel and System Call Interface	19
		2.1.3 Applications	20
		2.1.4 User Interfaces	26
	2.2 Overview of Modern OSs		30
		2.2.1 Desktop OSs	30
		2.2.2 Server OSs	30
		2.2.3 Embedded OSs	31
	2.3 Outstanding Features of GNU/Linux		31
		2.3.1 UNIX Design Philosophy Legacy	32
		2.3.2 Freedom and Openness	33
		2.3.3 Portability	35

xi

	2.4	Introduction to openEuler	36
		2.4.1 Architecture	36
		2.4.2 Innovative Features	37
		2.4.3 Open Source Contributions	38
	2.5	Hands-On with openEuler	39
		2.5.1 Huawei Cloud	39
		2.5.2 VMware Setup	39
		2.5.3 Docker Container Deployment	40
	2.6	Summary	40
3	**Getting Started with openEuler**		**43**
	3.1	Interaction Interfaces	44
		3.1.1 GUI	44
		3.1.2 CLI	47
	3.2	Using the CLI	48
		3.2.1 Console and Terminal	48
		3.2.2 System Login	49
		3.2.3 Remote Login	50
		3.2.4 Command Usage	52
		3.2.5 Getting Help	54
	3.3	Basic Command-Line Operations	57
		3.3.1 Directory Manipulation	58
		3.3.2 File Viewing	64
		3.3.3 File Management	71
		3.3.4 File Search	76
		3.3.5 System Information Query	79
		3.3.6 System Management	82
	3.4	Shells: Unleashing Command-Line Power	83
		3.4.1 Introduction to Bash	84
		3.4.2 Environment Variables	84
		3.4.3 Wildcards and Auto-Completion	87
		3.4.4 Command Combination	88
		3.4.5 Redirection	90
		3.4.6 Pipes	93
		3.4.7 Extended Commands	96
		3.4.8 Command-Line Editing	98
	3.5	Users and Permissions	99
		3.5.1 User Model	100
		3.5.2 Switching Users	100
		3.5.3 Permission Model	101
		3.5.4 Permission Modification	103
		3.5.5 Ownership Modification	104
	3.6	DDE Installation	104
	3.7	Summary	105

Contents

4 OS Principles and Practice..107
    4.1   OS Design Philosophy..108
    4.2   File Management..110
           4.2.1   File Tree..110
           4.2.2   Virtual File System 115
           4.2.3   Introduction to EulerFS...........................116
           4.2.4   Example 4.1: File System Operations.................117
    4.3   Memory Management...119
           4.3.1   Memory Protection 120
           4.3.2   Virtual Memory Management 123
           4.3.3   openEuler Memory Technologies 125
           4.3.4   Example 4.2: Memory Information Analysis..........126
    4.4   Process Management..127
           4.4.1   Parallelization Strategies 128
           4.4.2   Process Creation....................................129
           4.4.3   Process Scheduling 131
           4.4.4   IPC...132
           4.4.5   Thread Abstraction..................................134
           4.4.6   openEuler Process Technologies 136
           4.4.7   Example 4.3: Process Monitoring and Management......138
    4.5   Summary..141

5 openEuler Development Environment..........................143
    5.1   Text Processing 144
           5.1.1   Vim...145
           5.1.2   Nano..151
           5.1.3   Text Searching 152
           5.1.4   Text Replacement and Automated Editing..............155
           5.1.5   Text Analysis 157
           5.1.6   Text Formatting 160
           5.1.7   Using Git for Version Control 162
    5.2   Shell Scripting 163
           5.2.1   Number-Guessing Game 164
           5.2.2   Variables...166
           5.2.3   Expressions 168
           5.2.4   Branch Structures...................................169
           5.2.5   Loop Structures 171
           5.2.6   Functions 174
           5.2.7   Project 5-1: Install-Help Command....................174
    5.3   C/C++ Application Development.............................175
           5.3.1   my-nl 175
           5.3.2   Compilation and Debugging 176
           5.3.3   Building with Makefiles..............................181
           5.3.4   Building with CMake................................183
           5.3.5   Automated Testing..................................187

		5.3.6	Performance Optimization	188
		5.3.7	Project 5-2: my-utils Toolbox	190
	5.4	Portability Development and Docker Container Deployment		190
		5.4.1	POSIX Portability	191
		5.4.2	C/C++ Portability	193
		5.4.3	Docker Container Portability	194
		5.4.4	openEuler Multi-Scenario Portability	199
		5.4.5	Project 5-3: Cross-Platform Building of my-utils	199
	5.5	Learning in Open Source Communities		199
		5.5.1	Linux and Open Source	200
		5.5.2	openEuler Community	201
	5.6	Summary		201
6	**Embedded OS Development**			203
	6.1	Introduction to Embedded OSs		203
		6.1.1	Software Architecture of Embedded Systems	204
		6.1.2	Key Characteristics	205
		6.1.3	Common Embedded OSs	206
	6.2	Embedded Linux		207
		6.2.1	Embedded Linux Development Process	207
		6.2.2	Example 6.1: Embedded Development Environment Setup	209
	6.3	Linux Kernel Customization and Development		212
		6.3.1	Introduction to the Linux Kernel	213
		6.3.2	Kernel Build Mechanism	216
		6.3.3	Example 6.2: Kernel Compilation and QEMU Emulation	216
	6.4	Root File System Development		219
		6.4.1	Introduction to BusyBox	219
		6.4.2	Example 6.3: Root File System Compilation and QEMU Emulation	220
	6.5	openEuler Embedded		223
		6.5.1	Technical Architecture and Key Features	224
		6.5.2	Building with oebuild	226
		6.5.3	Example 6.4: Build and Emulation of openEuler Embedded with QEMU	227
		6.5.4	Embedded ROS Runtime	227
		6.5.5	Soft Real-Time Capabilities	229
	6.6	Summary		230
7	**Network Basics and Management**			233
	7.1	TCP/IP Network Model		233
		7.1.1	IP Addresses	236
		7.1.2	Ports	238

Contents

		7.1.3	Sockets	239
		7.1.4	Socket API	240
	7.2	Network Management Basics		243
		7.2.1	Basic Concepts	243
		7.2.2	Host Names	245
		7.2.3	Network Interface Names	246
	7.3	Network Management		247
		7.3.1	Tools	247
		7.3.2	Connection Configuration	252
		7.3.3	ifcfg Files	254
		7.3.4	Route Configuration	255
		7.3.5	Network Diagnosis	256
		7.3.6	Example 7.1: VLAN Creation	258
	7.4	Firewalls		260
		7.4.1	iptables	261
		7.4.2	firewalld	263
		7.4.3	Example 7.2: firewalld Configuration	267
	7.5	Classic Network Tools		269
		7.5.1	SSH	269
		7.5.2	wget	272
		7.5.3	cURL	272
		7.5.4	tcpdump	274
		7.5.5	netcat	275
		7.5.6	Nmap	276
	7.6	Summary		277
8	**Server OS Management**			279
	8.1	Typical Server OSs		280
		8.1.1	Windows Server	280
		8.1.2	Popular Linux Distributions for Servers	281
		8.1.3	The Rise of openEuler	282
	8.2	Users and User Groups		283
		8.2.1	User Management	284
		8.2.2	User Group Management	286
		8.2.3	Example 8.1: Batch User Creation	287
	8.3	Drives and Logical Volumes		287
		8.3.1	Drive Partitions	288
		8.3.2	MBR and GPT	288
		8.3.3	Example 8.2: Partition Creation and Mounting	289
		8.3.4	LVs	292
		8.3.5	Example 8.3: LV Creation and Mounting	293
	8.4	Software Packages		296
		8.4.1	Package Management with RPM	297
		8.4.2	Package Management with DNF	298
		8.4.3	Source Package Management	301

	8.5	System Services	302
		8.5.1 systemd	302
		8.5.2 systemctl	303
		8.5.3 .service Files	304
		8.5.4 SSH Service	306
		8.5.5 Example 8.4: LAMP Stack Installation	307
	8.6	Scheduled Tasks	308
		8.6.1 One-Time Tasks	309
		8.6.2 Periodic Tasks	309
	8.7	System Security	311
		8.7.1 Root Privileges	311
		8.7.2 Special File Permissions	312
		8.7.3 SELinux	314
		8.7.4 Logging System	315
		8.7.5 Security Auditing	321
	8.8	System Administration and Maintenance Examples	322
		8.8.1 Example 8.5: System Management with Cockpit	322
		8.8.2 Example 8.6: WordPress Blog Setup	324
	8.9	Summary	329
9	**Open-Source Innovation Within openEuler**		**331**
	9.1	Kernel	332
		9.1.1 SMT Expeller Free of Priority Inversion	333
		9.1.2 CPU QoS Priority-Based Load Balancing	333
		9.1.3 Tidal Affinity	334
	9.2	Fundamental Capabilities	334
		9.2.1 Lightweight Container Engine	335
		9.2.2 Virtualization	337
		9.2.3 High-Performance Service Management	338
		9.2.4 Kernel Live Upgrade	339
		9.2.5 Security and Reliability	342
	9.3	Scenario Enablement	346
		9.3.1 Server	347
		9.3.2 Cloud	351
		9.3.3 Embedded	355
		9.3.4 Edge	358
	9.4	Toolchains	360
		9.4.1 GCC for openEuler	360
		9.4.2 Compass-CI	361
		9.4.3 EulerLauncher	362
		9.4.4 A-Ops	363
		9.4.5 A-Tune	366

	9.5	Industry Applications	368
	9.5.1	Finance	368
	9.5.2	Energy	370
	9.5.3	Cloud Computing	370
	9.5.4	Scientific Research	371
	9.6	Summary	371

References ... 375

Chapter 1
Overview

Objectives

1. Understand the fundamental functions of operating systems and their impact on industries.
2. Grasp the basic evolution trajectory of operating systems.
3. Explore briefly the new ecosystem of the openEuler operating system.

1.1 OSs and the ICT Era

Operating system (OS) evolution is inextricably linked with advancements in information and communication technology (ICT). As the backbone software of a computer, OSs drive the next-generation digital infrastructure and anchor industrial progress, profoundly shaping its progression.

OSs power virtually every modern technology, from smartphones and tablets to vehicles and aircraft. In computers, OSs coordinate resources between the hardware and software sides over a standardized computing platform and user interfaces (UIs), ensuring the system operates reliably, securely, and effectively [1]. Microsoft Windows exemplifies the modern OS, dominating the PC landscape. Windows provides intuitive tools for file management and network connectivity and orchestrates essential services and seamless hardware compatibility across desktops and laptops by integrating components like hard drives, graphics cards, sound cards, and network adapters.

Our modern world is defined by the capabilities and data size of big data, artificial intelligence (AI), and Internet of Things (IoT) applications. Behind this change is the emergence of diverse processors—CPUs, GPUs, TPUs, and NPUs—that have created an extensive ecosystem, spanning from high-performance servers to AI edge solutions and energy-efficient embedded systems. This period has also seen the rise of revolutionary computing paradigms—from cloud-edge-device synergy to connectivity of everything—where AI reshapes computing services. This transformation has spawned diverse technological scenarios, such as cloud-native architecture, multi-core processing, and intelligent human–computer interaction. These seismic shifts in the ICT landscape must be complemented by advances in OS solutions [2].

Recognizing the importance of OSs as cornerstone infrastructure for the digital age, industry bodies, academic institutions, and research centers have channeled substantial resources into OS R&D. To better understand this technological marvel, we must begin by examining its origins and tracing its evolution.

1.2 Origin of OSs

When computers first emerged, numerous OSs were developed to manage computer resources and provide programmers with efficient development environments, including IBM System/360, DEC VMS, and MS-DOS. After extensive evolution, today's OS landscape primarily consists of two lineages: Windows OSs, evolved from MS-DOS, and UNIX-like OSs including Linux, BSD, and mobile OSs like Android, macOS, and iOS. These UNIX-like systems all comply with the Portable Operating System Interface (POSIX) requirements.

1.2.1 The Multics Project

In 1965, Massachusetts Institute of Technology (MIT), General Electric, and Bell Labs jointly launched the Multics (MULTiplexed Information and Computing Service) project to develop a multi-user, multi-tasking time-sharing OS for mainframes like the GE-645 [3]. The collaboration leveraged each partner's unique strengths: GE's hardware engineering prowess in time-sharing and multi-user computing systems, and Bell Labs' pioneering experience in OS development dating back to the 1950s. However, the project ultimately collapsed under its own weight in 1969. Its architects' quest for perfection led to an overly complex system that proved costly to develop and sluggish in operation, failing to attract market interest. Nevertheless, its influence on future OS development proved profound.

1.2.2 Birth of UNIX

In 1969, after Bell Labs withdrew from Multics, Ken Thompson at Bell Labs rewrote the "Space Travel" game on an idle DEC PDP-7 minicomputer [3]. He realized that he could create a complete OS with just three additional programs. During his wife's three-week vacation with their child, Thompson used assembly language to implement this bold idea. The three programs were a code editor, an assembler to convert code into executable files, and a "kernel shell" containing execution calls and shell interaction capabilities. This new OS, learning from Multics' failures, featured an elegantly simple design that quickly attracted attention from Dennis Ritchie and others.

The system was named UNICS (UNiplexed Information and Computing Service), emphasizing its contrast with Multics' complexity. Later renamed UNIX, it drew talented programmers at Bell Labs who continuously enhanced its functionality.

The first version, released in November 1971, included a Fortran compiler and many enduring utilities, including **ar**, **cat**, **chmod**, **chown**, **cp**, **dc**, **ed**, **find**, **ln**, **ls**, **mail**, **mkdir**, **mv**, **rm**, **sh**, **su**, and **who**.

Assembly language's constraints on UNIX development prompted Thompson and Ritchie to adopt BCPL (Basic Combined Programming Language) as their development platform. Their subsequent improvements to BCPL led to the creation of the B language, though this too proved inadequate for their needs. Ritchie and Brian Kernighan then engineered a revolutionary successor to B, introducing comprehensive data types and extensive operators. This breakthrough became the C programming language. The completion of C in 1973 enabled a complete rewrite of UNIX, yielding a stable, portable, and maintainable system. This transformation catalyzed UNIX's widespread adoption and enduring influence in computing.

The early days of UNIX development exemplified the challenges inherent in pioneering work. Running on the "outdated" PDP-7 in an era dominated by mainframes, the project faced severe hardware limitations. Bell Labs' management's indifference to OS development further constrained the team's access to resources. Fortune intervened when Bell Labs' patent department struggled with line-numbered documentation requirements for patent applications. This challenge prompted the purchase of a PDP-11, with the UNIX team commissioned to develop the necessary software tools. This pragmatic solution gave UNIX its foothold as a patent documentation system. The resulting text formatter, Nroff, became a cornerstone of UNIX-like OSs and shaped the evolution of document formatting technology. Figure 1.1 captures a historic moment: Thompson and Dennis Ritchie at work with early UNIX on the PDP-11.

UNIX's sixth iteration marked its maturity as a versatile, multi-user interactive OS with widespread adoption. At its heart lay an innovative, layered, detachable file system featuring highly compatible interfaces for both files and device I/O. The platform's robustness was evident in its support for over 100 subsystems and numerous programming languages. The system's implementation in C, a portable programming language, proved transformative, enabling UNIX to operate across diverse hardware platforms. This portability was revolutionary in an era when the computing landscape bore little resemblance to today's standardized environment. The industry, still in its infancy, lacked dominant players, and computer manufacturers produced machines with widely varying architectures and operating paradigms. Previously, programmers struggled with the burden of crafting separate code for each unique hardware configuration. UNIX's unified, portable interfaces

Fig. 1.1 Thompson and Ritchie at work with early UNIX on the PDP-11

dramatically streamlined software development, liberating programmers from hardware-specific constraints and establishing the foundation for modern computing's explosive growth.

1.3 Evolution of OSs

The evolution of OSs spans three distinct eras, each defined by its unique UI paradigm. The console era introduced text-based interfaces through basic display-and-keyboard setups, limiting users to character-based interactions. This gave way to the revolutionary desktop era, exemplified by Windows, where graphical interfaces transformed computers into accessible tools that penetrated both domestic and professional spheres. Today, we live in the ICT era of ubiquitous connectivity, where OSs adapt to various interface formats, enabling seamless access across interconnected devices.

1.3.1 Evolution of UNIX: From Academic Freedom to Copyright Battles

UNIX's initial distribution model pioneered what would later become the open source movement. Through innovative licensing agreements with universities, AT&T provided source code access for minimal fees, fostering a collaborative

1.3 Evolution of OSs

environment where academic institutions could freely study, modify, and share improvements [2, 3]. Figure 1.2 shows the UNIX family lineage.

This approach catalyzed rapid technological advancement and spawned vibrant user communities worldwide, exemplified by organizations like USENIX.

The Berkeley Software Distribution (BSD) emerged as a pivotal force in UNIX development, contributing fundamental technologies like the TCP/IP (Transmission Control Protocol/Internet Protocol) stack. BSD's development culture, immortalized in the tongue-in-cheek acronym "Because Sleep is Dumb," reflected the passionate dedication of its creators who routinely worked through the night at the computer labs of the University of California, Berkeley (UC Berkeley).

However, this period of open collaboration faced challenges when AT&T began restricting source code access in 1979, dramatically increasing licensing fees from $99 to $250,000 by the late 1980s.

This commercialization split UNIX into two distinct paths: AT&T's proprietary version and BSD's open source alternative. The ecosystem further diversified with numerous commercial variants like SunOS, IBM AIX, HP-UX, Xenix OS, and Solaris.

The 1990s marked a turbulent period of legal battles, beginning with AT&T's lawsuit against BSDi, established by the Computer Systems Research Group (CSRG) at UC Berkeley, over copyright infringement. This conflict forced BSD's complete rewrite, establishing it as an independent OS.

UNIX copyright disputes continued when Santa Cruz Operation (SCO) acquired partial UNIX rights through Novell (a Bell Labs' partner). In 2003, SCO sued IBM for $5 billion, alleging unauthorized use of UNIX code in Linux. An SCO victory

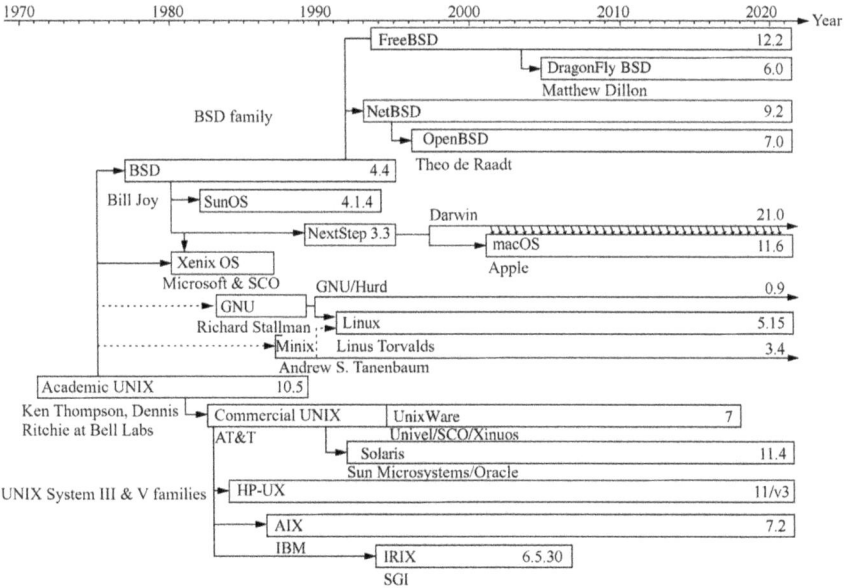

Fig. 1.2 UNIX family lineage

would have affected various OSs, including IBM AIX and Sun Solaris. This seven-year legal battle, ultimately resolved in IBM's favor, paradoxically strengthened the open source movement and accelerated Linux's adoption.

> BSD's lasting legacy extends beyond these legal conflicts. It broke new ground by introducing libraries that supported both the Internet protocol stack and Berkeley sockets. The seamless integration of sockets with UNIX file descriptors enabled developers to handle network communications as intuitively as local file operations, marking a fundamental shift in distributed computing.

1.3.2 Rise of Desktop OSs

The evolution of microprocessors and PCs ushered in a new era of desktop OSs [4]. While computers in the text-based era remained the domain of technical professionals, the advent of graphical user interfaces (GUIs) democratized computing, transforming it into an indispensable tool for both work and daily life. This transformation was not solely driven by declining hardware costs—the development of intuitive, user-friendly OSs played an even more crucial role.

Apple's 1984 launch of the Macintosh computer, featuring Macintosh System 1 (shown in Fig. 1.3), represented a watershed moment in computing history. Its revolutionary GUI introduced windows, mouse control, folder navigation, and

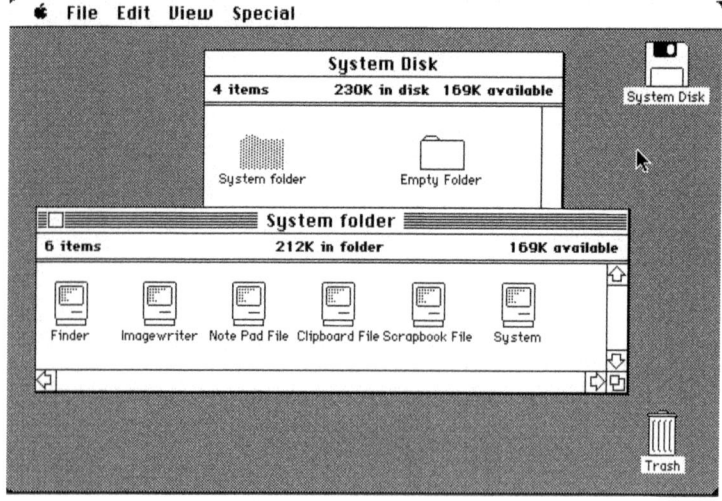

Fig. 1.3 GUI of Apple Macintosh System 1

1.3 Evolution of OSs

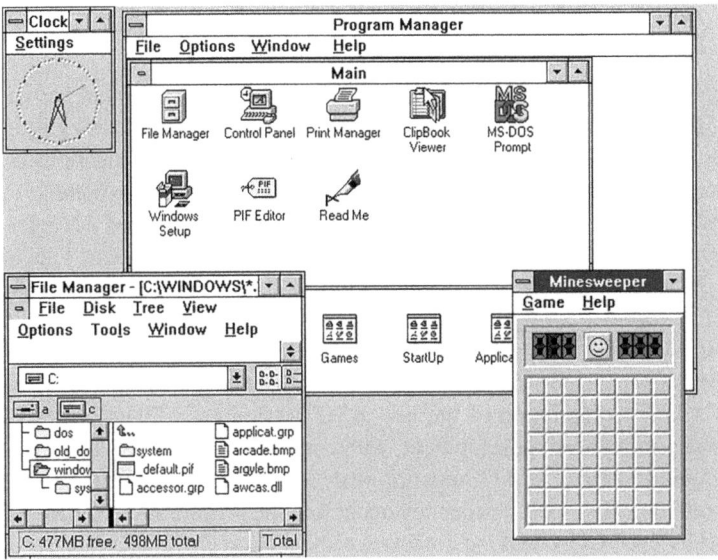

Fig. 1.4 GUI of Windows 3.1

drag-and-drop functionality, capturing the public's imagination and heralding the graphical desktop era. While macOS incorporated BSD code elements, maintaining its UNIX lineage, Apple's walled garden approach restricted hardware compatibility, focusing its adoption in creative professional sectors like graphic design and multimedia production. Today's macOS continues to command significant market share, distinguished by its robust stability, enhanced security protocols, distinctive interface design, seamless device integration, and comprehensive application ecosystem, including deep integration with cloud services like iCloud.

Microsoft's entry into the graphical computing space came in 1985 with Windows 1.0, bringing GUI capabilities to IBM PC-compatible OSs. The GUI of Windows 3.1 (shown in Fig. 1.4) exemplified early Microsoft design philosophy. Windows rapidly ascended to market dominance through its accessible interface and superior gaming and multimedia capabilities, appealing to both corporate and individual users—a position it maintains to this day. Although the initial reception of Windows 1.0 was tepid, Microsoft's aggressive development cycle yielded significant improvements, culminating in the landmark release of Windows 95, which introduced a refined architecture and pioneering tools like Internet Explorer and MSN Messenger. The 2001 release of Windows XP marked another pivotal moment in PC history. Contemporary Windows 10 stands as a testament to Microsoft's innovation, featuring advanced capabilities from device compatibility to artificial intelligence (AI) integration, cloud computing, and virtualization. The 2021 release of Windows 11 builds upon this foundation with architectural improvements and enhanced security features, though ongoing refinements to stability and compatibility continue.

1.3.3 Open Source Innovation of GNU/Linux

The renaissance of UNIX materialized through the remarkable ascent of GNU/Linux [5]. During the 1980s, the software landscape was dominated by proprietary solutions, requiring paid licenses and restricting users from modifications or extensions—creating technical barriers to UNIX's evolution and deployment.

A revolutionary shift began when pioneering hackers launched the open source movement, introducing an innovative paradigm for OS development. This transformation pivoted on two groundbreaking initiatives: the BSD project and the GNU project.

The BSD project emerged from UC Berkeley's liberal academic environment, where Thompson's UNIX creation found fertile ground. His fellow graduate student Bill Joy's 1977 compilation of the first BSD version established a precedent for transparency in software development, with comprehensive source code accessibility. The 1989 release of BSD's networking code served as a major milestone, catalyzing both the early open source movement and the proliferation of BSD variants.

The 1999 DEF CON hacking conference showcased OpenBSD founder Theo de Raadt's bold stance against the Back Orifice 2000 backdoor, pledging enhanced security measures in OpenBSD. This watershed moment elevated OpenBSD's reputation as a security-focused platform and highlighted the role of open source in addressing systemic trust issues.

Richard Stallman's 1983 GNU initiative aimed to create a freely modifiable and distributable UNIX-like OS. The establishment of the Free Software Foundation provided crucial financial backing for open source development. By 1990, GNU had assembled most essential UNIX components, including compilers, editors, and debugging tools, but lacked a viable kernel.

The missing piece emerged in 1991 when Linus Torvalds released his Linux kernel, which, combined with GNU utilities, created the comprehensive GNU/Linux OS [6]. Released under the GNU General Public License (GPL), this freely modifiable and distributable platform sparked unprecedented community engagement and rapid adoption across the expanding Internet landscape.

> While often under-appreciated, GNU's pivotal contribution lies in its comprehensive toolchain, fundamentally enabling unrestricted software development, modification, and distribution—cornerstones of the open source movement.

Community enthusiasm spawned numerous distinguished distributions, including Slackware, Debian, and Red Hat Linux, each packaging applications with the Linux kernel for streamlined deployment and management. Beyond cost efficiency, the robust community ecosystem ensures exceptional security, reliability, and stability. Corporate entities can tailor solutions to specific requirements, optimizing

1.3 Evolution of OSs

performance and adaptability. This compelling value proposition has attracted substantial investment from technology giants like Huawei, Google, IBM, and Intel, whose contributions to the Free Software Foundation continue to fuel open source innovation and growth.

1.3.4 OSs in the ICT Era

The digital transformation has made OSs ubiquitous in our connected world. They power everything from our smartphones and industrial robots to sensor-equipped devices and cloud containers, functioning wherever computation exists [4]. These silent workhorses continuously manage our digital assets and devices with remarkable efficiency.

(1) Mobile OSs

The dawn of the twenty-first century witnessed an unprecedented boom in mobile technology, fundamentally transformed by Apple's introduction of the iPhone in 2007 (Fig. 1.5). This revolutionary device redefined our expectations of mobile computing with its innovative multi-touch interface, robust connectivity, and rich ecosystem of applications. The term "smartphone" emerged to describe these sophisticated devices that offered users the freedom to customize their experience through downloadable applications.

The pre-iPhone landscape featured OSs like Palm OS, Windows Mobile, and Symbian, which primarily focused on basic resource management and simple applications. iOS of iPhone revolutionized this paradigm by delivering an unparalleled user experience characterized by intuitive navigation, fluid animations, and seamless transitions. Apple's carefully curated App Store ecosystem introduced a new standard for mobile applications, ensuring both quality and security through rigorous evaluation processes. The masterful integration of hardware and software optimization resulted in devices that outperformed competitors in terms of performance, stability, and battery efficiency.

This mobile revolution also marked a significant evolution in UNIX-like OSs. While iOS, descended from Mac OS X and BSD, remained proprietary to Apple devices, Android emerged in 2003 as the flag-bearer of open source mobile

Fig. 1.5 Apple's iPhone smartphone

computing. Built on the Linux kernel, Android provides a sandboxed Java virtual machine environment for applications. By exposing high-level APIs through Java, Android empowers developers to build mobile applications efficiently, eliminating common development complexities. The platform's continuous evolution, particularly the introduction of Android Runtime (ART) in version 5.0, dramatically improved application performance. By pre-compiling Java applications into executable files, ART significantly accelerates application launch times and responsiveness. Google's acquisition and Android's open source nature catalyzed its adoption across manufacturers, establishing it as the dominant force in mobile computing worldwide.

(2) IoT OSs

The vision of a fully interconnected world emerged in the late twentieth century, where sensors attached to everyday objects would monitor and analyze their conditions in real time, enabling precise control and optimization. This interconnected network of objects evolved into what we now call the IoT. To orchestrate these monitoring devices and streamline their communication, developers created specialized OSs that accommodate diverse communication protocols and optimize limited power resources.

The IoT ecosystem, including its OSs, remains in its nascent stage, still evolving toward maturity. While FreeRTOS has gained significant traction in IoT applications, it fundamentally operates on a real-time operating system (RTOS) kernel, falling short of true IoT system capabilities. Authentic IoT OSs must facilitate seamless communication across multiple dimensions: object-to-object, object-to-cloud, and object-to-human interactions.

As a telecommunications industry leader, Huawei has introduced innovative open source IoT solutions: LiteOS and OpenHarmony. LiteOS excels in powering lightweight, efficient IoT devices, while OpenHarmony pioneers a unified, open distributed OS platform (Fig. 1.6) that prioritizes seamless device collaboration and interoperability. These systems now drive advancements across

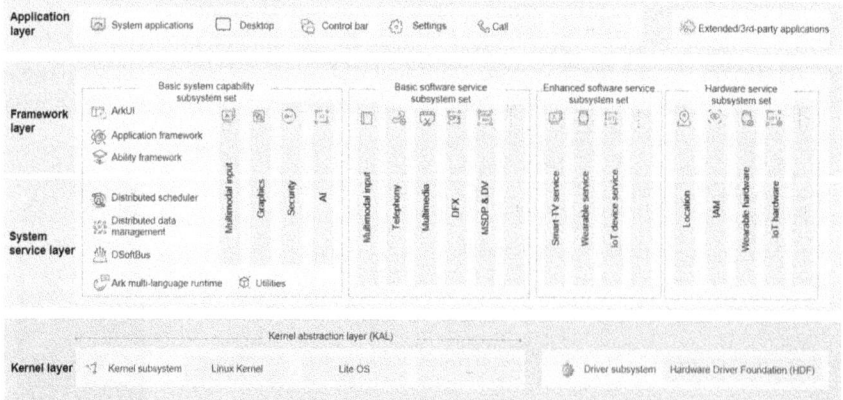

Fig. 1.6 OpenHarmony architecture

smart homes, cities, transportation networks, and industrial applications, laying the groundwork for an increasingly connected and intelligent world.

(3) Cloud OSs

The evolution of the Internet has transformed how enterprises deliver computing services. By leveraging Content Delivery Networks (CDN) and strategic data center placement, companies now position their servers closer to users for enhanced performance. This shift has spawned a new industry: cloud service providers who rent computing infrastructure to clients. These clients prioritize 24/7 access to reliable computing resources without managing the underlying hardware, while providers dynamically allocate various resources, including computing power (CPUs and GPUs), memory, storage, and network bandwidth. This service model demands sophisticated resource management, leading to the emergence of specialized cloud OSs.

Cloud OSs—the backbone of cloud service platforms—come in three categories: proprietary OSs (like Amazon's), commercial solutions (such as VMware vSphere and Microsoft Azure Stack), and open source platforms (including OpenStack and CloudStack). These OSs orchestrate and manage cloud infrastructure, forming the core of modern cloud computing services.

Huawei's FusionSphere exemplifies a comprehensive cloud OS. It unifies virtualization, storage, networking, and management capabilities to create a robust cloud platform. The OS excels in delivering high-performance virtualization environments, implementing flexible software-defined storage, and orchestrating network virtualization. These capabilities enable dynamic resource scheduling and streamline cloud management operations, empowering service providers to deliver efficient, secure, and scalable cloud solutions.

(4) Emerging OSs for cloud-edge-device synergy

The ICT era has ushered in a revolution in computing architecture, where data processing and intelligent services have become critical components of modern technology. At the forefront of this evolution is cloud-edge-device synergy, an innovative framework that harnesses the collective power of cloud computing, edge computing, and endpoint devices to deliver unprecedented efficiency in real-time data processing and analysis.

This sophisticated coordination system operates across three distinct layers, each serving specialized functions.

The cloud layer, comprising traditional data centers, excels at comprehensive data analysis and strategic decision support. These facilities process vast amounts of information over extended periods, providing crucial insights for business operations.

The edge layer bridges the gap between cloud and endpoint devices, enabling rapid local data processing and real-time decision-making.

The device layer—from smartphones to sensors—serves as the primary data collection point, performing initial data processing before transmission to higher computing layers.

The OSs powering this framework are equally specialized.

Cloud OSs are sophisticated platforms that orchestrate vast cloud infrastructure resources through advanced virtualization. They ensure secure, scalable operations while facilitating complex data processing workflows across distributed environments.

Edge OSs are specialized systems architected for efficiency at the edge of networks, prioritizing rapid response times and resource optimization. They incorporate dedicated frameworks to streamline application deployment and execution in resource-constrained environments.

Device OSs are streamlined systems designed for seamless device management and connectivity. These lightweight platforms enable efficient hardware control and communication protocols while supporting dynamic updates and diverse peripheral integration.

This architectural approach represents more than just a technological advancement—it is a fundamental shift in how we process and utilize data. Leading tech giants like Amazon, Alibaba, Huawei, and Apple are already embracing this paradigm, integrating these concepts into their service offerings and actively shaping the future of distributed computing systems.

As this framework continues to evolve, it promises to address key challenges in modern computing: reducing latency, enhancing scalability, improving information accessibility, and enabling more responsive business operations. This positions cloud-edge-device synergy as a cornerstone of next-generation ICT infrastructure.

1.4 openEuler's New Ecosystem

openEuler's evolving ecosystem unites open source communities, hardware vendors, and software developers around its core OS. This integrated framework drives the development of advanced digital infrastructure, specifically designed to power seamless cloud, edge, and device synergy in the modern ICT landscape [7].

1.4.1 openEuler Overview

openEuler stands as a versatile open source OS that evolved from the Linux kernel. Its robust architecture encompasses multi-platform support, advanced security features, and intelligent capabilities, serving diverse environments from enterprise servers to cloud-native applications, edge computing, and embedded systems. Under the stewardship of the OpenAtom Foundation and powered by Huawei's extensive contributions, openEuler spearheads the development of OSs for next-generation digital infrastructure.

openEuler's hardware compatibility spans an impressive range of architectures, creating a rich ecosystem that includes industry-standard x86 processors, Kunpeng

1.4 openEuler's New Ecosystem

series Arm processors known for their efficiency and performance, cutting-edge RISC-V processors, and indigenous Chinese innovations like LoongArch.

Through semi-annual innovation versions, openEuler swiftly incorporates cutting-edge community developments. This dynamic release cycle creates a feedback loop where user experiences inform technical refinements, fostering innovation and incubating emerging technologies. This synergy between distribution releases and technology incubation propels continuous evolution, as illustrated in Fig. 1.7.

The current long-term support version, openEuler 24.03 LTS, showcases the maturity of the platform. Built atop Linux kernel 6.6, it features advanced capabilities including the Distributed Soft Bus (DSoftBus) and KubeEdge+edge-cloud synergy framework. This release delivers superior digital infrastructure coordination, offering enterprise users a foundation that combines security, stability, and reliability in one comprehensive platform.

1.4.2 openEuler Community

The openEuler community stands at the forefront of open source innovation, driving the development of the openEuler OS. This collaborative platform unites developers globally to craft a software ecosystem that embraces diversity in both architecture and application. Its mission extends beyond mere development to revolutionizing digital infrastructure across all scenarios.

The journey began around 2010 when Huawei initiated EulerOS development. Following a decade of refinement and extensive internal deployment, Huawei made a landmark decision in 2019 to open-source the OS as openEuler, fostering a collaborative approach to digital infrastructure development based on joint construction, benefit, and governance.

Today, openEuler stands among China's most dynamic open source communities. Its ecosystem, depicted in Fig. 1.8, showcases extraordinary growth metrics: over 10,000 active contributors, more than 900 industry partners, and upwards of

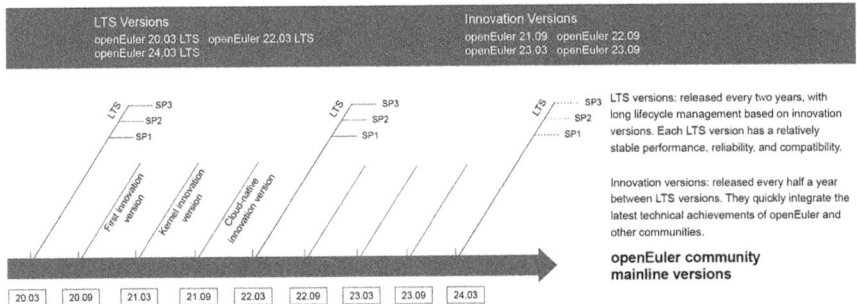

Fig. 1.7 openEuler version management

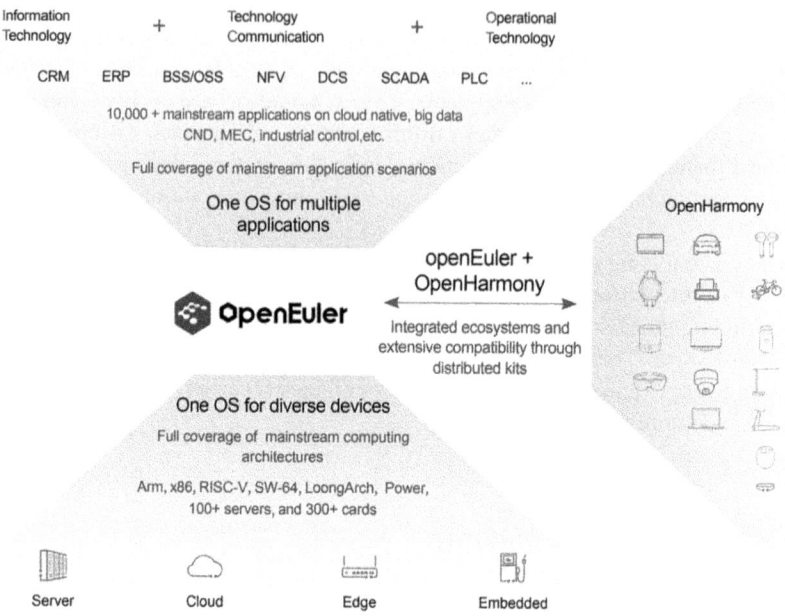

Fig. 1.8 openEuler ecosystem architecture

100 special interest groups (SIGs). The community's integration efforts with major global open source foundations have achieved 95% compatibility across projects. Native support extends to leading platforms like OpenStack, KubeEdge, OpenHPC, Hadoop, and Spark, encompassing essential domains from cloud-native applications to high-performance computing (HPC), ensuring seamless deployment worldwide.

The community's vision extends toward deeper engagement with international open source foundations, aiming to strengthen its role in the global open source landscape while making lasting contributions to worldwide technological advancement.

1.4.3 openEuler Software Ecosystem

The openEuler software ecosystem fosters robust connections throughout the technology stack, cultivating diverse partnerships and collaborative frameworks to drive systematic evolution. Major Chinese OS vendors, including KylinSoft, UnionTech, iSoft, Kylinsec, and TurboLinux, have embraced the openEuler platform, not only contributing to community initiatives but also launching innovative commercial distributions.

- Kylin Advanced Server Operating System harnesses the openEuler kernel to deliver powerful heterogeneous computing capabilities, specifically optimized for mission-critical operations and data-intensive workloads.
- iSoft marked its entry into the ecosystem with the purposefully designed iSoft Server OS for Kunpeng.
- UnionTech's deepinEuler V1.0 showcases advanced integration with Kunpeng processors, delivering superior performance through comprehensive hardware optimization.

Through dedicated SIGs, openEuler continuously expands its technological horizons beyond traditional server environments into emerging domains such as cloud computing, edge computing, and embedded systems. Notable initiatives include specialized distributions like openEuler Edge and openEuler Embedded.

openEuler aspires to achieve more than just technical progress, fostering a collaborative ecosystem where partners, users, and developers unite to enhance scenario-specific capabilities. This strategic approach aims to realize the ambitious goal of universal compatibility—enabling single-OS deployment across multiple devices and true write-once-run-anywhere application development.

1.5 Summary

This chapter traced the evolution of OSs, beginning with the emerging demands of the ICT era and progressing through the historical development from early OSs to UNIX and modern implementations. Special attention was given to Linux and other open source platforms, culminating in an exploration of the openEuler community's growth and its expanding technological ecosystem. In today's landscape of advancing digital infrastructure, openEuler has established strong footholds in cloud computing, edge computing, and embedded systems. These contemporary environments present unique challenges, demanding unprecedented levels of openness, cross-platform compatibility, and seamless edge-cloud integration.

This comprehensive overview illuminates not only the technical evolution of OSs but also their transformative impact across industries and sectors. As we navigate the ICT era, engaging with and contributing to open source OS development becomes increasingly crucial for technological advancement and innovation.

Open Access This chapter is licensed under the terms of the Creative Commons Attribution-NonCommercial-NoDerivatives 4.0 International License (http://creativecommons.org/licenses/by-nc-nd/4.0/), which permits any noncommercial use, sharing, distribution and reproduction in any medium or format, as long as you give appropriate credit to the original author(s) and the source, provide a link to the Creative Commons license and indicate if you modified the licensed material. You do not have permission under this license to share adapted material derived from this chapter or parts of it.

The images or other third party material in this chapter are included in the chapter's Creative Commons license, unless indicated otherwise in a credit line to the material. If material is not included in the chapter's Creative Commons license and your intended use is not permitted by statutory regulation or exceeds the permitted use, you will need to obtain permission directly from the copyright holder.

Chapter 2
Introduction to Operating Systems

Objectives

1. Understand the classical architecture of OSs.
2. Examine a couple of mainstream OSs.
3. Learn about the distinctive advantages of GNU/Linux.
4. Discover openEuler's innovative features and contributions to open source.

As ICT advances rapidly, operating systems (OSs) continue to evolve and break new ground in base software innovation. Both developers and system administrators must grasp not only the core components of OSs but also the distinctive features of established and emerging platforms. This chapter explores OS fundamentals, examines major OSs in current use, highlights distinctive advantages of GNU/Linux, and delves into openEuler's architecture, innovations, and contributions to the open source community.

2.1 Basic Components of OSs

OSs represent a specialized class of base software that serves a dual purpose: managing hardware resources while presenting users and applications with an intuitive, unified interface. Given their sophisticated internal architecture, understanding their structure requires careful examination. UNIX, widely regarded as the progenitor of modern OSs, serves as our primary example in exploring these basic components. The elegant simplicity of UNIX, conceived by pioneering developers, embodies the principle that true sophistication lies in simplicity—a philosophy that continues to inspire software practitioners today.

2.1.1 Typical Architecture

UNIX pioneered a fundamental architectural pattern that has become the blueprint for modern OSs. This architecture comprises three distinct software layers: the kernel, system call interface, and applications, including various management utilities [8].

Figure 2.1 demonstrates how the kernel provides the essential groundwork for this architecture, serving as the direct interface with computer hardware resources. Through the system call interface, it exposes system services to applications while presenting users with a consistent, abstracted computing environment. This elegant separation between hardware resources and applications has proven revolutionary, offering developers a standardized, portable development interface while maintaining a streamlined user experience. The success of this approach is evident in its widespread adoption across contemporary OSs.

UNIX implements robust security through a hierarchical protection scheme, establishing distinct operational domains, as depicted in Fig. 2.2. The kernel,

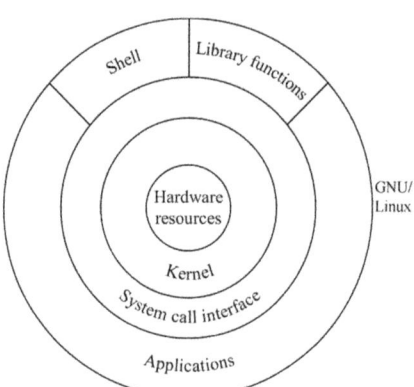

Fig. 2.1 Typical architecture of UNIX

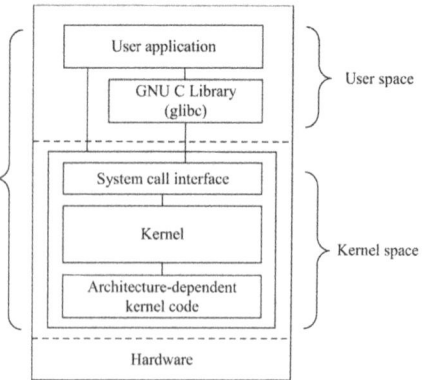

Fig. 2.2 Hierarchical structure of UNIX

operating in the kernel space, maintains exclusive direct access to hardware resources, including memory, storage devices, and peripherals. All other software executes in the user space, accessing physical resources solely through system services. This design ensures process isolation, with each application maintaining its own virtual environment and resource allocation, thereby guaranteeing both system stability and secure concurrent execution.

2.1.2 Kernel and System Call Interface

At the heart of every OS lies the kernel, a sophisticated component orchestrating critical functions including process management, memory allocation, file operations, and device control. Through its system call interface, the kernel exposes fundamental computing capabilities to applications [9].

Kernel architectures diverge into two primary designs: monolithic kernel and microkernel. Monolithic kernels consolidate all kernel modules into a unified kernel-mode task sharing a common address space. This streamlined architecture, utilizing direct function calls between modules, delivers optimal performance through simplicity. Microkernels take a modular approach, distributing functionality across independent modules in discrete address spaces, coordinating through message passing mechanisms. While this design enhances extensibility and reliability, the prevalent monolithic architecture continues to dominate modern systems despite the theoretical advantages of microkernels.[1]

The system call mechanism bridges applications and kernel services through a sophisticated interaction protocol. This process, though conceptually similar to a procedure call, involves complex operations including privilege-level transitions and hardware resource management, typically leveraging interrupt mechanisms. The system call interface defines this crucial boundary, specifying precise call signatures, parameter requirements, and return value formats. Windows OSs implement this through familiar calls like **CreateProcess** and **ReadFile**, while UNIX-based systems utilize commands such as **fork** and **read**.

Linux exemplifies the monolithic kernel design philosophy. Its open source foundation and adherence to POSIX standards[2] catalyzed widespread adoption,

---

[1] The historic controversy over kernel architecture sparked intense debate in the computing community. Minix proponents, including its creator, lambasted the monolithic design of Linux as archaic, dismissing it as a regression to 1970s computing paradigms. Linux defenders riposted by highlighting limitations of Minix in real-world applications, questioning its practical relevance despite its theoretical elegance.

[2] IEEE's POSIX standards, rooted in the UNIX architecture, established crucial standardization for OS interfaces. These standards revolutionized cross-platform compatibility among UNIX-like OSs, creating a unified framework for software development. Chapter 5 provides an in-depth exploration of POSIX standards.

while its synergy with the GNU project produced the robust GNU/Linux OS that powers countless systems today.

> OS design principles will be discussed in detail in Chap. 4. Linux source code structure, customization, compilation, and building will be covered in Chap. 6.

2.1.3 Applications

OSs come bundled with core system utilities—from compilers and common libraries to text editors and command shells. These tools enable effective system administration while supporting diverse applications across office productivity, entertainment, scientific computing, industrial automation, and middleware platforms [10].

The extensive collection of POSIX-compliant applications from the GNU project perfectly complemented Torvalds' Linux kernel, giving birth to GNU/Linux. These meticulously crafted tools function like skilled specialists, working in harmony to create a robust software ecosystem. Their reliability and effectiveness have earned them a devoted following in the programming community, fueling their continuous evolution and widespread adoption.

Compilers

Compilers serve as fundamental tools in application development, performing sophisticated transformations from human-readable source code to machine-executable instructions. This capability extends OS functionality through new applications. While originally created for UNIX, C compilers have evolved to support diverse OSs worldwide. Among the leading C/C++ compilers, GCC and Microsoft Visual C++ stand out as industry standards.

(1) GCC

GCC, the GNU Compiler Collection, dominates UNIX-like OSs as their default compiler. Beyond C/C++, it supports multiple languages, including Objective-C, Java, Ada, and Go, providing both compiler frontends and runtime libraries. This free software powerhouse works seamlessly across Linux, BSD, macOS, and even Windows through MinGW.

Operating through a command-line interface (CLI), GCC offers extensive optimization options and powerful functionality. When integrated with build automation tools like Makefile and CMake, it creates versatile, portable software solutions that have become cornerstone tools in open source development.

> Chapter 5 explores comprehensive C/C++ development in the Linux environment, focusing on GCC.

2.1 Basic Components of OSs

(2) Microsoft Visual C++

Microsoft Visual C++ distinguishes itself through comprehensive Windows ecosystem support, including native API access, DirectX graphics capabilities, and .NET Framework integration. Its sophisticated development environment features syntax highlighting, intelligent code completion, and robust debugging tools, making it invaluable for Windows software development.

The compiler landscape continues to evolve with innovative solutions.

Clang, Apple's open source compiler released in 2007 under the BSD license, revolutionizes C/C++ and Objective-C/C++ development. It excels with rapid compilation times, efficient memory management, and comprehensive error diagnostics. The compiler seamlessly integrates into various development environments while offering exceptional scalability for projects of any size. Its built-in static analysis tools, including Automatic Reference Counting, enhance code quality by identifying potential issues during compilation.

Huawei has emerged as a significant contributor with two notable releases. OpenArkCompiler, unveiled as open source in August 2019, introduces a revolutionary MapleIR-based framework for cross-language optimization. While currently supporting C compilation, its ongoing development paves the way for seamless Java-C integration. The compiler's roadmap includes expanding just-in-time (JIT) compilation capabilities across Java, C, and C++ intermediate representations (IRs).

Following this innovation, Huawei launched GCC for openEuler in April 2021. This specialized compiler builds upon GCC 10.3, introducing sophisticated hardware–software optimization techniques. It excels in performance optimization through advanced features including OpenMP implementation, Scalable Vector Extension (SVE), and math library enhancements. Designed specifically for Arm-based infrastructure, it delivers optimal performance on TaiShan servers equipped with Kunpeng 920 processors, supporting various Linux distributions including CentOS 7.6 and openEuler.

Common Libraries

Common libraries, particularly those for C/C++, serve as essential bridges between applications and OSs. Through compiler linking, these libraries seamlessly integrate with user applications, enabling sophisticated functionality through elegant encapsulation and efficient code reuse. By providing a unified extension mechanism, they dramatically simplify the challenges inherent in software development and cross-platform deployment. Built upon OS primitives and standardized interfaces like POSIX, these libraries transform complex system calls into clean, consistent APIs that work uniformly across different platforms. This abstraction layer accelerates development cycles while ensuring robust portability—a cornerstone of modern software architecture. The ecosystem encompasses several major implementations, including the ANSI standard libraries (libc), comprehensive offerings from GNU (glibc/libstdc++), and Microsoft's msvcrt, each contributing to a robust foundation for software development.

The libc library serves as the foundational implementation of the ANSI C standard, providing essential runtime functionality for C programs. It handles common needs such as data types and error handling, mathematical operations including floating-point and constant definitions, and core programming utilities. The scope of libc extends to crucial programming features: robust input/output (I/O) operations, extensive string manipulation capabilities, precise time and date handling, flexible variable argument processing, signal management, and sophisticated flow control through non-local jumps. It also supports internationalization programming with locale handling and includes diagnostic tools through program assertions, forming a complete ecosystem for C language development.

The GNU C Library (glibc) stands as a cornerstone of GNU/Linux, providing essential APIs that underpin the vast majority of applications, as depicted in Fig. 2.3. This comprehensive library extends beyond standard libc functionality, incorporating sophisticated POSIX-compliant system calls, including semaphores and interprocess communication mechanisms. Its implementation embraces virtually every established UNIX standard, showcasing its remarkable versatility.

glibc not only marks a crucial milestone in the evolution of GNU/Linux but also serves as an invaluable educational resource for C programming enthusiasts. Distributed under the GNU Lesser General Public License (LGPL), its source code remains fully accessible and free for study and examination. A prime example of its educational value lies in its implementation of the **strcpy** function, a topic

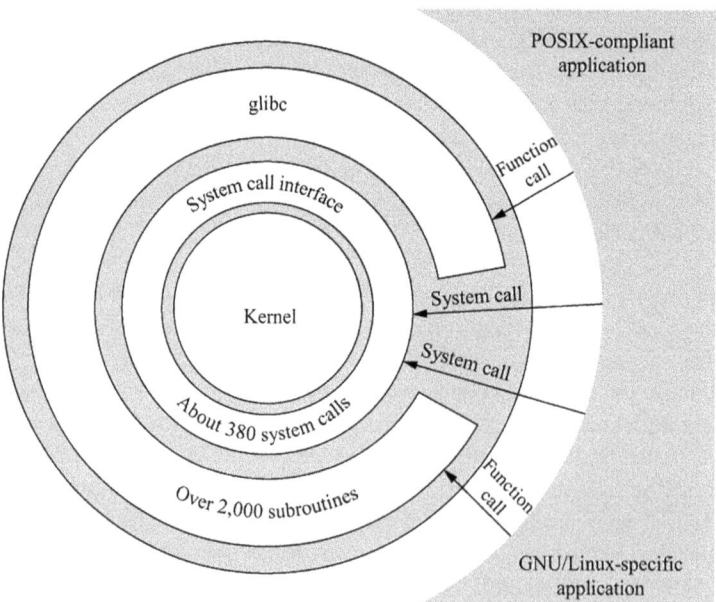

Fig. 2.3 glibc architecture

2.1 Basic Components of OSs

frequently discussed in software development interviews. The glibc approach to this function reveals an innovative code logic that differs significantly from conventional implementations, as demonstrated in the following core code.

```c
char *strcpy(char *dest, const char *src)
{
    char *s = src;
    const ptrdiff_t off = dest -s -1;
    do {
        s[off]=*s;
    } while (*s++ != '\0');
    return dest;
}
```

The actual implementation is more sophisticated and varies across CPU architectures. By examining this core code segment, what fundamental strategy does glibc employ in its implementations? Beyond this example, glibc contains numerous other function implementations, such as **strlen**, and interested readers are encouraged to delve into the source code to discover these implementations firsthand.

Text Editors

Text editors, essential tools for modifying text files, occupy dramatically different positions across OSs. While they might appear peripheral in Windows, they stand as cornerstone utilities in UNIX-like OSs, deeply integrated into daily operations.

In the GUI-centric world of Windows, text editors play a minimal role, particularly in contemporary mobile OSs where touch interfaces dominate and entertainment takes center stage. System administrators rely on specialized binary tools for configuration, while developers navigate through various editors embedded in integrated development environments (IDEs) such as MATLAB and Visual Studio. This fragmentation forces developers to constantly switch between different editing paradigms and workflows.

UNIX-like OSs present a stark contrast. Here, text editors emerge as foundational tools for both system maintenance and software development, crafted by hackers and programmers to address practical needs. These editors exemplify elegant design principles, delivering either remarkable efficiency or comprehensive functionality. Their evolution since inception demonstrates the enduring strength of UNIX culture, while their innovative approaches have elevated text editing to an art form. Users can achieve exceptional productivity by mastering just a handful of

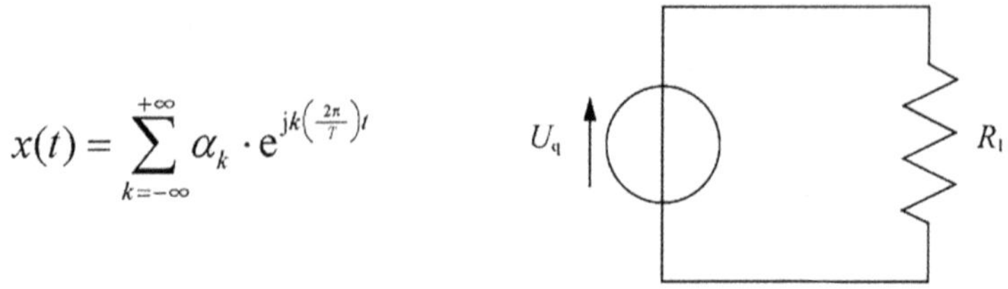

$$x(t) = \sum_{k=-\infty}^{+\infty} \alpha_k \cdot e^{jk\left(\frac{2\pi}{T}\right)t}$$

Fig. 2.4 Formula and circuit diagram generated by LaTeX using text files

editors and adapting them to their preferred workflow—a testament to the text-centric design philosophy of UNIX [11].

At its core, UNIX embraces text files over binary formats whenever feasible. Text files offer simplicity in parsing and universal accessibility through any text editor, eliminating concerns about file corruption or version incompatibility. This philosophy extends throughout the system, from configuration files to foundational Internet protocols like Hypertext Transfer Protocol (HTTP), Simple Mail Transfer Protocol (SMTP), Post Office Protocol Version 3 (POPv3), and File Transfer Protocol (FTP). The text-based approach enables efficient handling of complex tasks, from creating tables and graphs to composing technical documents and academic papers. As demonstrated in Fig. 2.4, even sophisticated outputs like math formulas and circuit diagrams can be generated from straightforward text input using tools like LaTeX.

```
\documentclass{article}
\begin{document}
\[ x(t)=\sum^{+\infty}_{k=-\infty}\alpha_k\cdot e^{jk(\frac{2\pi}{T})t} \]
\newpage
\begin{figure}[h!]
  \begin{circuitikz}
  \draw (0,0)
    to[V,v=$U_q$] (0,2)
    to[short] (2,2)
    to[R=$R_1$] (2,0)
    to[short] (0,0);
  \end{circuitikz}
\end{figure}
\end{document}
```

The fertile ground of UNIX philosophy spawned an exceptional generation of text editors, from ed, ex, and sed to vi, vim, nano, and Emacs. These pioneering tools introduced powerful and flexible capabilities that continue to influence editor design today. Modern editors like Notepad++, UltraEdit, Sublime Text, Atom, jEdit, and Visual Studio Code build upon this foundation, incorporating time-tested principles while introducing innovative features. Yet, despite the decades that have passed, these original editors maintain their classic status, with Vi and Emacs standing as towering figures representing two distinct and enduring approaches to text editing.

In 1976, UC Berkeley graduate student Bill Joy[3] revolutionized text editing with vi, the first full-screen console editor. This groundbreaking tool, dubbed the "god of editors," marked a significant departure from earlier line editors like Thompson's ed and George Coulouris' em.[4] The brilliance of vi lies in its ergonomic design philosophy: users can execute all editing commands while maintaining their fingers on the keyboard's central area. This powerful editor handles everything from system configurations to programming files across virtually any UNIX-like platform. Its distinctive approach has created a passionate following, though its learning curve has deterred many newcomers.

Building on vi's foundation, Bram Moolenaar[5] created Vim (vi IMproved), enhancing the original with sophisticated features. Vim introduces modern amenities like syntax highlighting, intelligent indentation, auto-completion, advanced pattern matching, block operations, and infinite undo capability. Its extensible architecture welcomes user-created scripts and plugins, enabling deep customization. The standout advantage of the vi family remains its universal consistency—users can work efficiently on any system without reconfiguring their environment. This versatility has established Vim as a cornerstone tool alongside Emacs in the UNIX ecosystem, particularly among system administrators and developers. Figure 2.5 demonstrates the sophisticated multi-buffer editing capability of Vim.

The 1970s witnessed the birth of Emacs at MIT's Artificial Intelligence Laboratory, where it emerged as a pioneering force in text editing and integrated development [11]. This versatile platform, revered as the "editor of gods," revolutionized document handling through its innovative "major modes" system. These specialized modes adapt the editor's behavior for different file types, from plain text and programming languages to Hypertext Markup Language (HTML) and LaTeX documents. At its core, Emacs embodies the philosophy of unlimited customization, offering users the power to define their own modes, keyboard shortcuts, and macros, while providing advanced capabilities like multi-window editing, comprehensive bookmarking, multiple clipboards, and sophisticated block operations. It even transcends traditional text editing by supporting rich media like images and PDFs.

---

[3] Joy earned the moniker "software god" through his extraordinary achievements. Beyond creating vi, he masterminded the development of BSD, TCP/IP, NFS, Java, and the SPARC microprocessor architecture. In 1982, he established Sun Microsystems as a co-founder and guided the company's technical vision as Chief Scientist for over two decades until 2003.

[4] For insights into the evolution from ed to em/vi, readers can explore various interviews with Joy.

[5] Moolenaar, who departed on August 3, 2023, leaves behind an enduring legacy. He dedicated nearly half his lifetime to developing Vim, profoundly impacting the open source community through his unwavering commitment.

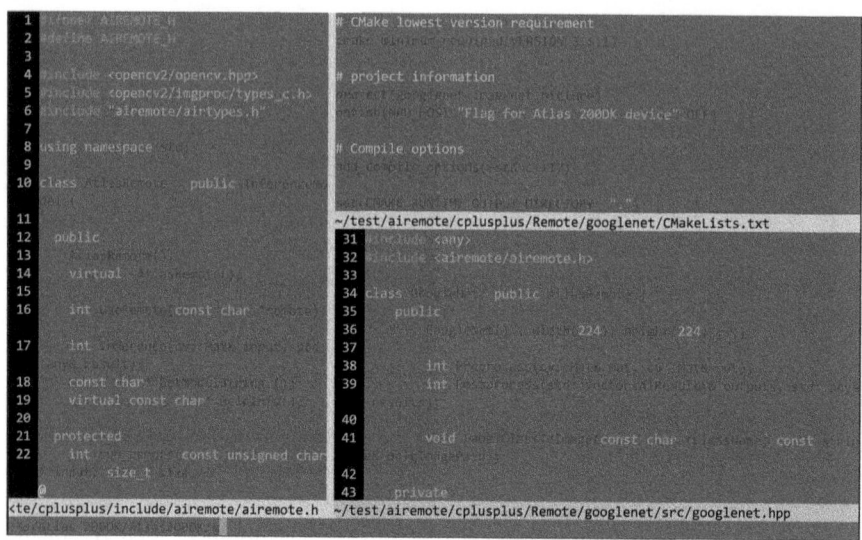

Fig. 2.5 Multi-buffer editing interface of Vim

In the modern computing landscape, Emacs demonstrates remarkable versatility, functioning seamlessly across GNU/Linux, Windows, Android, and iOS platforms. Its vast ecosystem of extensions transforms it into a Swiss Army knife for text manipulation tasks. Though initially daunting with its intricate command structure and challenging learning curve, Emacs rewards persistent users with unparalleled editing efficiency that becomes an essential part of their workflow. Figure 2.6 showcases this versatility, presenting a multi-buffer environment that exemplifies the powerful capabilities of Emacs.

The open source ecosystem also offers several lightweight alternatives, including nano, JOE, and Pico. These streamlined editors excel in resource-constrained scenarios, proving particularly valuable during system installations or on embedded platforms.

2.1.4 User Interfaces

The user interface (UI) serves as the crucial bridge between an OS and its users, providing an accessible means to utilize system services. In UNIX-like OSs, this interface manifests primarily through the shell, acting as the intermediate layer between users and the kernel [8]. Beyond its fundamental role of processing inputs and launching programs, the UI encompasses vital functions like directory

2.1 Basic Components of OSs

Fig. 2.6 Multi-buffer editing interface of EmacsNote: Top-left shows C++ code, bottom-left displays a shell interface, top-right contains a Markdown document, and bottom-right features a psychotherapist program and a mini-game

navigation, content viewing, and task management. At its core, it acts as the gateway through which users initiate other programs.

Modern computing environments feature two distinct interface paradigms: CLI and GUI. The CLI embraces a text-centric approach, where users interact through typed commands and receive textual feedback, exemplified by various shell implementations of UNIX-like OSs. In contrast, the GUI leverages visual elements and pointer-based interaction, as demonstrated by Windows File Explorer, macOS Finder, and desktop environments in UNIX-like OSs such as GNOME, KDE, and Xfce.

While Windows systems traditionally emphasize GUI interaction through File Explorer, offering an intuitive experience for general users, this approach often proves insufficient for developers seeking efficiency and automation capabilities. Although Windows initially provided limited command-line functionality through cmd.exe, the introduction of PowerShell in 2006 marked a significant advancement in CLI capabilities of Windows. Built on .NET Framework, PowerShell transcends traditional command interpretation, offering a sophisticated environment for both command execution and scripting. Its extensive command library, modular extensibility, and robust automation capabilities—spanning user management, continuous integration/continuous deployment (CI/CD) workflows, and cloud resource administration—have established it as the premier CLI solution in the Windows ecosystem.

UNIX-like OSs excel in providing developers with sophisticated interaction interfaces that, while demanding initial investment in learning, deliver exceptional productivity returns. These OSs emphasize CLI-based interaction, offering a powerful combination of command interpretation and scripting capabilities that

Fig. 2.7 ASCII art in CLI

streamline software development and automation workflows. The seemingly austere text-based environment has evolved into a rich ecosystem, spawning innovative applications from text-based menu systems to character art utilities (illustrated in Fig. 2.7), demonstrating remarkable versatility within command-line constraints.

The foundation of CLI rests on the shell, a sophisticated interface layer between users and the kernel. The watershed moment came in 1977 when Stephen Bourne introduced the Bourne Shell (sh for short) at Bell Labs for Version 7 UNIX. This groundbreaking shell introduced fundamental concepts like control flows, loops, and variables, while pioneering essential features such as pipes, redirection, and here documents.[6] Its elegant design and robust functionality established a lasting legacy, serving as the blueprint for modern shell development.

Contemporary shells, particularly Bourne-again shell (Bash), have elevated command-line interaction to new heights [12]. As the default shell in many GNU/Linux distributions including openEuler, Bash maintains compatibility with its predecessor while introducing advanced features like intelligent command completion, sophisticated editing capabilities, and comprehensive command history tracking. By incorporating the strengths of both csh and ksh, along with its powerful programming interface, Bash has transformed command-line interaction and script development into a remarkably efficient and productive experience.

In UNIX-like OSs, both CLI and GUI function as standard applications performing specialized interaction tasks. This elegant architectural choice simultaneously streamlines the system and empowers users with unprecedented flexibility. Users enjoy complete freedom to select their preferred interface, fine-tune it through window managers, and determine their GUI usage based on specific requirements. FVWM exemplifies this flexibility, offering virtually limitless GUI customization possibilities, as showcased in Fig. 2.8.

The GUI implementation in UNIX-like OSs builds upon the X Window foundation, developed at MIT in 1984. This system embodies a distinctive philosophy of providing mechanisms rather than enforcing policies [8]. It employs a unique architecture that separates GUI content generation from display management through X

---

[6] Here documents serve as a powerful text stream input redirection technique, enabling content I/O redirection to interactive programs or terminals, which greatly simplifies script writing.

2.1 Basic Components of OSs

Fig. 2.8 Customized desktop of FVWM

Client and X Server components. This client–server relationship presents an intriguing contrast to Windows Remote Desktop, with X Clients generating graphical content and X Servers managing I/O devices, including monitors, keyboards, and mouses. This separation, facilitated by the X protocol, enables distributed operation across different hosts, creating a remarkably flexible GUI framework that supports remote graphical interaction even without local display hardware.

> X11R6 was a widely adopted classic X protocol version, with XFree86 and Xorg being the primary X Server implementations on Linux. X Server can also run on Windows systems, allowing Linux X Client GUIs to display on Windows desktops. Setting up these connections is straightforward using SSH (Secure Shell) forwarding mechanisms, which are covered in Chap. 7.

These architectural decisions have created a UI ecosystem that many UNIX users celebrate for its exceptional customizability, efficiency, and ability to accommodate diverse personal preferences and workflows.

2.2 Overview of Modern OSs

OSs fall into three distinct categories based on their intended use: desktop, server, and embedded OSs.

2.2.1 Desktop OSs

Desktop OSs power PCs, prioritizing user-friendly interfaces and accessibility. The personal computing landscape divides along two primary lines: hardware (PCs versus Macs) and software platforms (Windows versus UNIX-like OSs).

The Windows family encompasses various iterations, from the early Windows 3.1 through Windows 95, XP, ME, 8, and 10.

The UNIX-based ecosystem includes Mac OS X and numerous Linux distributions, including Red Hat Enterprise Linux (RHEL), Debian, Ubuntu, openSUSE, and Fedora Linux.

While all these OSs employ monolithic kernel architectures and feature comprehensive application suites with GUIs, Windows and UNIX represent fundamentally different philosophies in OS design. Their divergent approaches manifest in OS architecture, extensibility, performance metrics, and user interaction models. UNIX-like OSs excel in stability, while Windows emphasizes intuitive GUIs for everyday tasks. UNIX-like OSs leverage CLIs, enhancing operational efficiency and providing deeper insights into system operations—particularly valuable for those learning programming and OS architecture.

2.2.2 Server OSs

Server OSs, designed for enterprise-grade hardware including web, application, and database servers, prioritize performance, security, and reliability. They comprise three main families:

1. UNIX variants: FreeBSD, Oracle Solaris, IBM AIX, and HP-UX
2. GNU/Linux distributions: Community Enterprise Operating System (CentOS), RHEL, Debian, and Ubuntu
3. Windows Server editions: from Windows NT through Server 2003, 2008, and 2022

While all these platforms support commercial deployments, they differ in their performance characteristics, reliability metrics, and maintenance requirements. UNIX variants dominate mission-critical sectors like banking and energy infrastructure. GNU/Linux continues to gain traction in educational and entertainment sectors, while Windows Server typically serves small to medium enterprises and modest web hosting operations.

2.2.3 Embedded OSs

Embedded OSs power specialized devices, prioritizing efficiency, power management, and real-time performance. These systems represent purpose-built computing platforms that integrate hardware and software components to meet specific requirements—from performance and reliability to cost constraints, physical dimensions, power efficiency, and environmental adaptability. Their presence pervades both industrial and consumer domains, driving everything from portable electronics like smartphones, tablets, and digital cameras to critical infrastructure, including medical devices, traffic control systems, avionics, and industrial automation equipment.

The embedded OS landscape encompasses specialized platforms such as μC/OS-III, Embedded Linux, Windows Embedded, and VxWorks. In the consumer electronics sector, particularly for smartphones and tablets, prominent systems include Android, iOS, Symbian, Windows Phone, BlackBerry OS, and the emerging IoT-focused OpenHarmony.

The mobile OS ecosystem particularly highlights the enduring influence of UNIX: Android builds upon GNU/Linux architecture, while iOS derives from BSD kernel foundations, exemplifying the versatility and robustness of UNIX-like OSs across the embedded computing spectrum.

2.3 Outstanding Features of GNU/Linux

Linux has emerged as one of the most pervasive OSs, powering everything from servers and cloud infrastructure to embedded systems. This widespread adoption stems from its elegant architecture, open source foundation, and remarkable portability.

The open source foundation empowers developers to explore, modify, and enhance the source code while customizing their development environment. This freedom breeds collaboration and drives innovation within the community. Linux excels in performance-critical scenarios, offering exceptional efficiency and scalability across diverse hardware architectures, making it the go-to choice for resource-intensive operations. Its robust CLI and scripting capabilities enable powerful automation, streamlining development processes.

The versatility of Linux shines through its deployment across multiple platforms. From PCs to IoT devices and supercomputers, its stability, security, and adaptability prove invaluable. Ubuntu has captured the hearts of desktop users with its intuitive interface, while Android—Google's Linux-based mobile OS—has revolutionized smartphone computing. Notably, since 2017, Linux powers all of the world's top 500 supercomputers.

The platform serves as an ideal learning ground for developers diving deep into software development. While Windows dominates the consumer market with its accessibility, its proprietary nature creates barriers between developers and the rich ecosystem of open source resources. In contrast, Linux continues to attract and inspire technology enthusiasts worldwide with its open architecture.

The triumph of Linux embodies the elegant fusion of UNIX philosophy with modern innovation, marking an extraordinary achievement in software evolution. This harmonious blend of traditional wisdom and progressive thinking has created an enduring legacy in computing history.

2.3.1 UNIX Design Philosophy Legacy

UNIX stands as a testament to elegant engineering, celebrated for its streamlined efficiency and architectural grace. At its core lies the "divide and conquer" philosophy—a principle so fundamental it has transcended its origins to become a cornerstone of software design, offering valuable insights even to developers outside the UNIX ecosystem [11].

Rather than a rigid methodology, the UNIX philosophy embodies a collective wisdom—an organic accumulation of engineering insights passed down through generations of developers. This approach emerged from Thompson's initial vision of creating an OS with minimal, well-crafted interfaces, and has evolved into a comprehensive set of guiding principles through the maturation of UNIX.

The "divide and conquer" ethos permeates every aspect of UNIX—from its architectural foundations to its programming paradigms, toolchains, and user interaction models. This philosophy champions modular design through clean interfaces, emphasizing simplicity, clarity, separation of concerns, composability, transparency, and consistency. By elegantly decomposing complex systems into manageable components, UNIX achieves remarkable flexibility and power while maintaining simplicity, resulting in a system that's both robust and adaptable.

Mike Gancarz, a pioneering figure in UNIX/Linux advocacy and X Window system development, codified these traditionally oral principles in his seminal work *Linux and the UNIX Philosophy*. His systematic documentation transformed these time-tested practices from tribal knowledge into accessible wisdom, revealing several fundamental concepts:

(1) Small is beautiful
Programs should embrace minimalism, focusing on executing a single task efficiently while delegating other functions elsewhere. This approach yields code that is intuitive, maintainable, and readily integrated with other tools. Linux exemplifies this philosophy through its core toolkit—mastering these few dozen utilities unlocks the full potential of the system.

(2) Make each program do one thing well
The commitment to a singular purpose extends beyond mere size constraints. Each program should excel at its designated function, mirroring the single-responsibility principle (SRP) found in modern software design. This laser focus on excellence in simplicity drives the effectiveness of UNIX and Linux.

(3) Write programs that work together
The innovative pipe system of UNIX revolutionized program interaction, enabling complex operations through elegant combinations of simple tools.

2.3 Outstanding Features of GNU/Linux

These programs function as sophisticated filters, transforming data while preserving its fundamental structure.

(4) Provide mechanism, not policy

The architecture of UNIX carefully separates mechanisms from policies, distinguishing between core functionality and its implementation. This separation enhances flexibility and maintainability, allowing programs to evolve independently as requirements change.

(5) Store data in plain text files

Text streams embody a universal format. Unlike binary formats, they can be read and edited with any preferred text editor. This philosophy represents UNIX's commitment to accessibility and resilience, as demonstrated by its use of plain text for system configurations. The approach markedly differs from the binary registry system of Windows, which demands specialized tools and complicates recovery in the case of data corruption.

The prevalence of text-based formats extends far beyond OSs. Core Internet protocols, including HTTP and various Internet Engineering Task Force (IETF) standards, utilize text-based communication. This practice flourishes in contemporary technologies, from data interchange formats like Extensible Markup Language (XML) and JavaScript Object Notation (JSON) to document preparation systems such as Markdown and LaTeX—with LaTeX maintaining particular prominence in academic publishing.

(6) Everything is a file

This paradigm unifies system resource access through a consistent interface. This elegant abstraction simplifies interaction with diverse system elements, from directories to network interfaces, proving remarkably powerful in practice.

These principles converge on the fundamental KISS (Keep It Simple, Stupid) principle, emphasizing elegant simplicity in problem-solving (Fig. 2.9). This philosophy remains the cornerstone of UNIX design thinking.

2.3.2 Freedom and Openness

The principles of freedom and openness ignite passionate dedication among UNIX enthusiasts and stand as pillars of the remarkable success of Linux. These fundamental values continue to inspire software enthusiasts worldwide to delve into GNU/Linux [5].

Fig. 2.9 KISS, the fundamental principle of UNIX design philosophy

The journey of UNIX began with open source code distribution before commercialization captured its early momentum. BSD maintained the torch of openness, catalyzing the nascent open source software movement and eventually spawning a diverse ecosystem of modern OSs, including the robust FreeBSD and NetBSD, alongside Apple's sophisticated Mac OS X.

UC Berkeley, an institution synonymous with intellectual freedom, gave birth to BSD. In 1977, Joy's compilation of programs became the first Berkeley Software Distribution (1BSD), initially an extension of Version 6 UNIX. The following year's 2BSD release introduced Joy's groundbreaking vi text editor (a visual version of ex) and C shell—tools that remain fundamental to UNIX-like OSs today. By 1983, 4.2BSD emerged as a technological tour de force, notably featuring a pioneering TCP/IP implementation.

The landscape shifted dramatically in 1991 with Net/2's release—a clean-room implementation free from AT&T code. This milestone spawned two significant projects: William Jolitz's free 386BSD and BSDi's commercial BSD/OS. Although the direct influence of 386BSD was brief, it laid the foundation for NetBSD and FreeBSD.

A protracted legal battle between BSDi and UNIX System Laboratories (USL), a subsidiary owned by AT&T, cast a shadow over BSD development from 1992 to 1994. This dispute, centered on UNIX System V copyright and the UNIX trademark, effectively froze BSD and free software evolution for two years. During this legal paralysis, Linux flourished unencumbered, gaining crucial momentum in the open source landscape.

> Linux and 386BSD started almost simultaneously. Linux creator Torvalds later remarked, "If 386BSD had been available when I started on Linux, Linux would probably never had happened."

4.4BSD emerged in June 1994 with dual releases: the unrestricted 4.4BSD-Lite, purged of AT&T code, and 4.4BSD-Encumbered, which maintained AT&T licensing requirements. The BSD journey culminated in 1995 with 4.4BSD-Lite Release 2, marking the dissolution of the CSRG. This transition ushered in the era of community-driven development through FreeBSD, OpenBSD, and NetBSD projects.

The influence of BSD extends far beyond its direct descendants, thanks to its permissive license. This openness enabled both free and commercial systems to leverage BSD code, notably the TCP/IP stack of Windows and various networking utilities that persist today. BSD's legacy thrives in academia, commercial ventures, and increasingly in embedded systems. Its architectural elegance, pristine code quality, and exemplary documentation—particularly the renowned "man pages"—have established it as an invaluable learning resource for generations of programmers.

Parallel to the evolution of BSD, the GNU project emerged with the ambitious goal of creating a free UNIX alternative. By 1990, GNU had assembled an impressive collection of free software tools, including the revolutionary GCC compiler, lacking only a kernel to complete its vision. Torvalds' 1991 introduction of the POSIX-compliant Linux kernel proved transformative, perfectly complementing the existing framework of GNU. The GPL license of Linux fostered unprecedented collaboration, pioneering the "bazaar model"[7] of distributed development through Internet-enabled tools, including email communication and version control systems. This innovative approach accelerated kernel development, enabling rapid adaptation across diverse computing platforms.

> Good programmers know what to write. Great programmers know what to rewrite (and reuse).—Eric S. Raymond

Linux exemplifies code reuse at its finest, supported by vast open source communities maintaining petabytes of freely accessible code. This rich ecosystem offers unparalleled opportunities for finding and adapting existing solutions, fundamentally transforming software development practices and benefiting countless projects through its commitment to openness.

2.3.3 Portability

Portability measures how readily code can migrate between different architectures. Linux excels in this aspect through its thoughtfully engineered kernel, robust C runtime libraries, and extensive suite of POSIX-compatible applications, enabling seamless deployment across diverse computing platforms.

While portability and performance traditionally present competing priorities, Linux strikes an elegant balance. The system implements most interfaces and core functionality in architecture-agnostic C code, selectively optimizing kernel features for specific hardware architectures only where performance demands are paramount. Performance-critical and hardware-specific components leverage assembly

---

[7] For deeper insights, see *The Cathedral and the Bazaar* by Eric S. Raymond—a pioneering hacker, open source advocate, and preeminent theorist of hacker culture. This seminal work weaves together riveting narratives from the open source revolution with time-tested wisdom and revolutionary concepts that continue to illuminate the path for software developers worldwide.

language, achieving an optimal compromise between cross-platform compatibility and computational efficiency.

Furthermore, the modular architecture of Linux enables precise system customization, allowing developers to tailor deployments to specific resource constraints and service requirements. This flexibility makes Linux equally well-suited for desktop environments, enterprise servers, and resource-constrained embedded systems.

2.4 Introduction to openEuler

openEuler stands at the forefront of digital infrastructure as a versatile open source OS. Through groundbreaking innovations in the Linux kernel and system applications, it seamlessly integrates with diverse computing environments—from traditional servers to cutting-edge cloud platforms, edge computing systems, and embedded devices. The system excels in bridging operational technology (OT) applications with ICT1, creating a unified technological ecosystem [7].

The OS traces its roots to EulerOS, originally developed for Huawei's enterprise servers. Built on Linux kernel 4.19, EulerOS demonstrates remarkable versatility by supporting both x86 and Arm architectures, serving diverse computational needs from database management to AI applications. Over nearly a decade, EulerOS has earned international recognition by delivering exceptional security, stability, and performance across Huawei's product portfolio. The exponential growth of cloud computing, particularly through Huawei Cloud, elevated the strategic importance of server OSs, catalyzing EulerOS's advancement. The OS gained additional significance as the natural software foundation for Huawei's innovative Kunpeng processors. In a strategic move to accelerate ecosystem development and foster global technological advancement, Huawei transformed EulerOS into openEuler through open-sourcing in late 2019.

2.4.1 Architecture

The overall architecture of openEuler, depicted in Fig. 2.10, showcases both conventional and innovative elements. At its core, this multi-scenario OS incorporates standard components: memory management, process management, interprocess communication (IPC), file systems, networking, device management, and virtualization with container support. However, openEuler distinguishes itself through advanced features that surpass traditional server OSs. These innovations include sophisticated multi-core scheduling mechanisms, seamless hardware–software synergy, efficient lightweight virtualization, optimized instruction-level processing, and an intelligent tuning engine.

2.4 Introduction to openEuler

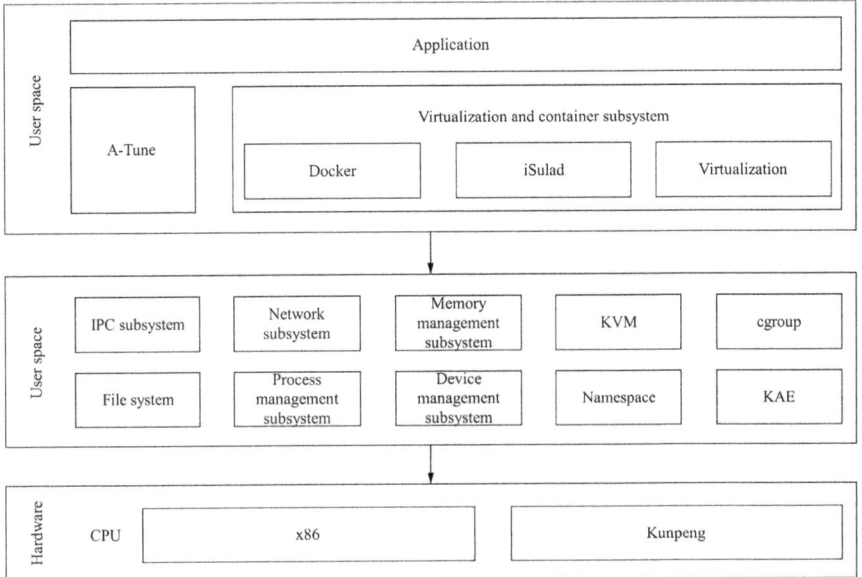

Fig. 2.10 Overall architecture of openEuler

2.4.2 Innovative Features

openEuler represents a paradigm shift in OS design by unifying support for mainstream computing architectures under a single framework. This breakthrough enables diverse computing capabilities while advancing GNU/Linux innovation.

openEuler's core innovations encompass multiple dimensions. Its sophisticated multi-kernel architecture dramatically improves concurrent processing in multi-core systems, while cutting-edge features—including AI-driven tuning, tiered memory expansion, and the lightweight iSulad container engine—deliver superior performance and scalability. Security receives comprehensive treatment through full-stack Chinese cryptographic algorithms (also known as ShangMi algorithms, or SM for short) and advanced policy tools. System administration becomes streamlined through AI-powered maintenance and hot service capabilities. The innovative Lego-style architecture, combined with full-stack atomic decoupling, enables unprecedented flexibility in version customization and service deployment.

In pioneering all-scenario computing, openEuler introduces a unified architecture spanning traditional servers to edge devices. This comprehensive approach integrates diverse hardware platforms while supporting varied applications through a common framework. The distributed soft bus (DSoftBus) technology enables seamless integration with platforms like OpenHarmony, facilitating ecosystem interconnectivity and enabling true cloud-edge-device synergy, as illustrated in Fig. 2.11.

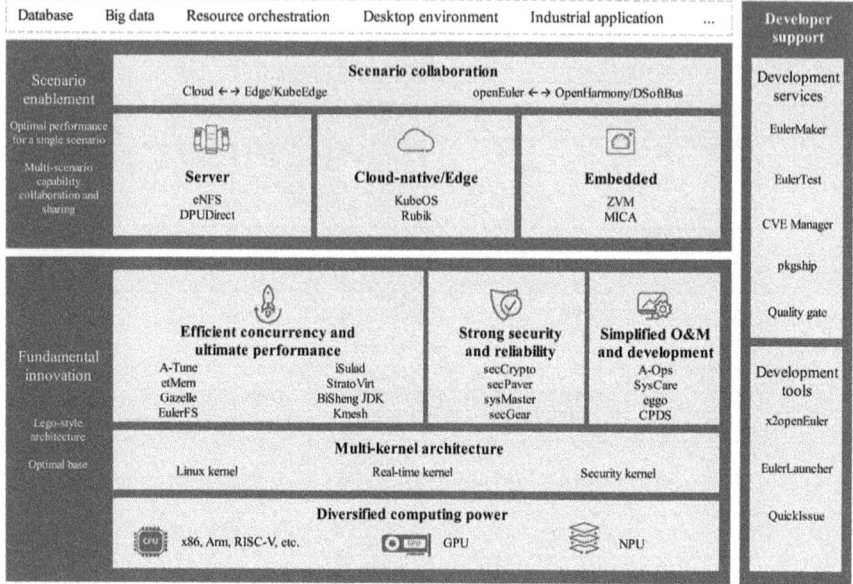

Fig. 2.11 openEuler: open source OS for digital infrastructure

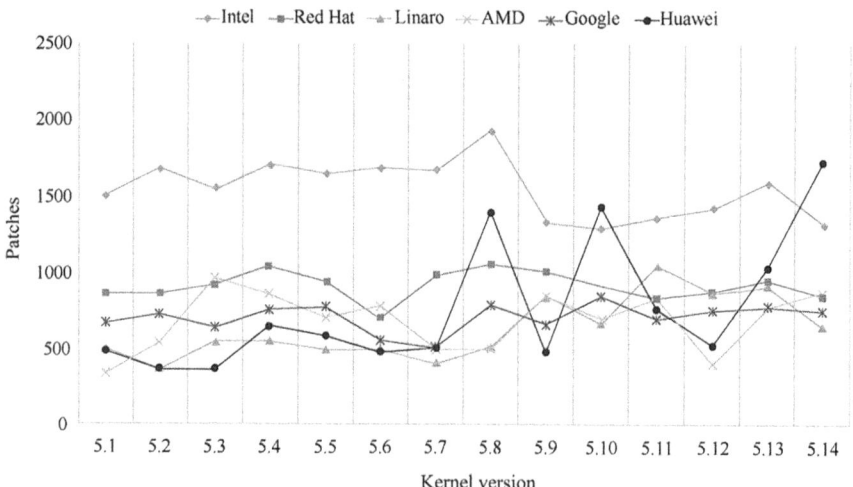

Fig. 2.12 openEuler's contributions to the Linux kernel

2.4.3 Open Source Contributions

openEuler has established itself as the leading contributor to Linux kernel versions 5.10 and 5.14, as depicted in Fig. 2.12. These substantial contributions, spearheaded by Huawei, span crucial areas including processor architecture optimization, Advanced Configuration and Power Interface (ACPI) implementation, memory management enhancement, file system improvements, multimedia capabilities, kernel documentation, comprehensive quality assurance, and architectural refinements.

openEuler maintains development momentum through semi-annual innovation versions, efficiently incorporating cutting-edge open source advancements. Community-validated features undergo systematic integration into distributions, with new capabilities packaged as discrete open source projects—ensuring accessibility for developers and interoperability across the open source ecosystem.

2.5 Hands-On with openEuler

This book focuses on openEuler 24.03 LTS. For those new to openEuler, we strongly recommend starting with a virtual environment before moving to physical hardware. Below are three virtual environment options for exploring openEuler. Choose the method that best suits your needs to create your learning and development environment.

2.5.1 Huawei Cloud

Users with Huawei Cloud vouchers or those interested in leasing or purchasing Elastic Cloud Servers (ECSs) can access detailed setup and login instructions on the Huawei Cloud website.

Huawei Cloud ECSs deliver instantly available, scalable computing power, combining CPUs, memory, images, and cloud storage to create a secure, dependable, and efficient platform for applications.

2.5.2 VMware Setup

VMware Workstation enables desktop virtualization, allowing users to run multiple virtual machines (VMs) on Windows or Linux systems. OSs like Windows, Linux, and BSD can be easily installed in these VMs. A free 30-day trial with full functionality is available through VMware Workstation Pro or Player.

Most modern PCs exceed VMware Workstation's modest requirements of 2 GB memory and 10 GB storage space per VM.

VMware Workstation offers the most comprehensive openEuler installation experience at no cost. Detailed setup instructions are provided in the appendix.

2.5.3 Docker Container Deployment

For users familiar with Docker, this represents the most streamlined approach to experiencing openEuler.

1. Pull the openEuler image:

```
$ docker pull openeuler/openeuler:24.03-lts
```

2. Create and run the openEuler container:

```
$ docker run -tid --name openEuler24 --hostname=openEuler24 openeuler/openeuler:24.03-lts
```

3. Run the container interactively:

```
$ docker exec -it openEuler24 bash
```

2.6 Summary

This chapter explores the foundational elements of OSs, beginning with their classic architecture and core components: the kernel, applications, and UI. It examines various OS types—desktop, server, and embedded systems—before delving into UNIX design principles and distinctive features of GNU/Linux. The discussion culminates with an in-depth look at openEuler's architecture, innovations, open source contributions, and practical implementation.

openEuler stands out for its versatility, extending beyond traditional Linux kernel and server operations. It pioneers solutions for emerging technologies like edge computing, embedded systems, and IoT through its real-time kernel capabilities. This unified yet flexible architecture accommodates diverse applications, marking a significant departure from conventional OSs.

Upon completing this chapter, readers should have gained comprehensive insights into kernel functionality, system calls, application integration, and UI design. Readers will understand the philosophical underpinnings of UNIX and GNU/Linux, appreciate open source community dynamics, and recognize openEuler's technological innovations and competitive advantages.

Reflection and Practice

1. Outline the core components of UNIX and illustrate its logical structure.
2. Identify primary functions of the kernel.
3. Examine the UI–kernel relationship and the rationale behind their separation.
4. Enumerate the key principles of UNIX design philosophy.
5. Analyze the catalysts behind the rapid evolution of GNU/Linux.
6. Detail openEuler's innovative features.
7. Establish a working environment with openEuler 24.03 LTS using your preferred method.

Open Access This chapter is licensed under the terms of the Creative Commons Attribution-NonCommercial-NoDerivatives 4.0 International License (http://creativecommons.org/licenses/by-nc-nd/4.0/), which permits any noncommercial use, sharing, distribution and reproduction in any medium or format, as long as you give appropriate credit to the original author(s) and the source, provide a link to the Creative Commons license and indicate if you modified the licensed material. You do not have permission under this license to share adapted material derived from this chapter or parts of it.

The images or other third party material in this chapter are included in the chapter's Creative Commons license, unless indicated otherwise in a credit line to the material. If material is not included in the chapter's Creative Commons license and your intended use is not permitted by statutory regulation or exceeds the permitted use, you will need to obtain permission directly from the copyright holder.

Chapter 3
Getting Started with openEuler

Objectives

1. Explore the two interaction interfaces of openEuler.
2. Master essential command-line operations.
3. Become proficient with advanced shell features
4. Understand users and permissions.
5. Learn DDE installation procedures.

Developed on the Linux kernel, openEuler advances Linux innovations while maintaining familiar usage operations. openEuler is equipped with both a GUI and CLI to meet distinct purposes: the GUI executes point-and-click operations, particularly for web browsing, email, and media entertainment, but lacks advanced system administration and development support, while the CLI, though initially daunting to newcomers, is invaluable for processing complex operations through concise command combinations. This chapter examines the various command-line options within the dynamic world of Linux.

This chapter introduces the openEuler Xfce desktop environment, examines basic and essential UNIX CLI commands, and analyzes the roles of the commands within areas like advanced shell features, user permission model, and permission management. This information is compounded through hands-on experience, underscoring the fundamentals of the UNIX design and openEuler CLI. For example, the openEuler command set offers sophisticated options for task execution, while shell pipes and redirection allow for combinations of multiple commands, enabling more complex operations and workloads that surpass any single graphical application. By chaining commands together, you can achieve powerful functionality and efficiency far beyond that of typical graphical interfaces.

Mastering openEuler requires neither shortcuts nor rote memorization—rather, it demands consistent hands-on practice. Through dedicated practice, study, and persistence, you will be able to gain a full understanding of UNIX CLI commands and related operations.

3.1 Interaction Interfaces

openEuler, in keeping with its UNIX-based counterparts, offers both GUI and CLI, enabling users to select the most appropriate interface for their specific needs. While newcomers often find the GUI more approachable, deeper engagement with openEuler reveals the compelling advantages of command-line operations.

openEuler defaults to the CLI upon installation, with the GUI available for custom installation and configuration according to user preferences.

3.1.1 GUI

The Linux graphical environment is delivered through desktop environments such as GNOME, KDE, Xfce, and LXDE, enabling users to effortlessly accomplish everyday computing operations from web browsing to multimedia entertainment.

The GUI proves more approachable than the CLI, especially for those transitioning from Windows or macOS. openEuler accommodates diverse user preferences through multiple desktop environments—UKUI, DDE, Xfce, and GNOME—and even supports custom desktop environment development for ambitious users.

This section explores the Xfce desktop environment, covering its core components and encouraging hands-on experimentation.

(1) Home screen

Upon logging in graphically, users encounter openEuler's home screen (Fig. 3.1), featuring familiar elements like the desktop, taskbar, application launcher, workspace switcher, and status bar. While operation mirrors other graphical systems, Linux distinguishes itself through extensive customization options, from window manager selection to sophisticated desktop zone configuration.

(2) File management

The file manager mirrors Windows File Explorer's functionality (Fig. 3.2), handling local file operations and network sharing with familiar ease.

(3) Text editing

openEuler provides intuitive text editors like gedit and mousepad (Fig. 3.3 shows gedit in action), complemented by sophisticated development environments like Visual Studio Code.

(4) Terminal access

The terminal emulator (Fig. 3.4) bridges the GUI and CLI, accessible via **Ctrl+Alt+T** or the context menu, offering command-line power within the graphical environment.

Despite its advantages in accessibility and visual feedback, the GUI presents several limitations for professional users.

3.1 Interaction Interfaces

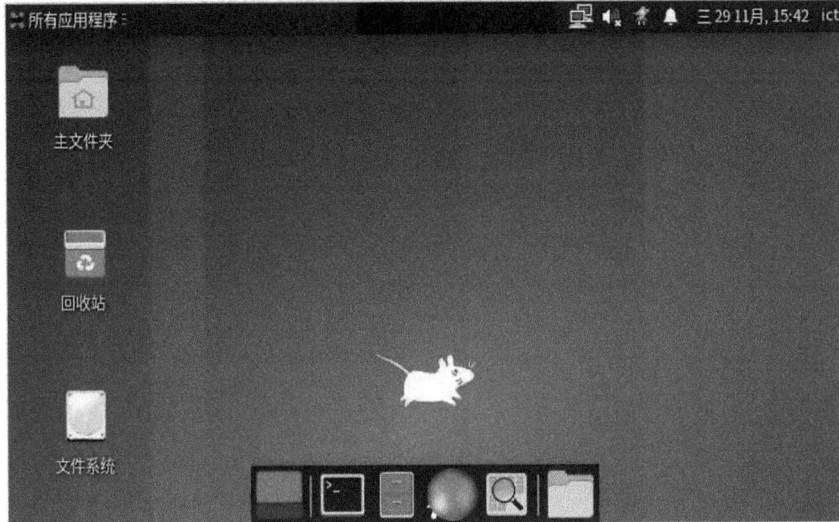

Fig. 3.1 Home screen

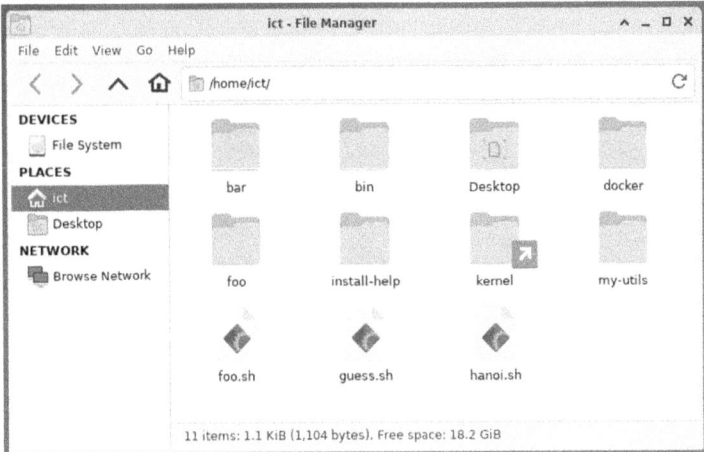

Fig. 3.2 File manager on openEuler

- Operational inefficiency: While mouse-driven interfaces excel at discoverability, they can impede efficiency in repetitive tasks and resist automation. For example, configuring network connections may require repetition of multiple menu navigations and mouse movements.
- Limited flexibility: Graphical applications typically offer rigid workflows and restricted customization, constraining users to predetermined patterns.

Fig. 3.3 gedit

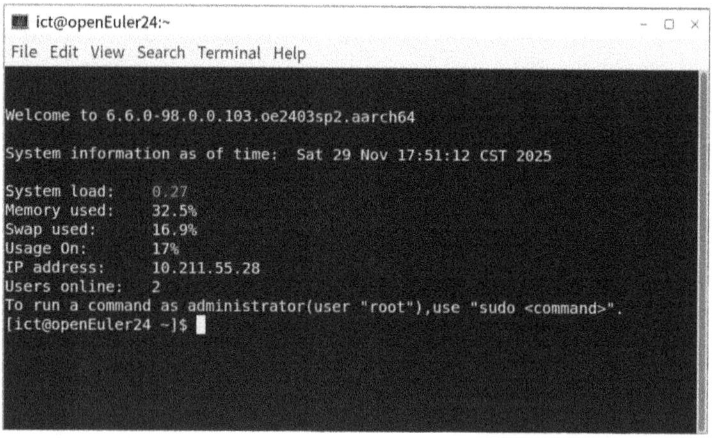

Fig. 3.4 Terminal

Consider word processors like Word—users cannot integrate their preferred text editors or export documents beyond the prescribed formats, illustrating the fundamental inflexibility of graphical tools.

– Resource intensity: GUI development and maintenance demand significant resources, both in creation and operation.

- Restricted applicability: GUIs require display hardware and substantial network bandwidth, limiting their use in embedded systems, industrial controls, and remote operations.
  These constraints explain why UNIX-like OSs favor CLIs. Even in OSs renowned for graphical excellence, like macOS, experienced users frequently leverage terminal capabilities for enhanced productivity while benefiting from graphical conveniences.

3.1.2 CLI

The CLI stands as the cornerstone of UNIX-like OSs. For computing enthusiasts, CLI embodies true user-friendliness, with many of its classic tools remaining indispensable and actively used even after half a century, continuing to inspire Linux users worldwide.

Departing from the graphical paradigm, the CLI operates through textual commands rather than mouse interactions. Users communicate directly with the system via keyboard input, making it the standard interface for UNIX servers, which typically operate without GUIs.

As openEuler's default interface and the tool of choice for professionals and system administrators, CLI offers distinct advantages:

- Streamlined execution: Commands provide immediate task completion without navigating menus or switching between input devices. This keyboard-centric approach not only enables swift operation but also supports automation through scripting, dramatically improving efficiency for repetitive tasks.
- Robust toolchain: The extensive collection of Linux utilities can be ingeniously combined through pipes, redirection, and automation scripts, enabling sophisticated operations beyond the scope of GUIs.
- Extensive customization: Users can tailor their environment to match their workflow precisely. Whether editing source code, crafting Markdown documents, or composing emails, users can employ their preferred tools and compilers with granular control over options and configurations.
- Universal compatibility: Thanks to POSIX compliance, CLI operations remain consistent across UNIX-like OSs, facilitating seamless transitions between distributions and enabling straightforward software portability.

The UNIX CLI ecosystem transcends simple tool collection—it represents an elegant synthesis of kernel design, system interfaces, and powerful utilities. This comprehensive command-line environment delivers exceptional productivity for server management and software development, embodying the UNIX philosophy of powerful, composable tools working in harmony.

3.2 Using the CLI

The perception that command lines are intimidating to newcomers belies their true nature. Over five decades of evolution and refinement have elevated CLIs into powerful tools that showcase the full interactive potential of Linux. This section explores the fundamental elements of command-line usage, including consoles and terminals, system access, command structure, administrative software installation, and essential help resources.

3.2.1 Console and Terminal

Both Console and Terminal enable command-line interaction with Linux, though they serve distinct purposes in the system architecture.

The console, rooted in the early days of computers, traditionally represents the physical I/O devices directly connected to a computer—typically a monitor and keyboard combination—providing direct system interaction, message display, and command execution capabilities.

Terminals, by contrast, function as abstract character devices enabling remote system access. They allow users to connect and execute commands from diverse physical devices. Serial interface terminals exemplify this flexibility, facilitating system debugging, data collection, and remote login capabilities. While terminals can emulate console functionality, they often extend beyond these basic features with enhanced capabilities.

In contemporary UNIX-like OSs, including Linux, both interfaces operate through software simulation.

Linux implements multiple virtual consoles to enhance user experience and system security. Users can navigate between consoles using **Ctrl+Alt+F**n key combinations (where n represents console numbers). Distribution-specific configurations vary—Ubuntu 20.04 allocates consoles 1–3 to GUI and 4–6 to CLI, while openEuler assigns GUI to console 1 and CLI to the remaining five.

Virtual terminals manifest either as GUI terminal emulators or as text-based interfaces accessed through network connections. GNOME Terminal exemplifies this concept, providing command-line functionality within the graphical GNOME environment.

In practical usage, the terms console and terminal often overlap, both referring to command-line interaction tools, unless specific hardware distinctions require emphasis.

3.2.2 System Login

Upon booting a standard openEuler installation, users encounter the CLI login interface on the virtual console by default.

```
    | Authorized users only. All activities may be monitored
and reported.                                                    |
    | Activate the web console with: systemctl enable --now
cockpit.socket                                                   |
    | openEuler24 login:                                          |
```

System access requires entering a username followed by a password at the respective prompts. For security, password characters remain invisible during entry.

Logging in as the **root** user grants superuser privileges. The **root** user password, configured during OS installation, requires careful safekeeping. A successful **root** login displays:

```
    | Authorized users only. All activities may be monitored
and reported.                                                    |
    | Activate the web console with: systemctl enable --now
cockpit.socket                                                   |
    | openEuler24 login:r
oot                                                              |
    | Passwd:                                                     |
    | ......                                                      |
    | [root@openEuler24 ~]#                                       |
```

Given the extensive system privileges of **root** in UNIX-like OSs, it is prudent to create and utilize common users for routine operations. This practice helps prevent accidental system modifications.

After logging in as **root**, execute these commands (following "#") sequentially, pressing **Enter** after each line. The commands will create common user **ict**, assign it to the **wheel** group, configure its password, and exit the session.

```
[root@openEuler24 ~]# adduser -g wheel ict
[root@openEuler24 ~]# passwd ict
[root@openEuler24 ~]# exit
```

Subsequently, log in as the newly created user:

```
-----------------------------------------------------------------
 | Authorized users only. All activities may be monitored
and reported.                                                    |
 | Activate the web console with: systemctl enable --now
cockpit.socket                                                   |
 | openEuler24 login:
ict                                                              |
 | Passwd:                                                       |
 | ......                                                        |
 | [ict@openEuler24 ~]$                                          |
----------------------------------------------------------------|
```

While virtual console access serves its purpose, remote login capabilities offer greater convenience and flexibility, particularly for system administrators and newcomers alike.

3.2.3 Remote Login

Remote login enables users to connect to remote computer systems through terminal devices for interactive sessions. This method is particularly popular among system administrators and software developers, while also serving as an excellent starting point for beginners learning Linux through familiar desktop environments like Windows.

UNIX was designed with multi-tasking and multi-user capabilities at its core. During the 1970s, when computing resources were scarce and expensive mainframes dominated the landscape, the remote login and time-sharing capabilities of UNIX proved invaluable for serving multiple users efficiently.

Remote login gives users the same command execution capabilities they would have locally. Users can run their own computing tasks while sharing system resources, with the system managing everything to maintain efficiency and stability. While early UNIX systems relied on telephone lines and plain text Telnet protocol with modems for signal conversion, modern OSs predominantly use the SSH protocol over computer networks.

3.2 Using the CLI

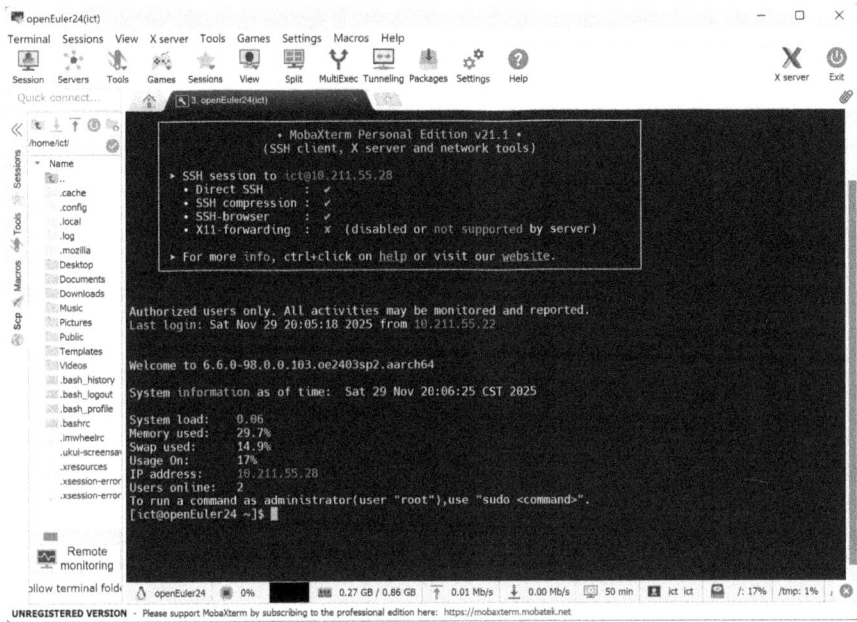

Fig. 3.5 MobaXterm remote login interface (1)

(1) Secure Sessions with SSH

Modern remote access benefits from encryption features of SSH and higher speeds and reliability of Ethernet and fiber optic networks. This allows users to securely access and manage Linux systems from anywhere using SSH client software [13].

openEuler comes with SSH service enabled, supporting both command-line tools like OpenSSH and graphical clients such as PuTTY, MobaXterm (Fig. 3.5), and Xshell. Beginners often find it helpful to access openEuler remotely from desktop environments like Ubuntu or Windows, as this enables easy text manipulation through copy and paste functions.

All command-accepting interfaces are collectively known as CLI, whether they are pure character-based, GUI terminal windows, or remote terminals accessed via serial interfaces or networks.

(2) Working with multiple terminal windows

Command-line operations often require multiple terminal windows. Users can achieve this in two ways.

The first approach involves creating multiple SSH connections, each providing a new terminal session, as demonstrated in MobaXterm (Fig. 3.6). However, this method is vulnerable to network disruptions. The second approach utilizes tools like Screen or Tmux, which offer more robust features, including virtual window division and session persistence during network interruptions. These tools maintain active tasks and allow session recovery after reconnection.

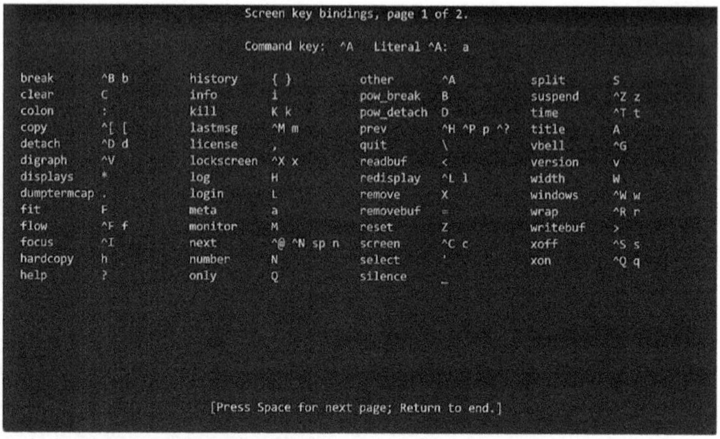

Fig. 3.6 MobaXterm remote login interface (2)

3.2.4 Command Usage

After logging in, users can begin interacting with the system through commands. Understanding command basics, structure, and root privilege usage is essential before proceeding.

(1) Command prompt

The Linux command prompt provides key information about your current environment. A typical prompt includes your username, host name, current directory, and a status symbol. For example:

```
[ict@openEuler24 ~]$
```

This prompt shows user **ict** logged in to a host named **openEuler24**, working in the user's home directory (~).

The $ indicates standard user status, while a # indicates **root** user status—a deliberate distinction to encourage careful operation with root privileges.

Users can enter commands after the prompt to interact with the system. After each interaction, the system displays the prompt again, ready for the next command. Users can customize the prompt according to their preferences.

In subsequent examples, commands entered in the CLI or terminal window follow the # or $ prompt, while lines without prompts show command output.

3.2 Using the CLI

(2) Command execution
Commands are entered after the prompt and executed by pressing **Enter**. Consider this basic example:

```
[ict@openEuler24 ~]$ date
Mon Jan  2 18:01:31 CST 2025
```

Notice how the first line displays the **date** command following the **$** prompt, while the output appears on the subsequent line without a prompt.
Consider another common command that illustrates the Linux command structure:

```
[ict@openEuler24 ~]$ ls -t --color /usr
  bin   libexec  sbin     share    lib64    include   local    src
lib   games   tmp
```

This example demonstrates entering **ls -t --color /usr** after the **$** prompt, with its output shown below.
These examples highlight the versatility of Linux commands: they can incorporate not just the command name itself, but also various options and arguments.

(3) Options and arguments
Linux commands follow a structured syntax where command names, options, and arguments are separated by spaces:

```
$ command [options] [arguments]
```

The square brackets ([]) denote optional elements that vary by command. Remember that pressing **Enter** executes the command.
The command structure consists of three main components:

- The command name itself
- Options, which come in two formats: short (single-letter) options beginning with "**-**" or long (full-word) options beginning with "**--**"
- Arguments, which specify the targets for command operations
  For instance, in the previous examples, **date** and **ls** are command names, **-t** and **--color** are options, while **/usr** is an argument.
  Linux command syntax offers notable flexibility: it is case-sensitive, and options can be combined (**-abc** equals **-a -b -c** or **-ab -c**). Unlike macOS, which mandates options before arguments, Linux allows options anywhere

in the command line. However, placing options before arguments remains a best practice for consistency.

For handling lengthy commands, Linux provides line continuation using backslashes ("\"):

```
[ict@openEuler24 ~]$ file \
> /usr/share/grub/grub-mkconfig_lib
/usr/share/grub/grub-mkconfig_lib: ASCII text
```

(4) Root privilege usage

Operating as a common user provides optimal security for both novices and system administrators. However, certain system management tasks—such as modifying system time or installing software—require root privileges.

The **sudo** command empowers common users to execute privileged commands without switching to the **root** user. On openEuler, this capability extends to members of the **wheel** group (known as the **admin** group in some Linux distributions). Our example user **ict** belongs to the **wheel** group, granted **sudo** access. Using **sudo** is straightforward: prefix your command with **sudo** and authenticate with your user password when prompted. The system then executes your command with administrative privileges.

Software installation exemplifies the need for root access. openEuler employs DNF, a sophisticated package manager that streamlines software deployment by:

- Automatically downloading and updating packages
- Managing software dependencies
- Handling installation and removal processes

To install software, common users run **sudo dnf install** *package*_name, where *package_name* comes from the repository of the OS. You can discover available packages through **dnf search** *keyword*.

Administrators can grant **sudo** access to other users (such as **foo**) by adding them to the **wheel** group: **sudo usermod -g wheel foo**.

Remember: While **sudo** provides necessary administrative access, exercise caution—even temporary root privileges demand careful consideration of potential system impacts.

3.2.5 Getting Help

Linux's comprehensive help system serves as an invaluable knowledge base, offering quick access to command documentation and functionality guides.

3.2 Using the CLI

While openEuler's **/bin** directory houses thousands of commands, memorizing every detail is neither necessary nor practical. Even power users typically utilize only a subset of available features. The recommended approach combines hands-on practice with documentation review, allowing users to naturally expand their command knowledge through practical application.

openEuler provides help documentation through two main channels:

1. Built-in help documentation accompanying commands
2. Manual (man) pages available through package installation

(1) Help documentation

Most openEuler commands include built-in documentation accessible via the **--help** option.

Here is an example using the **date** command:

```
[ict@openEuler24 ~]$ date -help
Usage: date [OPTION]... [+FORMAT]
   or:  date [-u|--utc|--universal] [MMDDhhmm[[CC]YY][.ss]]
Display date and time in the given FORMAT.
With -s, or with [MMDDhhmm[[CC]YY][.ss]], set the date and time.

Mandatory arguments to long options are mandatory for short options too.
    -d, --date=STRING          display time described by STRING, not 'now'
    --debug                    annotate the parsed date,
                               and warn about questionable usage to stderr
    -f, --file=DATEFILE        like --date; once for each line of DATEFILE
    ......
```

For easier navigation, append | **less** to view documentation page by page. Press **f** or the space bar to advance, and **b** to return to previous pages. This utilizes pipe functionality, detailed in Sect. 3.4.6.

Note that while **--help** is widely supported, some less common commands may lack this option. For these cases, consult the man pages. For Bash built-in commands (like **pwd** and **cd**), use the **help** command (for example, **help pwd**). Running **help** alone displays all available Bash built-in commands.

(2) Man pages

The man page system serves as a comprehensive reference tool for system commands, development documentation, and technical information. This robust documentation framework provides detailed insights into commands and utilities across UNIX-like OSs.

Dating back to the early 1970s, man pages emerged alongside UNIX and have matured into an indispensable documentation resource. Today, they are integral to UNIX-like OSs, including Linux distributions and macOS, offering instant access to technical documentation.

Man pages feature detailed entries for command names, functionality, parameter usage, practical examples, and command comparisons. Content is systematically organized into thematic sections, each offering in-depth coverage of specific topics. When users enter keywords, the man command conducts searches across these sections. To pinpoint specific information, users can append section numbers to their queries, particularly useful when keywords appear in multiple sections.

To access the **man** command documentation:

```
[ict@openEuler24 ~]$ man
```

Navigation is streamlined through intuitive shortcuts:

- **Page Up/Page Down** or **b/f** for page navigation
- Arrow keys or **k/j** for line-by-line movement
- **q** for exit
- **h** for keyboard shortcut help

While openEuler does not include man pages for basic commands by default, they are easily installable:

```
[ict@openEuler24 ~]$ sudo dnf install -y coreutils-help binutils-help
```

This installation unlocks documentation for essential commands like **date**, **ls**, and other utilities covered in this chapter.

For additional command documentation, install specific help packages. For instance, to add **dnf** command documentation:

```
[ict@openEuler24 ~]$ sudo dnf install -y `rpm -qf \`which dnf\` | sed 's/-[0-9].*//'`-help
```

This command identifies and installs the appropriate documentation package. Simply substitute **dnf** with any command name to install its corresponding documentation.

This command utilizes advanced shell features detailed in Sects. 3.4.4, 3.4.6, 3.4.7, and 3.5.2.

Beyond man pages, users can access supplementary resources through the openEuler community documents and various Linux technical support materials.

3.3 Basic Command-Line Operations

The CLI is the primary gateway to mastering Linux. One of the distinguishing features of Linux is its exceptional CLI efficiency, where well-chosen commands enable users to execute complex tasks—from system administration to file processing and computational operations—with remarkable flexibility and power.

openEuler's extensive command suite empowers users with comprehensive system control. Table 3.1 showcases common commands for basic operations. These time-tested tools, largely inherited from early UNIX systems and standardized through POSIX standards of IEEE, constitute the essential toolkit for every Linux user.

These commands exemplify the elegant minimalism of early UNIX design philosophy. Their concise names reflect an era of limited computing resources, where brevity in command naming served both memory conservation and operational efficiency. This consistent, abbreviated naming convention enhances command memorability, readability, and ease of use.

Table 3.1 Common commands for basic operations

Operation	Commands
Directory manipulation	ls, pwd, cd, mkdir, rmdir, du
File viewing	ls, cat, less, tail, cut, nl, diff, hexdump, file, lsof
File management	cp, mv, rm, ln, tar
File search	which, whereis, locate, find
System information query	uname, who, last, free, df
System management	date, timedatectl, halt, poweroff, reboot, shutdown

It is worth noting that while these commands might appear limited in function and cumbersome to use for beginners, they are actually designed to be concise and consistent. Their true power and efficiency become particularly evident when combined with advanced shell features like pipes and redirections.

3.3.1 Directory Manipulation

Directory manipulation stands as one of the most fundamental tasks in Linux. A distinctive feature of the elegant Linux architecture is that directories themselves are implemented as files, showcasing the commitment to simplicity in UNIX design.

Directories are the building blocks of the file system, orchestrating the organization of files and subordinate directories. Files function as the primary units in the OS for data storage, access, and management, encompassing everything from text documents to binary executables. In Linux, directories exist as specialized files containing directory entries—data structures that maintain file names, inode pointers, and hierarchical relationships within the file system.

Linux implements a hierarchical directory structure, visualized as an inverted tree stemming from the root directory (/). This tree-like architecture branches out to encompass all system files and directories, with each node (directory) potentially hosting both child nodes (subdirectories) and leaf nodes (files). This intuitive organization streamlines file operations and system maintenance. The structure seamlessly integrates various storage devices—including physical drives, external storage, USB devices, optical media, and network-mounted volumes—as branches within this unified tree.

Directory hierarchies are denoted using the forward slash ("/") as a path separator. For instance, **/bin** indicates the bin directory beneath the root directory, establishing / as the parent and **bin** as its child directory.

The root directory houses system-critical directories, detailed in Table 3.2, with each subdirectory named to reflect its core function. This structured arrangement creates a logical organization of system files, facilitating efficient system administration and user interaction.

Linux maintains a structured user environment by allocating dedicated home directories. The **root** user resides in **/root**, while common users receive personalized spaces under **/home**, identified by their usernames.

Though all directory entries in Linux are files, they serve distinct purposes through different types:

- Regular files: The foundation of data storage, handling both text and binary content.

3.3 Basic Command-Line Operations

Table 3.2 Common system directories

Directory	Purpose	Directory	Purpose
/bin	Contains common command programs (binary executables).	/root	Home directory for the **root** user.
/boot	Stores essential files for the Linux system boot.	/run	Temporary file system for system runtime information.
/dev	Contains device files for hardware.	/sbin	Stores system administration programs.
/etc	Contains system configuration files.	/srv	Stores data for services after startup.
/home	Contains common users' home directories.	/sys	Mount point for the sysfs file system.
/lib	Contains essential shared libraries.	/tmp	Stores temporary files.
/media	Mount point for automatically detected devices.	/usr	Stores UNIX software resources.
/proc	Virtual file system providing system and process information.	/var	Contains frequently modified files, including logs.

Table 3.3 Common ls options

Option	Description	Option	Description
-l	Display detailed information in list format.	-t	Sort by modification time (newest first).
-h	Used with **-l** to show file sizes in human-readable format.	-S	Sort by file size (largest first).
-a	Show all files and directories, including hidden ones (starting with .).	-r	Reverse sort order.
-d	Show only directories (without recursing into them).	-i	Display inode numbers.

- Directory files: Specialized containers that maintain hierarchical organization through metadata about their contents, enabling efficient file management.
- Link files: Advanced reference mechanisms that provide flexible access to files and directories. While conceptually similar to Windows shortcuts, Linux links offer enhanced functionality and versatility.

Directory manipulation forms the backbone of file system interaction, encompassing essential tasks such as content viewing, location awareness, navigation, creation, and removal. These fundamental operations enable users to maintain an organized and efficient file system structure.

(1) Viewing directory contents

The **ls** command (list) is a fundamental tool for displaying directory contents in Linux. This versatile command presents file and subdirectory information in a customizable format, ranging from simple name lists to comprehensive detailed views with color-coding and various sorting options.

When invoked without parameters, **ls** displays the contents of the current directory. The command supports an extensive set of options to tailor its output, as detailed in Table 3.3.

Options can be combined for enhanced functionality (for example, **ls -lh** or **ls -l -h**).

The **-l** option reveals comprehensive file attributes. Here is an example examining the root directory:

```
[ict@openEuler24 ~]$ ls -lh /
total 66K
lrwxrwxrwx.    1 root root    7 May 27 2025 bin -> usr/bin
dr-xr-xr-x.    9 root root 4.0K Nov 20 22:20 boot
drwxr-xr-x.   19 root root 3.3K Dev  7 13:07 dev
drwxr-xr-x.  108 root root  12K Nov 30 11:09 etc
drwxr-xr-x.    6 root root 4.0K Nov 17 22:37 home
......
```

The detailed output includes:

- File type identifiers: **-** for regular files, **d** for directories, and **l** for symbolic links
- Access permissions: displayed as **rw-r--r--** (detailed in Sect. 3.5)
- Ownership information: both user (first **root**) and group (second **root**)
- Size metrics: displayed in bytes by default, or human-readable with **-h**
- Temporal data: last modification or creation timestamp
- Name and link information: including target paths for symbolic links indicated by arrows (->) (covered in Sect. 3.3.2)

Users can streamline their workflow by creating custom aliases for frequently used options. The command **alias ll=ls -lh --color** creates a shorthand **ll** that eliminates the need to type multiple options repeatedly.

The default alphabetical sorting of **ls** can be customized to sort entries by various attributes—size, modification time, access time, or creation time—providing flexible ways to analyze directory contents.

The **touch** utility serves dual purposes: updating file timestamps and creating empty files, making it an essential tool for file management tasks.

Command output redirection in Linux is straightforward. For example, the following command saves **ls** output to a file:

3.3 Basic Command-Line Operations

```
[ict@openEuler24 ~]$ ls > ls_output.txt
```

This demonstrates the shell redirection capability (detailed in Sect. 3.4.5) using the > operator.

Since its introduction in UNIX V1, **ls** has remained an indispensable tool. Its comprehensive functionality and efficiency surpass GUI file managers, offering unmatched directory exploration capabilities.

For more **ls** usage details, use **ls --help** or **man ls**.

Paths are integral to directory operations, representing the sequence of sub-directories needed to access a file or directory. Path navigation employs two methods: absolute and relative addressing. Absolute paths provide complete routes from the root directory, while relative paths navigate from the current location using **.** (current directory, which can be omitted) and **..** (parent directory) as reference points. Table 3.4 illustrates both approaches:

When working from **/home/ict**, **../** references **/home** while **../../** reaches the root directory, making **../../bin** a valid path to **/bin**.

Choose between relative and absolute paths based on directory relationships—relative paths excel for nearby locations, while absolute paths offer clarity for distant or unrelated destinations.

(2) Viewing the current working directory

The **pwd** (print working directory) command reveals your current location in the file system through its absolute path. This essential UNIX tool includes two specialized options:

– **-L**: Displays the logical path (default behavior), maintaining symbolic links in the output.
– **-P**: Reveals the physical path by resolving any symbolic links to show their actual destinations.

When **pwd** is executed in the **/bin** directory:

Table 3.4 Examples of absolute and relative paths

Scenario	Current directory	Target directory	Absolute path	Relative path
Scenario 1	/	/bin	/bin	bin, ./bin
Scenario 2	/home/ict	/bin	/bin	../../bin

```
[ict@openEuler24 bin]$ pwd
/bin
[ict@openEuler24 bin]$ pwd -P
/usr/bin
```

This command proves invaluable in script programming, enabling precise location awareness for file operations by identifying the execution directory of commands.

(3) Navigating directory structures

Your current working directory represents your active location in the CLI. While Linux initially places you in your home directory at login, you can freely navigate to other locations as your tasks demand.

The shell prompt is your constant navigator, displaying your current location and updating automatically with each directory change.

The **cd** (change directory) command enables this navigation with elegant simplicity. Rather than utilizing complex options, it focuses on straightforward directory arguments. Without any argument, it returns you to your home directory. Table 3.5 outlines the essential navigation commands.

Several special symbols facilitate navigation: ~ represents your home directory, .. points to the parent directory, and . indicates the current directory.

The CLI emphasizes efficiency. For instance, **cd -** provides instant toggling between your current and previous locations, streamlining your workflow.

(4) Creating directories

Since Linux maintains its system directories for specific purposes, users should establish their own directory structures for personal files.

The **mkdir** (make directory) command serves as your directory creation tool, offering flexibility in both simple and complex directory structures. It excels at creating both individual directories and elaborating nested hierarchies. Without specified paths, new directories appear in your current location.

A particularly powerful feature is the **-p** (**--parents**) option, which streamlines the creation of multiple directory levels simultaneously. Combine this with **-v**

Table 3.5 Directory navigation commands

Command	Function
cd dir	Navigate to the **dir** directory. For example, **cd /** moves to the root directory
cd, cd~	Return to your home directory
cd ..	Move up one directory level
cd -	Return to the previous working directory

3.3 Basic Command-Line Operations

for detailed progress feedback—a common verbose flag across Linux commands.

Here is an example creating parallel directory structures (**bar_a** and **bar_b** under **/tmp/foo**):

```
[ict@openEuler24 ~]$ mkdir -pv /tmp/foo/bar_{a,b}
mkdir: created directory '/tmp/foo'
mkdir: created directory '/tmp/foo/bar_a'
mkdir: created directory '/tmp/foo/bar_b'
```

(5) Removing directories

Maintaining a clean file system requires regular removal of obsolete directories. The **rmdir** (remove directory) command specifically handles the removal of empty directories. This safety-focused tool only succeeds when directories contain no files or subdirectories.

The **-p** (or **--parents**) option enables recursive cleanup of directory hierarchies. It automatically removes parent directories that become empty after their subdirectories are deleted, continuing upward until it encounters occupied space.

Exercise caution with **rmdir** operations. Always verify your target directories and maintain backups of critical data. Double-check both your working location and removal targets to prevent unintended removal.

For recursive deletion of non-empty directories, refer to Sect. 3.3.4.

(6) Analyzing directory space usage

While GUIs usually offer basic storage information, CLI tools provide superior flexibility in analyzing drive space usage.

The **du** (disk usage) command is a powerful tool for storage analysis and system maintenance. It excels at providing detailed insights into how your storage space is utilized, making it invaluable for system cleanup operations. Table 3.6 outlines its most practical options.

Here is an example analyzing **/usr/src** and its level-1 subdirectories:

```
[ict@openEuler24 ~]$ du -hd1 /usr/src
4.0M    /usr/src/kmod-kvdo-8.1.0.316-1
102M    /usr/src/kernels
106M    /usr/src/
```

Table 3.6 Common du options

Option	Description	Option	Description
-a	Displays space usage for every file and subdirectory.	-c	Provides a comprehensive listing plus a total usage summary
-h	Converts sizes to human-friendly format (KB, MB, GB).	-s	Summarizes total usage without individual breakdowns
--d	Limits output to the specified directory depth.	--time	Reveals last modification timestamps across the directory tree

3.3.2 File Viewing

UNIX embraces a distinctive "everything is a file" philosophy, having abstracted both data content representation and storage interfaces. Linux supports an array of file types beyond the conventional regular files, directories, and symbolic links—including character device files, block device files, pipes, and socket files. It maintains a consistent interface across all these types, making them remarkably straightforward to work with.

In the Linux environment, file names offer considerable flexibility, accommodating letters, numbers, hyphens, and underscores in nearly unlimited length combinations. These file names maintain case sensitivity, adding an extra layer of precision to file organization. While file names may include extensions (. followed by a suffix) to denote file types or purposes, Linux takes a more flexible approach than Windows—extensions remain optional, even for executable files.

True to UNIX traditions, files prefixed with . remain hidden from standard directory listings (running **ls** without arguments). These hidden files typically serve as configuration files or system-maintained documents, deliberately tucked away to prevent casual interference with their specialized functions.

(1) Viewing Basic File Information

While commonly associated with directory listings, **ls** actually reveals information about any file type—directories being just one special case. Consider this example with the **/bin** file:

```
[ict@openEuler24 ~]$ ls -l /bin
lrwxrwxrwx. 1 root root 7 May 27 2025 /bin -> usr/bin
```

This output reveals a symbolic link of 7 bytes, with **/bin** pointing to **usr/bin**. The relative path notation indicates that both locations share the root directory as their parent, effectively linking **/bin** to **/usr/bin**.

This elegant linking mechanism ensures command accessibility across traditional system locations. Take **mkdir** for example—whether accessed via **/usr/bin/mkdir** or **/bin/mkdir**, it references the same executable file, eliminating redundancy and potential confusion. Notice how the **mkdir** command executable eschews a file extension. Link files will be covered in detail in later sections.

3.3 Basic Command-Line Operations

The capabilities of **ls** extend far beyond these basics. It can reveal a wealth of file attributes: access timestamps, modification records, creation dates, actual storage block usage, and even internal system details like inode numbers. The full potential of this command can be explored through its comprehensive documentation.

(2) Viewing text file contents

Linux boasts an extensive arsenal of file viewing commands, with particularly sophisticated options for text files. This variety lets users choose tools that best match their viewing preferences and requirements (Table 3.7).

The **cat** command excels at displaying complete file contents and frequently partners with shell redirection. It offers useful options like **-s** to suppress repeated empty lines and **--show-tabs** to represent tab characters as ^I. Here is an example viewing system information:

```
[ict@openEuler24 ~]$ cat /etc/os-release
NAME="openEuler"
VERSION="24.03 (LTS-SP2)"
ID="openEuler"
VERSION_ID="24.03"
PRETTY_NAME="openEuler 24.03 (LTS-SP2)"
```

For CPU details, **cat /proc/cpuinfo** reveals comprehensive runtime information.

The cleverly named **tac** command reverses the functionality of **cat**, displaying content from bottom to top—its name itself a reverse spelling of cat.

The **less** command transforms file viewing into an interactive experience. Unlike the rapid-fire output of **cat**, **less** enables controlled, page-by-page navigation through file content. As an enhanced successor to more, it supports sophisticated features including bidirectional scrolling, multiple search pat-

Table 3.7 Common text file viewing commands

Command	Purpose	Applicable scenario
cat	Display entire file content.	View small files or concatenate multiple files.
less	Display file content page by page.	View large files with substantial content.
head	Display file header content.	Quick view of file beginnings.
tail	Display file ending content.	View log files, where the latest logs are at the end.
cut	Display partial line content.	View specific column content.

terns, and flexible navigation options. Users can scroll with arrow keys, advance pages with the space bar, move line-by-line with **Enter**, and access help via **h**. **less** smoothly handles both drive-based text files and command outputs. Consider these examples:

```
[ict@openEuler24 ~]$ ls --help | less
[ict@openEuler24 ~]$ ls -lh / | less
```

These commands demonstrate the shell pipe functionality, channeling output between commands via the | symbol.

The **head** and **tail** commands serve as precise surgical tools for viewing file segments. While **head** focuses on file beginnings, **tail** specializes in endings, with both offering sophisticated control over output size and format. Their default 10-line output can be adjusted—for instance, to 5 lines with **-n5**. The standout feature of **tail** is its live monitoring capability, making it invaluable for tracking active log files.

Consider this example examining the last 5 users in openEuler's user database:

```
[ict@openEuler24 ~]$ tail -n5 /etc/passwd
sshd:x:74:74:Privilege-separated SSH:/var/empty/sshd:/sbin/nologin
ict:x:1002:1002::/home/ict:/bin/bash
nginx:x:986:986:Nginx web server:/var/lib/nginx:/sbin/nologin
apache:x:48:48:Apache:/usr/share/httpd:/sbin/nologin
mysql:x:27:27:MySQL Server:/var/lib/mysql:/sbin/nologin
```

Each line presents crucial user information: username, password status (x indicates secure storage elsewhere), user ID, group ID, full name, home directory, and login shell.

The **cut** command excels at data extraction, offering precise control over output through several key options:

- **-b**: Extracts by byte position, specifying range (for example, **-b 10-20** outputs bytes 10 to 20).
- **-c**: Selects specific characters, specifying range (for example, **-c 2-5** outputs characters 2 to 5).
- **-d**: Defines custom field separators (the default is tab).
- **-f**: Used with **-d** to specify which fields to display.

3.3 Basic Command-Line Operations

Here is **cut** extracting usernames and home directories:

```
[ict@openEuler24 ~]$ cut -d: -f1,6 /etc/passwd
...
sshd:/var/empty/sshd
ict:/home/ict
nginx:/var/lib/nginx
...
```

Two additional tools complete the text-viewing toolkit: **wc** and **nl**.
wc provides quick file statistics, counting lines, words, and characters in files. Here is a directory count:

```
[ict@openEuler24 ~]$ ls -A /bin/ | wc -l
1589
```

nl adds sophisticated line numbering:

```
[ict@openEuler24 foo]$ nl /etc/os-release
     1  NAME="openEuler"
     2  VERSION="24.03 (LTS-SP2)"
     3  ID="openEuler"
     4  VERSION_ID="24.03"
     5  PRETTY_NAME="openEuler 24.03 (LTS-SP2)"
```

Despite its apparent simplicity, **nl** boasts 11 customization options, perfecting the art of line numbering through features like width control, alignment options, and selective numbering patterns.

> **nl** perfectly exemplifies the UNIX philosophy of "small is beautiful."

The thoroughness of **nl** eliminates the need for alternatives, allowing developers to channel their energy into innovations. This focused approach has helped drive open source development forward. Chapter 5 will explore these principles hands-on by creating a simple **.my-nl** tool, offering valuable insights into command design and implementation.

(3) Comparing text files

In the world of system administration and software development, tracking changes in text files—whether configuration files, documents, or source code—can be a complex challenge. When things go wrong, such as configuration failures, compilation errors, or unexpected bugs, manual inspection often falls short. This is where file comparison becomes invaluable, offering a reliable way to verify modifications against original or backup versions.

Enter the **diff** command, a powerful tool that has become indispensable for system maintenance and software development. It performs lightning-fast, precise comparisons between text files, presenting differences in an organized format. For instance, the notation "4,5c4,7" precisely indicates where changes occur—between lines 4–5 in the original file and lines 4–7 in the new version—making differences immediately apparent.

Using **diff** is remarkably straightforward: simply provide two file names as arguments, with the older file first. Table 3.8 outlines its most useful options.

Perhaps the most revolutionary application of diff was in creating patches—an elegant solution that transformed how software updates were distributed. A patch file, containing only the differences between versions, allows users to re-create the new version by applying these changes to their existing files using the patch utility. This approach dramatically reduced bandwidth requirements and simplified code distribution compared to sending complete source packages.

Before Git revolutionized version control, patch files were the backbone of software distribution in the Linux ecosystem, handling everything from security updates to feature enhancements. While modern tools have largely superseded this approach, understanding patch creation and usage remains valuable for those interested in Linux technical heritage.

(4) Viewing binary file contents

Linux provides powerful tools for examining binary files through its text-based CLI, essential for security analysis and debugging. Two primary commands, **hexdump** and **od**, transform binary data into human-readable formats, including American Standard Code for Information Interchange (ASCII), decimal, hexadecimal, or floating-point representations.

hexdump excels at presenting binary content in a structured hexadecimal format, organizing output into rows that display memory addresses, raw data, and corresponding ASCII characters. Using the **-C** option demonstrates this capability beautifully, as shown in this example of viewing system user information:

Table 3.8 Common diff options

Option	Description	Option	Description
-u	Outputs unified header information.	-B	Ignores blank lines
-i	Ignores case differences.	-w	Ignores all whitespace

3.3 Basic Command-Line Operations

```
[ict@openEuler24 ~]$ hexdump -C /etc/passwd
00000000  72 6f 6f 74 3a 78 3a 30 3a 30 3a 72 6f 6f 74 3a
|root:x:0:0:root:|
00000010  2f 72 6f 6f 74 3a 2f 62 69 6e 2f 62 61 73 68 0a
|/root:/bin/bash.|
00000020  62 69 6e 3a 78 3a 31 3a 31 3a 62 69 6e 3a 2f 62
|bin:x:1:1:bin:/b|
00000030  69 6e 3a 2f 73 62 69 6e 2f 6e 6f 6c 6f 67 69 6e
|in:/sbin/nologin|
```

The **od** command offers even greater flexibility, supporting multiple output formats and sophisticated display options. Users can specify byte counts, offsets, and create customized output formats, making it invaluable for detailed binary analysis.

From the output above, we can see that text files contain more than printable characters. For example, at the end of the second line is "0a," with ASCII value 10, which is the newline character (\n) commonly used in the **printf** function of the C language.

Complementing these tools is the **strings** command, a specialized utility that extracts printable character sequences from binary files. This proves invaluable when investigating programs, shared libraries, or other binary objects, often revealing crucial information for debugging and analysis.

(5) Examining file type information

Understanding file type information enables more thorough analysis of target files, facilitating proper command selection and platform compatibility verification. This knowledge proves essential for both system administrators and software developers.

Linux stores detailed file type information and metadata within the file content, contrasting with the simpler extension-based identification system on Windows. Files exist in numerous formats: plain text appears as "ASCII text," images as "JPG" or "PNG," and executables as "ELF" (short for "Executable and Linkable Format," the native executable format on Linux).

The **file** command examines file headers to determine their nature—whether text, image, executable, or other formats—and provides detailed characteristics. This proves particularly useful when troubleshooting execution errors, such as when attempting to run x86 executables on Arm development boards. The command reveals crucial details about executable files, including their instruction set architecture and OS requirements.

```
[ict@openEuler24 ~]$ file /usr/bin/pwd
/usr/bin/pwd: ELF 64-bit LSB pie executable, x86-64,
version 1 (SYSV), dynamically linked, for GNU/Linux 3.2.0,
stripped
```

This output reveals that **pwd** is a 64-bit ELF executable designed for the x86-64 architecture, runs on Linux systems, and utilizes system dynamic libraries as indicated by the "dynamically linked" attribute.

(6) Monitoring dynamic file information

Tracking real-time file access by users and programs, along with monitoring critical files' dynamic information, plays a vital role in system security management, development debugging, and analysis.

The **lsof** (list open files) command provides comprehensive visibility into all open files and their usage details, including user and program information. Its scope encompasses both every currently opened file and all file types—from regular files to directories, device files, pipes, and network files.

This powerful utility boasts an extensive set of options that showcase its versatility. It defaults to generating a consolidated list of all open files in repeat mode, continuously updating until user interruption. Beyond human-readable output, it produces data that other programs can parse and process.

```
openEuler requires manual installation of lsof via sudo dnf
install -y lsof.
```

To examine files accessed by user **ict**, use the **-u** option as shown:

```
[ict@openEuler24 ~]$ lsof -u ict
   COMMAND     PID USER    FD    TYPE   DEVICE  SIZE/OFF
NODE NAME
   sshd     331715  ict   cwd     DIR    253,0
4096        2 /
   sshd     331715  ict   txt     REG    253,0    921584 1720448
/usr/sbin/sshd
   sshd     331715  ict   mem     REG    253,0    591984 1705843
/usr/lib64/libm.so.6
   ...
```

Further chapters will explore the capabilities of **lsof** in examining device and network files.

> Since **lsof** typically needs to access kernel memory and various files, running it with root privileges allows full utilization of its capabilities.

In the file-centric Linux architecture, **lsof** serves as a powerful tool for monitoring all active file usage. It enables administrators to track resource utilization by specific users, examine file and network connections of running programs, and take necessary actions like terminating unnecessary processes or removing unauthorized users.

3.3.3 File Management

The GUI excels at simple file operations—copying, deleting, or compressing multiple files with a few mouse clicks. However, consider a more complex scenario: selectively copying files to the foobar directory, including only those files that are either newer than their counterparts in foobar or do not exist there yet.

While graphical file managers might struggle with such specific requirements, the CLI handles this task effortlessly. This capability stems from the foundational design of UNIX, which incorporated elegant and consistent tools and commands to facilitate efficient file management across all contexts.

This section explores common file operations in the CLI environment, addressing both directories and regular files under the unified concept of files in UNIX systems.

(1) Backing up filesCreating backup copies is a crucial safeguard before modifying important files, protecting against accidental changes or unexpected issues. These backups provide both reference material and a restoration point when needed.

The **cp** (copy) command functions as the primary backup tool, enabling users to copy files to specific destinations or directories. This command accommodates various copying tasks through multiple options and parameters. The fundamental syntax follows this structure:

```
cp [options] src dest
```

The command operates with multiple parameters: *src* specifies the source files or directories to copy, while *dest* indicates the target location. When *dest* represents a directory, *src* can encompass multiple files. Table 3.9 outlines the commonly used options.

Table 3.9 Common cp options

Option	Description	Option	Description
-a	Used when copying directories, preserves links, timestamps, and other attributes while copying all contents; equivalent to combining **-d**, **-p**, and **-r**	-u	Only copies files that are newer than their counterparts in the destination
-d	Preserves links during copying instead of copying the files they point to	-p	Preserves source file permissions, ownership, and timestamps
-r	Copies directories and all their subdirectories and files; required for directory copying	-f	Forces copying, overwriting existing destination files without prompting
-i	Prompts before copying; asks for confirmation to overwrite if the destination file exists	-l	Creates link files instead of copying files

Consider this example, where we create a backup from the home directory. The task involves creating a **bak** directory and backing up the **.ssh** and **/etc/profile.d/** directories, while selectively copying files based on their timestamps and preserving all relevant attributes:

```
[ict@openEuler24 ~]$ mkdir ~/bak
[ict@openEuler24 ~]$ cp -pru .ssh/ /etc/profile.d/ bak
```

Exercise caution when executing backup operations to prevent accidentally overwriting valuable files, which could result in data loss or corruption.

Beyond cp, Linux provides specialized backup utilities for more specific requirements, including **cpio**, **dump**, and **dd**.

(2) Moving files

File movement operations in Linux handle both file relocation and renaming through a unified approach.

The **mv** (move) command facilitates file and directory transfers while also supporting rename operations. Its straightforward syntax follows this pattern:

```
mv [options] src dest
```

The command processes multiple parameters: *src* designates the files or directories to move, while *dest* specifies the target location. The system behavior varies based on the nature of *dest*: when *dest* exists as a directory, *src* moves inside it; when *dest* exists as a regular file, *src* overwrites its content; when *dest* does not exist, *src* relocates and assumes the *dest* name. Multiple files specified in *src* transfer into *dest* when *dest* exists as a directory.

3.3 Basic Command-Line Operations

Table 3.10 details the versatile options of **mv**.

The **mv** command excels through its intuitive syntax and versatile functionality. It efficiently handles individual files, directories, or complete directory structures, providing precise control over file organization and management tasks.

(3) Removing files

Regular cleanup of temporary compilation files, outdated logs, and other unnecessary data maintains system efficiency and prevents file system congestion, storage waste, and performance issues.

The **rm** command (remove) eliminates files or directories from the file tree while reclaiming drive space. It accepts multiple target parameters and features these essential options:

- **-i**: requests user confirmation before deletion (interactive mode).
- **-f**: Forces removal even for read-only items without confirmation.
- **-r**: Removes directories and their entire contents (recursive deletion).

The **rm** command executes irreversible operations, making file recovery extremely difficult. Users must verify their intentions before proceeding.

> A particularly destructive operation is executing **rm -rf/** as **root**, which will delete all files across the entire file system without warning until the entire system and all data are destroyed.

To safeguard against accidents, implement these best practices: use relative paths instead of absolute paths with **rm**, and position the **-rf** option after the directory specification. This approach limits potential damage and prevents catastrophic deletions that might occur from hitting Enter prematurely while typing absolute paths.

(4) Linking files

UNIX-like OSs implement a practical mechanism through file linking, enabling synchronized access to source files through link files—a fundamental skill for Linux users.

The **ln** (link) command creates two distinct link types: hard links and symbolic links (soft links). UNIX files abstract data content in different ways through

Table 3.10 Common mv options

Option	Description
-b	Creates a backup of the destination file before overwriting it
-i	Asks for confirmation before overwriting files with the same name (interactive mode)
-f	Overwrites destination files without prompting (forced movement)
-n	Never overwrites existing files or directories
-u	Moves only when source files are newer than destination files or when destination files do not exist

these links. Hard links function as file aliases (analogous to C++ references), directly accessing the same data content as the source file and matching its size. Symbolic links operate as special files, similar to shortcuts (analogous to C++ pointers), storing only path information to the source file rather than actual data. This makes their size minimal—typically just a few to dozens of bytes. When deleting a source file, hard links preserve access until their complete removal triggers system storage release. Symbolic links become inactive but persist as "broken links," maintaining their presence while losing access capability.

Symbolic links dominate practical applications. openEuler demonstrates this prevalence with over 200 symbolic links in **/bin/** and more than 700 in **/lib64/**. These links deliver several key benefits:

- Streamlined management: Symbolic links enable multi-path access without file duplication, conserving storage space and eliminating synchronization overhead. Centralizing multiple links that reference files across different locations creates an efficient access point, significantly simplifying file organization.
- Enhanced compatibility: Symbolic links accommodate any file system target. Source file relocations or name changes require only link re-creation, maintaining consistent file access patterns. Their widespread implementation in command tools and libraries insulates users from software changes while preserving system stability.
- File system flexibility: Symbolic links transcend file system boundaries. This capability enables dynamic storage expansion through new drive integration and root file system linking when physical space constrains growth. Network and distributed systems leverage symbolic links extensively, creating unified access despite diverse physical storage locations.

Creating symbolic links follows this syntax: **ln -s** *src dest*. The **-s** option specifies symbolic linking, with *src* indicating the source file and *dest* the link file. Omitting *dest* creates a same-name link in the current directory. Existing *dest* names prevent creation unless overridden with **-f**.

This example demonstrates creating quick access to **usr/local/bin** through a symbolic link named **ulb**:

```
ln -s /usr/local/bin ulb
```

Critical considerations: Source file operations (moving/deletion) invalidate symbolic links. Link relocation or copying may break functionality without immediate detection. Implementation requires careful path selection (absolute/relative) based on specific requirements. Production environments should employ verification tools like symlinks for regular system-level link validation.

3.3 Basic Command-Line Operations

(5) Packaging files

Packaging multiple or large files into a single unit proves essential for backup and network transmission, significantly reducing storage requirements and transfer times. Modern software installations and source code distributions typically arrive as single packaged files. This practice traces back to early UNIX development, when storage costs and transmission limitations made efficient packaging crucial for file management.

The **tar** command stands as the predominant archiving utility in UNIX-like OSs. It consolidates multiple files and directories into unified archives, integrating seamlessly with compression utilities like **gzip** and **bzip2** to minimize archive size. This versatility makes **tar** instrumental for file management, backup operations, and compression tasks.

Introduced in Version 7 UNIX (1979) for tape archiving, **tar** evolved into a standard system utility. The current GNU implementation primarily serves drive-based and network operations. **tar** uniquely handles special files—such as device files in **/dev** that resist direct **cp** command copying—enabling their transfer through archive packaging.

tar implements extensive functionality through various options, detailed in Table 3.11.

For directory packaging with gzip compression, consider this example compressing **/etc**:

```
[ict@openEuler24 ~]$ tar -czvf etc.tar.gz /etc
```

Extraction demonstrates equal flexibility. This command unpacks **etc.tar.gz** into **/tmp**:

```
[ict@openEuler24 ~]$ tar -xzvf etc.tar.gz -C /tmp
```

tar achieves enhanced functionality through pipeline integration, enabling sophisticated packaging operations.

Table 3.11 Common tar options

Option	Description	Option	Description
-c	Creates an archive file (package).	-r	Appends files to the archive end
-x	Extracts files from an archive file (unpack).	-v	Displays the execution process
-z	Uses gzip compression/decompression.	-f	Specifies an archive file
-j	Uses bzip2 compression/decompression.	-C<*dir*>	Specifies the target directory
-t	Lists archive contents.	--help	Displays help information

The **zip** and **unzip** utilities present alternative packaging and unpacking solutions. **zip** creates compressed archives directly from multiple files and directories. While it offers advanced compression algorithms and adjustable compression levels, **zip** has several limitations: slower processing speed, potential compatibility issues with legacy systems, and possible character encoding problems with non-English text.

3.3.4 File Search

Linux incorporates multiple sophisticated search commands that streamline file location tasks. These tools enable users to track down executable files, locate files based on attributes like modification dates and sizes, or conduct searches using complex text patterns. Each command brings unique strengths to specific search scenarios.

This section examines four classic commands for common search operations, detailed in Table 3.12.

(1) Finding executable files

System maintenance, security analysis, debugging, and script development often demand identifying the specific executable file behind a command or determining its complete path.

The **which** command pinpoints executable files and outputs their full paths. It operates within system-defined paths, ensuring quick results through focused searching. By default, it displays the first match only, though the **-a** option reveals all matching paths.

```
[ict@openEuler24 ~]$ which pwd tar
/usr/bin/pwd
/usr/bin/tar
```

(2) Finding executable files, source code, and documentation

The **whereis** command extends beyond executable files to identify source code and documentation. While it defaults to searching system-defined paths, it accommodates additional search locations through optional parameters.

Table 3.12 Classic search commands

Command	Purpose
which	Find executable files in system-defined paths
whereis	Find executable files and related documentation, source code in system-defined paths
locate	Quickly find files (using a file name index database)
find	Precisely search for files in specified directories

3.3 Basic Command-Line Operations

```
[ict@openEuler24 ~]$ whereis tar stdio.h
tar: /usr/bin/tar /usr/share/man/man1/tar.1.gz /usr/
share/info/tar.info-1.gz
/usr/share/info/tar.info-2.gz /usr/share/info/tar.info.gz
stdio.h: /usr/include/stdio.h
```

(3) Searching for files globally
locate enables swift system-wide file discovery, displaying paths for successful matches. It achieves rapid results by consulting a pre-compiled file name index database. Though it examines the entire database by default, users can refine searches through specific file name patterns.

```
[ict@openEuler24 ~]$ locate pwd
/etc/.pwd.lock
/usr/bin/pwd
/usr/include/pwd.h
/usr/lib64/python3.11/lib-dynload/spwd.cpython-311-x86_
64-linux-gnu.so
...
```

openEuler requires manual installation of **locate** via **sudo dnf install -y mlocate && updatedb**.

The index database updates automatically on a schedule, causing a slight delay before newly created or added files become searchable. The **root** users can trigger immediate database updates by executing the **updatedb** command.

(4) Searching for files precisely
find ranks among the most versatile search utilities, featuring comprehensive matching criteria and recursive directory traversal to pinpoint files meeting specific requirements. Beyond basic searching, it enables operations like file deletion. The command evaluates conditions including file names, types, sizes, timestamps, and other attributes. Its ability to combine multiple criteria creates sophisticated search patterns for exact file location, making it indispensable for various tasks.

When executing **find**, users specify one or more target directories, separated by spaces. Without explicit directory parameters, the command examines the current working directory. The command offers extensive matching options, with Table 3.13 highlighting the most frequently used ones.

Table 3.13 Common find options

Option	Description
-name	Searches by file name, supporting wildcards * and ?
-type	Searches by file type: **f** (regular file), **d** (directory), **l** (symbolic link), etc
-size	Searches by file size, using **+** or **-** to indicate greater or less than the specified size; units include **c** (byte), **w** (word), **b** (block), **k** (KB), **M** (MB), and **G** (GB)
-mtime	Searches by modification time, using **+** or **-** to indicate before or after the specified day
-newer	Searches by comparing timestamps with reference files or specified timestamps
-print	Outputs all matching file names or writes results to the specified file
-exec	Executes external programs for operations like deletion or other processing on matching files

Interestingly, **find** employs a distinctive option format using single hyphens and strings—a legacy from its UNIX V1 origins. This format persists since Version 7 UNIX to maintain compatibility with countless system scripts, underscoring its fundamental role in UNIX-like OSs.

Consider this example that locates C source files modified within the past day throughout the working directory tree and archives them into **latest.tgz**:

```
[ict@openEuler24 ~]$ find -mtime -1 \( -name "*.c" -or -name "*.h" \) -exec tar -rvf \
> latest.tgz {} \;
```

This example uses the escape character ("\") four times to pass subsequent symbols to **find** rather than the shell for processing. Additionally, if you anticipate a lengthy search but want to continue with other commands, append **&** to run the search in the background. The system will display a notification upon completion.

Here is how to locate and remove all files in the system log directory that pre-date the **ttt** file and exceed 10 MB (**!** negates the following expression):

```
[ict@openEuler24 ~]$ find /var/log/ \! -newer ttt -size +10M -type f -delete
```

This command identifies broken symbolic links within the **/usr** directory hierarchy (limited to 3 levels deep):

```
[ict@openEuler24 ~]$ find /usr -type l -maxdepth 3 -exec test ! -e {} \; -print
```

3.3 Basic Command-Line Operations

The command scans for symbolic links (**-type l**) and validates each link through the **test ! -e** command. {} represents actual file names, while \; marks the **-exec** command boundary.

While these tasks prove straightforward with **find**, they present significant challenges for graphical file managers. GUI applications excel at common operations but struggle with specialized tasks. CLI tools impose no such limitations, offering unrestricted access to their rich feature sets.

The capabilities of **find** extend far beyond these examples. When combined with pipes and regular expressions, it enables precise search patterns that efficiently handle complex file location tasks.

Another powerful file-related command is **grep**, which searches for strings in text files according to specified matching rules and displays all matching lines. Chapter 5 will cover this in detail.

3.3.5 System Information Query

Linux features comprehensive commands for system information retrieval, enabling users to monitor and understand their system environment effectively. These utilities provide insights into OS details, active user sessions, memory utilization, drive usage, and beyond.

(1) Viewing OS information
   The **uname** utility reveals detailed system information, including OS characteristics, kernel data, host name, and additional system parameters.
   While **uname** includes multiple options for displaying specific system informa-

```
[ict@openEuler24 ~]$ uname -a
Linux openEuler24 6.6.0-98.0.0.103.oe2403sp2.x86_64 #1
SMP Wed Jun 25 23:16:20 CST 2025
x86_64 x86_64 x86_64 GNU/Linux
```

tion, the **-a** flag outputs comprehensive details, as outlined in Table 3.14.

For detailed hardware insights, users can examine CPU specifications through **cat /proc/cpuinfo**, memory statistics via **cat /proc/meminfo**, and Peripheral Component Interconnect (PCI) device details using **lspci**.

Table 3.14 uname output

Category	Output	Category	Output
Kernel	Linux	Processor type	x86_64
Kernel release	6.6.0-98.0.0.103.oe2403sp2.x86_64	Hardware architecture	x86_64
OS version and time	#1 SMP Wed Jun 25 23:16:20 CST 2025	OS type	GNU/Linux
Hardware platform	x86_64	Network host name	openEuler

(2) Monitoring user sessions

System administrators can track user activity through login queries, enabling informed decisions about system management. Two key commands facilitate this monitoring: **who** and **last**. These tools display essential session data, including usernames, terminal identifiers, login timestamps, and contextual information such as source IP addresses.

The **who** command displays active user sessions, as demonstrated here:

```
[ict@openEuler24 ~]$ who -H
NAME         LINE        TIME                    COMMENT
ict          tty1        2025-01-01 08:58
ict          pts/0       2025-01-01 08:17  (10.211.55.2)
```

This output reveals two active sessions: a local login by user **ict** on console 1 (**tty1**), and a remote connection from IP address 10.211.55.2.

The **last** command reveals user login history by examining the **/var/log/wtmp** file. It presents comprehensive session data, including time, duration, and connection origins. When specified with a username, it filters records for that particular user. The command includes versatile options: **-a** appends source information to output lines, while **-d** resolves IP addresses to host names.

Example of **root** user's login history:

```
   [ict@openEuler24 ~]$ last root
   root       tty1                                       Fri
Nov 24 14:31 -01:34 (5+11:03)
   root       pts/0         10.211.55.2                  Sat Nov
18 16:12 -17:53 (01:40)
   root       pts/1         10.211.55.2                  Fri Nov
17 22:20 -22:20 (00:00)
   wtmp begins Fri Nov 17 21:14:46 2025
```

(3) Analyzing memory usage

The **free** command provides detailed insights into memory allocation across physical memory, swap space, shared segments, and kernel buffers. This diag-

3.3 Basic Command-Line Operations

nostic tool enables performance optimization and helps troubleshoot system slowdowns after application launches.

Table 3.15 outlines the primary options available with **free**:

The **-h** option automatically scales output to appropriate units (Mi for MB, Gi for GB). For continuous monitoring, **-s** establishes a refresh interval. This example refreshes every 3 seconds until interrupted by **Ctrl+C**:

```
[ict@openEuler24 ~]$ free -ht
          total    used    free    shared   buff/cache   available
Mem:      942Mi    414Mi   75Mi    22Mi     562Mi        528Mi
Swap:     2.1Gi    15Mi    2.0Gi
Total:    3.0Gi    429Mi   2.1Gi
```

(4) Monitoring drive space

The **df** (disk free) command monitors file system storage utilization. This essential maintenance tool enables proactive storage management through regular monitoring, helping administrators identify and address space constraints through cleanup operations or storage reallocation.

df displays comprehensive information about mounted file systems, including space utilization metrics and file system characteristics (Table 3.16).

```
[ict@openEuler24 bin]$ df -h /
Filesystem                    Size Used Avail Use%  Mounted on
/dev/mapper/openeuler-root    40G  5.9G 32G   16%   /
```

Table 3.15 Common free options

Option	Description	Option	Description
-h	Displays memory usage in appropriate units	-g	Displays memory usage in GB
-k	Displays memory usage in KB	-t	Adds a line showing column totals
-m	Displays memory usage in MB	-s<N>	Refreshes display every N seconds

Table 3.16 Common df options

Option	Description	Option	Description
-a	Shows drive usage for all file systems, including **/proc**.	-t, --type	Shows drive usage only for specified file system types
-h	Displays drive usage in appropriate units.	-T	Adds a line showing column totals

For additional block device insights, the **lsblk** command displays comprehensive information, including device identifiers, capacity specifications, type classifications, and mount points.

3.3.6 System Management

Linux provides an extensive array of command-line tools for system management [14]. This section introduces fundamental administrative operations, with more advanced topics following in subsequent chapters. All system management commands require root privileges for execution.

(1) Setting system date and time

openEuler supports two methods for managing system time: **date** and **timedatectl**.

The **date** command modifies the current time using the format **date --set="MMM DD YYYY HH:MM:SS"**. For instance, to set the time to January 1, 2025, 00:00:00, run **date --set="Jan 01 2025 00:00:00"**.

However, changes made through **date** remain temporary and may reset after system restart. For permanent changes, synchronize with the hardware clock using **hwclock -w**.

timedatectl represents the preferred approach on openEuler, offering comprehensive control over date, time, timezone, and Network Time Protocol (NTP) synchronization with persistent changes. Examples include:

Time adjustment: **timedatectl set-time "2025-01-01 00:00:00"**

Timezone configuration: **timedatectl set-timezone "Asia/Shanghai"**

NTP activation: **timedatectl set-ntp yes**

Exercise caution when adjusting system time settings, as incorrect configurations might trigger data loss or system irregularities.

(2) Restarting and shutting down the systemWhile Linux systems rarely require restarts or shutdowns, these operations become essential during maintenance. Special consideration applies in multi-user environments to minimize disruption.

Linux implements three shutdown-related procedures:

Halt: Initiates shutdown sequence by disabling logins and network services, performs cleanup tasks including process termination and data synchronization, then halts kernel operations.

Power off: Completes halt procedures before signaling power management through ACPI to cut power.

Restart: Executes halt procedures followed by kernel reinitiation until system readiness.

openEuler maintains UNIX traditions with four commands: **halt**, **poweroff**, **reboot**, and **shutdown**. Each targets specific use cases while supporting all shutdown behaviors and broadcasting warnings through the **wall** command.

The first three commands operate without arguments and share common options, defaulting to their namesake actions. Key options include:

--halt: Forces system halt.
--poweroff: Triggers power shutdown.
--reboot: Initiates system restart.
--force: Expedites execution without full service termination; double specification bypasses shutdown procedures.

The **shutdown** command defaults to power off but accommodates halt and restart operations. It uniquely enables scheduled execution and customized notifications through two optional parameters: time and message content. Time accepts **hh:mm** or **+n** format, defaulting to one one-minute delay. Using **now** or **+0** triggers immediate execution, matching halt, poweroff, or reboot behavior. On openEuler, **systemctl** underlies all these operations. These commands function as symbolic links to **/bin/systemctl**, maintaining interface familiarity and script compatibility.

> **systemctl** stands as a cornerstone of modern Linux system management, orchestrating services, system events, and daemons. Its extensive capabilities and options support comprehensive system administration, as detailed fully in Chap. 8.

3.4 Shells: Unleashing Command-Line Power

Shells form the primary interface for UNIX-like OSs. The CLI available through a console or terminal operates through a shell, which interprets and executes all entered commands.

While the previous sections demonstrated the capabilities of shells through various commands, they only scratched the surface by illustrating basic command interpretation and execution functions. Shells encompass numerous advanced interactive features that enhance command-line flexibility and power, delivering a genuinely intuitive interface.

Shells emerged from UNIX designers' vision for an intuitive UI. Developed as a standard application, it builds upon the elegant kernel architecture and leverages streamlined yet robust system call interfaces. Through command-line interaction, shells deliver flexibility and power within a coherent framework. UNIX enthusiasts continuously enhance shell capabilities and develop distinct shell variants to create more intuitive interfaces. This symbiotic relationship highlights how UNIX established the groundwork for shell design, while shells propelled the advancement of UNIX.

3.4.1 Introduction to Bash

Shells trace their origins to 1971 when Thompson created the first shell at Bell Labs [12]. This pioneering shell operated as a standalone program outside the kernel, incorporating features reminiscent of Multics. It introduced groundbreaking concepts like wildcards (***.txt**) and streamlined syntax for redirection (<, >, and >>) and pipes (| and ^). Though the V6 Shell excelled primarily as an interactive command interpreter, its scripting capabilities remained limited.

The evolution of UNIX spawned multiple shell variants, each maintaining core functionality while introducing unique features to accommodate diverse user needs and scenarios. Notable shells include:

- Bourne shell (sh): This interactive command interpreter and scripting language emerged from Stephen Bourne's work at Bell Labs. Introduced in Version 7 UNIX in late 1977, it became the standard UNIX shell. Today, this straightforward shell primarily handles system-level scripting and automation tasks.
- C shell (csh): Joy developed this shell with C-inspired syntax. It incorporates C-like control structures, mathematical operations, built-in functions, and customizable prompts. Through special characters and syntax, it manages CLI behavior, including execution order, history access, aliases, and parameter expansion. While prevalent in BSD systems, its syntax differs from other shells.
- Bourne-again shell (Bash): This widely adopted shell, developed by Brian Fox for GNU, debuted in 1989. Initially targeted for GNU systems, Bash now runs across most UNIX-like OSs. It combines practical interactive features with robust programming capabilities, including command-line editing, variable substitution, and control structures. Importantly, it maintains complete compatibility with sh scripts, ensuring legacy code runs without modification.

The recent emergence of fish (friendly interactive shell) brings modern conveniences through its intuitive interface. It integrates command suggestions, syntax highlighting, auto-completion, and history search capabilities without requiring plugins, enhancing the interactive experience.

Bash stands out for its exceptional performance in both command-line interaction and script programming. This widespread adoption has established it as the standard shell across Linux distributions, supported by extensive applications and a robust user community. This book explores common advanced interactive features that shell brings to CLI, using Bash as the primary example.

3.4.2 Environment Variables

Environment variables play a fundamental role in shell operations, defining parameters for user interaction and application environments. These global variables, preconfigured in the system, accommodate various application scenarios. Their scope

3.4 Shells: Unleashing Command-Line Power

extends beyond the current shell instance, remaining accessible to all launched programs and subshells.

These variables store critical information, including system configurations, search paths, and user details, which influence the behavior of all programs and scripts within the system. System administrators configure system-level variables, while users define their personal variables, enabling straightforward implementation of flexible, multi-level customization in UNIX-like OSs.

(1) Viewing environment variables

The **env** command displays environment variables. Running it without options or parameters lists all current environment variables. Here are some typical examples:

```
[ict@openEuler24 ~]$ env | less
HOSTNAME=openEuler
LANG=zh_CN.UTF-8
HOME=/home/ict
USER=ict
PATH=/home/ict/.local/bin:/home/ict/bin:/usr/local/bin:/usr/bin:/usr/local/sbin:/usr/sbin
```

Table 3.17 describes common environment variables and their purposes.

While **env** displays all environment variables, you can view individual variable values using the **echo** command with the syntax **echo $*VARIABLE***—for example, **echo $PWD**. Following convention, environment variables, being global in nature, use uppercase letters in their names.

(2) Using environment variables

$PATH is a vital environment variable that defines search paths for executable files. To view its value, use the **echo $PATH** command:

```
[ict@openEuler24 ~]$ echo $PATH
/home/ict/.local/bin:/home/ict/bin:/usr/local/bin:/usr/bin:/usr/local/sbin:/usr/sbin
```

Table 3.17 Common environment variables

Variable	Meaning	Variable	Meaning
SHELL	Path of the current shell file	USER	Current login user
PWD	Working directory	PATH	Search paths for executable files
HOME	Default user home directory	LANG	System language (Chinese, English, etc.)

These default system paths eliminate the need to specify full paths when entering commands. The shell systematically searches through the paths listed in **$PATH**, beginning with the first entry. When a command cannot be located after all paths are examined, the shell generates a "command not found" error message.

Consider a scenario where **/home/ict/bin** exists in **$PATH**. If this directory contains an executable file named **find**, the shell will execute it before checking other locations. The **type** command reveals the category of a command and, for non-built-in commands, displays their absolute paths.

```
[ict@openEuler24 ~]$ type find
find is /home/ict/bin/find
```

This behavior demonstrates how earlier paths in the search sequence take precedence over later ones, potentially overriding system commands with identically named files.

It is important to note that the current directory is not included in **$PATH**. Therefore, even if an executable file **foo** exists in the current directory, it must be run using **./foo**. This security mechanism prevents accidental execution of malicious programs with the same name.

(3) Setting environment variables

Bash provides two methods to set environment variables: the **export** command for temporary variables and configuration scripts for permanent variables. These scripts include system-wide configurations in **/etc/profile.d/*** and user-specific files such as **~/.bashrc** and **~/.profile**.

- Temporary setting: Using the **export** command to set an environment variable in the current Bash session affects all subsequent commands until session termination.

```
[ict@openEuler24 ~]$ export PATH=/home/ict/tools/bin:$PATH
```

- Permanent setting: Environment variables configured in Bash configuration files activate automatically upon each user login. The following commands append the environment variable setting to **~/.bashrc** and implement it immediately.

```
[ict@openEuler24 ~]$ echo "export PATH=/home/ict/tools/bin:$PATH" >> ~/.bashrc
[ict@openEuler24 ~]$ . ~/.bashrc
```

To maintain optimal compatibility, create new configuration scripts in the **/etc/profile.d/** directory for automatic system loading rather than modifying system-level configuration scripts like **/etc/profile** or **/etc/bashrc**.

Another type of variable in Bash, known as a "shell variable," exists exclusively within the current shell instance. These variables remain inaccessible to subshells or other launched programs. The command prompt utilizes shell variables **$PS1** and **$PS2**. For additional information about shell variables, refer to the **man bash** command documentation.

3.4.3 Wildcards and Auto-Completion

Wildcards and auto-completion streamline command-line input in shells. Wildcards enable quick selection of multiple files through simple patterns, while auto-completion minimizes keystrokes for entering commands or parameters. These features enhance command-line efficiency and surpass mouse-based interactions in both flexibility and speed.

(1) Wildcards

The * wildcard rapidly selects files matching specific patterns. For example, ***.txt** matches all text files in the current directory without individual selection. ****/*.log** matches all log files across the current directory and its subdirectories—an efficient operation impractical with mouse interactions.

When combined with command-line tools (such as **ls**, **cp**, **mv**, and **rm**), wildcards enable bulk file operations. For instance, **rm *.bak** eliminates all backup files with the .bak extension. Multiple files matching specified patterns can be viewed:

```
[ict@openEuler24 ~]$ ls -dl /*bin
lrwxrwxrwx. 1 root root 7 May 27 2025 /bin -> usr/bin
lrwxrwxrwx. 1 root root 8 May 27 2025 /sbin -> usr/sbin
```

Bash translates wildcards into matching file names (with paths) and passes them as parameters to commands like **rm**, eliminating manual file name entry. Beyond *, which matches zero or more characters, Bash implements **?** to match any single character. These wildcards work together—**a?** matches two-character file names beginning with **a**; **a??** matches three-character file names starting with **a**; **??c*** matches file names containing **c** as the third character. These patterns expedite interactive tasks, enhancing efficiency and user experience.

> To pass wildcards directly to commands, enclose them in quotes or precede with the escape character \. For example, wildcards following **-name** in find commands require direct processing by find rather than Bash interpretation.

(2) Auto-completion

Auto-completion expands partial input strings into complete commands or file names through several methods:

- Tab-based completion: Enter a partial command or file path and press **Tab**. A unique match completes automatically; multiple options display with a second **Tab** press. Continue typing and pressing **Tab** until reaching the desired completion.
- Command history completion: Navigate previous or next commands with **Ctrl+P** or **Ctrl+N**; initiate history search with **Ctrl+R** and keywords. Cycle through matches with repeated **Ctrl+R** presses, or exit with **Ctrl+G**.
- Custom completion rules: Users can implement personalized auto-completion by creating and storing custom scripts in designated directories. These scripts activate automatically during partial command entry, following user-defined completion patterns to boost productivity.
- Completion tools: Third-party enhancements like the bash-completion package extend the built-in completion capabilities of Bash with additional features.

3.4.4 Command Combination

Bash implements multiple command combination methods, creating a streamlined and efficient command-line environment.

(1) Command chaining

When tasks require executing several related commands sequentially, command chaining minimizes interactions and wait times.

Consider developers working on large software projects who regularly need to enter the source code directory, fetch the latest version from the version control system, compile files, and run tests upon successful compilation. Traditional methods require entering and waiting for each command individually. This approach leads to extended idle periods between commands, with the system pausing after command completion if the user steps away.

The **&&** operator addresses this by chaining multiple commands with an "AND" relationship. Each subsequent command executes only after successful completion of its predecessor; failure halts the entire chain. For example:

3.4 Shells: Unleashing Command-Line Power

```
[ict@openEuler24 foo]$ pwd && mkdir /foo && pwd
/home/ict/foo
mkdir: cannot create directory '/foo': Permission denied
```

This chain terminates early because the **ict** user lacks root directory permissions, causing the second command to fail.

The || operator establishes an "OR" relationship, executing the second command only if the first fails. For independent commands, the ; operator executes all commands regardless of previous outcomes.

The shell determines command success through the **$?** variable, storing the exit status of the previous command. A value of 0 indicates success; any other value signals failure. For C programs, this status matches the return value of the **main** function. The shell maintains this result to enable conditional processing based on command outcomes. This explains the default return value of 0 in the **main** function written in C.

(2) Command substitution

Command substitution through backticks ("`") channels one command output into another command input. For instance, storing a temporary file name from **mktemp** in a shell variable (ensuring no spaces around the "=" assignment operator):

```
[ict@openEuler24 ~]$ tmpf=`mktemp -u /tmp/tmp.XXXX` && echo $tmpf
/tmp/tmp.6PYJ
```

Alternatively, $ and () achieve the same result - **$(pwd)** functions identically to `pwd`.

The man page installation in Sect. 3.2.5 demonstrated command substitution:

```
[ict@openEuler24 ~]$ sudo dnf install -y `rpm -qf \`which dnf\` | sed 's/-[0-9].*//'`-help
```

This command employs nested substitution: **rpm** processes the output of **which dnf** to query package names, while **dnf install** uses the output of **sed** to install man pages. Note the escape characters required for nested substitution.

An alternative syntax:

```
[ict@openEuler24 ~]$ sudo dnf install -y `rpm -qf $(which
dnf) | sed 's/-[0-9].
*//'`-help
```

(3) Command groups
Parentheses "()" create command groups executing in subshells and enable multiple commands to function as a single unit when chaining.
Subshell execution maintains isolation from the current shell environment:

```
[ict@openEuler24 ~]$ (cd /tmp; pwd) && pwd
/tmp
/home/ict
```

The output demonstrates that changing directories within the subshell leaves the working directory of the current shell unchanged.

3.4.5 Redirection

Redirection, a groundbreaking innovation from early UNIX, remains fundamental across UNIX-like OSs today [3]. This feature lets users modify program input and output sources through different files or devices, enabling dynamic control over program I/O streams for diverse interactive tasks.

UNIX-like OSs equip each program with three abstract standard I/O channels: standard input (stdin), standard output (stdout), and standard error (stderr). The keyboard typically supplies standard input, while the display handles both standard output and standard error by default. In C programming, **scanf** reads from standard input, and **printf** writes to standard output.

This technology employs straightforward methods to modify default settings of these standard I/O channels, enabling precise control over program I/O and separation of normal output from error messages, bringing remarkable flexibility to command-line operations.

(1) Output redirection
Output redirection routes the default standard output of a command to a file through the > and >> operators. Both create new files when necessary. With existing files, > overwrites the content, while >> adds new output at the end.
For example, **echo** typically displays text on screen, but redirection can write it to a file:

3.4 Shells: Unleashing Command-Line Power

```
[ict@openEuler24 ~]$ echo "Hello, openEuler!" > hello.txt
```

This command writes the string directly to **hello.txt** instead of displaying it. Error messages still appear on screen by default. To channel both error messages and standard output to the same destination, use **&>**:

```
[ict@openEuler22 ~]$ echo "Hello, openEuler!" &> hello.txt
```

This approach redirects standard error to standard output, which then flows to the file. In UNIX, file descriptors 0, 1, and 2 represent the three standard I/O channels.

To suppress error messages entirely, redirect standard error to the "black hole" file with **2>**:

```
[ict@openEuler24 ~]$ echo "Hello, openEuler!" > hello.txt 2> /dev/null
```

The **tee** command offers unique functionality by reading standard input and duplicating it to both standard output and multiple specified files.

(2) Input redirection

Input redirection shifts the default standard input of a program from keyboard to a file using the **<** operator.

The **wc** command demonstrates this by counting lines, words, and characters. Without arguments, it accepts standard input, which can come from a file:

```
[ict@openEuler24 ~]$ wc < hello.txt 1 2 18 hello.txt
```

Programs can combine input and output redirection:

```
[ict@openEuler24 ~]$ wc < hello.txt > wc.txt
```

The redirection technology of UNIX brings elegance and consistency to command-line programs. Developers can focus on core functionality without implementing multiple I/O methods, while users gain flexibility beyond built-in I/O features. These three standard I/O channels form the backbone of command-line programs across UNIX-like OSs, enabling versatile I/O redirection capabilities.

(3) Example

Managing changes across thousands of files in large software projects like the Linux kernel presents a significant challenge. Tracking modified files and specific changes becomes nearly impossible manually. To share these modifications, sending entire software packages proves impractical due to their size and network constraints. The **diff** command offers an elegant solution by generating compact patch files that recipients can easily apply using the **patch** command. Here is how to create a patch file by recursively comparing the **kernel** and **kernel.new** directories:

```
[ict@openEuler24 ~]$ diff -uNr kernel kernel.new > kernel.patch
```

Recipients can replicate these changes by placing the patch file in their **kernel** directory and running:

```
[ict@openEuler24 kernel]$ patch -p1 < kernel.patch
patching file ...
```

The Yocto project leverages patch files extensively as key building blocks for software package construction, streamlining Linux customization and porting processes.

(4) Here documents

Here documents provide a specialized form of redirection that streamlines the process of passing multiple data lines to a command input stream. This feature proves invaluable in automation scripts. The syntax follows this structure:

```
[command] <<[-] ['DELIMITER' | DELIMITER]
    HERE-DOCUMENT
DELIMITER
```

- The structure begins with an optional command, followed by the << redirection operator and an end delimiter. Users can optionally include - and choose whether to quote the delimiter identifier.
- The end delimiter accepts any string, though "EOF" and "END" remain popular choices.
- Within the HERE-DOCUMENT block, users can freely mix commands, variables, and various input types.
- The final delimiter line must contain the unquoted DELIMITER without any preceding spaces or characters.

  Here documents excel when paired with the **cat** command for writing content to files without launching an editor. Consider this example that demonstrates appending text and environment variables to **hello.txt**:

```
[ict@openEuler24 ~]$ cat << EOF >> hello.txt
> Hello, $(whoami)@$HOSTNAME
> EOF
[ict@openEuler24 ~]$ cat hello.txt
Hello, ict@openEuler24.03
```

Beyond basic file operations, here documents enable automation of multiple interactive inputs in programs, a capability that becomes particularly relevant in shell scripts discussed in Chap. 8.

3.4.6 Pipes

Pipes stand as one of the most revolutionary UNIX innovations and continue to define shell interaction in UNIX-like OSs [3]. They introduce a system-level mechanism for command collaboration that combines simplicity with efficiency, unlocking flexible command combinations and robust data stream processing capabilities.

In the CLI, the | symbol represents pipes, connecting two commands. A pipe channels the standard output of one program into the standard input of another, creating an elegant and powerful collaboration mechanism.

(1) Basic usage

This example illustrates connecting the **echo** command output to the **wc** command input:

```
[ict@openEuler24 ~]$ echo "Hello, openEuler!" | wc
      1       2      18
```

In Sect. 3.2.5, we encountered pipes during man page package installation:

```
[ict@openEuler24 ~]$ sudo dnf install -y `rpm -qf \`which
dnf\`` | sed
's/-[0-9].*//'`-help
```

Here, the **rpm** command outputs a package name that flows through the pipe to the **sed** command. **sed** strips away all characters beginning with the version number (marked by "-"), producing the core package name. Adding **-help** creates the man documentation package name for **dnf install**.

Pipes enable multiple commands to work in concert, achieving sophisticated operations. Consider this example that orchestrates four commands to manipulate the **/etc/passwd** file:

```
[ict@openEuler24 ~]$ cat /etc/passwd | sort | tee -a /tmp/
passwd | nl > nlpasswd
```

This demonstrates the key strength of the **tee** command: branching the data stream to capture intermediate results in log files for analysis while maintaining uninterrupted data flow.

Pipes brilliantly facilitate command combinations to create new functionality without developing standalone programs. At their core, pipes transfer data streams between programs, enabling continuous processing operations and extensive functional expansion.

The power of pipes manifests in two key ways. First, they create a text-processing pipeline where programs can chain together seamlessly. When a program outputs text data, any text processor accepting standard input can further manipulate it, creating an infinitely extensible CLI. This capability highlights why UNIX heavily favors text-based protocols.

No complex program alone can anticipate every user demand, but pipes enable unlimited functional growth, perfectly complementing the "small is beautiful" UNIX philosophy.

Second, pipes handle large data volumes efficiently through stream processing rather than loading entire datasets into memory. This "read-while-write" approach proves invaluable when using backup commands like **dd** or **dump** and **restore** on large file systems, significantly reducing drive usage and processing time. This efficiency extends to database remote backup and network transmission applications.

For programs resistant to direct command-line connection, users can create named pipes through **mkfifo**, then redirect input and output through these pipe files.

(2) Examples

The tar command showcases the versatility of pipes when they are paired with compression utilities. This approach unlocks unlimited compression capabilities—each new compression algorithm simply requires a new command.
Here is how to compress file packages using **gzip** and **xz**:

```
[ict@openEuler24 ~]$ tar -cvf bak.tar ~/bak | gzip > bak.tar.gz
[ict@openEuler24 ~]$ tar -cvf bak.tar ~/bak | xz > bak.tar.gz
```

Combining **find** with other commands through pipes unlocks sophisticated operations. This command locates and archives all shell scripts in the working directory and its subdirectories:

```
[ict@openEuler24 ~]$ find -type f -name "*.sh" | tar -cvf sh.tar -T
```

This command identifies all C source files in the current directory tree, calculates their sizes individually and in total, then displays them in ascending order:

```
[ict@openEuler24 ~]$ find . -name "*.c" | du -ch | sort -k1 -n
```

Here, **du** reports drive usage, while **sort -k1 -n** arranges results numerically by the first column.

The **xargs** command amplifies the power of pipes by bridging programs that do not naturally fit into pipelines. It reads standard input and transforms it into arguments for other commands.

xargs proves invaluable for commands that cannot accept standard input or multiple arguments. Commands like **file** or **mv** have valid reasons for this limitation—they specifically need file names as input, and general text would not make sense as arguments. Moreover, **mv** arguments play distinct roles.

This example finds all C source and header files, then counts lines in each:

```
[ict@openEuler24 ~]$ find -type f \(-name "*.c" -or -name "*.h" \) | xargs wc -l
```

Without **xargs**, this would count the lines of output rather than the contents of each file.

This command locates all script files and adds a ".bak" extension to each:

```
[ict@openEuler24 ~]$ find . -maxdepth 1 -type f -name '*.sh' | xargs -I % mv % %.bak
```

The **-I %** flag introduces a placeholder, replacing each % in **mv % %.bak** with matched file names.

Food for thought: How would you tackle these tasks in a Windows GUI environment?

Pipes represent elegant, efficient collaboration, connecting programs that handle standard input/output to process data streams seamlessly. They grant the command line nearly limitless extensibility—something monolithic applications rarely achieve.

While these commands might look daunting, you can streamline frequent operations by creating aliases, shell functions, or shell scripts to craft your own custom commands.

3.4.7 Extended Commands

Shells provide various mechanisms for extending existing commands to deliver enhanced or more user-friendly functionality.

Commands in shells fall into three primary categories:

- Built-in commands exist as functions within the shell program itself, optimizing execution speed for frequently used operations as integral parts of the shell.
- External commands come from standalone executable files outside the shell environment. These may be binary programs compiled from languages like

3.4 Shells: Unleashing Command-Line Power

C/C++ or shell/Python scripts, functioning across different shell implementations. For instance, **pwd** and **cd** operate as built-in commands, while **ls** and **cat** located in the **/bin** directory function as external commands.
- Alias commands represent user-defined shortcuts created with the **alias** command. For example, running **alias ll='ls -lh --color'** creates an alias command **ll**.

The **type** command identifies the category of a command:

```
[ict@openEuler24 ~]$ type cd cat ls
cd is a shell builtin
cat is /usr/bin/cat
ls is aliased to `ls --color=auto'
```

Shell function commands represent another extension method beyond external and alias commands, implementing functionality through shell script functions.

Let's explore shell function commands by creating one that streamlines man page installation.

In Sect. 3.2.5, we encountered a complex command for installing man pages. We can simplify this process through a shell function command.

Here is the original complex command:

```
[ict@openEuler24 ~]$ sudo dnf install -y `rpm -qf \`which dnf\` | sed 's/-[0-9].*//'`-help
```

Creating a custom extension command involves two straightforward steps:

(1) Write the shell function.
   Create **~/.install-help.rc** containing:

```
function install-help() {
  dnf install -y `rpm -qf \`which dnf\` | sed 's/-[0-9].*//'`-help
}
```

(2) Load the shell function.
   Import the **install-help** function into the current shell environment:

```
[ict@openEuler24 ~]$ . ~/.install-help.rc && type install-help
install-help is a function
```

Once loaded, **install-help** becomes available as a command. For permanent availability, either load **~/.install-help.rc** or incorporate the function code directly into **~/.bashrc**.

The **install-help** command streamlines man page installation:

```
[ict@openEuler24 ~]$ sudo -i install-help xargs && man xargs
```

Note: Using **sudo** with **ict** user's extended commands fails because the **root** user's shell environment lacks the **install-help** command. To resolve this, mirror the modifications in **root** user's Bash configuration file at **/root/.bashrc**.

This showcases shell function commands as another powerful command type, executing within the current shell environment. While alias commands handle simple shortcuts, shell functions excel at extending moderately complex, frequently used operations. For more sophisticated features, developers can create C/C++ programs or shell scripts as external commands. Chapter 5 delves deeper into shell scripting techniques.

3.4.8 Command-Line Editing

Bash offers powerful command-line editing capabilities that enhance interactive use. These features enable rapid text manipulation through keyboard shortcuts while entering commands, significantly improving user experience. For instance, pressing **Ctrl+A** instantly moves the cursor to the line beginning, while **Ctrl+E** moves the cursor to the line end. Mastering these keyboard shortcuts can dramatically boost productivity and make command-line operations more intuitive.

This section outlines essential command-line editing shortcuts that minimize repetitive typing and reduce hand movement. We strongly encourage incorporating these shortcuts into your daily workflow until they become automatic.

(1) Quick cursor movement

These shortcuts minimize dependence on arrow keys or mouse navigation, optimizing cursor movement efficiency, as shown in Table 3.18.

(2) (Command editing

These shortcuts streamline command editing without requiring mouse interaction, as shown in Table 3.19.

(3) Terminal control

These shortcuts enable vital control over the terminal or interactive device, as shown in Table 3.20.

3.5 Users and Permissions

Table 3.18 Quick cursor movement shortcuts

Key combination	Description	Key combination	Description
Ctrl+A	Move cursor to line beginning	Ctrl+B	Move cursor back (left) one character
Ctrl+E	Move cursor to line end	Alt+F	Move cursor forward (right) one word
Ctrl+F	Move cursor forward (right) one character	Alt+B	Move cursor back (left) one word

Table 3.19 Command editing shortcuts

Key combination	Description	Key combination	Description
Ctrl+D	Delete character at cursor; exit shell if line is empty	Ctrl+K	Delete from cursor to line end
Ctrl+H	Delete character before cursor (equivalent to **Backspace**)	Ctrl+U	Delete from cursor to line beginning

Table 3.20 Terminal control shortcuts

Key combination	Description	Key combination	Description
Ctrl+L	Clear screen (same as the **clear** command)	Ctrl+C	Terminate current task
Ctrl+M	Submit command	Ctrl+S	Pause screen output (useful for large compilations)
Ctrl+Z	Suspend current task (use the **bg** command to continue in the background)	Ctrl+Q	Resume screen output

3.5 Users and Permissions

A common error message that frustrates beginners is "Permission denied"—a classic permission-related issue.

One of the fundamental UNIX design principles centered on creating a multi-user OS where everything exists as a file. UNIX extensively utilizes human-readable text files for system configurations, user settings, and various applications. These files directly influence system stability and user privacy. Consequently, implementing effective access control for these files remains essential to the security architecture of UNIX [14].

UNIX-like OSs pioneered an elegant user and permission model in their early development stages. This model delivers efficient access control over system resources for all users while maintaining simplicity, clarity, and ease of management—principles that hold true to this day.

3.5.1 User Model

In multi-tasking OSs, the allocation of system resources hinges on user identity, with the system controlling resource usage accordingly. These resources encompass CPUs, memory, and drives. While administrators require nearly unlimited access to all resources, common users need appropriate restrictions. The OS must authenticate whether users accessing resources hold legitimate ownership or authorization, thus safeguarding all users' resources against unauthorized access, modification, or removal.

Linux implements an elegant two-tier structure of users and user groups. Individual users can participate in multiple groups, while groups can encompass multiple users. Users log in to the system using their usernames and passwords. The system tracks users through unique user IDs (UIDs), providing each with a dedicated home directory. The **/etc/passwd** text file stores essential user information, while **/etc/group** maintains group details, including group names and group IDs (GIDs).

The **root** user stands as the primary user of Linux, wielding supreme authority. Distinguished by the username "root" and UID 0, this user commands almost unrestricted access to all files. Its use should remain limited to essential tasks like system maintenance.

Conducting routine operations under root privileges invites considerable dangers: inadvertent commands can trigger system-wide disasters, program execution risks Trojan infiltration, and password security becomes compromised. Therefore, root access warrants use only when absolutely necessary. Following this principle, regular service programs should operate without root privileges to shield the system from potential software vulnerability exploitation.

3.5.2 Switching Users

Linux offers streamlined commands for switching users, enabling efficient task execution without repeated system logins.

While logging in as root is generally discouraged, certain system administration tasks—such as software installation and removal—demand root privileges. Furthermore, some applications should operate under virtual users to minimize security risks.

(1) Temporary identity changes

Authorized common users can temporarily adopt other user identities through the **sudo** command, which defaults to root privileges when no specific user is designated.

```
[ict@openEuler24 ~]$ sudo whoami ; sudo file ~ ; sudo -u
openEuler whoami ;
  [sudo] password for ict:
  root
  /home/ict: directory
  openEuler
```

Upon entering and validating the current user's password, commands execute under the alternative identity.

The second command output reveals that the home directory remains linked to the **ict** user, indicating these commands run with root privileges within the current user's shell context. The **-l** option enables access to **root** user's environment.

sudo permissions flow from the **/etc/sudoers** configuration file. On openEuler, **wheel** group membership automatically grants **sudo** privileges. Beyond basic group access, **/etc/sudoers** supports fine-grained control, including command restrictions for root access and password requirement exceptions for specific users.

For multiple root-privileged commands, use syntax like:

```
[ict@openEuler24 ~]$ sudo sh -c "cd /var/log && du -hs"
  12M.
```

The **root** user can leverage the **runuser** command to launch service applications under different identities, enhancing security.

(2) Identity switching

The **su** command allows all logged-in users to switch identities for entire sessions, defaulting to **root** when no argument is provided. It offers two variants based on the **-** option:

- **su [user]**: Shifts user identity while preserving the current shell environment.
- **su -[user]**: Changes both identity and shell environment to match the target user, mirroring a fresh login.

  The **exit** command returns users to their original session. Remember that **su** requires the target user's password for authentication.

3.5.3 Permission Model

Permissions form the cornerstone of resource access control in OSs. UNIX-like OSs treat all resources as files, applying three fundamental permissions: read, write, and execute. This framework, combined with multi-user capabilities, establishes distinct access levels for file owners, groups, and other users, creating a robust yet flexible system for managing resource access.

The interplay of user identities, group memberships, and file permissions determines access rights throughout the system. Whether a user can read, modify, or execute a file hinges on the permissions granted to them and their groups. This same principle extends to processes, where access to system resources mirrors the permissions of the initiating user.

(1) Permission notation

Linux employs three basic permissions: read, write, and execute, expressed through either symbolic notation ("rwx") or octal numbers, as detailed in Table 3.21.

Execute permission unlocks file execution and directory access capabilities. Without execute permission on a directory, its contents remain inaccessible.

The **root** user bypasses all permission restrictions except file execution constraints.

(2) Permission granularity

Linux implements a layered permission model based on users and groups, as outlined in Table 3.22. Each file or directory links to an owner and a group. By defining specific permissions for owners, groups, and others, the system shields sensitive data from unauthorized operations.

(3) File permissions

Nine permission bits govern file access, arranged in three triplets (one octal digit each), defining read, write, and execute permissions for owners, groups, and others. The **ls -lh** *file* command reveals these permission settings.

Table 3.21 Permission notation

Symbolic notation	Octal notation	Binary notation	Access rights
rwx	7	111	read+write+execute
rw-	6	110	read+write
r-x	5	101	read+execute
r--	4	100	read
-wx	3	011	write+execute
-w-	2	010	write
--x	1	001	execute
---	0	000	None

Table 3.22 Permission granularity

Level	Symbol	Description
Owner	u (user)	File owner, typically the creator
Group	g (group)	All users in the owner's group
Others	o (other)	All other users
All	a (all), equals u+g+o	All users

3.5 Users and Permissions

```
[ict@openEuler24 ~]$ ls -lh / | head -n 3
total 68K
lrwxrwxrwx.   1 root root   7 May 27  2025 bin -> usr/bin
drwxr-xr-x. 109 root root 12K Jan  2 05:47 etc
drwxrwxrwt.  13 root root 400 Jan  2 03:46 tmp
```

Consider **/etc** with rwxr-xr-x permissions: the owner (**root**) holds complete access (read, write, execute), while group members and others can only read and execute. This pattern, represented as octal number 755, appears frequently in system configurations.

Sharp-eyed readers might spot unique permissions of **/tmp**—these special cases will be explored in Chap. 8.

3.5.4 Permission Modification

When newcomers encounter "Permission denied" errors, they typically need to adjust file permissions. This might happen when executable files lose their execute permissions or when shell scripts become inoperable.

The **chmod** (change mode) command alters file permissions through flexible and comprehensive permission patterns. Its basic syntax follows:

```
$ chmod mode file...
```

The *mode* parameter defines permission patterns using either symbolic or octal notation, while *file* accepts one or multiple file names. The **-c** option reports only when permissions change, and **-R** modifies permissions recursively through directories and their contents.

(1) Symbolic notation

Symbolic notation follows this pattern: **[ugoa][[+-=][rwxX]...][,...]**. Multiple permission changes link together with commas. Table 3.23 illustrates common commands.

Table 3.23 Symbolic notation

Command	Description	Command	Description
chmod +x file	Grant execute permission to all users	chmod -R u=rwx dir	Recursively grant all permissions to the owner
chmod -x file	Remove execute permission from all users	chmod g-x,o-x file	Remove execute permission from group members and others

(2) Octal numeric notation
   While symbolic notation enables targeted permission changes, octal notation modifies all nine permission bits at once.
   This example finds files with 777 permissions and removes execute permissions from group members and others:

```
[ict@openEuler24 ~]$ find ~/bin/ -type f -perm -777 -exec chmod g-x,o-x {} \;
```

These complementary notation methods balance convenience with precision in permission management.

3.5.5 Ownership Modification

Beyond execution permissions, ownership issues frequently trigger "Permission denied" errors. Files created through **sudo** commands default to root ownership, blocking access from common users.

The **chown** (change owner) command updates file ownership and group assignment. Its syntax reads:

```
$ sudo chown -R user[:[group]] file...
```

The **-R** option propagates ownership changes throughout directory structures. While this command demands root privileges, it maintains a straightforward interface.

This command transfers ownership of **~/bin** and its contents to **ict**:

```
[ict@openEuler24 ~]$ sudo chown -R ict: ~/bin
```

3.6 DDE Installation

While openEuler ships without a desktop environment by default, it supports multiple options for users who prefer mouse-based operations: DDE, Xfce, UKUI, and GNOME.

- DDE, engineered by UnionTech, brings together dozens of powerful desktop applications in a comprehensive, independently developed environment.

- Xfce offers a lightweight alternative to traditional desktop environments. It distinguishes itself from GNOME and KDE through minimal resource consumption, maximizing system performance.
- UKUI, crafted by KylinSoft, builds on GTK and Qt foundations. This desktop environment prioritizes usability and responsiveness, featuring modular components that function independently.
- GNOME ranks among the most popular desktop environments for UNIX-like OSs, blending comprehensive functionality with an intuitive design. As a GNU project-endorsed environment, it caters to both users and developers.

For newcomers, DDE and Xfce emerge as particularly compelling choices. Below, we detail DDE installation. For Xfce and other GUIs, consult the openEuler documents.

DDE installation follows these straightforward steps:

```
# Switch to root by entering root password.
[ict@openEuler24 ~]$ su -
[root@openEuler24 ~]# dnf update     # Update software
                                      repositories.
[root@openEuler24 ~]# dnf             # Install the DDE package.
install dde
# Set the GUI as default and
restart the system.
[root@openEuler24 ~]# systemctl set-default graphical.
target && reboot
```

Once DDE is installed, access DDE by logging in with the **ict** user. Remember that DDE blocks root login for security reasons. You can also use the default DDE user (username and password: **openeuler**).

DDE creates a versatile computing environment where you can navigate multimedia applications and web browsers through an intuitive interface while retaining access to powerful command-line tools through virtual terminals.

3.7 Summary

openEuler seamlessly integrates with other Linux distributions, facilitating smooth transitions for users from mainstream Linux systems. The CLI presents an extensive array of commands with versatile options, delivering robust functionality for text processing, system management, and operational control. These tools blend sophisticated capabilities with intuitive operation, empowering users to work according to their preferences.

The brilliant shell design, especially the pipe mechanism, lets users create sophisticated data processing pipelines by linking commands—achieving a level of flexibility that surpasses individual graphical applications. Redirection techniques amplify command capabilities by transforming how commands handle input and output. The shell further enriches the command-line experience through various mechanisms that boost functionality and streamline interaction. These features highlight the elegant UNIX design principles while exemplifying the hallmark Linux traits of simplicity, adaptability, efficiency, and consistency.

This chapter explored the distinctions between GUI and CLI interfaces, introduced essential command-line concepts, outlined Linux user and permission models, and guided through DDE installation. This foundation prepares readers to appreciate openEuler's command-line advantages and sets the stage for exploring OS fundamentals in Chap. 4.

Reflection and Practice

1. Gain hands-on experience with openEuler by establishing remote SSH connections from Windows.
2. Identify and explain your preferred common commands from the basic operation set.
3. Master Bash fundamentals and design your personalized command prompt.
4. Apply wildcards and command combinations to streamline familiar operations.
5. Design and implement a custom task using here documents and redirection techniques.
6. Create advanced workflows by combining common commands through pipes.
7. Optimize your workflow by mastering command-line editing capabilities.
8. Experiment with permission and ownership modifications, validating changes through practical tests.

Open Access This chapter is licensed under the terms of the Creative Commons Attribution-NonCommercial-NoDerivatives 4.0 International License (http://creativecommons.org/licenses/by-nc-nd/4.0/), which permits any noncommercial use, sharing, distribution and reproduction in any medium or format, as long as you give appropriate credit to the original author(s) and the source, provide a link to the Creative Commons license and indicate if you modified the licensed material. You do not have permission under this license to share adapted material derived from this chapter or parts of it.

The images or other third party material in this chapter are included in the chapter's Creative Commons license, unless indicated otherwise in a credit line to the material. If material is not included in the chapter's Creative Commons license and your intended use is not permitted by statutory regulation or exceeds the permitted use, you will need to obtain permission directly from the copyright holder.

Chapter 4
OS Principles and Practice

Objectives

1. Grasp fundamental design principles of OSs.
2. Master file management methodologies and organizational structures.
3. Comprehend memory management concepts and techniques.
4. Understand process fundamentals and management strategies.

When you power up your computer, the OS provides your first interactive interface. Acting as a master coordinator, the OS orchestrates all hardware resources while protecting personal data stored within. Understanding OS concepts and principles is essential for effectively managing any environment, whether it is embedded systems or large-scale clusters.

The UNIX philosophy has made a lasting impact on modern OSs. It emphasizes component simplicity and interface consistency, which together foster modularity and reusability. These are foundational elements of contemporary software engineering, offering flexible and maintainable systems. This approach has influenced modern software development practices, with many prominent applications embodying these principles.

This chapter focuses on essential hardware—drives, memory, and CPUs—and their relationship to file, memory, and process management. What follows presents three real-world examples that demonstrate Linux core principles and architecture in practice, transforming abstract concepts into tangible applications, strengthening your proficiency with Linux distributions such as openEuler.

Computers connect with these core hardware components and various external devices, but despite the diversity in form and function, OSs typically follow the same UNIX principles to create meaningful abstractions. For those interested in a more in-depth exploration of the kernel architecture, we encourage you to explore the relevant literature, which offers comprehensive coverage of topics beyond this discussion.

4.1 OS Design Philosophy

Linux, released under a free software license, promotes source code sharing and modification to address diverse user needs. It features extensive configuration options and modular design, enabling users to tailor and optimize according to their specific requirements and hardware environment. While these configuration options increase system design complexity, the separation of mechanisms and policies dramatically reduces coupling between modules and the kernel. Each module needs only to adhere to the interface specifications to fulfill system requirements. This approach keeps all modules internally straightforward, while sophisticated interface design ensures minimal coupling between modules and powerful performance [6].

(1) Key features
Modern OSs demonstrate these essential characteristics:

- Concurrent multi-user login and multi-tasking support, accommodating simultaneous users; parallel task processing capabilities, supporting multiple processes, threads, and even coroutines
- Integration of UNIX-like file systems, incorporating various file system types including ext4, Btrfs, and XFS, delivering high performance and reliability
- Runtime memory isolation, creating independent address spaces for execution units to maintain data security between them
- Virtual memory management, integrating physical memory and drive space to offer expanded address spaces and enhanced system stability
- Rich network functionality and protocol support, encompassing the TCP/IP protocol stack, network device drivers, and network services

(2) Design principles
To fulfill these key features and user requirements, OS design adheres to these principles:

- Modular design: Implement modular architecture with standardized interfaces, partitioning functionality into independent modules for autonomous development, maintenance, and expansion.
- Portability: Engineer kernel with portability in mind, enabling deployment across diverse hardware platforms and supporting multiple hardware architectures.

4.1 OS Design Philosophy

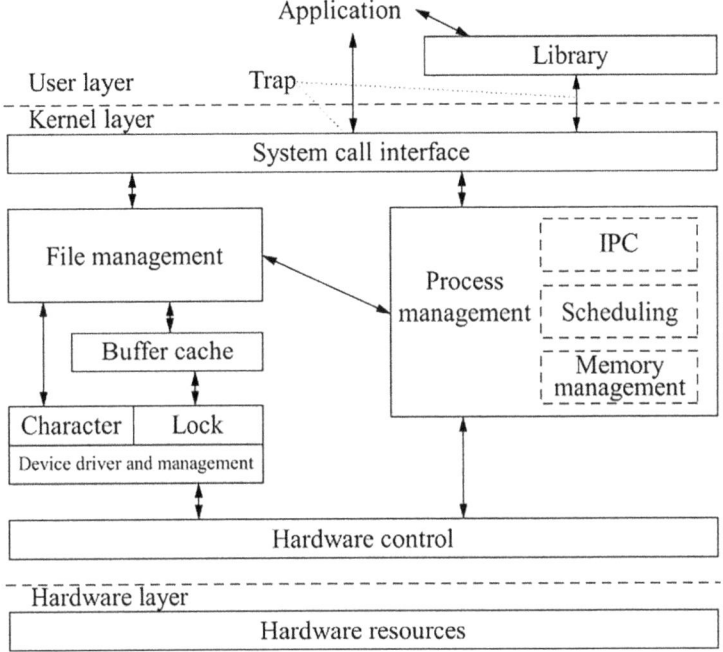

Fig. 4.1 Typical monolithic kernel structure

- Open standard compliance: Follow standards such as POSIX, ensuring compatibility with UNIX applications and seamless operation and migration across platforms.

(3) System architecture

The classic OS architecture (typical monolithic kernel structure), illustrated in Fig. 4.1, comprises process management, memory management, file management, and device management modules. It orchestrates underlying computer hardware resources while offering a simple, consistent, and portable system call interface for upper-layer applications [15]. Applications access kernel services through these interfaces. The kernel layer sits between the user layer and hardware layer, much like filling in a sandwich. Through elegant interface design, the kernel layer unifies various hardware functions and exposes them to users. It converts user calls into appropriate driver calls, directing specific hardware through driver programs to achieve software design goals. Consequently, drivers occupy the lowest layer of the system, maintaining direct hardware interaction. The kernel layer also provides essential protection and scheduling functions, including memory management and IPC.

> The previously discussed shell program is also a common type of application.

4.2 File Management

OSs face the complex challenge of managing vast computing resources while maintaining user accessibility. Traditional approaches to device management, where each device requires its own interface and methods, prove inadequate for modern systems. While this straightforward method works well in microcontroller designs—exemplified by functions like uart_write and spi_read—it becomes unwieldy when dealing with multiple devices or frequent hardware changes. The complexity of maintaining separate protocols for each device variation makes this approach unsustainable.

UNIX designers revolutionized resource management by identifying common patterns and implementing the elegant principle of "everything is a file." This concept draws a clever parallel with paper documents—just as you can write to or read from a paper, file operations follow the same fundamental pattern of writing and reading data. This analogy extends naturally to external devices: transmitting data to a serial interface mirrors a write operation, while receiving data corresponds to a read operation. This unified approach allows all devices to function as "files" with consistent read and write capabilities.

This abstraction transforms user experience from managing diverse devices to interacting with standardized file objects, known as device files. Users need only utilize system-provided functions for reading and writing to these device files. These functions constitute the system call interface, which maintains stability to ensure OS compatibility.

The need for cross-platform compatibility led to the development of POSIX, an IEEE standard collection that defines OS interfaces. POSIX encompasses specifications for system calls, commands, and related formats. OSs that implement POSIX standards streamline application development and portability, earning the designation of POSIX-compliant systems. This standardization represents a crucial step toward universal software compatibility.

4.2.1 File Tree

After abstracting all devices as files, OSs need only focus on organizing and managing these files effectively. The challenge lies in handling such a vast number of files efficiently. Throughout history, humans have excelled at organizing through hierarchical classification—just as biology organizes eukaryotes into kingdoms (animal, plant, fungi) with subsequent divisions into subkingdoms, superphyla, phyla, and subphyla. OSs adopt this intuitive approach by organizing files into a comprehensive hierarchical tree structure.

Within this file tree, directories function as special files capable of containing other files, while regular files store data but cannot contain other files. Regular files typically reside at the tree's bottom level, with directory files occupying the

4.2 File Management

intermediate layers. The tree's apex features the root directory, denoted by a forward slash ("/") in POSIX-compliant OSs. This root directory provides access to all files within the system. For instance, the **ls** command discussed in Chap. 3 exists as a file typically located at **/usr/bin/ls**. The leading "/" represents the root directory, while subsequent slashes separate the directories **usr** and **bin** in the path. This path structure prohibits the use of forward slashes in file names to prevent ambiguity in the system.

> Note that besides the forward slash, characters such as backslash ("\"), colon (":"), asterisk ("*"), question mark ("?"), and double quote (""") cannot be used in file names.

In essence: each file possesses a unique file name; directories function as special files that contain other files; paths constructed with file names and "/" characters locate specific files; and all file paths originate from the root directory /.

POSIX-compliant OSs implement a standardized directory hierarchy that maintains consistency across all systems that adhere to the POSIX standards. As illustrated in Fig. 4.2, the root directory encompasses multiple subdirectories, each fulfilling distinct roles.

- The **bin** directory houses system-level binary executables. Its name originates from "binary," and similar directories like **/usr/bin** throughout the system typically share this purpose of storing executable files.
- The **lib** directory contains shared libraries in the system. Though these libraries exist as binary files, they differ from executables in that they provide callable functions rather than direct execution. Both **lib** and **bin** directories maintain their distinct roles consistently throughout the file system.

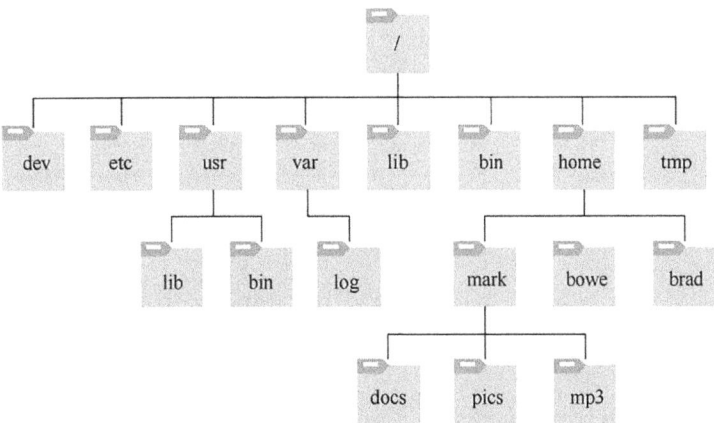

Fig. 4.2 File tree in a POSIX-compliant OS

- The **etc** directory holds system configuration files that dictate system behavior and operation. Critical files such as **/etc/passwd** for user accounts and **/etc/network/interfaces** for network settings reside here. Due to their vital nature, this directory typically remains read-only, with modifications limited to root user access.
- The **usr** directory hosts user-accessible software and data vital for everyday operations. Notably, this directory often mirrors the **bin** and **lib** structure found at the root directory level. Some OSs align **/bin** and **/lib** with their **/usr/bin** and **/usr/lib** counterparts. To streamline management and optimize storage, engineers implemented symbolic links, enabling single-file storage with multiple access points. We will explore this mechanism in detail later.
- The **tmp** directory functions as temporary storage, with files automatically purged during system shutdown or reboot. This location explicitly excludes any files requiring permanent retention.
- The **dev** directory implements unified naming conventions and access interfaces for system devices. All device files reside here, offering a comprehensive view of system devices through directory listing.
- The **var** directory manages dynamic system data that evolves during operation. For instance, **/var/log** maintains system logs, providing crucial insights into system behavior and troubleshooting information.
- The **home** directory allocates dedicated storage space for individual users. Each user receives a personal directory matching the username, serving as the primary location for personal files, including images, videos, documents, and code. For instance, **/home/mark** in Fig. 4.3 represents the exclusive storage space for user **mark**.

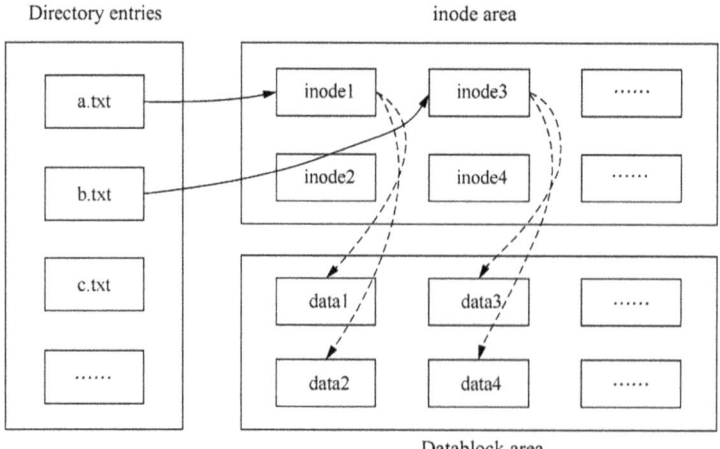

Fig. 4.3 Relationship between inodes

4.2 File Management

(1) File naming conventions

OSs implement different file naming conventions. Here are the standard conventions in Linux:

- Character set: File names incorporate Unicode characters, encompassing letters, numbers, and special characters. For optimal compatibility across systems, using ASCII characters exclusively remains the best practice.
- Length limit: Linux imposes a 255-character limit on file names.
- File extensions: File names may incorporate extensions to identify file type or content, appearing after the final period in the file name. Linux maintains flexibility by supporting extensionless files, particularly common with binary executables discussed earlier.

> Files without extensions are called "extensionless files," and their type and purpose can be determined using the **file** command. The **file** command displays comprehensive file attributes, including file type, encoding format, CPU architecture, and other information.

- Case sensitivity: Linux distinguishes between uppercase and lowercase letters, treating them as distinct characters. Thus, **file.txt** and **File.txt** are separate files—a key distinction from Windows systems.
- Special characters and spaces: Linux restricts certain special characters and spaces in file names. When necessary, these characters must undergo escaping or encoding, typically achieved by prefixing the character with a backslash.

  Given the diversity of conventions across OSs, adhering to universal naming practices ensures maximum compatibility and reliability when creating file names.

(2) inodes

Linux OSs utilize inodes (index nodes) as their foundational data structure for file data storage. Each file and directory maintains a unique inode encompassing several crucial elements:

- File type: determines whether it represents a regular file, directory, symbolic link, or other variant.
- Permissions: define access rights for the owner, group members, and others.
- Owner and group: pinpoints who owns the file and its group association.
- File size: measures content volume in bytes.
- Timestamps: capture access, modification, and status change moments.
- Link count: counts hard link references to the inode.
- Data block pointers: maps locations of the physical content of the file.

  This architecture enables instantaneous metadata retrieval without file system traversal, as depicted in Fig. 4.3. During file or directory creation, the system generates a fresh inode with a unique identifier, facilitating streamlined management while delivering outstanding flexibility and performance.

Inodes embody the true essence of files, with file names functioning as mere aliases. Multiple file names can point to one inode. Consider how **/bin/ls** and **/usr/bin/ls** often represent identical files with different paths, sharing a single inode number. The **stat** command exposes this relationship

```
[ict@openEuler24 ~]$ stat /bin/ls
  File: /bin/ls
  Size: 138208         Blocks: 272        IO Block: 4096     regular file
Device: 10302h/66306d  Inode: 11403944    Links: 1
Access: (0755/-rwxr-xr-x)  Uid: (    0/    root)   Gid: (    0/   root)
Access: 2025-11-26 17:46:54.057391761 +0800
Modify: 2025-06-18 21:53:09.000000000 +0800
Change: 2025-11-25 15:58:55.365080207 +0800
 Birth: 2025-11-25 15:58:54.939101573 +0800

[ict@openEuler24 ~]$ stat /usr/bin/ls
  File: /usr/bin/ls
  Size: 138208         Blocks: 272        IO Block: 4096     regular file
Device: 10302h/66306d  Inode: 11403944    Links: 1
Access: (0755/-rwxr-xr-x)  Uid: (    0/    root)   Gid: (    0/    root)
Access: 2025-11-26 17:46:54.057391761 +0800
Modify: 2025-06-18 21:53:09.000000000 +0800
Change: 2025-11-25 15:58:55.365080207 +0800
 Birth: 2025-11-25 15:58:54.939101573 +0800
```

Symbolic links and hard links showcase distinct characteristics despite both creating file connections. Changes propagate across all links, yet their implementations diverge significantly. Symbolic links manifest as specialized files storing target paths, boasting unique inodes and link-type markers. Hard links generate new directory entries wielding the original inode number, mirroring the source file almost perfectly. The **ls -l** command highlights symbolic links with an arrow (->) followed by their destination:

```
$ ls -l /
lrwxrwxrwx 1 root root          7 Dec 9 2025 bin -> usr/bin
```

Deleting target files transforms symbolic links into "broken links," while hard links persist undisturbed when their counterparts vanish. The system monitors these connections through the link count of the inode. Once this count zeroes out, signaling no remaining pathways, the system frees the associated drive space for future allocation.

4.2.2 Virtual File System

Contemporary file systems interpret high-capacity storage devices as expansive arrays housing both essential data and organizational metadata. The diversity of storage devices, each optimized for different priorities—whether read performance, write reliability, or scalability—necessitates careful consideration of data management approaches. This has led to the development of multiple file system formats, including ext4, XFS, Btrfs, and NTFS, each implementing unique data structures for high-capacity storage management [10].

Linux addresses this multiplicity through its Virtual File System (VFS) mechanism. This abstraction layer presents every storage device as a directory within VFS, regardless of its underlying file system. The actual data access occurs only when users interact with these directories, triggering coordination between the specific file system driver and device access driver, as depicted in Fig. 4.4.

This abstraction extends to device files, which integrate seamlessly into VFS with standardized access functions. Linux provides a unified set of file operations—**write**, **read**, **open**, and **close**—handling common tasks across file systems. However, devices often require specialized configurations. For instance, serial interfaces need parameters like baud, stop bit length, and parity settings. The ioctl function handles these device-specific operations.

The **/dev** directory houses special files beyond standard and device files, including pseudo-devices, pipes, and sockets. These represent virtual devices or program utilities within the kernel. Notable examples include **/dev/zero** (outputting zeros), **/dev/null** (discarding input), and **/dev/random** (generating random numbers).

Two distinctive directories reside in the root directory: **/proc** and **/sys**. The **/proc** directory mirrors current system status through its files—**/proc/cpuinfo**, for instance, details processor specifications including architecture, frequency, cache, core count, and instruction sets. The **/sys** directory presents runtime device information in a hierarchical structure based on device categories. For example, **/sys/dev/block** contains mass storage devices, while **/sys/bus/pci** manages PCI bus components.

Unlike drive letters in Windows, Linux represents storage devices as files in **/dev** (such as **/dev/sda**, **/dev/sdb**). These devices become accessible through mounting—attaching them to any directory in the file hierarchy. For example:

```
[ict@openEuler24 ~]$ sudo mount /dev/sdb1 /mnt
```

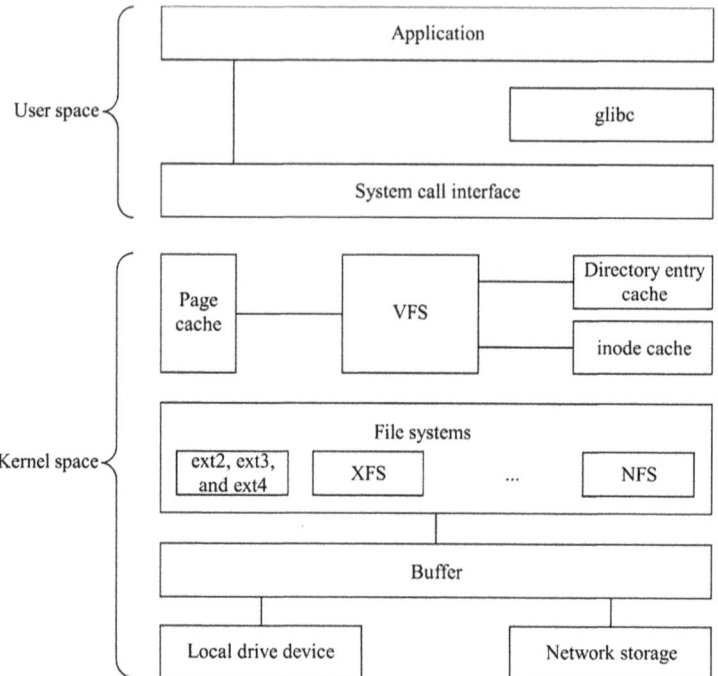

Fig. 4.4 Kernel architecture with VFS

The **dd** command enables comprehensive drive operations. These commands illustrate drive backup and cloning operations, processing data in 1 MB blocks:

```
[ict@openEuler24 ~]$ sudo dd if=/dev/sdb of=/mnt/usb/sdb.img bs=1M
[ict@openEuler24 ~]$ sudo dd if=/dev/sdb of=/dev/sdc bs=1M
```

4.2.3 Introduction to EulerFS

EulerFS is an open-source distributed file system that distributes files across multiple computer systems [16]. Its core capabilities distinguish it in several key areas:

- Auto-sharding and scaling: EulerFS distributes files automatically across multiple physical storage nodes and adapts dynamically as new nodes join the system.
- Strong consistency: Every EulerFS node maintains a complete and unified file system view, delivering an experience similar to local drive access.

- High reliability: Through its replication mechanism, EulerFS ensures data availability even when individual nodes fail.
- High performance: With its thread pool implementation, EulerFS handles concurrent access efficiently, supporting high-volume read and write operations.
- Easy scalability: The modular architecture of EulerFS enables seamless integration and removal of backend storage.
- Rapid failure recovery: Using the snapshot technology, EulerFS quickly recovers data from system crashes or corruption.
- Open source and free: Released under Apache License 2.0, EulerFS gives users complete freedom to use and modify its source code.

As a comprehensive solution, EulerFS excels in distributed storage scenarios demanding high capacity, minimal latency, and maximum throughput. Its distributed architecture overcomes the limitations inherent in traditional file systems by eliminating single points of failure.

4.2.4 Example 4.1: File System Operations

OSs offer a comprehensive suite of tools that streamline file system management. These tools handle essential tasks like partition manipulation, file system formatting, and directory tree mounting. Beyond local operations, OSs enable the integration of both local files and remote drives into the local directory tree, treating them as directory files. These powerful capabilities stem from the sophisticated abstraction layer of VFS.

(1) Create, format, and mount a partition

In Linux, mounting a drive partition integrates it into the file tree by linking the root directory of the partition to a standard system directory. The process involves three key steps: partitioning, formatting, and mounting. Let's walk through these steps, beginning with partition verification:

```
[ict@openEuler24 ~]$ ls /dev/sdb*    # List all partitions on the sdb drive.
/dev/sdb
```

The presence of file names like **/dev/sdb1** in the output indicates existing partitions, which should be modified with caution. To create partitions, use **fdisk /dev/sdb** to launch the interactive partitioning tool. After creating partitions, run the previous command again to confirm the new partitions in the **/dev** directory.

```
[ict@openEuler24 ~]$ sudo fdisk /dev/sdb
Command (m for help):n
Partition type
  p   primary (0 primary, 0 extended, 4 free)
  e   extended (container for logical partitions)
Select (default p):p
Partition number (1-128, default 1):1
First sector (34-5860533134, default 2048): 2048
Last sector, +/-sectors or +/-size{K,M,G,T,P}
(2048-5860533134, default 5860533134): +1G
Created a new partition 2 of type 'Linux filesystem' and
of size 1 GiB.
```

Next, format the partition with a file system. Linux typically employs the ext4 file system:

```
[ict@openEuler24 ~]$ sudo mkfs.ext4 /dev/sdb1
```

With formatting complete, mount the partition. While you can mount it anywhere in the file tree, non-system drives typically reside under the **/mnt** directory:

```
[ict@openEuler24 ~]$ sudo mount /dev/sdb1 /mnt/data    #
Ensure that /mnt/data exists.
```

Contents of the partition are now accessible through the **/mnt/data** directory.

Direct access to files and directories through **/dev/sdb1** is impossible before mounting—the content becomes accessible only after successfully mounting the partition.

(2) Mount network shared drives to the file tree.

Network file servers enable drive content sharing, letting users within a network access files across multiple computers seamlessly. Linux leverages its robust VFS architecture to integrate network-shared drives into the local file tree, creating a unified experience where remote files feel like local ones. This integration happens through the **mount** command, as shown in the following example.

Take a server with IP address 192.168.1.100 running the Network File System (NFS) service, which shares its **/shared** directory. The **mount** command below integrates this remote directory into the local system at **/mnt/nfs**. During file operations in this directory, the OS transparently manages all drive operations through the NFS protocol, creating a seamless experience where the remote nature of the files remains invisible to users.

```
[ict@openEuler24 ~]$ sudo mount -t nfs 192.168.1.100:/shared /mnt/nfs
```

(3) Virtualize files as drives.

In the elegant "everything is a file" philosophy, drive devices exist as files and mount as directories. This same principle extends to regular files, which can transform into virtual drives. While the **mkfs** command typically formats drive partitions, it also handles regular files. To format a regular file as a drive partition, you must first convert it into a loop device partition. The following commands walk through this transformation process. After completing these steps, you can inspect all loop devices using the **lsblk** command.

```
    # Create a 10 GB file filled with zeros to ensure space
allocation.
    [ict@openEuler24 ~]$ sudo dd if=/dev/zero of=/media/disk.img bs=1G count=10
    # Virtualize the created /media/disk.img file as a loop
device /dev/loop0 and its partition /dev/loop0p1.
    # The '0' in loop0 is an automatically assigned number.
    [ict@openEuler24 ~]$ sudo losetup -fP /media/disk.img
    # Format the loop device partition /dev/loop0p1.
    [ict@openEuler24 ~]$ sudo mkfs.ext4 /dev/loop0p1
    # Ensure that /mnt/vdisk exists before mounting.
    [ict@openEuler24 ~]$ sudo mount /dev/loop0p1 /mnt/vdisk
```

4.3 Memory Management

Memory forms a cornerstone of computer systems, housing all programs and data. OSs must implement essential memory-related functions: allocation, reclamation, and compression [9]. Through memory allocation, the system designates specific memory regions to applications, creating exclusive access zones that logically separate data across different applications. Memory reclamation retrieves previously allocated memory from processes, enabling efficient resource utilization through the recycling of unused memory spaces. Memory compression techniques maximize available space by compressing existing data in memory.

However, logical isolation of memory alone proves insufficient for security. Malicious actors or faulty programs might exploit OS vulnerabilities to initiate attacks, potentially compromising or destroying data belonging to other applications. To establish robust security measures, OSs must employ hardware protection mechanisms. Furthermore, when physical memory runs low, the OS must maintain application functionality without forced terminations. This challenge is typically addressed by implementing virtual memory, which leverages larger but slower drive space to extend memory capacity.

4.3.1 Memory Protection

Memory protection safeguards system stability and data integrity by establishing barriers against unauthorized memory access and modification [4]. To illustrate its significance, consider a scenario without such protection: a payment application stores user passwords at memory address 0×1000. In an unprotected environment, any program could freely access this address, enabling malicious actors to steal sensitive credentials. This vulnerability would expose not only application data but also critical OS information to potential theft.

Linux implements hardware-based protection mechanisms to enforce application privileges, creating secure boundaries between programs. This architecture prevents direct memory access between applications, requiring all data exchanges to flow through OS services, as depicted in Fig. 4.5.

The need for memory protection extends to multiple instances of the same application. For example, when several Discord windows run simultaneously in Windows with different user accounts, each instance must maintain data independence to prevent communication mix-ups. These running instances, known as processes, operate within multi-tasking OSs—systems capable of concurrent process

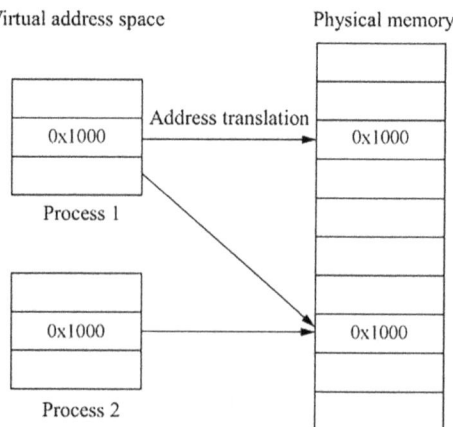

Fig. 4.5 Virtual address mapping

4.3 Memory Management

execution. Address mapping enforces memory isolation between these processes. Since applications must interface with the OS for all data exchanges, robust security measures protect these essential interactions.

(1) Address mapping

Before address mapping eme5rged, programmers wrote applications that targeted a single address space. This address space encompassed all accessible physical memory addresses—for example, on a computer with 1 MB of memory, applications could access addresses from 0×00000 to 0xFFFFF. This limitation meant systems could typically run only one application (or process) at a time. Attempting to run multiple processes simultaneously created significant problems.

Imagine multiple applications storing data at address 0×1000. When process 1 and process 2 both use this address, any modifications by one process directly impact the other. This interference undermines the intended program logic, resulting in errors and security vulnerabilities.

OS designers tackled this challenge by implementing an address mapping mechanism. This system might map address 0×1000 in process 1 to physical address 0×1000, while directing the same address in process 2 to physical address 0×11000. Though both processes reference address 0×1000 in their code, they access different physical memory locations during execution. We call the pre-mapped location a virtual address and the actual memory location after mapping a physical address. This architecture achieves process isolation by ensuring that identical virtual addresses in different processes point to distinct physical locations.

From a programming perspective, developers need only focus on the correctness of their process-internal logic, without worrying about multi-process interactions. This process-level memory management significantly simplifies multi-tasking program design.

> Once compiled, an application cannot alter its data addresses or detect other processes, making address mapping impossible within the application itself.

In essence, address mapping transforms virtual addresses into physical addresses, playing a crucial role in modern computing. It enables OSs to provide each process with an independent address space mapped to physical memory, ensuring process isolation and data protection. This technology also establishes a foundation for system optimization and memory management, enhancing overall system performance and efficiency. In Linux, this address mapping primarily relies on paging.

(2) Paging

The implementation of virtual-to-physical address mapping raises two fundamental questions. First, how should the mapping relationships be recorded and accessed? Second, what constitutes an appropriate minimum mapping unit? A unit too small creates excessive mapping overhead, while one too large wastes memory. Paging resolves these challenges by dividing both virtual and physical address spaces into fixed-size pages. The mapping relationships reside in dedicated page tables under OS management, with actual address translation performed by the hardware Memory Management Unit (MMU). Pages typically measure 2^n bytes (n being a natural number)—commonly 4 KB, 2 MB, or 1 GB, with 4 KB emerging as the standard due to hardware characteristics and historical precedent.

In the paging system, virtual addresses are split into two components: the page number and the page offset. Consider a 4 KB page system where an application accesses virtual address 0 × 11384. The page number comprises the bits above position 12 (0 × 11), while the page offset consists of the lower 12 bits (0 × 384). This division point shifts with the page size—a system with 8 KB pages uses 13 bits for the split. During address translation, the MMU substitutes the virtual page number with its corresponding physical page number, then combines it with the unchanged offset to create the physical address. For example, if virtual page number 0 × 11 corresponds to physical page number 0 × 32, the final physical address becomes 0 × 32384, preserving the original offset of 0 × 384. Figure 4.6 depicts this translation mechanism.

This architecture aligns perfectly with digital circuit implementation. The bitwise division naturally supports page sizes of 2^n bytes, while limiting translation to page numbers dramatically reduces the mapping information required.

Considering the previous example from a different perspective, a virtual address range of 0 × 11000 to 0 × 11FFF maps to physical addresses 0 × 32000 to

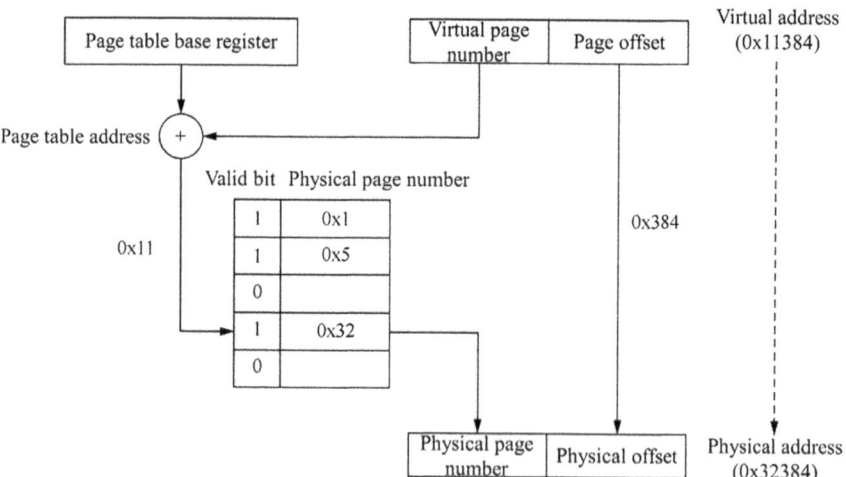

Fig. 4.6 Paging mechanism

0 × 32FFF, while addresses outside this range, like 0 × 12000, need distinct mappings. This illustrates how paging operates at the granularity of its page size—the memory allocation of a process must occur in page-size increments. Even when a process requires just a single byte, it consumes an entire page. While larger pages risk increased memory waste, smaller pages multiply the number of page numbers, potentially degrading mapping performance. Page size optimization requires careful consideration from both OS and hardware engineers, as it faces constraints from both domains.

The OS and MMU maintain page tables to track mappings between virtual and physical page numbers. These tables contain entries that record not only the mapping relationships but also additional control information. The system typically uses virtual page numbers as direct indexes into the page table—an elegant design that translates efficiently to digital circuits. During process execution, the MMU loads the unique page table of that process to handle address translation. Thanks to the specialized design of the MMU for address translation within the CPU, this mapping occurs with minimal impact on application performance.

The OS can allow multiple processes to share physical address space through memory-sharing mechanisms. This special memory region enables simultaneous access and modification by multiple processes, facilitating data storage and IPC through common memory addresses. Shared memory offers notable benefits: it enables lightning-fast data transfer between processes by eliminating the need for data copying through traditional IPC mechanisms, and it streamlines IPC by allowing direct memory access without complex message-passing protocols. However, shared memory implementation requires careful attention. The simultaneous access by multiple processes necessitates robust synchronization and mutual exclusion mechanisms to maintain data consistency and prevent race conditions. Furthermore, effective shared memory management demands meticulous planning to prevent memory leaks and unauthorized access attempts.

4.3.2 Virtual Memory Management

Computer memory provides fast access speeds but often comes with limited capacity due to cost constraints. Users commonly encounter application terminations due to memory exhaustion, and in some systems, this can trigger OS crashes. To address this limitation, OS designers leveraged the vast storage capacity of drives by implementing virtual memory management. This innovation enables applications to access memory space that far surpasses the physical memory capacity. Acting as an efficient system manager, the OS implements these mechanisms transparently, ensuring they neither alter application behavior nor burden developers. In the ideal scenario, applications interact solely with their virtual address space, remaining oblivious to whether the data resides in physical memory or on the drive, as depicted in Fig. 4.7.

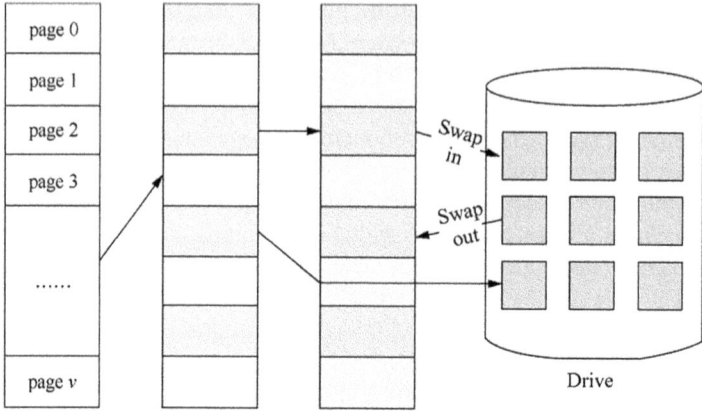

Virtual memory   Memory mapping   Physical memory

Fig. 4.7 Virtual memory layout

The paging mechanism discussed in Sect. 4.3.1 accomplishes this functionality. The OS and MMU include a valid bit within page table entries to indicate data presence in physical memory. When an address access finds a valid bit of 0, signaling the absence of data from physical memory, the MMU triggers a page fault (specifically, page not present). The OS responds by suspending the faulting application, locating the target page data on the drive, and identifying a victim page in memory (either unused or modified). It then orchestrates a swap by saving the victim page data to the drive and loading the target page data into the freed space—an operation called page replacement. Following this, the OS updates the page table to reflect the validity of the newly loaded page and resumes execution of the application at the previous address, preserving its logical flow. This entire fault handling sequence operates through the exception handling mechanism of the CPU without any application awareness, achieving complete transparency to running programs.

During page replacement, the OS must select a victim page. Choosing a page that will soon be needed can trigger frequent swapping, degrading overall system performance since handling page faults and replacements consumes significant time. Several algorithms exist for selecting victim pages: first in first out (FIFO), least recently used (LRU), and least frequently used (LFU). While these algorithms employ different selection criteria, they all aim to identify pages unlikely to be active in the upcoming program execution. Linux defaults to the LRU algorithm, choosing pages that have not been accessed recently for replacement. This approach mirrors human memory patterns—information unused for extended periods becomes harder to recall and eventually fades from memory. Recognizing that different applications may require different replacement strategies, the Linux kernel enables customization of the victim page selection algorithm.

Virtual memory resides on drive storage but remains distinct from the file system. The OS designates a specific swap partition or file for memory extension. This swap space exclusively stores memory pages and cannot accommodate other files. While solid-state drives (SSDs) deliver superior performance as swap space compared to hard disk drives (HDDs) due to faster access times, their limited write endurance poses a challenge. High-frequency write operations can significantly shorten the lifespan of an SSD. To enhance system reliability, administrators can opt for swap files instead of dedicated partitions. This approach allows the OS to dynamically relocate swap space if specific SSD sectors deteriorate from repeated writes, maintaining system stability. The following output from the **swapon** command displays current swap configurations:

```
[ict@openEuler24 ~]$ swapon --show
NAME       TYPE       SIZE  USED PRIO
/dev/sdd5  partition  63.9G 437.2M -1
```

4.3.3 openEuler Memory Technologies

openEuler has refined memory management for multi-tenant cloud environments, particularly optimizing huge page memory handling to support expansive memory scenarios [16]. The distribution boasts several cutting-edge memory technology advantages:

- Streamlined memory management: By implementing sophisticated virtual memory management mechanisms, advanced page replacement algorithms, and intelligent memory allocation, openEuler efficiently orchestrates system memory resources. This approach ensures applications receive optimal memory allocation while maintaining system stability and peak performance.
- Intelligent memory compression: openEuler integrates memory compression technology that dynamically compresses memory pages. This innovative approach maximizes memory utilization, minimizes page swapping, and ultimately boosts system responsiveness and efficiency.
- Robust NUMA architecture optimization: openEuler delivers comprehensive support for Non-Uniform Memory Access (NUMA) architectures. By intelligently managing memory access across multiple nodes, it significantly reduces latency and enhances performance in complex multi-processor environments.
- Advanced huge page capabilities: With support for expansive page sizes (2 MB and beyond), openEuler dramatically reduces page table complexity. This optimization decreases Translation Lookaside Buffer (TLB) cache misses, accelerating memory access—particularly beneficial for memory-intensive applications like databases.
- Comprehensive memory security: Security remains paramount in openEuler's memory management strategy. Through granular access control and rigorous address space isolation, openEuler creates a robust defense against unauthorized access and potential memory-based attacks.

These sophisticated memory technologies position openEuler as a high-performance, adaptable platform capable of meeting diverse computational demands with exceptional efficiency and reliability.

4.3.4 Example 4.2: Memory Information Analysis

Memory serves as a fundamental computing resource. Modern OSs offer an array of tools for monitoring memory usage, enabling users to track allocation purposes, process consumption, virtual memory locations, and size distributions.

(1) **/proc/meminfo**

Building on the introduction to the **/proc** directory in Sect. 4.2.2, the **meminfo** file stands out as a crucial resource for monitoring system memory utilization. This file provides essential diagnostic data for system operations and maintenance. Accessing the file through the cat command reveals kernel-processed information in a readable format. The output displays key metrics including:

- Total system memory (**MemTotal**)
- Free memory space (**MemFree**)
- Available memory (**MemAvailable**)
- Buffer allocations (**Buffers**)
- Swap space capacity (**SwapTotal**)
- File mapping usage (**Mapped**)

While these metrics offer valuable insights, interpreting them requires foundational knowledge of kernel memory management principles. Note that all values display in KB units, which can prove cumbersome when analyzing modern systems with substantial memory capacity. For more practical analysis, the **free** command offers a more streamlined approach to memory statistics.

```
[ict@openEuler24 ~]$ cat /proc/meminfo
MemTotal:        131629944 KB
MemFree:         118051680 KB
MemAvailable:    127552784 KB
Buffers:            126132 KB
Cached:            9799204 KB
SwapCached:              0 KB
......
SwapTotal:         2097148 KB
SwapFree:          2097148 KB
Dirty:                 688 KB
Mapped:             441848 KB
......
DirectMap4k:        390324 KB
DirectMap2M:       8781824 KB
DirectMap1G:     124780544 KB
```

4.4 Process Management

(2) **free** command

The free command provides a quick overview of system memory usage, as illustrated below:

```
[ict@openEuler24 ~]$ free -h
              total        used        free      shared  buff/cache   available
Mem:          125Gi       2.6Gi       112Gi        69Mi        10Gi       121Gi
Swap:         2.0Gi          0B       2.0Gi
```

The **-h** option transforms raw byte values into human-readable formats. For instance, **131629944 KB** becomes the more intuitive **125Gi** (125 GB). The output displays two critical rows: the first (**Mem:**) details physical memory metrics, while the second (**Swap:**) outlines swap partition statistics.

The columns break down memory utilization:

- **total**: overall capacity
- **used**: memory currently in use
- **free**: immediately available memory
  The additional columns offer nuanced insights:
- **shared**: memory segments shared across processes
- **buff/cache**: kernel cache space that can be dynamically reallocated
- **available**: actual memory reservable by applications, serving as a key indicator of system memory overhead

(3) **mkswap** command

To convert a partition or file into a swap partition, use the **mkswap** command. For example, to designate **/dev/sdb1** as a swap partition:

```
[ict@openEuler24 ~]$ sudo mkswap /dev/sdb1
[ict@openEuler24 ~]$ sudo swapon /dev/sdb1
```

You can also substitute the device path with a file path. Crucially, maintain root ownership and restrict permissions to 600 (read-write for **root** only) to preserve system data integrity. The **swapon** command activates the swap partition.

4.4 Process Management

A process represents the runtime execution of a program on a specific data collection and is the fundamental unit of resource allocation in computer systems. The core objective of process management is to ensure systematic, efficient process execution, ultimately enhancing system performance and user experience [10].

Each process encompasses unique attributes: a process ID, virtual address space, program counter, register snapshots, file descriptors, and associated system resources. The OS meticulously manages these elements through several critical stages:

1. Process creation: The OS allocates essential structures like process IDs, page tables, and file descriptor lists.
2. Process scheduling: The OS employs scheduling algorithms to load runnable processes into ready queues, select and assign CPU resources, distribute time slices, and record comprehensive context information.
3. Process execution: The OS dynamically manages virtual address spaces, interprocess synchronization, communication mechanisms, and process state transitions.
4. Process termination: The OS systematically handles resource cleanup by releasing physical memory, clearing file descriptors, updating process data structures, modifying process tables, and de-allocating associated resources.

Fundamentally, Linux process management orchestrates the entire lifecycle of processes—from creation through execution to termination—ensuring optimal system resource utilization and performance.

4.4.1 Parallelization Strategies

As discussed in Sect. 4.3.1, a process represents a running application instance. Modern software architectures enable multiple instances of the same application to run concurrently, with individual instances potentially containing multiple processes working in tandem to complete complex tasks. From a design perspective, this approach embodies parallel programming principles.

Contemporary OSs typically employ three primary parallelization strategies: processes, threads, and coroutines. While process-based parallelism offers robust isolation, its comprehensive resource management—including independent virtual address spaces—demands substantial computational and memory overhead.

To address these limitations, OS designers developed more lightweight mechanisms: threads and coroutines. Despite their architectural complexity, these approaches have gained substantial traction in high-performance computing (HPC) environments due to their exceptional efficiency.

Understanding parallel computing requires examining fundamental processing paradigms. At its core, parallel computing leverages multiple computing resources to accelerate problem-solving through two primary strategies:

- Temporal parallelism: Implementing pipeline techniques
- Spatial parallelism: Executing computations across multiple processors simultaneously

4.4 Process Management

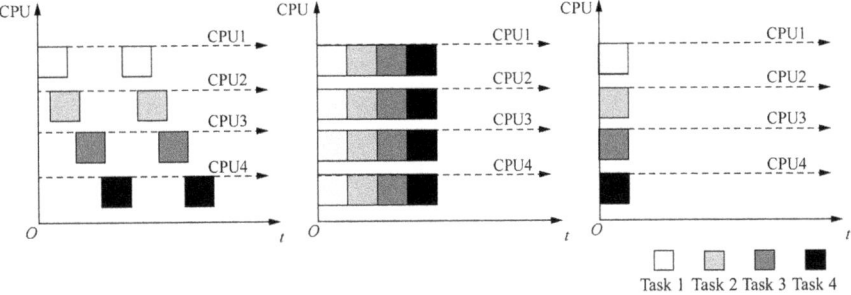

Fig. 4.8 Parallel computing scheduling methods

A practical analogy illuminates these concepts:

- Serial computing: One chef preparing a meal sequentially
- Parallel computing: Multiple chefs collaborating—simultaneously washing, preparing, and cooking—each handling a distinct task

CPU cores function like a versatile culinary team. While one core processes task A, another tackles task B, dramatically reducing overall completion time. This approach maximizes computational efficiency by distributing workloads across available processing units—a critical advantage in multi-core computing architectures, as shown in Fig. 4.8.

The historical UNIX design exemplified temporal parallelism through time-sharing technologies, enabling concurrent process execution. As multi-core processors evolved, Linux demanded sophisticated scheduling strategies. openEuler has notably advanced this domain, introducing innovative multi-core scheduling and coroutine support within system kernels.

4.4.2 Process Creation

The **fork** system call offers a simple mechanism for spawning new processes. When an application invokes **fork**, the current process divides into two processes that both continue execution post-fork. One process remains the original (parent), while the other is the newly created child process. By duplicating the entire context of the parent—including code, data, and stack—the child process effectively mirrors its parent, with the crucial distinction of possessing a unique process ID (PID).

PIDs serve as unique identifiers, enabling process differentiation. The **ps** command provides comprehensive insights into system processes.

```
[ict@openEuler24 ~]$ ps    -ef
    UID        PID     PPID C STIME TTY          TIME CMD
    root         1            0  0  2025 ?           00:00:50 /
usr/lib/systemd/systemd --switched-root
    root         2            0  0  2025 ?           00:00:00
[kthreadd]
    ......
    root      1025        1  0  2025 ?           00:00:00 sshd: /usr/
sbin/sshd -D [listener] 0 of
    root     36471     1025  0 Jan03 ?           00:00:00 sshd:
ict [priv]
    ict      36474    36471  0 Jan03 ?           00:00:01 sshd:
ict@pts/0
    ict      36475    36474  0 Jan03 pts/0       00:00:01 -bash
    ict      41829    36475 99 04:30 pts/0       00:00:00 ps -ef
```

The output unveils a hierarchical process structure: systemd (PID 1) stands as the root, with PID 1025 emerging as a systemd child and parent to PID 36471. This lineage extends through the command-executing process (PID 41829).

In fact, Linux organizes processes in a tree-like structure, mirroring the file system. The pstree command elegantly visualizes this hierarchy. Child processes stem from parent processes, with each parent potentially spawning multiple children. This tree-based approach facilitates efficient system process management.

Processes typically have unique tasks, but after **fork** is invoked, both processes continue executing identical code. To distinguish between them, the **fork** call returns 0 to the child process, enabling the application to identify its process type. By examining this return value, programs can execute distinct tasks based on their process role. The following code demonstrates this mechanism:

```
pid_t pid;
// Child process creation
pid = fork();
if (pid == -1) {                   //Error handling
    perror("fork");
    return 1;
} else if (pid == 0) {             // The child process
```

```
executes task 1.
    task_child();
} else {                    // The parent process
continues.
    task_parent();
}
```

Moreover, as previously mentioned, each process has an independent virtual address space and external resources, making direct data exchange between processes challenging. However, processes often require communication for data exchange or synchronization. The OS provides multiple IPC technologies to meet these needs, including pipes, shared memory, message queues, and semaphores. Each technology is designed with specific communication requirements in mind.

Shared memory facilitates high-performance data exchange between processes by allowing them to share large data volumes. Pipes and message queues are primarily used for small-scale data transmission, with pipes supporting unidirectional communication and message queues enabling bidirectional communication. Semaphores serve synchronization control, ensuring processes execute in a predetermined sequence.

In certain scenarios, the OS can impose resource limitations on processes, such as maximum memory usage or maximum number of open files. These restrictions prevent processes from abusing system resources or crashing the system. In the following example, the **ulimit** command restricts the maximum open file count for a process to 512, with **-n** specifying the limit type. Using **-a** reveals all possible parameters.

```
[ict@openEuler24 ~]$ ulimit -n 512
```

4.4.3 Process Scheduling

From an application's viewpoint, multiple processes seem to execute simultaneously and in parallel. Yet, with only one CPU core, only a single application truly runs at a time. The OS manages switching between processes, creating the illusion of concurrent execution. Linux employs a time-slice round-robin scheduling algorithm, allocating each process a brief time slice (typically milliseconds) to ensure fair CPU time distribution. This process scheduling allows the OS to determine which process runs during a specific time interval.

Process switching involves intricate mechanisms. The classic Lions Book (*A Commentary on the UNIX Operating System*) features a famous comment "/* You are not expected to understand this */" (shown in Fig. 4.9), underscoring the complex and often cryptic nature of process switching.

The OS cannot arbitrarily interrupt application execution. It gains CPU core control only under two conditions: when an application triggers an interrupt or exception, or when an application invokes a system function.

Traditionally, the OS awaits a system function call, enabling the scheduling algorithm to decide whether to suspend the current process and allow others to continue. Such non-preemptive OSs passively intervene in process scheduling, with unpredictable switching times. The OS switches processes opportunistically, waiting when no opportunity exists.

Despite higher overall efficiency, non-preemptive systems pose challenges for time-sensitive tasks. Imagine a music playback process blocked by another process continuously occupying the CPU core—resulting in intermittent audio.

Preemptive OSs emerged to address these limitations. They use timers to generate periodic interrupts, actively interrupting the current process. During interrupt handling, the OS schedules and switches processes, preventing any single process from monopolizing the CPU. This approach ensures responsive multitasking, though the interrupt processing introduces minimal performance overhead.

4.4.4 IPC

In parallel computing, applications typically focus on defining task execution flows for individual processes without delving into execution sequences or process switching mechanisms. Initially, processes operate independently, with task completion times being unpredictable. However, certain scenarios demand that one process wait for another's completion or rely on its computational output, necessitating IPC.

IPC is a critical technology that enables independent processes in multi-tasking OSs to exchange information securely and collaborate effectively. Linux, building

```
2225    /* Switch to stack of the new process and set up
2226     * his segmentation registers.
2227     */
2228    retu(rp->p_addr);
2229    sureg();
2230    /*
2231     * If the new process paused because it was
2232     * swapped out, set the stack level to the last call
2233     * to savu(u_ssav). This means that the return
2234     * which is executed immediately after the call to aretu
2235     * actually returns from the last routine which did
2236     * the savu.
2237     *
2238     * You are not expected to understand this.
2239     */
2240    if(rp->p_flag&SSWAP) {
2241            rp->p_flag =& ~SSWAP;
2242            aretu(u.u_ssav);
2243    }
2244    /* The value returned here has many subtle implications.
2245     * See the newproc comments.
2246     */
2247    return(1);
2248 }
```

Fig. 4.9 Process switching code of Version 6 UNIX

4.4 Process Management

upon UNIX's robust design, offers sophisticated and efficient communication mechanisms tailored to diverse usage scenarios.

(1) Semaphores

Semaphores function as a synchronization control mechanism to address IPC challenges by orchestrating process execution sequences. A process pauses until a specific semaphore triggers its continuation, while other processes can manipulate these triggers through semaphore operations. When conditions require a process to wait, it self-blocks through a semaphore until another process performs the necessary operations to release it. By modifying semaphore values, processes can trigger or influence other waiting processes, effectively coordinating execution sequences and resource allocation.

At their core, semaphores act as data operation locks that enable mutual exclusion and synchronization. They maintain an integer value to govern resource access: positive values indicate available resources, zero signifies full allocation, and negative values reveal waiting processes or threads.

(2) Signals

Signals are software interrupts, alerting processes to events or exceptions while facilitating inter-process communication and coordination through notifications, synchronization, and resource management.

As an asynchronous communication mechanism, signals allow processes to communicate without waiting for recipient completion. Processes can capture, handle, or redirect signals as needed. Upon receiving a signal, a process may execute specific handlers, terminate, or perform custom operations.

The **kill** function exemplifies signal usage, enabling targeted process termination through command-line interfaces.

(3) Pipes

Pipes, built upon ring buffers, connect the output of a process output to the input of another, enabling IPC. Pipes maintain a fixed size, typically 4 KB, adjustable via system calls.

Writing to a pipe populates its ring buffer, overwriting existing data. Reading from a pipe retrieves data sequentially from the start of the buffer, cycling back to the beginning upon reaching the end.

Pipes provide efficient IPC, bypassing kernel space. However, restrictions include supporting only related processes and solely unidirectional communication.

Pipes frequently appear in shell scripts, chaining the standard output and input of small programs for complex data stream manipulation.

(4) Sockets

Sockets offer a universal IPC mechanism, supporting communication across different hosts. They empower both local and network communication, extending to distributed and parallel computing systems.

Socket types include stream, datagram, and raw sockets, catering to various communication needs. For instance, TCP/IP leverages stream sockets for reliable data transmission, while datagram sockets using the User Datagram Protocol (UDP) handle unreliable transfers or broadcast/multicast scenarios.

Sockets abstract low-level communication details through a unified interface, presenting simple, consistent APIs. This allows developers to concentrate on application logic. Sockets feature ease of use, scalability, cross-platform compatibility, efficiency, and flexibility, establishing them as powerful, versatile network programming tools. In Linux, they also facilitate communication between service daemons.

(5) Shared memory

Shared memory provides a potent IPC mechanism, enabling multiple processes to access the same physical memory. It excels in scenarios demanding substantial data exchange, such as real-time systems, parallel computing, and multi-threaded applications.

Shared memory maps the same physical memory region into the address space of each participating process, granting all processes direct access. When one process writes to this shared region, all other processes instantly perceive the changes. Reciprocally, reading from the shared memory retrieves data written by any other participant.

Shared memory delivers exceptional efficiency, real-time performance, and synchronization capabilities. Bypassing data copying, as the data resides directly in physical memory, boosts communication speed. Because the data is shared, processes exchange and share information instantaneously. However, shared memory requires careful synchronization to maintain data consistency and integrity when accessed concurrently.

> Linux IPC offers efficiency, flexibility, reliability, scalability, and cross-platform compatibility. Consequently, it finds widespread use in cloud computing, distributed systems, and network communication.

4.4.5 Thread Abstraction

Parallel computing within a process can be achieved using multiple threads, each executing a different task. These threads share resources like the virtual address space of the process, simplifying IPC, and incur lower creation and switching overhead (CPU time) than processes. Thread switching, managed by the OS, changes only the thread execution context (register values, stack location, thread status, priority, and scheduling information) while leaving the virtual address space of the process and open file handles unchanged. This smaller context results in significantly less overhead compared to process switching, as illustrated in Fig. 4.10.

POSIX provides functions like **pthread_create**, **pthread_exit**, and **pthread_join** for thread management. However, shared access to the virtual address space of the process by all threads introduces potential thread safety issues. For instance, if

4.4 Process Management

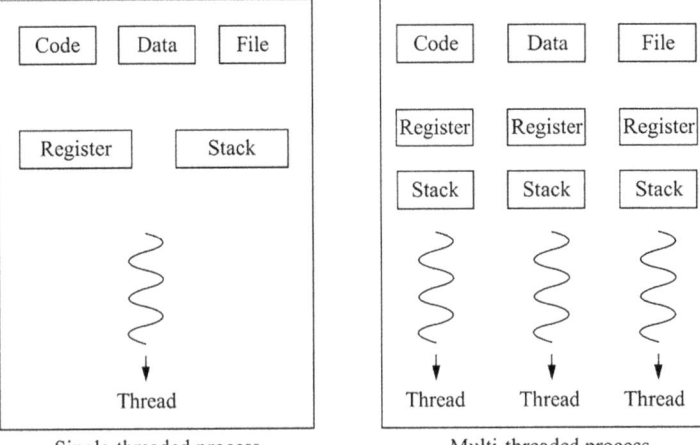

Fig. 4.10 Multi-threaded resource overhead

the global variable **IsRunning** is set to **True** in thread A and used in a conditional statement, a context switch to thread B could change **IsRunning** to **False**, leading to unexpected behavior when thread A resumes. Functions relying on global variables for data passing or control are deemed thread-unsafe. To ensure thread safety, consider the following:

- Avoid global variables: Their shared nature can cause race conditions (as demonstrated with IsRunning). Minimize their use or protect them with locking mechanisms.
- Use local variables or thread-local storage: Provide each thread with independent data copies to prevent contention.
- Use mutex locks: Protect critical sections accessing shared resources. Acquire the lock before entering and release it after exiting, preventing concurrent access. Locking IsRunning before assignment in thread A would prevent modification by other threads.
- Use atomic operations: Ensure atomicity for simple operations like integer addition and assignment, preventing race conditions.
- Employ thread-safe library functions: Guarantee proper handling of concurrent access within the function implementation.
- Leverage OS synchronization mechanisms: Use tools like condition variables and semaphores to manage thread execution order and cooperation.

In essence, while more complex to manage due to safety considerations, threads offer a lightweight approach to concurrency and are crucial for performance-sensitive applications.

4.4.6 openEuler Process Technologies

openEuler features a highly optimized multi-core scheduler and technologies like openEuler coroutines, designed specifically for multi-core processors [16]. These enhancements maximize system resource utilization, minimize process waiting times, and boost system throughput, ultimately improving process scheduling efficiency and responsiveness.

(1) Multi-core scheduler

Managing process allocation across multiple CPU cores presents a significant scheduling challenge for OSs. openEuler's multi-core scheduler within the Linux kernel prioritizes load balancing, affinity, scheduling optimization, and scalability to deliver efficient and stable multi-core processing. This approach maximizes hardware resource utilization, improving both user experience and performance. The key features of the multi-core scheduler include:

- Multi-core load balancing: The scheduler distributes tasks efficiently across multiple cores to fully utilize processing power. It dynamically adjusts task allocation, ensuring balanced core loads and preventing performance bottlenecks.
- Multi-core affinity: The scheduler supports task-core affinity, binding tasks to specific cores to reduce context switching overhead and improve overall system efficiency.
- Multi-core task scheduling optimization: The scheduler uses optimization strategies to improve multi-core task efficiency and performance. It intelligently schedules based on task type, priority, and resource needs, and leverages task parallelism to accelerate completion times by running parallel tasks concurrently.
- High scalability: The scheduler adapts to multi-core systems of varying sizes and configurations. From small embedded systems to large servers, it effectively manages core resources for reliable, high performance.

These features allow openEuler to maximize multi-core processor performance, offering a significant advantage in server applications.

(2) openEuler coroutines

openEuler supports coroutines within its kernel. Coroutines enable concurrent execution of multiple tasks within a single thread, as depicted in Fig. 4.11.

Key features include:

- Lightweight: openEuler coroutines offer a lightweight concurrency model. Compared to threads, they consume fewer system resources. Multiple coroutines can run concurrently within a single thread, eliminating the need for additional threads and improving efficiency for handling numerous concurrent tasks.
- User-space scheduling: openEuler coroutines use a user-space scheduling mechanism. Coroutine scheduling is managed by the user program, not the OS kernel scheduler, offering greater flexibility and customization.

4.4 Process Management

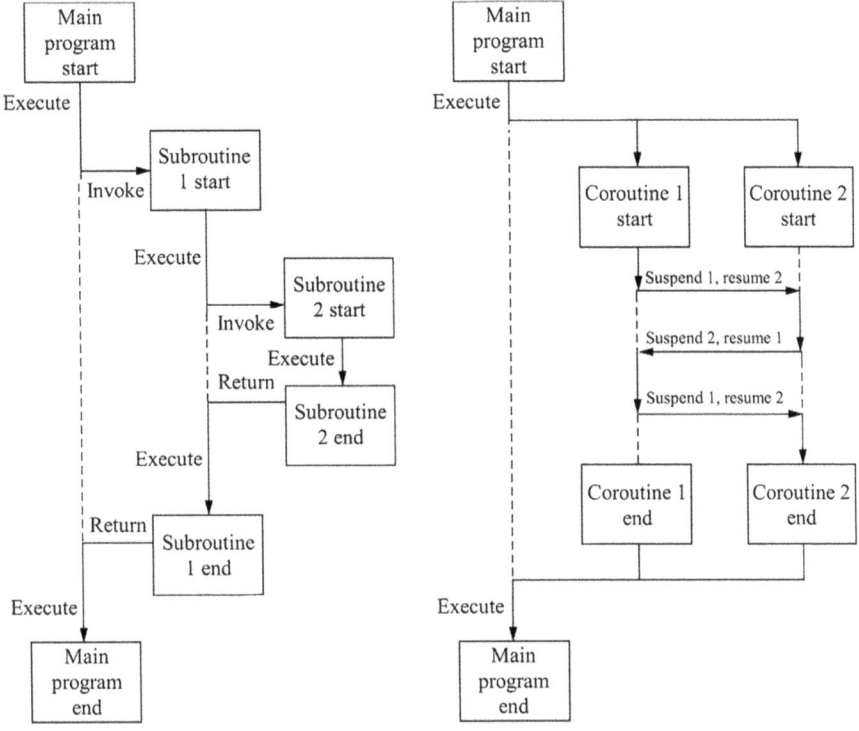

Fig. 4.11 Coroutine working principle

- Non-preemptive scheduling: openEuler coroutines employ non-preemptive scheduling. Context switching occurs explicitly at points determined by the program, enhancing control and reducing overhead.
- Cooperative scheduling: openEuler coroutines implement cooperative scheduling. Coroutines switch context through explicit cooperation points. When a coroutine relinquishes control, the scheduler selects another executable coroutine, enhancing system stability and reliability by preventing race conditions and resource contention.
- Asynchronous programming support: openEuler coroutines facilitate asynchronous programming. Their suspend and resume mechanism simplifies asynchronous task handling, avoiding the complexities of callback-based programming. Coroutines can pause during I/O or computations and resume upon completion, enabling efficient asynchronous operations.

In summary, openEuler coroutines are lightweight, leverage user-space and cooperative non-preemptive scheduling, and support asynchronous programming. These features create an efficient, flexible, and controllable concurrency model well-suited for managing concurrent tasks and asynchronous operations.

4.4.7 Example 4.3: Process Monitoring and Management

Linux offers command-line tools for monitoring the system and managing processes, allowing users to inspect, modify, and terminate computer system resources and processes. This example uses four common commands: **top**, **ps**, **lsof**, and **kill**. These commands are versatile, and readers should explore their usage and underlying design.

This example demonstrates using **top** to check CPU and memory usage, **ps** to inspect the real-time status of each process, **lsof** to examine files opened by the watch process, and **kill** to stop the process.

(1) **top**: monitoring system status in real time

The **top** command provides an interactive, real-time view of system status and process activity. It displays CPU and memory usage, process status, and other real-time data. Numerous shortcuts allow users to customize their view and even modify process priorities.

To sort by memory usage, execute the following command. **top** defaults to sorting by process ID. Use the **-o** option upon startup or keyboard shortcuts during operation to change the sort order.

```
[ict@openEuler24 bar]$ top -o %MEM
top -23:55:25 up 3 days, 1:59, 2 users, load average: 0.05, 0.08, 0.02
    Tasks: 125 total, 1 running, 123 sleeping, 1 stopped, 0 zombie
    %Cpu0 : 0.3 us, 0.3 sy, 0.0 ni, 99.3 id, 0.0 wa, 0.0 hi, 0.0 si, 0.0 st
    %Cpu1 : 0.0 us, 0.3 sy, 0.0 ni, 99.7 id, 0.0 wa, 0.0 hi, 0.0 si, 0.0 st
    MiB Mem : 942.4 total, 514.0 free, 257.2 used, 265.1 buff/cache
    MiB Swap: 2100.0 total, 1902.5 free, 197.5 used. 685.2 avail Mem
        PID USER PR NI VIRT RES SHR S %CPU %MEM TIME+ COMMAND
        39549 ict 20 0 21536 2372 2088 T 0.0 0.2 0:00.00 watch
            1 root 20 0 179176 8544 4576 S 0.0 0.9 0:47.50 systemd
            2 root 20 0 0 0 0 S 0.0 0.0 0:00.20 kthreadd
    ......
```

top displays both summary system information and detailed process information. The first line of the summary shows system uptime, logged-in users, and system load. The second line details process counts: **total**, **running**, **sleeping**, **stopped**, and **zombie**. The third and fourth lines show per-CPU usage, broken down by user (**us**), system (**sy**), niced (**ni**), idle (**id**), waiting (**wa**), hard interrupt (**hi**), soft interrupt (**si**), and steal time (**st**). The fifth and sixth lines show physical

4.4 Process Management

Table 4.1 Common ps options

Option	Description	Option	Description
-aux	Displays all processes for all users.	-auf --user ict	Displays process information for user **ict**
-axf	Displays comprehensive process information.	-eo pid,ppid,cmd,%mem,%cpu	Displays custom process information

memory and swap usage, with **total**, **free**, **used**, **buff/cache**, and **avail Mem** representing total capacity, free memory, used memory, buffered/cached memory, and available swap, respectively.

Each line in the detailed process information section represents a process. The data includes the process ID (**PID**), user (**USER**), priority (**PR**), virtual memory (**VIRT**), resident memory (**RES**), and shared memory (**SHR**).

top is feature-rich. Besides startup options, users can press **F** to select columns, **O** to filter, **R** to adjust priorities, **K** to send signals, and **Q** to quit.

The **-b** option saves the output of top to a file for later analysis.

(2) **ps**: inspecting process status

The **ps** (process status) command quickly shows all running processes, their detailed state (ready, running, paused, zombie, and more), and their associated commands. While **top** focuses on real-time system monitoring, **ps** is suitable for both interactive use and scripts.

A powerful process management tool originating in Version 4 UNIX, **ps** supports numerous options due to backward compatibility. Table 4.1 lists some common options.

The command below displays information for all processes run by user **ict**, including resource consumption, state, and the initiating command.

```
[ict@openEuler24 bar]$ ps uf --user ict
USER       PID   %CPU  %MEM  TTY     STAT    START    TIME   COMMAND
ict      36474   0.0   0.5   ?       S       Jan03    0:01   sshd: ict@pts/0
ict      36475   0.0   0.6   pts/0   Ss      Jan03    0:01   \_ -bash
ict      42197   100   0.4   pts/0   R+      06:00    0:00   \_ ps uf --user ict
ict      33376   0.0   0.4   ?       S       Jan03    0:02   sshd: ict@pts/3
ict      33377   0.0   0.5   pts/3   Ss+     Jan03    0:01   \_ -bash
ict      39549   0.0   0.2   pts/3   T       Jan03    0:00   \_ watch -n 1 ls /bin
ict      30374   0.0   0.7   ?       Ss      Jan03    0:00   /usr/lib/systemd/systemd --user
......
```

Process states include: **R** (running), for processes actively running or queued; **S** (sleeping), for processes waiting on a condition or signal; **T** (stopped or traced), for paused or traced processes; and **Z** (zombie), for terminated processes whose parent has not yet released system resources.

The **pstree** command displays the hierarchical relationship of processes, which is helpful for process analysis.

(3) **lsof**: inspecting open files

While **top** and **ps** reveal the CPU and memory consumption of processes, they do not show open files, which can impact system security and debugging. The **lsof** command lists all files opened by a process. These can include regular files, device files, network files, or even sensitive system files.

Execute the following command to list all files opened by the **watch** process:

```
[ict@openEuler24 bar]$ lsof -p 39549
    COMMAND    PID   USER     FD     TYPE DEVICE SIZE/OFF    NODE NAME
    watch     39549  ict      cwd    DIR  253,2     4096     392449 /home/ict
    watch     39549  ict      rtd    DIR  253,0     4096     2 /
    watch     39549  ict      txt    REG  253,0     68104    1709754 /usr/bin/watch
    watch     39549  ict      mem    REG  253,0     1661144  1705840 /usr/lib64/libc.so.6
    ......
```

The output shows that the **watch** process has opened directories, its executable, and the **libc** shared library. If this process accesses sensitive or unrelated files, further analysis is necessary to determine if malicious activity, security flaws, or unreleased file resources exist.

(4) **kill**: terminating processes

Linux lets users terminate (or kill) processes directly from the command line. This is useful for processes that will not exit normally or present security risks. The **kill** command stops one or more processes based on their process IDs. For example, run the following command to stop the **watch** process:

```
[ict@openEuler24 bar]$ kill 39549
```

The **kill** command sends a signal to the specified process to control its behavior; termination is only one possible action. The command above sends the default

TERM signal, instructing the process to stop. Some processes might ignore this signal (if they have not implemented the corresponding signal handler). In this case, send the **SIGKILL** signal to force termination:

```
[ict@openEuler24 bar]$ kill -9 39549
```

The **SIGHUP** signal typically notifies a process to restart or reread its configuration files and is frequently used with server daemons. Use **kill -l** to list all supported signals.

Using **kill** requires appropriate permissions to prevent accidents or malicious activity. Common users can only terminate the processes they started. The **root** user can terminate processes started by others and its own regular processes, but not essential system processes like init or systemd.

4.5 Summary

This chapter introduced the OS design philosophy and, guided by this philosophy, briefly described the design goals and implementations of file, memory, and process management. Each section also highlighted openEuler's improvements and features addressing various system requirements.

This chapter should give readers an understanding of the management strategies, challenges, and solutions related to resources like hard drives, memory, and CPUs. Readers should now grasp the characteristics of these three key OS components and understand the technical innovations and advantages of openEuler. More importantly, we hope readers have grasped the essence of OS design principles and can apply these ideas to future software designs, achieving highly cohesive and loosely coupled software. We also hope readers can better apply Linux to both system administration and software development.

Reflection and Practice

1. Using the file system as an example, consider how UNIX ensures operational consistency through its interface design.
2. Implement system backup and recovery using simple file operation commands.
3. Build an NFS file server and mount the shared folder at **/mnt/share** on another machine.
4. Run **watch -n 1 ps** to display the status of all running processes every second. Observe the process ID of the **watch** command and check for any child process IDs.
5. Use the **lsof** command to view all files opened by a specific process.

Open Access This chapter is licensed under the terms of the Creative Commons Attribution-NonCommercial-NoDerivatives 4.0 International License (http://creativecommons.org/licenses/by-nc-nd/4.0/), which permits any noncommercial use, sharing, distribution and reproduction in any medium or format, as long as you give appropriate credit to the original author(s) and the source, provide a link to the Creative Commons license and indicate if you modified the licensed material. You do not have permission under this license to share adapted material derived from this chapter or parts of it.

The images or other third party material in this chapter are included in the chapter's Creative Commons license, unless indicated otherwise in a credit line to the material. If material is not included in the chapter's Creative Commons license and your intended use is not permitted by statutory regulation or exceeds the permitted use, you will need to obtain permission directly from the copyright holder.

Chapter 5
openEuler Development Environment

Objectives

1. Understand common text processing tools and methods in openEuler.
2. Master shell script programming.
3. Master C/C++ application development on openEuler.
4. Understand portability development and open source communities.

Linux is one of the world's most popular development environments, owing to its powerful command-line tools, cross-platform compatibility, custom features, portability, and open source principles. This chapter uses openEuler to showcase a typical Linux development environment.

openEuler fully inherits and enhances the strengths of the UNIX development environment. The elegant design and concise interface of UNIX provide consistency, openness, and extensibility. Concepts like text streams and small tools, coupled with OS interface standards, form the bedrock of a productive development environment, further energized by the open source movement. Beyond the portability of scripts and applications developed in openEuler, the development and deployment environments themselves are also highly portable.

This chapter covers text processing, shell script programming, C/C++ development, and openEuler portability. The text processing section explores the Vim editor, regular expressions, text stream processing tools like **grep**, **tr**, **sed**, **sort**, and **gawk**, and command-line formatting tools; in shell script programming, we use a number-guessing game to illustrate the basic syntax and programming structures and demonstrate iterative development with the **install-help** script; to explore C/C++ development, we describe command-line operations using GCC, Makefiles, and CMake, including optimization tools and minimal code examples with build processes; and the final section looks at the portability of the openEuler development and deployment environments.

openEuler provides an entry point into the developer-friendly nature of Linux, offering an excellent selection of tools and features. These include, but are not limited to, powerful text stream processing, script automation, flexible compilation and build systems, rich open source ecosystem, and wide portability.

5.1 Text Processing

Text files remain relevant and widely used. They power diverse applications, from program source code and web pages to Linux configuration files, log files, and data records. Common formats like HTML, comma-separated values (CSV), JSON (often used for web service APIs), YAML (frequently used for configuration and data exchange), and Markdown (a lightweight markup language popular in open source projects) exemplify the continued importance of text files.

UNIX-like OSs offer powerful text processing capabilities through a rich collection of command-line tools. Editors like ed, Vi, Emacs, and nano, along with filters like **cat**, **less**, **sort**, **cut**, **grep**, **sed**, and **awk**, have become enduring classics. Users select editors based on personal preference, regardless of the content—from general program output to source code in C, Java, or Python. Filters, individually or combined via pipes, enable complex operations like extracting, sorting, transforming, and analyzing text.

> UNIX arguably owes its early survival to text processing. Despite lacking resources like computer hardware, UNIX secured funding thanks to troff. This software efficiently formatted text for printers and character terminals, proving invaluable for typesetting complex patent applications. troff served as the core of the UNIX document processing system for an extended period and remains in use today.

UNIX embraces a concise and consistent text-based interface. Its I/O model champions simple, text-based, stream-oriented, and device-independent formats. Most programs function as simple filters, converting input text streams into output text streams. Douglas McIlroy, the inventor of the UNIX pipe, articulated the UNIX philosophy: small is beautiful; do one thing well; write programs to work together; provide mechanisms, not policies; store data in plain text files; everything is a file [11].

The creators of UNIX foresaw the enduring relevance of text, promoting text streams as the universal interface and developing numerous tools around text processing. Many of these tools, nearly as old as UNIX itself, remain widely used and deserve exploration by any computer enthusiast.

5.1 Text Processing

5.1.1 Vim

If you are interested in programming, explore Vim. This powerful text editor, with its rich advanced features, stands as one of the premier editors in UNIX. Mastering Vim grants the ability to edit any text file on any UNIX-like OS.

The man pages describe Vim as "a programmer's text editor," suitable for editing all plain text, particularly program code.

```
VIM(1)         General Commands Manual         VIM(1)
NAME
       vim -Vi IMproved, a programmer's text editor
   ...

DESCRIPTION
       Vim is a text editor that is upwards compatible
to Vi. It can be
       used to edit all kinds of plain text. It is
especially useful for
           editing programs.
```

The editing style of Vim, however, differs significantly from GUI applications like Notepad and Word, which can initially intimidate beginners. But embrace Vim, practice diligently, and you will discover its speed and efficiency, and derive long-term benefits.

(1) Vim and vi

Vim, built upon the vi editor, shares its core command set, which has remained consistent for decades.

vi, an early UNIX program released in 1976 with BSD, remains widely used. Its core design keeps the user's hands on the keyboard's central area, enabling all editing actions without searching for a misplaced mouse. vi's small size, powerful features, and efficient commands quickly propelled its popularity.

vi discourages personalized configurations. This "virtue" ensures immediate usability on any new system without prior setup. Its robust built-in functionality and consistent command set facilitate immediate use across different versions without altering user habits. vi is readily available on virtually all UNIX-like OSs.

Vim enhances vi with features like multi-level undo/redo (with unlimited actions), multiple windows and buffers, syntax highlighting, command-line editing, file name completion, online help, and visual selection. It supports diverse platforms, including Linux, Windows, and Mac OS X. Furthermore, Vim supports custom scripts and plugins for extended functionality. On most Linux distributions, **vi** is likely a symbolic link to Vim.

Fig. 5.1 Multi-window C++ editing in Vim

Beginners can experience this powerful tool by focusing on the basics. openEuler defaults to a streamlined Vim installation, accessible as **vi**. This chapter covers basic usage of Vim, referring to it as vi.[1]

(2) Working modes

vi offers numerous startup options, enabling users to tailor its initial behavior and appearance, including selecting different working modes. Figure 5.1 displays multi-window C++ editing in Vim.

The versatility of vi stems from its diverse working modes, catering to various editing tasks. These include normal, insert, replace, visual, command-line, easy, read-only, diff, and recovery modes. Users can specify these modes through options before launching vi or switch between them using commands afterward. Three core modes are normal, insert, and command-line. Their functions and basic operations are described below.

- Normal mode: vi launches in normal mode by default. This mode facilitates quick cursor navigation, deletion, cutting, copying, pasting, undo/redo actions, and string searches. Pressing keys like **I**, **A**, **C**, **R**, or **O** activates insert mode, while **:** enters command-line mode.
- Insert mode: This encompasses both insert and replace modes. Insert mode adds text at the cursor location, whereas replace mode overwrites existing text. Pressing **Esc** returns to normal mode.
- Command-line mode: This mode executes complex commands, such as accessing help, saving, exiting, finding and replacing strings, and configuring parameters. Pressing **Esc** reverts to normal mode.

---

[1] Consult the official Vim website for a comprehensive tutorial.

5.1 Text Processing

Fig. 5.2 Switching between Vim working modes

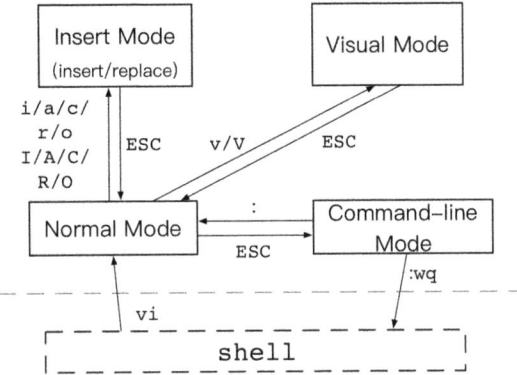

Figure 5.2 depicts the transitions between these modes. Note that insert and command-line modes do not allow direct switching; transitions occur through normal mode. Other documentation may use different names for these modes.

> If the current mode is unclear, pressing **Esc** will always return to normal mode, from which other modes can be accessed.

These three modes distinguish vi from most other editors. This section emphasizes normal and command-line modes—the defining features of vi. Vim also features visual mode, enabling users to visually select a text region for operations. This includes not only multiple lines, but also rectangular blocks (a capability uncommon in most editors).

Carefully review this section, compare shortcut key configurations, and consider the design philosophy of the vi editor. Then, practice these concepts.

> On openEuler, the fastest way to learn these fundamentals is through the integrated vi tutorial (**vimtutor**), accessible from the shell, which takes only 25–30 min.

(3) Normal mode

When vi launches, it enters normal mode by default. Every keystroke initiates a command instead of inserting text. For example, pressing **I** activates insert mode, not inputting the letter "i."

Normal mode forms the core of the vi experience, providing numerous commands and combinations for powerful editing. Beginners do not need to memorize all commands immediately. Focusing on a few useful commands and progressively expanding their repertoire is sufficient. The commands share a common underlying logic, making diverse actions possible through clever combination.

Normal mode enables various operations, including cursor navigation, deleting and cutting text, copying and pasting, entering insert mode, performing undo/redo actions, and searching.

The versatile cursor movement system of vi is arguably its most notable feature. It allows rapid cursor manipulation using three fingers of the right hand, keeping the user's hands on the keyboard's central area and maintaining touch-typing efficiency. The following tables detail the keys for various operations (Tables 5.1, 5.2, 5.3, 5.4, 5.5 and 5.6).

Most vi commands can be prefixed with a number to specify repetitions. For example, **3w** moves the cursor to the start of the third word to the right.

vi provides unlimited undos, reverting changes until no further undos are possible.

It is also worth mentioning the . command, which repeats the last edit. This includes actions like inserting, replacing, copying, pasting, undoing, and redoing. Remember to experiment with this powerful command.

Table 5.1 Cursor movement commands

Key	Description	Key	Description
h	Moves the cursor left one character	Ctrl + b	Scrolls up one page (same as **Page Up**)
j	Moves the cursor down one character	Ctrl + f	Scrolls down one page (same as **Page Down**)
k	Moves the cursor up one character	Shift+g	Moves the cursor to the last line
l	Moves the cursor right one character	n+Shift+g	Moves the cursor to line n (**20G** goes to line 20)
w	Moves the cursor to the next word beginning	gg	Moves the cursor to the first line (same as **1G**)
b	Moves the cursor to the previous word beginning	n+Enter	Moves the cursor down n lines

5.1 Text Processing

Table 5.2 Deletion and cut commands

Key	Description	Key	Description
x	Deletes the character behind the cursor, same as **Delete**	dd	Cuts the current line. Paste with **p** or **Shift+p**
Shift+x	Deletes the character in front of the cursor, same as **Backspace**	ndd	Cuts n lines from the current line downward. For example, **2dd** cuts two lines. Paste with **p** or **Shift+p**

Table 5.3 Copy and paste commands

Key	Description	Key	Description
yy	Copies the current line	p	Pastes the copied content below the current line
nyy	Copies n lines from the current line downward. For instance, **20yy** copies 20 lines	Shift+p	Pastes the copied content above the current line

Table 5.4 Entering insert mode

Key	Description	Key	Description
i	Enters insert mode at the cursor	cw	Deletes the word from the cursor forward and enters insert mode
Shift+i	Enters insert mode at the first non-whitespace character of the line	r	Enters replace mode, overwriting one character, then returns to normal mode
a	Enters insert mode after the cursor	Shift+r	Enters replace mode, overwriting subsequent characters
Shift+a	Enters insert mode at the end of the line	Shift+o	Inserts a new line above the current line

Table 5.5 Undo and redo commands

Key	Description	Key	Description
u	Undoes the last change	Ctrl+r	Redoes the last undone action
Shift+u	Undoes all changes to the current line	3+Ctrl+r	Redoes the previous three actions

Table 5.6 String search commands

Key	Description	Key	Description
/+word	Searches down for **word**	n	Repeats the last search
?+word	Searches up for **word**	Shift+n	Repeats the last search in the reverse direction

Pressing **/** or **?** activates command-line mode, where you can enter words to execute the search.

(4) Command-line mode

Command-line mode distinguishes vi, offering an interface for advanced commands. Actions like replacing strings, saving, exiting, and configuring parameters occur primarily within this mode. Notably, Vim also facilitates direct interaction with shell commands in command-line mode, enabling operations such as executing shell commands and inserting the results, or processing the file contents.

The format for string replacement, detailed in Table 5.7, generally follows this structure:

```
:[range]s/{pattern}/{string} [count]
```

This command locates **{pattern}** within each line of the given **[range]** and substitutes it with **{string}**. The optional **[count]** parameter, a positive integer, controls how many replacements to make. Omitting **[range]** and **[count]** replaces only the first occurrence of **{pattern}** on the current line. By default, the search differentiates between uppercase and lowercase characters; "FOO" will not match "FOo."

When you open a Windows-generated text file with vi, ^M often appears at each line end. Use **:%s/^M$//g** to eliminate these. % represents the entire file. Input ^M using **Ctrl+v** followed by **Ctrl+m**. The trailing $ matches the line end, effectively deleting it through replacement with an empty string.

Command-line mode also supports string searches using syntax comparable to normal mode (Tables 5.8 and 5.9).

The **:r** *some_file* command inserts the contents of a specified file at the cursor. This also works with shell commands. For instance, **:r !date** inserts the date and time, while **:r !ps -aux** inserts process information.

Table 5.7 String replacement commands

Key	Description	Key	Description
:s/foo/bar/	Substitutes **bar** for the first instance of **foo** on the current line	:3,$/s/foo//	Deletes the first instance of **foo** from line 3 to the file end
:2-5s/foo/bar/g	Substitutes **bar** for all instances of **foo** from lines 2 through 5	:%s/^M$//g	Removes all ^M characters within the file

Table 5.8 Saving and exiting commands

Key	Description	Key	Description
:w	Saves the file. Specify a file name to save as.	:wq	Saves the file and exits
:q	Exits; prompts if unsaved changes exist.	:q!	Forces exit without saving

Table 5.9 Parameter setting commands

Key	Description	Key	Description
:set nu	Shows line numbers	:set ignorecase	Enables case-insensitive searching
:set nonu	Hides line numbers	:set noignorecase	Enables case-sensitive searching

5.1 Text Processing

(5) Visual mode
Visual mode provides a straightforward way to select and work with text regions. It has three variations:
Character mode: Select individual characters by pressing **v** in normal mode.
Line mode: Select entire lines by pressing **Shift+v** in normal mode.
Block mode: Select rectangular blocks of text by pressing **Ctrl+v** in normal mode.
In visual mode, use navigation commands to adjust the selected area and perform actions like deleting, cutting, copying, pasting, and replacing. For example, **x** deletes the selection, **y** copies it, **p** pastes, and **r** replaces characters within the selection.

> vi offers a wealth of commands; this is just a small sample. This does not mean every user needs to know them all, or that vi/Vim is inherently complex. The commands follow a consistent logic, allowing users to choose a subset based on the needs. With practice, proficiency comes quickly. Besides **vimtutor**, Vim offers help documents accessible via **:help** in command-line mode.
> Emacs provides even greater power, featuring extensive customizability, extensibility, and a steeper learning curve. Users can customize every keybinding, access unlimited clipboards, and use Lisp scripting for extensions. Its extensive plugin system enables rapid development of custom enhancements, making it suitable for efficiently editing virtually any type of text.

5.1.2 Nano

nano is a small, user-friendly text editor included in most Linux distributions by default (Fig. 5.3). Compared to vi and Emacs, nano presents a simpler interface and easier navigation, making it well-suited for users unfamiliar with command-line editing and ideal for those new to Linux.

nano creates or opens text files for editing. For instance, the **nano test.c** command creates the **test.c** file if it does not already exist or opens it if it does.

The top section of the nano interface is the text editing area, where users can add, delete, modify, search, and replace text. The bottom section displays keyboard shortcuts. These shortcuts use two combination types:

^<*capital letter*>: ^ stands for the **Ctrl** key. For example, save a file with **^O** (**Ctrl+o**) and exit nano with **^X** (**Ctrl+x**).

M-<*capital letter*>: M- stands for the **Alt** key. For example, undo with **M-u** (**Alt+u**) and redo with **M-e** (**Alt+e**).

> While shortcuts display in uppercase, users should execute them using lowercase letters. nano provides numerous shortcuts. Access the complete documentation by pressing Ctrl+G.

```
┌─────────────────────────────────────────────────────────────┐
│                      ict@openEuler24 ~                ^ _ □ × │
│ File  Edit  View  Terminal  Tabs  Help                        │
│  GNU nano 8.4                      test.c *                   │
│ #include <stdio.h>                                            │
│                                                               │
│ int main(void)                                                │
│ {                                                             │
│         printf("Hello, openEuler \n"};                        │
│         return 0;                                             │
│ }                                                             │
│                                                               │
│ ^G Help    ^O Write Out  ^F Where Is  ^K Cut    ^T Execute   ^C Location │
│ ^X Exit    ^R Read File  ^\ Replace   ^U Paste  ^J Justify   ^/ Go To Line │
└─────────────────────────────────────────────────────────────┘
```

Fig. 5.3 Nano

5.1.3 Text Searching

Text searching relies on string matching. Regular expressions (regexes) provide a robust method for defining string-matching patterns. These patterns govern how large volumes of text and strings are processed. Regexes are widely used in diverse areas, including text manipulation (searching and replacing), natural language processing, automated testing, data cleaning and preprocessing, text formatting, lexical analysis, and compilers.

Many UNIX command-line utilities, including the previously mentioned vi and Vim, as well as **grep**, **sed**, **gawk**, and shell scripts, support regexes. This section demonstrates the basic application of regexes in text searching, using the **grep** command as an example.

(1) **grep**

grep (global regular expression print) searches text efficiently by matching patterns within files or streams. It outputs matching lines to standard output, leveraging powerful regex capabilities for precise pattern matching.

While both **grep** and the **find** command (introduced in Chap. 3) perform searches, their core functions differ. **find** locates files within the file system based on file names, attributes, or other criteria. **grep**, conversely, searches within the content of text files or streams for matching text lines based on string patterns. However, both commands share a common strength: they execute their respective tasks effectively.

The basic syntax for **grep** is as follows:

```
grep [options] pattern [files...]
```

pattern represents the search string or regex. It can be followed by one or more file names. If no files are specified, **grep** reads text from standard input. Commonly used options are listed in Table 5.10.

5.1 Text Processing

Table 5.10 Common options for pattern

Option	Description	Option	Description
-i	Ignores case during matching	-s	Suppresses error messages
-n	Displays the line number of matching lines	-v	Inverts the match; outputs only non-matching lines
-l	Outputs only the names of matching files	-c	Outputs only the count of matching lines

The following example demonstrates using **grep** to locate processes by their names.

Executing the command below searches the process information listed by **ps** for the **watch** string.

```
[ict@openEuler24 ~]$ ps -aux | grep watch
root      92  0.0  0.0    ?      S   Jan 07  0:00 [watchdogd]
ict    39549  0.0  0.2  pts/3    T   05:46   0:00 watch -n 1 ls /bin
ict    39581  0.0  0.2  pts/3    S+  05:46   0:00 grep --color=auto watch
```

This search returns three lines. The second line represents the process initiated by the **ict** user, with a process ID of 39549. For automated tasks requiring the process ID directly, a more precise matching pattern is necessary.

(2) Character classes

Character classes provide a basic matching mechanism within regexes. Defined by square brackets ([]), these classes match literal characters as shown in Table 5.11.

Let's illustrate the use of character classes by retrieving the process ID of a specific command, **watch**.

Examining the earlier output of processes named watch reveals a unique identifier in the target line: digit + space + **watch**. We can leverage this pattern with the following command:

```
[ict@openEuler24 ~]$ ps aux | grep "[0-9] watch"
ict 39549 0.0 0.2 pts/3 T 05:46 0:00 watch -n 1 ls /bin
```

This precisely targets the correct process information. Piping this output to **cut** enables direct extraction of the process ID:

Table 5.11 Character class expressions

Expression	Description	Example
[0–9]	Matches a single digit	[123] matches **1**, **2**, or **3**
[a–z]	Matches a lowercase letter	[a–c] matches **a**, **b**, or **c**
[A–Z]	Matches an uppercase letter	[ABC] matches **A**, **B**, or **C**
[_]	Matches an underscore	[_] matches an underscore character
[^...]	Matches any single character except those listed	[^abc] matches any character other than **a**, **b**, or **c**

Table 5.12 Escape character expressions

Expression	Description	Expression	Description
\\	Matches a backslash	\d	Matches a digit (equivalent to [**0-9**])
\n	Matches a newline character	\w	Matches a word character (equivalent to [**A-Za-z0-9_**])
\(	Matches an opening parenthesis	\b	Matches a word boundary (**\bCha** matches the start of **Chapter**)

```
[ict@openEuler24 ~]$ ps aux | grep "[0-9] watch" |
cut -d' ' -f9
39549
```

(3) Escape characters

Regexes use the backslash \ to escape characters, indicating the subsequent character possesses a special meaning. These meanings are outlined in Table 5.12.

While escape characters appear in various contexts like C and shell scripts, their specific functions can vary, requiring careful consideration.

(4) Metacharacters

Metacharacters are essential components of regexes, serving as special characters with designated meanings, as detailed in Table 5.13.

Important considerations: Inside brackets, ^ inverts the selection; outside brackets, it matches the string beginning. Use .*, not the shell wildcard *, to match multiple characters. Escape literal metacharacters with a backslash (for example, \^ matches the ^ symbol).

Let's illustrate metacharacter usage by searching for patterns within files.

The following command locates lines beginning with **/* openEuler** within all C source files in the current directory tree:

```
[ict@openEuler24 ~]$ find -name "*.c" -exec grep "^/*
openEuler.*" {} \;
```

5.1 Text Processing

Table 5.13 Metacharacters

Metacharacter	Description	Example
^	Signifies the start of a string	^\d identifies strings starting with a digit
$	Signifies the end of a string	\d$ identifies strings ending with a digit; abc$ identifies strings ending with **abc**
*	Matches zero or more occurrences of the previous character	**zo*** matches **z** and **zoo**
+	Matches one or more occurrences of the previous character	**zo+** matches **zo** and **zoo**, but not **z**
?	Matches zero or one occurrence of the previous character	**do(es)?** matches **do** or **does**
|	Represents an OR condition, matching either option	**(P|p)ython** matches both **Python** and **python**
.	Matches any character except a newline	**ag.** matches strings like **agag** and **agaag**

find can also search file paths for patterns. This command finds files with paths containing **src/openEuler/** followed by one or more digits and ending in **.txt**:

```
[ict@openEuler24 ~]$ find $HOME -regex ".*/src/openEuler/[0-9]+.txt$"
```

grep utilizes regexes to identify and output lines matching specific patterns within text streams.

Regexes provide a robust set of pattern-matching rules. They empower diverse text processing tasks, including searches, replacements, and in-depth text analysis.

5.1.4 Text Replacement and Automated Editing

Beyond simple output, text matching empowers text replacement and automated editing, significantly enhancing efficiency and saving time.

While interconnected, text replacement and automated editing serve distinct purposes in automated text file processing. Text replacement substitutes specific content while automated editing executes a series of modifications.

Commonly, text replacement leverages basic string or regex matching with tools like **tr** and **sed**. Automated editing, frequently employing **sed**, performs non-interactive batch processing through scripts or automated commands.

(1) **tr**

The **tr** (translate) command provides convenient character conversion, replacing or removing specified characters from an input stream. The command follows this basic syntax:

```
$ tr [options] set1 [set2]
```

set1 and *set2* define the character sets, either as single characters or ranges. **tr** substitutes characters in *set1* with their corresponding characters in *set2*. Providing only *set1* instructs **tr** to delete those characters.

```
[ict@openEuler24 ~]$ echo "openEuler" | tr 'a-z' 'A-Z'
OPENEULER
```

Vim also leverages **tr** for similar functionality. For instance, executing **2,4 !tr 'a-z' 'A-Z'** in command-line mode converts lowercase letters in lines 2 through 4 to uppercase.

tr also addresses the challenges of varying newline formats across OSs. Linux employs **\n** (newline), Windows uses **\r\n** (carriage return and newline), while older macOS versions relied on **\r** (carriage return), though modern macOS adheres to the Linux standard. These inconsistencies can introduce formatting problems. Windows text files opened in Linux might exhibit ^M characters at line endings or display as a single continuous line.

To remove carriage return characters from a Windows text file and save it in the Linux format, run:

```
[ict@openEuler24 ~]$ tr -d '\r' < windows.txt > linux.txt
```

(2) **sed**

sed (stream editor) offers efficient, non-interactive processing of input streams and files. It executes specified editing actions like find and replace, delete, and insert operations, making it highly effective for applying the same edits to many files. The flexible editing capabilities and powerful integration with regexes make **sed** a versatile tool for complex text transformations within Unix-like OSs. Its basic syntax is:

```
sed [options] [actions] [files]
```

Table 5.14 describes common **sed** options.
Table 5.15 outlines common **sed** actions.

5.1 Text Processing

Table 5.14 Common sed options

Option	Description	Option	Description
-i	Directly modifies the file (backs up the original if an extension is provided)	-f *script_file*	Reads **sed** actions from a script file
-n	Prints only processed lines	-e *script*	Specifies sed actions (script) on the command line

Table 5.15 Common sed actions

Action	Description	Action	Description
a	Appends a new line containing the following string	I	Inserts a new line containing the following string
c	Replaces the entire line with the following string	p	Prints the line (usually used with the **-n** option)
d	Deletes lines matching the specified pattern	s	Substitutes strings, often leveraging regexes

Note: While **i** represents both an option and an action in **sed**, their meanings differ. Use the following command to delete carriage return characters from the Windows text file:

```
[ict@openEuler24 ~]$ sed -i 's/\r$//' windows.txt
```

sed often partners with **find** via pipes to process groups of files. The example below searches the working directory for all C header files, inserting specific text at the beginning and globally replacing occurrences of the target string:

```
[ict@openEuler24 ~]$ find . -name \*.h |xargs sed -i -e
'1i/#define __ICT__' \
> -e 's/OpenEuler/openEuler/g'
```

5.1.5 Text Analysis

Unix-like OSs extensively use text files to store diverse information, including computation results, monitoring data, and system logs. These text files often contain significant insights. Text analysis tools empower users to extract value from these files through various operations such as presenting file content, isolating key data, conducting statistical computations, and more.

(1) **sort**

The **sort** command efficiently sorts lines of text from an input stream. It can sort lexicographically or numerically by specified fields or keywords in ascending or descending order. Outputting to standard output, **sort** simplifies analysis and clarifies text data for users.

Despite its simple functionality, the numerous options available in **sort** demonstrate its thoroughness. Commonly used options appear in Table 5.16.

For example, this command finds all C source files (.c and .h) in the current directory and subdirectories, counts lines in each file, sorts the results in descending order, and displays them (note the required space after the closing parenthesis):

```
[ict@openEuler24 ~]$ find -type f \( -name "*.c" -or -name "*.h" \) | xargs wc -l | sort -rn
```

This command displays process information, sorts it by ascending CPU usage, and displays the final five lines:

```
[ict@openEuler24 ~]$ ps aux|sort -k2 -n | tail -5
```

Piping to **sort** provides a generic line-sorting analysis for any program that utilizes standard output. This eliminates redundant development of sorting functions, except perhaps in heavily used commands like **ls**.

The uniq command, closely related to sort, reports or removes duplicate lines in text streams. They are frequently combined for data cleaning and report generation.

uniq removes consecutive duplicate lines by default, retaining only the first instance. It also offers many options. The **-c** option prefixes each line with its occurrence count, while **-d** shows only duplicate lines.

Using **sort** before **uniq** typically yields clearer results by ensuring correct duplicate removal.

(2) **gawk**

gawk is a powerful command-line tool for text analysis, enabling extraction and computation of text data according to user-defined rules. Using regexes and conditional statements, **gawk** performs complex analyses, processes data, and automates report generation.

Table 5.16 Common sort options

Option	Description	Option	Description
-k	Specifies one or more sort keys; use commas to separate multiple keys.	-t	Specifies the field delimiter (defaulting to tabs).
-n	Sorts numerically, not lexicographically.	-b	Ignores leading whitespace.
-r	Sorts in reverse (descending) order.	-m	Merges presorted files.

5.1 Text Processing

gawk provides basic text formatting, outputting data in various simple formats such as text, CSV, and HTML. Further enhancing its versatility, **gawk** functions as a scripting language, complete with variables, arrays, control structures, and functions, allowing for complex data manipulations.

The basic syntax of the **gawk** command is:

```
gawk [options] 'BEGIN{ command1 } pattern{ command2 } END{ command3}' [files]
```

gawk offers various options and arguments to control aspects like input/output field separators and multi-file processing sequence. Its commands are divided into three main sections:

- **BEGIN** block (optional): performs preprocessing or prints headers.
- *pattern* block: iterates through and processes each line of input.
- **END** block (optional): executes final actions like report generation.

gawk reads input line by line, splitting each line into fields based on the input field separator (defaulting to spaces or tabs). Each field is then stored in a built-in variable. This process continues until all lines are processed. Table 5.17 lists the predefined variables.

This example splits the input string "Hi, openEuler!" into two fields using the default space delimiter and prints the second field:

```
[ict@openEuler24 ~]$ echo "Hi, openEuler!" | gawk '{print $2}'
openEuler!
```

This example locates all C source files (.c and .h) in the current directory and its subdirectories, counts the lines of each, and then calculates the total number of lines:

```
[ict@openEuler24 ~]$ find -type f \(-name "*.c" -or -name "*.h" \) | xargs wc -l \
>| gawk 'NR>1 {toal += $1} END {print "Total lines: ", total}'
```

Table 5.17 Predefined gawk variables

Variable	Description	Variable	Description
$0	Entire current line	$2	Second field of the current line
$1	First field of the current line	$9	Ninth field of the current line

The following example calculates the total memory usage percentage of all processes running under user **ict**:

```
[ict@openEuler24 ~]$ ps --user ict au --sort=-%mem \
> | gawk 'NR>1 {total_mem += $4} END {print "Total memory used:", total_mem}'
  Total memory used: 5.5
```

After the **ict** user starts and logs in to the Xfce graphical interface with **sudo systemctl start lightdm,** the output changes to:
```
Total memory used: 69.9
```

Regexes are a powerful, unified mechanism for text searching, replacement, and analysis. Together with commands like **find**, **grep**, and **sed**, they provide robust and efficient text manipulation capabilities within UNIX-like OSs.

5.1.6 Text Formatting

Document creation has always been a core function of modern computing. Users rely on computers to structure information into a variety of document types, including reports, spreadsheets, and academic papers. In modern non-UNIX OSs, WYSIWYG ("what you see is what you get") editors are the dominant paradigm.

UNIX text formatting adheres to a distinctly different approach, centered around markup. In fact, one of the original uses of UNIX was as a document preparation system, specifically designed to aid Bell Labs in drafting patent applications. The UNIX approach involves storing the user's input as plain text files rather than proprietary binary data. Specialized tools then format and typeset this text based on the markup it contains, producing output in either text or binary formats. Furthermore, a range of text processing tools allows conversion of these documents into diverse output formats. For instance, a document written using the lightweight Markdown language can be converted into formats such as TXT, TeX, HTML, or PDF using tools like Pandoc.

(1) LaTeX

LaTeX, based on TeX, provides a powerful and efficient typesetting system. Supporting diverse typesetting options and styles, it easily creates various documents, including reports and presentations.

> Frustrated with available typesetting software while writing *The Art of Computer Programming*, Donald Knuth developed TeX. He later open-sourced it.

LaTeX uses a specialized markup language for precise and elegant formatting, particularly excelling at rendering mathematical equations. This makes it ideal for academic papers and mathematics-related documents.

Even without typesetting or programming experience, users can harness the power of TeX through LaTeX. It can produce publication-ready documents quickly, adeptly handling complex tables and mathematical formulas.

As Sect. 2.1.3 shows, LaTeX, using packages like TikZ, enables graphic and table creation directly within documents using its markup language.

(2) Pandoc

Pandoc is a versatile document conversion utility that seamlessly transforms files between various formats, including Markdown, HTML, Word, and PDF. Supporting multiple markup languages, it offers extensive customization options that enable users to precisely tailor document formatting and styles.

Pandoc is simple to use: specify input/output formats and execute the command-line tool. Supporting batch processing, it converts multiple documents simultaneously. Pandoc is cross-platform, working on Windows, macOS, and Linux.

Beyond format conversion, Pandoc handles tables, footnotes, and citations. It integrates with tools like Git and Jekyll, facilitating version control and static website generation.

The first draft of the book, written in Markdown using Pandoc, allows output in formats like DOC and PDF. The command below generates the preview PDF:

```
[ict@openEuler24 ~]$ pandoc chap*.md -o eulerbook.
pdf --pdf-engine=xelatex \
  > --number-sections -H style.tex --filter=pandoc-crossref
```

(3) groff

groff, the GNU implementation of troff, produces high-quality output in various formats, including text, mathematical formulas, and charts. It is powerful and flexible.

> troff, launched in 1971, is a UNIX document formatting tool that generates high-quality output using a unique command syntax. It was a key component in the document processing system of UNIX and remains one of the oldest software tools still in use today.

groff employs a macro-like syntax to define custom text formats and styles, supporting diverse fonts and typesetting options. It handles complex layout elements like tables, charts, and mathematical formulas, streamlining document creation.

Beyond its core capabilities, groff integrates with numerous extensions and tools, including man page and document generation utilities. The compatibility with systems like LaTeX underscores its flexibility as a robust document formatting solution.

5.1.7 Using Git for Version Control

Text files offer a significant advantage through effective version management tools like Git.

Version management is a systematic approach to tracking, controlling, and documenting variations in software, documents, and projects. It enables precise change tracking, facilitates version recovery, and supports collaborative workflows by ensuring file consistency and traceability.

Text files excel in version control systems, allowing granular modification tracking and clear, text-based difference visualization. While binary files can be managed, their opaque change representations diminish the core purpose of version tracking.

Git, developed by Linux creator Torvalds, revolutionized version control with its distributed architecture. Unlike centralized systems, Git enables developers to commit changes locally without constant central repository synchronization. This approach enhances development flexibility, allowing work continuity even without network connectivity.

Key strengths of Git include:

- Robust branch management: Ultra-fast branch creation and switching support parallel development, enabling teams to explore new features without disrupting the main development line.
- Outstanding performance: Efficient algorithms of Git ensure rapid local and remote operations, making pushing, pulling, and merging seamless.
- Extensive community support: Widely adopted in open source projects, Git provides robust community resources and serves as a reliable enterprise-grade code hosting platform.

Beyond software source code, Markdown, LaTeX, and other text-based files benefit from the sophisticated version management capabilities of Git.

5.2 Shell Scripting

Shell scripting dramatically boosts CLI work efficiency. As the command interpreter for UNIX-like OSs, the shell fundamentally translates user commands into executable actions. Beyond interactive mode, the shell provides a robust programming language enabling users to craft scripts that extend commands, create system services, and automate complex tasks, thus empowering CLI capabilities.

At its core, a shell script is a text file containing a sequence of commands. The shell reads and executes these commands sequentially, mirroring manual CLI interactions. Any command-line task can be automated through scripting.

Shell scripts deliver remarkable advantages:

- Lightweight design: Featuring concise syntax and basic high-level language constructs, shell scripts integrate seamlessly with command-line operations. They are intuitive to write and execute without compilation.
- Processing power: Shell scripts directly leverage command-line tools like **find**, **grep**, **sed**, and **gawk**, combined with native pipe and redirection features. This enables sophisticated system management and text processing programs.
- Extensibility: Shell scripts can easily invoke third-party programs through command-line calls, supporting integrations with languages like C, Python, and Ruby while maintaining simplicity.
- Platform universality: Standard across UNIX-like OSs, shell scripts ensure broad compatibility and portability.
- Debugging accessibility: Shell scripts are editable via standard text editors, with built-in commands like **echo** and **set** facilitating variable tracking and breakpoint identification without specialized debugging tools.

These characteristics make shell scripts invaluable for system administrators and developers, driving automation in command extension, system management, and data processing. Many of openEuler's system tools exemplify effective shell programming.

For context, 222 commands in openEuler's **/bin** directory are script-based, verifiable through this command:

```
[ict@openEuler24~]$ file /bin/* |grep 'shell script' | wc -l
222
```

Shell scripts can transform complex commands into user-friendly utilities. The **install-help** command illustrates this, simplifying man page installation with three options and multiple parameters:

```
[ict@openEuler24~]$ install-help --help
Usage: install-help [OPTION]... [CMD-NAME]...
Install manual documents for commands.

Options:

  -h|--help     Display this help and exit
  -y|--yes      Set -y for dnf install
  -v|--verbose  Display some errors during processing
     --version  Output version information and exit
```

The subsequent sections will explore shell scripting through a number-guessing game example and demonstrate **install-help** command development across three iterative versions, providing hands-on learning opportunities.

5.2.1 Number-Guessing Game

To provide readers with a quick, intuitive grasp of shell scripting, we will start with a simple number-guessing game. The complete shell script below can be understood even by those who have never programmed before.

```
 1 #!/bin/sh
 2 echo "***Welcome to the Number-Guessing Game! [`date`]***"
 3 target=$(( RANDOM % 100 + 1 ))
 4 attempts=0
 5 while [[ $guess -ne $target ]]
 6 do
 7     read -p "Guess a number (1-100):" guess
 8     if [[ $guess -lt $target ]]; then
 9         echo "Too low!"
10     elif [[ $guess -gt $target ]]; then
11         echo "Too high!"
12     fi
13     attempts=$((attempts + 1))
14 done
15 echo "Congratulations! You guessed it in $attempts tries."
```

Next, you can run the number-guessing game and then analyze it step by step.

(1) Quick experience

Remove the line numbers from the shell script and save it as **~/bin/guess.sh** using vi or nano. Ensure you strictly maintain the original format, especially avoiding spaces around the = sign.

A quick way to run the script is:

```
[ict@openEuler24~]$ bash ~/bin/guess.sh
***Welcome to the Number-Guessing Game! [Tue Jan 09 19:41:26 CST 2025]***
Guess a number (1-100):
```

Enter your guess and press **Enter**. Try to guess the number in the fewest attempts.

(2) Comments and the shebang line

The comment symbol in the shell is "#". Everything from the first character after the comment symbol to the end of the line is a comment, which the shell will not interpret. Comments can start from any position in a line.

The first line is typically a special comment starting with "#!". This combination is called "shebang," and the line is known as the shebang line. It specifies the shell program to interpret and execute the script. In guess.sh, the specified shell is **/bin/sh**. Shebang lines first appeared in sh scripts and are now used in multiple scripting languages like Python.

Writing a shebang line is a standard practice. When a script starts in the user's shell, the current shell will read the shebang line and launch the specified shell to interpret and execute the script. Different shell scripting languages may not be compatible, so developers should explicitly specify to ensure the script runs correctly. For example, a script written in csh syntax cannot be interpreted in Bash. Additionally, the shell allows users to forcibly specify a different shell program to run the script. When running the script with **bash ~/bin/guess.sh**, the shebang line will be ignored, and the script will run directly in Bash.

(3) Execution permissions and search path

To run the script as a command, you need to modify execution permissions and the search path. A shell script must have execute permission to become a command, and the shell must find the script in its search path.

Since the **~/bin** directory is already in the search path of Bash, you only need to use **chmod** to add execute permission for all users.

```
[ict@openEuler24 ~]$ chmod +x ~/bin/guess.sh
[ict@openEuler24 ~]$ guess.sh
***Welcome to the Number-Guessing Game! [Tue Jan 09 19:52:33 CST 2025]***
Guess a number (1-100):
```

When you run **guess.sh** this way, the current Bash shell will start the sh shell specified in the shebang line to actually run the script, which means the script runs in a new shell instance.

Adding the script to system directories like **/usr/bin/** and **/usr/local/bin/** makes it available to all users. Additionally, file extensions are not required; using an extension is mostly for historical compatibility.

Shell scripts can also be run using the **source** command, which is typically used to load configuration scripts. It simply reads and executes the statements in the script in the current shell without creating a subshell. The example of implementing extended commands in Chap. 3 used this method to load scripts. **source** is an internal command. You can also use a dot . in place of the command name.

5.2.2 Variables

Shell variable naming follows conventions similar to most programming languages: they can include numbers, letters, and underscores, must begin with a letter or underscore, and cannot use shell keywords.

When initializing or modifying variables, you must assign a value:

```
attemps=0
```

Here, **attempts** is the variable name, and **0** is its assigned value. Variable initialization does not require specifying a type. Importantly, no spaces are allowed on either side of the = sign.

To read a variable, simply prefix it with the **$** symbol, using the same method as reading shell environment variables:

```
echo "Congratulations! You guessed it in $attempts tries."
```

If a value contains whitespace (spaces or tabs), it must be enclosed in quotes. Single and double quotes differ in their handling of content:

Single quotes provide literal representation. Content within single quotes (variables or constants) undergoes no substitution, rendering exactly what is typed.

Double quotes allow partial substitution. Variables and commands within double quotes are evaluated before output, meaning the final content reflects their resolved values.

5.2 Shell Scripting

```
[ict@openEuler24 ~]$ echo '$SHELL' && echo "$SHELL" $SHELL
$SHELL
/bin/bash
```

Another method to assign variable values is by obtaining user input from the keyboard. The **read** command allows data retrieval from standard input.

```
read -p "Guess a number (1-100):" guess
```

The **guess** variable stores input data, which can be single or multiple items, space-separated during entry. The **-p** option displays a prompt message.

The shell also includes default variables, with the most common listed in Table 5.18.

Leveraging the variable knowledge from this section, the man page installation command can be transformed into an **install-help-v1** script.

```
1  #!/bin/sh
2  # Retrieve execution path for the specified command.
3  bin_file=`which $1`
4  # Derive software package name from execution path.
5  help_name=`rpm -qf $bin_file | sed 's/-[0-9].*//'`-help
6  # Install package via dnf.
7  echo "Installing with dnf for $help_name ..."
8  dnf install -y $help_name
```

The script simplifies a complex command into three steps and adds informative output. By saving it as **/usr/local/bin/install-help-v1** with execute permission, it becomes a system command.

Table 5.18 Common built-in shell variables

Variable	Description	Variable	Description
$0	Current script file name	$@	List of all parameters
$1–$9	Values of parameters 1–9	$*	All parameters as a single string
$#	Total number of script parameters	$?	Return value of the last command (0 indicates success; non-zero values indicate failure.)

```
[ict@openEuler24 ~]$ sudo install-help-v1 dnf
Installing with dnf for dnf-help ...
   Last metadata expiration check: 0:00:19 ago on Tue 09 Jan
2025 10:41:26 PM CST.
   Package dnf-help-4.16.2-8.oe2403sp2.noarch is already
installed.
   Dependencies resolved.
   Nothing to do.
   Complete!
```

This compact script, involving two variable assignments and three variable reads, exemplifies powerful shell scripting techniques. By directly invoking commands and transforming multi-step interactions into streamlined processes, it showcases the potential of scripts for command simplification.

Despite its brevity, the script reveals inherent limitations. Absent parameters could trigger **dnf** errors, and it cannot install man pages for multiple commands at a time. Addressing these constraints requires more advanced shell programming constructs.

5.2.3 *Expressions*

Expressions serve as computational and conditional evaluation tools, synthesizing variables, operators, and constants into powerful constructs. The shell supports diverse expression types: arithmetic, relational, logical, and file test expressions.

(1) Arithmetic expressions

Arithmetic expressions facilitate fundamental mathematical operations. Operators (+, -, *, /, %) handle addition, subtraction, multiplication, division, and modulo calculations with precision.

Double parentheses "(( ))" enable integer expansion—a syntactic shortcut for streamlining numeric computations. This mechanism automatically parses variables without $prefixes, offering flexible formatting with relaxed spacing constraints.

```
target=$(( RANDOM % 100 + 1 ))
```

(2) Relational expressions

Relational expressions compare values, returning boolean outcomes based on precise evaluation criteria. They encompass integer and string comparison operators.

Integer operators (**-gt**, **-ge**, **-lt**, **-le**, **-eq**, **-ne**) systematically compare variables, representing comparative relationships: greater than, greater than or equal, less than, less than or equal, equal, and not equal.

String operators (**=**, **!=**, **-z**, **-n**) validate string equivalence and emptiness, providing nuanced text comparison capabilities.

(3) Logical expressions

Logical expressions orchestrate complex conditional logic through AND, OR, and NOT operations. Operators (**&&**, **||**, **!**) interconnect relational expressions, with alternative representations **-a** and **-o** supporting traditional logical combinations.

(4) File test expressions

The shell provides unique file test expressions to evaluate file and directory attributes, such as existence, readability, writability, and executability. These expressions return true when conditions are met, and false otherwise. Table 5.19 lists the most common file test operators.

(5) Conditional test expressions

Shell conditional tests combine test expressions with square brackets, utilizing two distinct bracket forms: single [] and double [[]].

Single brackets handle basic conditional tests, supporting string and numeric comparisons along with file test operators. While their syntax remains straightforward, functionality remains somewhat constrained. Expressions require careful spacing and occasional special character escaping.

Double brackets offer enhanced capabilities, providing advanced comparison and logical operators, string length evaluation, and regex matching. Their syntax allows more complex conditional processing, enabling variable expansion and sophisticated pattern matching.

The selection between bracket types depends on specific testing requirements. Single brackets suit simple tests, while double brackets excel in handling intricate conditional logic and text processing.

A critical implementation detail: always maintain spaces between brackets and expressions.

5.2.4 Branch Structures

Branch structures dynamically execute different code blocks based on conditional expression evaluations. These test expressions can encompass relational, logical, and file test expressions.

Table 5.19 Common file test operators

Operator	Function	Operator	Function
-e *file_name*	Checks file or directory existence	-r *file_name*	Checks file readability
-f *file_name*	Verifies a regular file	-w *file_name*	Checks file writability
-d *file_name*	Confirms directory existence	-x *file_name*	Checks file executability
-L *file_name*	Identifies a symbolic link	-s *file_name*	Checks non-zero file size

Common branching mechanisms include if-else and case structures, both supporting nested implementations.

(1) If-else branches

If-else branching provides conditional execution control analogous to other programming languages. It supports single, dual, and multi-branch variations with distinct syntax. The **guess.sh** example demonstrates a dual-branch approach:

```
7       if [[ $guess -lt $target ]]; then
8           echo "Too low!"
9       elif [[ $guess -gt $target ]]; then
10          echo "Too high!"
11      fi
```

The shell evaluates conditions following the **if** keyword, executing corresponding code blocks based on test results. True conditions trigger immediate block execution, while false conditions prompt skipping. The **elif** construct enables complex, multi-condition testing, with an optional **else** capturing unmatched scenarios.

Critical implementation details include maintaining spaces around bracket delimiters and allowing multiple statements per block via semicolons or line breaks.

Transforming **install-help-v1** demonstrates practical branch structure application, adding robust parameter validation:

```
  1 #!/bin/sh
+ 2 if [ $# -eq 0 ]; then          # Check parameters.
+ 3 echo -e "\nUsage: sudo install-help cmd\n" && exit 1;
+ 4 fi
  5 # Retrieve execution path for the specified command.
  6 bin_file=`which $1 2>/dev/null`
+ 7 if [ ! -x "$bin_file" ]; then  # Check if the file exists and is executable.
+ 8 echo "Binfile not found for $1" && exit 2;
+ 9 fi
  10 # Derive software package name from execution path.
  11 help_name=`rpm -qf $bin_file | sed 's/-[0-9].*//'`-help
  12 # Install package via dnf.
  13 echo "Installing with dnf for $help_name ..."
  14 dnf install -y $help_name
```

This implementation introduces new features: first, checking for missing parameters, where **$#** represents the number of parameters, and providing a help prompt and exiting if no parameters are provided; second, checking parameter validity, where **$1** represents the value of parameter 1, and providing an error prompt and exiting if the command is invalid. These features prevent potential downstream errors.

Despite these improvements, the script remains limited—lacking option support, multi-parameter handling, and bulk man page installation capabilities. Addressing these constraints requires incorporating case branches and iterative structures.

(2) Case branches

Case branching provides multi-branch conditional execution based on variable values. Its syntax follows this structure:

```
case $variable in
    pattern1)
        # Commands for pattern1
        ;;
    pattern2)
        # Commands for pattern2
        ;;
    ...
esac
```

The mechanism systematically compares input against predefined patterns, executing corresponding code blocks upon successful matches. Patterns support flexible representations including strings, numeric values, and regexes. Each pattern terminates with a right parenthesis and double semicolons (;;).

Pattern-statement pairs form the structural core. If a pattern does not have corresponding execution statements, you can add two semicolons after that pattern to skip it.

Dual semicolons serve as definitive block terminators, ensuring precise control flow and preventing unintended statement execution across patterns. When no explicit match occurs, the wildcard pattern ("*") provides a default fallback mechanism.

5.2.5 Loop Structures

Loop structures provide a powerful mechanism for iterative execution, enabling repeated statement blocks until specified termination conditions are met. Developers can leverage for and while loops, selecting the most appropriate variant based on computational requirements.

(1) For Loops

For loops excel at systematic traversal of collections, offering precise iteration over numeric sequences or object collections with predictable iteration counts.

```
for variable in list
do
      # Execution statement block
done
```

The construct designates a loop variable that sequentially assumes values from a predefined list. Elements—whether numeric or textual—are space-delimited, forming the iteration domain. The region between **do** and **done** constitutes the loop body, representing statements executed during each iteration.

The for loop mechanism operates systematically: it initially assigns the first element of the list to the variable, executes the corresponding statement block, then progressively cycles through subsequent elements. Upon exhausting all list members, the loop terminates, allowing program execution to resume beyond the **done** delimiter.

(2) While loops

While loops provide a dynamic iteration mechanism, executing code segments repeatedly under specified conditions—often with unbounded or indeterminate iteration counts. The **guess.sh** script exemplifies the flexible nature of this construct.

```
5   while [[ $guess -ne $target ]]
6   do
7         read -p "Guess a number (1-100):" guess
8         if [[ $guess -lt $target ]]; then
          ... ...
14  done
```

Each iteration evaluates the condition expression: true conditions trigger statement execution, while false conditions bypass the block. Continuous true conditions sustain loop progression until the termination criterion emerges.

Prudent while loop implementation demands meticulous condition management to prevent infinite iterations. Developers can strategically integrate conditional logic and control flow statements to regulate loop behavior.

Leveraging case branches and iterative structures, **install-help-v2** undergoes transformation and becomes **install-help-v3**, gaining robust multi-option and multi-parameter capabilities:

5.2 Shell Scripting

```
1  #!/bin/sh
2  usage="\nUsage: sudo install-help [-y] cmd ...\n"
3  # Parameter validation
4  if [ $# -eq 0 ]; then echo -e $usage; exit 1; fi
5  # Variable initialization
6  cmd_list=""; help_list=""; yes=""
7  # Option and parameter parsing
8  while [ -n "$1" ]; do
9    case "$1" in
10     -y|--yes)    yes="-y" ;;
11     -h|--help)   echo -e $usage; exit 0 ;;
12     -*)   shift; break ;;
13     *)    cmd_list="$cmd_list $1" ;;
14   esac
15   shift
16 done
17 # Package query across the parameter list
18 for cmd in $cmd_list; do
19   # Retrieve execution path for the specified command.
20   bin_file=`which $cmd 2>/dev/null`
21   # Existence verification
22   if [ -z "$bin_file" ]; then echo "''$cmd'' not found"; continue; fi
23   # Derive software package name from execution path.
24   help_name=`rpm -qf $bin_file | sed 's/-[0-9].*//'`-help
25   help_list="$help_list $help_name"
26 done
27 # Package name validation
28 if [ -z "$help_list" ]; then echo -e $usage; exit 2; fi
29 # Install package via dnf.
30 echo "Installing with dnf for $help_list ..."
31 dnf install $yes $help_list
```

Lines 8–16 orchestrate nuanced option and parameter parsing, strategically populating the **yes** and **cmd_list** variables. The shift mechanism progressively moves the parameter list left, transforming **$2** to **$1**, and so on. Lines 18 to 26 enable comprehensive multi-parameter processing, extracting command names from the **cmd_list** variable, performing validity checks, and storing man page package names in the **help_list** variable.

The script evolves from a basic command to a sophisticated, flexible utility supporting diverse invocation patterns. Despite this enhancement, potential refinements remain—particularly regarding code modularity and reduction of repetitive constructs—which could be addressed through shell functions.

5.2.6 Functions

Shell scripting introduces functions as modular, reusable code constructs capable of parameter reception and value return. By encapsulating complex operations, functions mitigate code redundancy, significantly enhancing script readability and maintainability.

The canonical function definition syntax appears as follows:

```
function func_name( )
{
    # Function body
}
```

Parameter acquisition occurs through positional notation: **$1** represents the first argument, **$2** the second, progressively indexing input parameters. Function-scoped variables default to global visibility, with return status accessible via **$?** after invocation.

Consider the following implementation for a help function in **install-help**:

```
function print_help()
{
   printf "\n%s\n" "Usage: sudo install-help [-y] cmd ..."
}
```

Deploying **print_help** in place of repetitive **echo -e $usage** statements, specifically in lines 4, 11, and 28 of **install-help-v3**, yields immediate benefits: code concision, reduced redundancy, and enhanced future extensibility.

5.2.7 Project 5-1: Install-Help Command

Transform the **install-help-v3** script into a robust, user-centric command with enhanced functionality.

Beyond implementing the **print_help** function, refactor option parsing using **getopts** and extract the help_list generation logic (currently in lines 18–26) into a dedicated function to bolster code readability and future maintainability.

Configure suitable script permissions, deploy the script to the system-wide search path **/usr/local/bin/**, and perform comprehensive validation.

5.3 C/C++ Application Development

Beyond initial stages of requirement analysis and software design, C/C++ application development encompasses source code creation, compilation, building, debugging, and optimization. Linux stands out as an exceptionally developer-friendly OS, particularly for C/C++ application developers.

While Windows developers typically rely on IDEs like Visual Studio—which consolidate source code editors, compilers, and debuggers into a unified GUI workflow—Linux offers similar environments such as Eclipse, Code::Blocks, CodeLite, and NetBeans. However, most Linux developers prefer CLIs for C/C++ application development.

Since the rewrite of UNIX in C, the language has remained the primary tool for developing UNIX and its application utilities. The CLI and lightweight tools of UNIX have profoundly shaped C application development patterns. Developers can flexibly combine editors, compilers, debuggers, and command-line tools, tailoring their environment to personal preferences and application requirements. Leveraging rich tool options and integrating script and build tools enables comprehensive automation of compilation and development processes.

Performance analysis and optimization tools further enhance software quality, enabling developers to refine and release high-performance applications.

Linux development tools and software libraries maintain robust compatibility with UNIX open source implementations, predominantly adhering to POSIX standards and delivering exceptional portability [17]. Developers can seamlessly transfer development skills across Linux distributions and UNIX-like OSs, often with minimal code modifications. The open source nature of Linux and its ecosystem provides an invaluable learning resource for emerging developers.

This section explores compilation, debugging, automated testing, and performance optimization techniques for C/C++ applications in the Linux CLI, using minimal implementations of classic utilities **nl** and **wc** as instructive examples. Readers are encouraged to engage in hands-on practice alongside the content.

5.3.1 my-nl

my-nl represents a minimalist implementation of the **nl** command that reads text lines from standard input, numbers them, and outputs the result to standard output without supporting any options. As such, **my-nl** functions as a text stream filter.

```
 1  #include <stdio.h>
 2  int main(void)
 3  {
 4      char *line = NULL;
 5      size_t cap = 0;
 6      ssize_t len = 0;
 7      int no = 0;
 8      while ((len = getline(&line,&cap, stdin)) != -1){
 9          if (len > 1)
10              printf("\x1b[32m%6d \x1b[39m", ++no);
11          printf("%s", line);
12      }
13      return 0;
14  }
```

This source code is straightforward, and even if readers are not familiar with the **getline** function, it will not impede the compilation and build process. To distinguish the output, **my-nl** renders line numbers in light green.

Readers are advised to use Vim to enter the source code (disregarding line numbers) and save it as **~/my-utils/my-nl.c**. Compilation, building, and testing will follow.

5.3.2 Compilation and Debugging

Linux distributions feature several prominent C compilers, including GCC, Clang, C++ Compiler, and LLVM. These tools support multiple programming languages like C, C++, Objective-C, and Fortran, delivering robust optimization and extensive platform compatibility.

Clang stands out as an LLVM-based compiler for C, C++, and Objective-C, boasting high extensibility and a modular architecture that provides superior error reporting and diagnostics. Intel's C++ Compiler focuses on optimizing performance for Intel processors. LLVM emerges as a versatile compiler infrastructure supporting languages such as C, C++, Objective-C, and Rust.

This section will leverage GCC for compilation and offer a concise introduction to GNU Symbolic Debugger (GDB). Notably, openEuler has developed a GCC variant specifically optimized for China-developed processors like Kunpeng.

1. GCC

    GCC is a compiler suite developed by GNU. Originally created for GNU, it has become one of the most widely used C/C++ compilers on Linux and comes pre-installed with most Linux distributions.

GCC supports multiple programming languages, including C, C++, Objective-C, Fortran, Java, Ada, and Go, along with their corresponding library functions. Designed for cross-platform compatibility, GCC can run on virtually all major CPU architectures and efficiently convert source files into target code specific to various hardware platforms. Additionally, GCC features an extensible architecture and plugin system that allows developers to customize and extend its functionality according to their needs.

GCC offers perhaps the most extensive set of options among all software, with over 2000 available options (viewable using the **gcc --help -v | grep "^ -" | wc** command). These options are categorized into 12 groups: overall options, language options, preprocessor options, assembler options, linker options, directory options, warning options, debugging options, optimization options, target options, machine-dependent options, and code generation options.

When using GCC from the command line, developers can control compiler behavior through various command-line parameters, such as specifying source files, defining output formats for target code, and setting optimization options. GCC is supported by comprehensive documentation and an active community, enabling developers to thoroughly learn and utilize its capabilities.

2. Compiling **my-nl**

   Navigate to the **my-utils** directory, compile **my-nl.c** to generate the **my-nl** executable, and verify it using **ls** and **file** commands as shown:

```
[ict@openEuler24 ~]$ cd my-utils && gcc -o my-nl my-nl.c
&& ls -l my-nl && file my-nl
    -rwxr-xr-x. 1 ict 71040 Jan 10 23:33 my-nl
    my-nl: ELF 64-bit LSB executable, ARM aarch64, version 1
(SYSV), dynamically linked,
    interpreter /lib/ld-linux-aarch64.so.1, BuildID[sha1]=
af13528bf572b785091d248d3af22b019
    c9cc197, for GNU/Linux 3.7.0, not stripped
```

This indicates that **my-nl** has been successfully generated. The usage is as follows:

```
[ict@openEuler24 my-utils]$ cat /etc/passwd | ./my-nl
| head -3
         1  root:x:0:0:root:/root:/bin/bash
         2  bin:x:1:1:bin:/bin:/sbin/nologin
         3  daemon:x:2:2:daemon:/sbin:/sbin/nologin
```

As you can see, this small tool compiled by GCC can now work with pipes in text streams.

Additionally, careful readers might have noticed that **./my-nl** is used to execute **my-nl**, while system commands like **cd** and **pwd** are executed without specifying a path. This is because the shell searches for system commands in default system paths. For system security, the current working directory is not added to the system default paths.

> You can view the system default paths by running **echo $PATH**.

3. GCC Compilation Process

   The seemingly simple command **gcc -o my-nl my-nl.c** actually involves four distinct steps: preprocessing, assembly, compilation, and linking, as detailed in Table 5.20.

> GCC generates temporary files with .i, .s, and .o extensions during compilation. These intermediary files get automatically removed when compilation completes in a single step.

You can run each step independently to examine intermediate outputs.

– Preprocessing: The C preprocessor (CPP) handles header file inclusion (**#include**), macro expansion (**#define**), and directive processing. The resulting my-nl.i file expands to over 3000 lines.
– Assembly: The assembler program (as) converts preprocessed code into machine-specific assembly code.
  On ×86 platforms, running **gcc -S -masm=intel my-nl.i -o my-nl.s** generates Intel syntax assembly code. A snippet from the **main** function illustrates this:

```
call      getline
mov       QWORD PTR [rbp-16], rax
cmp       QWORD PTR [rbp-16], -1
jne       .L4
mov       eax, 0
leave
```

Table 5.20 Steps to generate my-nl

Step	Command	Function	Output File
Preprocessing	$ gcc -E my-nl.c -o my-nl.i	Preprocess source code.	my-nl.i
Assembly	$ gcc -S my-nl.i -o my-nl.s	Generate assembly code.	my-nl.s
Compilation	$ gcc -c my-nl.s -o my-nl.o	Create the object file.	my-nl.o
Linking	$ gcc my-nl.o -o my-nl	Create the executable.	my-nl

The eax register stores function return values, available for other functions or programs to read. The shell uses this mechanism to check the execution status of recent commands.
- Compilation: The compiler proper (cc) transforms assembly code into object files. While commonly called a compiler, GCC actually encompasses the entire toolchain for preprocessing, assembly, compilation, and linking.
- Linking: The linker program (ld) combines object files with library files into an executable. Modern programs often link multiple source files and libraries, including libc. The **ldd** command reveals shared library dependencies:

```
[ict@openEuler24 my-utils]$ ldd my-nl
    linux-vdso.so.1 (0x0000ffff8e084000)
    libc.so.6 => /usr/lib64/libc.so.6 (0x0000ffff8de98000)
    /lib/ld-linux-aarch64.so.1 (0x0000ffff8e047000)
```

The use of the eax register for return values explains the single return value limitation of C functions.

The term "build" typically refers to the entire process of generating executables, distinguishing it from the compilation step that produces object files.

4. GDB
    GDB stands as the flagship command-line debugger from the GNU project, offering robust support for C, C++, Objective-C, and other programming languages. This versatile tool streamlines software development through essential debugging features like breakpoints, step execution, and real-time variable monitoring.
    GDB excels with capabilities spanning multiple domains:

    - Language flexibility across major programming platforms
    - Interactive command interface for runtime control and inspection
    - Strategic execution control via breakpoints and watchpoints
    - Flexible breakpoint system with granular stepping control
    - Real-time variable monitoring during program pause
    - Complete visibility and control in multi-threaded environments
    - Cross-machine debugging through remote connections

    Developers typically debug by strategically placing breakpoints and stepping through code while monitoring program state through variables and memory inspection. This systematic approach helps narrow down issues efficiently until the root cause emerges.
    Compiling with the **-g** option enables source-level debugging capabilities.

5. Debugging **my-nl**

   A practical debugging session demonstrates the GDB workflow. Debug **my-nl** by recompiling with the **-g** option and loading it into GDB. View the source code with the **list** command and set a breakpoint at line 12 using **break 12**. Execute the program with **run < /etc/os-release**. The program runs until it hits the breakpoint at line 12 after entering the main function. Step to the next line using **n** (next). At each pause, inspect variables with **print** or perform other debug operations.

```
[ict@openEuler24 my-utils]$ gcc -g -o my-nl my-nl.c
[ict@openEuler24 my-utils]$ gdb my-nl
GNU gdb (GDB) openEuler 11.1-6.oe2203sp2
......
For help, type "help".
Type "apropos word" to search for commands related to "word"...
Reading symbols from my-nl...
(gdb) list
1   /* my-nl: A very simple ``nl'' for learning openEuler */
2   #include <stdio.h>
3   #include <unistd.h>
......
10      int      no=0;
(gdb) break 12
Breakpoint 1 at 0x40079c: file my-nl.c, line 12.
(gdb) run < /etc/os-release
Starting program: /home/ict/my-utils/my-nl < /etc/os-release
[Thread debugging using libthread_db enabled]
Using host libthread_db library "/usr/lib64/libthread_db.so.1".
Breakpoint 1, main () at my-nl.c:12
12          while ((len = getline(&line, &cap, stdin)) != -1){
(gdb) n
13              if (len > 1) fprintf(stdout, "\x1b[32m%6d \x1b[39m", ++no);
(gdb) print len
$3 = 17
```

GDB serves as a crucial tool for bug detection in software development. It enables developers to launch and control program execution, set breakpoints for pausing, examine program state during pauses, and inspect or modify variables and memory values.

5.3 C/C++ Application Development

GDB provides extensive debugging capabilities through numerous control commands, all accessible via the **help** command in the debug interface.

5.3.3 Building with Makefiles

Modern software projects employ modular programming principles, often comprising hundreds or thousands of source files across multiple modules. Compiling each file individually, as in the **my-nl** example, would prove inefficient and tedious—an approach UNIX developers reject.

Makefiles automate the build process and manage large software projects efficiently. They enable developers to define comprehensive compilation rules and execute them through a single **make** command, streamlining the entire compilation workflow. Makefiles implement intelligent compilation by targeting only modified files and their dependencies, vastly improving build efficiency.

The Makefile system leverages file timestamps to determine compilation needs. Linux updates the timestamp of a file upon modification. When **make** is executed, the system compares source and target file timestamps—newer source timestamps trigger recompilation. The system tracks file dependencies comprehensively: when a target file requires recompilation, all dependent files undergo recompilation as well. This selective compilation approach ensures optimal build performance.

Makefiles originated in the 1970s at Bell Labs, where Stuart Feldman developed this tool to automate program building. Prior to Makefiles, program building involved manual, error-prone processes. The introduction of Makefiles brought automation and reproducibility to build processes, eventually establishing itself as a cornerstone tool for software development in UNIX and Linux environments [11].

1. Using a Makefile to build **my-nl**
   Makefile employs a syntax of rules, targets, and commands to describe how to build software. Each rule defines dependencies for a target file and specifies commands for generating and updating it.
   A Makefile rule follows this structure:

   ```
   target [attributes]separator [dependencies]
       commands
   ```

   The target specifies the output file or module to create. Commands must start with a tab character and execute through the system shell, enabling the use of system variables and command-line arguments. Critical syntax requirements include using colons to separate targets from dependencies and tabs (not spaces) to indent commands.

Here is the Makefile for **my-nl**, saved as **~/my-utils/Makefile**:

```
CC=gcc
CFLAGS=-Wall
my-nl: my-nl.o
    $(CC) $(CFLAGS) -o my-nl my-nl.o
my-nl.o: my-nl.c
    $(CC) $(CFLAGS) -c my-nl.c
clean:
    rm -f *.o my-nl
```

This Makefile defines three targets:

- **my-nl**: builds the final executable by using GCC to link **my-nl.o**.
- **my-nl.o**: creates the intermediate object file by using GCC to compile **my-nl.c**.
- **clean**: removes generated object files and executables using the rm command. The **make** command automates the build process, eliminating the need for manual **gcc** commands.

```
[ict@openEuler24 my-utils]$ rm my-nl && make && ls -l my-nl
gcc -Wall -o my-nl my-nl.o
-rwxr-xr-x. 1 ict ict 71040 Jan 11 01:10 my-nl
```

Beyond compilation, Makefile supports preprocessor, assembler, and linker customization. It enables additional tasks like packaging and installation through custom targets.

Makefile offers several advantages: rich functionality for customized builds, clear text-based configuration, and cross-platform compatibility. Its widespread adoption is evident in the Linux kernel 6.6, which contains thousands of Makefiles, and in tools like Yocto that use Makefiles for package customization.

```
[ict@openEuler24 my-utils]$ find /usr/src/kernels/ -name Makefile|wc -l
2702
```

2. Limitations of Makefiles
   While Makefiles excel at automating C/C++ application builds, creating Makefiles for complex software projects presents significant challenges. Makefiles exhibit several key limitations.

   – Its complex syntax and poor readability create a steep learning curve that particularly impacts novice developers.
   – Cross-platform compatibility issues emerge between different OS and platforms, necessitating specific adjustments and adaptations.
   – Debugging rule configuration errors proves tedious and requires supplementary tools.

   The Automake project addresses these limitations through automatic generation of complex Makefiles, enabling developers to concentrate on code development rather than build management. It requires developers to write predefined macros, which Automake processes into **Makefile.in** files. Autoconf then converts these into a **configure** shell script. On the target platform, running the **configure** script automatically generates environment-specific Makefiles.

   Though Automake partially resolves manual Makefile creation issues, its complexity has led to its gradual replacement by CMake.

5.3.4 Building with CMake

CMake is a cross-platform build automation system that provides developers a unified approach to rapidly create projects across multiple platforms and tools. At its core, CMake defines build processes through concise description files (typically **CMakeLists.txt**) and automatically generates platform-specific Makefiles.

Key advantages of CMake include:

– Automated end-to-end build process: CMake streamlines source code compilation, testing, and packaging, enabling developers to concentrate on coding and problem-solving instead of managing builds manually.
– Intuitive learning curve: CMake employs clear, straightforward syntax that helps developers quickly become productive and handle complex projects efficiently.
– Cross-platform compatibility: CMake generates platform-specific build files, facilitating direct software project builds across Linux, Windows, macOS, and other OSs.
– Seamless integration: CMake automatically detects and incorporates third-party libraries and build tools, supporting both static and dynamic linking methods.

To use the CMake command (**cmake**) on openEuler, simply execute **sudo dnf install -y cmake**.

1. Using CMake to build **my-nl**
   Create a CMake description file with the following content and save it as **~/my-utils/CMakeLists.txt**:

```
cmake_minimum_required(VERSION 2.9)
project(my-utils)
add_executable(my-nl my-nl.c)
INSTALL(TARGETS "my-nl" RUNTIME DESTINATION bin)
```

CMake uses **CMakeLists.txt** by default to generate the Makefile automatically. Best practice involves creating a **build** subdirectory alongside the description file to store intermediate files generated during compilation. Execute these commands:

```
[ict@openEuler24 ~]$ cd ~/my-utils/ && mkdir -p build && cd build
[ict@openEuler24 build]$ cmake .. && ls
CMakeCache.txt CMakeFiles cmake_install.cmake Makefile
```

During file generation, CMake detects C/C++ compilers and creates a comprehensive Makefile spanning hundreds of lines. This Makefile includes multiple targets like **all** and **install**. The **all** target, set as default, typically builds all object files, while **install** copies generated files to system paths. Run **make help** to view all available targets.
Next, build and install **my-nl**:

```
[ict@openEuler24 build]$ make && sudo make install
[100%] Built target my-nl
[100%] Built target my-nl
Install the project...
-- Install configuration: ""
-- Installing: /usr/local/bin/my-nl
```

Now **my-nl** exists as a system command, accessible without the **./** prefix.

```
[ict@openEuler24 build]$ cat /etc/passwd | my-nl | head -3
     1  root:x:0:0:root:/root:/bin/bash
     2  bin:x:1:1:bin:/bin:/sbin/nologin
     3  daemon:x:2:2:daemon:/sbin:/sbin/nologin
```

5.3 C/C++ Application Development

The concise **CMakeLists.txt** significantly reduces developer build effort. Moreover, CMake description files automatically generate platform-specific Makefiles, enabling cross-platform compilation without complex configuration requirements.

2. Using CMake to build the **my-libc** shared library

    CMake offers a straightforward approach to building shared libraries, unlike most integrated development environments.

    Shared libraries serve as executable modules that provide common code across multiple executables, playing a vital role in modular software projects. These libraries eliminate code redundancy and enhance project maintainability. A prime example is glibc, a fundamental runtime library that provides shared functions like **printf** for C/C++ applications.

    Let's build a basic shared library containing a single function, **my-strlen**, to calculate input string lengths. The implementation simply iterates through each character until reaching \0, then calculates the character count by finding the difference between two pointer positions.

    Save this code as **~/my-utils/my-libc.c**:

```
/* my-strlen: A very simple ``strlen'' for learning openEuler */
    #include <stdio.h>
    int my_strlen(const char *s)
    {
        const char *p = s;
        while (*p++) ;
        return (p-s-1);
    }
```

To verify the shared library functionality, we will create **my-wc**, a minimal version of the **wc** command. Save this code as **~/my-utils/my-wc.c**:

```
/* my-wc: A very simple ``wc'' for learning openEuler */
1 #include <stdio.h>
2 #include <string.h>
3 int my_strlen(const char *s);
4 int main(void)
5 {
6     char *line = NULL;
7     size_t cap = 0;
8     ssize_t len = 0;
9     int lines = 0, words = 0, chars = 0;
```

```
10    while ((len = getline(&line,&cap, stdin)) != -1){
11        chars += my_strlen(line);
12        lines++;
13    }
14    printf("%8d%8d\n", lines, chars);
15    return 0;
16 }
```

The **my-wc** tool processes text from standard input, leverages **my_strlen** to count characters, and displays both line and character counts.

Update **CMakeLists.txt** to incorporate **my-libc.c** and **my-wc.c** into the **my-utils** project:

```
cmake_minimum_required(VERSION 2.9)
project(my-utils)
add_executable(my-nl my-nl.c)
add_executable(my-wc my-wc.c)
add_library(my-libc SHARED "my-libc.c")
target_link_libraries(my-wc my-libc)
INSTALL(TARGETS "my-nl" RUNTIME DESTINATION bin)
INSTALL(TARGETS "my-libc" LIBRARY DESTINATION lib)
```

The configuration remains minimal yet clear, defining the **my-libc** shared library target and establishing the link between **my-wc** and **my-libc**. Run the **cmake**, **make**, **cat**, and **my-wc** commands sequentially to see results:

```
    [ict@openEuler24 build]$ cmake .. && make && cat /etc/
os-release | ./my-wc
    --Configuring done
    --Generating done
    --Build files have been written to: /home/ict/
my-utils/build
    ... ...
    [ 66%] Built target my-libc
    ... ...
    [100%] Built target my-wc
           7       136
```

5.3 C/C++ Application Development

The **my-wc** output mirrors **wc** command results, though it lacks word-counting functionality. Readers can extend the program to include word-counting features.

The **ldd** command reveals shared library dependencies of **my-wc**, including **my-libc**. Linux maintains a standard naming pattern for shared libraries: "lib" prefix and ".so" (shared object) suffix.

```
[ict@openEuler24 build]$ ldd my-wc
        linux-vdso.so.1 (0x0000ffff979d5000)
        libmy-libc.so => /home/ict/my-utils/build/libmy-libc.so (0x0000ffff97977000)
        libc.so.6 => /usr/lib64/libc.so.6 (0x0000ffff977c8000)
        /lib/ld-linux-aarch64.so.1 (0x0000ffff97998000)
```

5.3.5 Automated Testing

CMake provides two approaches for automated testing, enabling developers to automatically build and run test cases for software validation and quality assurance.

The first method adds the **add_test** command to **CMakeLists.txt** for implementing simple tests. This command defines a test name and execution command, typically referencing a test executable previously created through **add_executable** or **add_library**. These tests can then be executed with **make test** or **ctest**.

The second method employs the standalone **ctest** tool for comprehensive testing, encompassing unit tests, performance tests, and integration tests. This approach offers enhanced flexibility with additional options, letting users select specific tests and configure test environments. **ctest** functions as the main CMake testing interface and seamlessly integrates with CI/CD systems for test automation.

Let's explore the simpler first approach using **my-wc** as an example.

Add these three lines to **CMakeLists.txt** to implement automated testing:

```
enable_testing()
add_test(test_my-wc sh -c "./my-wc < /etc/os-release" )
set_tests_properties(test_my-wc PROPERTIES PASS_REGULAR_EXPRESSION " 7 136")
```

The second line creates a test command that runs **my-wc** through sh with input redirection, while the third line establishes the test case parameters and output verification.

After regenerating the Makefile, execute the compilation, build, and test sequence:

```
[ict@openEuler24 build]$ cmake .. && make && make test
--Configuring done
--Generating done
--Build files have been written to: /home/ict/
my-utils/build
[ 66%] Built target my-libc
Consolidate compiler generated dependencies of
target my-wc
[100%] Built target my-wc
Running tests...
Test project /home/ict/my-utils/build
    Start 1: test_my-wc
1/1 Test #1: test_my-wc ....................... Passed
0.00 sec
100% tests passed, 0 tests failed out of 1
Total Test time (real) = 0.00 sec
```

Readers interested in expanding their knowledge can further explore CMake automated testing capabilities through additional resources.

5.3.6 Performance Optimization

1. GCC performance optimization
   GCC provides comprehensive performance optimization capabilities that developers can control through optimization flags to enhance program execution efficiency.
   GCC features four primary optimization levels, ranging from **-O0** (no optimization) to **-O3** (full optimization). Each level targets specific optimization goals:
   - **-O1** implements basic optimizations without increasing compile time significantly. It performs constant folding and dead code elimination, reducing executable size and build time.
   - **-O2**, the recommended level, builds upon **-O1** optimizations and adds features like constant propagation, basic block reordering, and loop unrolling to enhance runtime performance.
   - **-O3** includes all **-O2** optimizations plus advanced features such as function inlining, loop optimization, and automatic vectorization. These enhancements particularly benefit computationally intensive programs.
     GCC also offers additional optimization options like **-fPIC** for position-independent code, **-fPIE** for position-independent executables, and **-fno-inline** to disable function inlining. Developers can combine these options to meet specific performance requirements.

2. Valgrind error detection
   Valgrind functions as an essential debugging and performance analysis toolkit. It provides comprehensive tools for analyzing memory, cache, stack, and multi-threading issues to improve program reliability.
   The toolkit comprises seven specialized tools: a memory error detector, two thread error detectors, a cache and branch prediction analyzer, a call-graph generator with cache analysis, and two heap analyzers. Valgrind detects memory leaks, uninitialized memory usage, and invalid memory operations. It analyzes program execution flow, identifies performance bottlenecks, evaluates cache utilization, detects thread synchronization issues, and monitors heap allocation.
   Here is an example using Valgrind to detect memory errors in **my-nl**:

```
[ict@openEuler24 build]$ valgrind --leak-check=summary ./my-nl < /etc/os-release
==45950== Memcheck, a memory error detector
==45950== Copyright (C) 2002-2017, and GNU GPL'd, by Julian Seward et al.
==45950== Using Valgrind-3.16.0 and LibVEX; rerun with -h for copyright info
==45950== Command: ./my-nl
... ...
==46032== LEAK SUMMARY:
==46032==    definitely lost: 120 bytes in 1 blocks
==46032==    indirectly lost: 0 bytes in 0 blocks
==46032==      possibly lost: 0 bytes in 0 blocks
==46032==    still reachable: 0 bytes in 0 blocks
==46032==         suppressed: 0 bytes in 0 blocks
==46032== Rerun with --leak-check=full to see details of leaked memory
... ...
```

The analysis reveals a memory leak in **my-nl**. After reviewing the **getline** function requirements, adding this code after the **while** loop eliminates the leak:

```
if (line) free(line);
```

Note: The glibc-debuginfo package must be installed through **dnf** on default openEuler systems before you can run these commands.

3. **gprof**
   gprof is a robust performance analysis tool in GNU systems, designed specifically for analyzing C, C++, Pascal, and Fortran programs. The tool proves

invaluable for optimizing code, enhancing runtime efficiency, and identifying performance bottlenecks.

By sampling program counter values during execution, **gprof** pinpoints CPU-intensive sections of code. It tracks comprehensive function call metrics, including invocation counts and execution times. The tool produces two key outputs: a flat profile detailing function call frequencies and CPU time consumption, and a call graph illustrating function interdependencies with timing data.

To profile a program with **gprof**:

1. Compile with specific flags (like **-pg**) to embed profiling instrumentation.
2. Run the program to generate a **gmon.out** performance data file.
3. Run **gprof** to analyze the data file and extract function call metrics.

Important limitations: **gprof** primarily measures CPU usage and may not accurately detect I/O bottlenecks. In multi-threaded applications, it typically captures performance data only from the main thread. Understanding these constraints helps ensure appropriate use of the tool.

5.3.7 Project 5-2: my-utils Toolbox

Building upon the **my-nl** and **my-wc** utilities covered earlier, implement a new **my-tee** utility. Base it on the **/usr/bin/tee** command to provide core functionality: read data from standard input, write it to specified files, and simultaneously copy it to standard output.

Extend the utilities by implementing command-line options through the **getopt** function to expand their feature set.

Use CMake to automate the build process across all utilities and develop comprehensive automated tests.

5.4 Portability Development and Docker Container Deployment

Software portability is the ability of software to transition between different environments. Its key aspects include adaptability, coexistence, replaceability, and ease of installation. Portable software runs on various platforms, adapting to diverse hardware architectures and OSs. This reduces development costs, enhances user experience, and promotes cross-platform usage.

Linux offers a highly favorable environment for portability development. Linux itself is highly portable, running on nearly all common hardware platforms and improving the hardware adaptability of user applications. Adherence to POSIX standards provides a foundation for cross-platform development. The POSIX-compliant kernel, system calls, and system libraries of Linux ensure consistency

5.4 Portability Development and Docker Container Deployment

across different systems for tools like the shell and GCC, enhancing the portability of both the development tools and the resulting applications. Furthermore, Linux supports native applications like Docker containers, enabling high-performance and portable development and deployment, further bolstering the portability of these environments.

It is important to note that portability does not guarantee a program will run on any computer without modification. Instead, it means programs require minimal changes to adapt to new environments. Good portability simplifies the process of adapting existing programs to new hardware and software.

5.4.1 POSIX Portability

POSIX represents a set of UNIX OS interface standards established by IEEE, widely referenced as POSIX standards in engineering practice.

The standard carries the official designation IEEE Std 1003 or ISO/IEC/IEEE 9945. POSIX.1 (IEEE Std 1003.1) stands as the most recognized version, serving as the core standard that defines essential OS interfaces. POSIX specifies mandatory standard interfaces for OSs, encompassing system calls, library functions, shells, and command-line tools. These interfaces ensure consistent behavior across UNIX-like OSs, enabling developers to build portable applications using reliable tools and libraries. This standardization reduces development and maintenance costs while enhancing software reusability and reliability.

POSIX initially aimed to bridge the gaps between different UNIX-like OSs and ensure interoperability. Its scope expanded significantly with the emergence of the GNU project and Linux [17].

Linux maintains strict POSIX compliance, which grants it strong portability and compatibility characteristics, establishing a robust foundation for cross-platform software development. Through its POSIX-compliant development tools and libraries, Linux ensures applications built on its platform remain compatible with other POSIX-compliant OSs.

(1) Shell portability

Shell stands as a vital component of UNIX-like OSs and a cornerstone of POSIX standards, exhibiting portability through both interactive usage and script programming.

sh, the original UNIX shell, evolved into the foundation for POSIX standards through its streamlined syntax and powerful programming capabilities. Its consistent presence and behavior across POSIX-compliant systems let users interact with sh in a uniform manner. Scripts written in sh execute across different systems with minimal adjustments while maintaining consistent behavior.

Though sh lacks features like command history, command aliases, and arithmetic operations, it remains integral to all UNIX-like OSs as a POSIX-mandated tool. It maintains widespread use in system administration and script development. openEuler includes hundreds of POSIX shell scripts within the **/bin** directory.

Bash, another widely adopted POSIX-compliant shell, implements numerous POSIX-standard features. It supports standard command syntax and semantics, including file name wildcards, command substitution, and pipes. Bash incorporates POSIX-compatible built-in commands and utilities such as **echo**, **test**, and **expr**. This adherence to POSIX standards enables Bash's portability, reliability, and capability, ensuring scripts execute consistently across OSs.

(2) Basic command portability

POSIX standards establish comprehensive specifications for basic commands and their behaviors, encompassing detailed requirements for options and parameters. These commands maintain consistency and functionality across all POSIX-compliant OSs.

Common Linux commands adhere to POSIX standards: file operations (**ls**, **cd**, **pwd**, **cp**, **mv**, **rm**, **cat**), process management (**top**, **ps**, **kill**), and text processing (**cut**, **sort**, **find**, **grep**, **tr**, **sed**, **awk**). POSIX standards precisely define each command and tool to guarantee uniform operation across UNIX-like OSs.

These commands demonstrate predictable behavior, enabling developers to work seamlessly across POSIX OSs without learning new commands, thus creating a consistent development environment.

(3) Programming interface portability

POSIX standards define unified programming interfaces that abstract underlying OS details, providing consistent behavior and standardized interfaces independent of specific platforms.

The POSIX programming interface includes system interfaces, C library functions, fundamental data types, and constants. System interfaces provide low-level access to kernel functionality, managing processes, files, network communication, threads, and synchronization. C library functions extend system calls with higher-level capabilities for string manipulation and math operations.

Common programming interfaces include:

- System interface functions: **open**, **close**, **read**, **write**, **fork**, **exec**, **wait**, **exit**, **socket**
- C library functions: **printf**, **scanf**, **strlen**, **strcpy**, **strcmp**, **rand**, **srand**
  These C interfaces implement core functionality for file I/O, process control, file operations, and network programming.

> Open source tools like Cygwin and MSYS2 enable POSIX compatibility on Windows, facilitating Linux application portability.

5.4.2 C/C++ Portability

C/C++ languages possess inherent portability, enhanced by glibc, the Linux C runtime library, for application development.

glibc implements POSIX-compliant interfaces. These specifications define essential OS interfaces for applications, covering file operations, process control, and IPC. Through glibc implementation, C applications achieve compatibility across POSIX-compliant systems.

Beyond POSIX compliance, glibc delivers additional capabilities through its dynamic linker, thread library, and math library, optimizing application performance and development efficiency.

Licensed under the GNU Lesser General Public License (LGPL) as part of the GNU project, glibc enables free use and modification. It serves as the primary C runtime library for many Linux distributions and underpins numerous open source projects. Its widespread adoption and ongoing maintenance establish glibc as a cornerstone library in Linux systems.

The example below illustrates a minimal **cat** utility using system call interfaces, reading from standard input or a specified file and outputting to standard output.

```
/* my-cat: A very simple ``cat'' for learning openEuler */
1 #include <stdio.h>
2 #include <unistd.h>
3 #include <fcntl.h>
4 int main(int argc, char * argv[])
5 {
6     char buf[1024];
7     int fd, nbytes;
8     int rc = 0;
9     fd=(argc < 2) ? STDIN_FILENO : open(argv[1], O_RDONLY);
10    do {
11        nbytes=read(fd, buf, sizeof(buf)); // Read data from source file.
12        if (nbytes < 0) {
13            perror("read"); rc = -1; break;
14        }
15        write(STDOUT_FILENO, buf, nbytes); // Write read data to standard output.
16    } while (nbytes);
17    close(fd);
18    return rc;
19 }
```

This C program employs the **read** and **write** system interface functions for file operations. While functional on POSIX-compliant systems, it fails on Windows platforms.

For improved portability, developers should utilize ANSI/ISO C standard library functions such as **fread** and **printf**. This approach ensures compatibility across all systems supporting the C standard library, as shown in the **my-nl** implementation.

5.4.3 Docker Container Portability

Docker containers deliver portable development environments and cross-platform deployment capabilities.

Docker, an open source Linux application container engine, empowers developers to package applications with dependencies into portable containers deployable across Linux and Windows platforms. Built on the LXC technology, Docker ensures consistent container behavior across OSs, guaranteeing application portability.

Docker container environments excel through multiple advantages. They enable swift creation of uniform development environments, package runtime environments for instant deployment, and leverage kernel-level virtualization for near-native performance. A single machine can host thousands of containers, which run seamlessly across physical hardware, virtual machines, and cloud platforms supporting Docker.

This section examines the creation of Docker container-based development environments and introduces a unified, portable approach to development and deployment.

(1) Core Docker concepts

Docker revolves around three core concepts: images, containers, and registries. Images form the cornerstone of Docker operations. Each image functions as a read-only template for creating Docker containers, comprising multiple file system layers, application code, and runtime environments. Dockerfile specifies the build instructions for Docker images through a script that defines application environments, dependencies, and configurations.

Containers represent running instances derived from images, with capabilities for starting, stopping, and removal. Each container executes in isolation, ensuring platform security. Think of a container as a streamlined Linux environment featuring root privileges, process space, user space, and network space, plus the applications it hosts.

Repositories act as centralized image storage platforms, available in both private and public formats. These platforms enable users to push and pull images, facilitating image distribution and management.

(2) Development environment setup

Setting up a Docker container-based development environment involves three key steps: Docker installation, image creation, and container deployment. This

5.4 Portability Development and Docker Container Deployment

section demonstrates the process using the **my-utils** toolbox as an example. For comprehensive Docker instructions, see the official documentation or online resources.

On openEuler, Docker installation and execution require just a few commands.

```
[ict@openEuler24 ~]$ sudo dnf install -y docker
[ict@openEuler24 ~]$ sudo systemctl enable --now docker
[ict@openEuler24 ~]$ sudo docker run hello-world
Unable to find image 'hello-world:latest' locally
latest: Pulling from library/hello-world 478afc919002:
Pull complete
  Digest: sha256:4bd78111b6914a99dbc560e6a20eab57ff6655aea4a80c50b0c5491968cbc2e6
  Status: Downloaded newer image for hello-world:latest
  Hello from Docker!
  This message shows that your installation appears to be working correctly.
```

The initial command installs Docker software, followed by launching the Docker system service—a topic covered extensively in Chap. 8. The final command executes a minimal test container. On first run, Docker automatically fetches the image from the repository, launches the container, executes the program, and terminates, confirming proper Docker operation.

While repository images serve well for testing purposes, development environments typically demand customized images tailored to specific project requirements.

Docker facilitates image creation through a script-based approach, enabling developers to easily customize and modify development environments.

The **my-utils** project requires only **gcc** and **cmake**. Create a **~/docker/Dockerfile.dev** file with these contents:

```
FROM openeuler/openeuler:24.03-lts-sp2
RUN dnf update -y && dnf install -y gcc gcc-c++ make cmake
```

Execute the following commands in the **~/docker/** directory to build a custom development image based on the **openeuler:24.03-lts-sp2** base image.

```
[ict@openEuler24 docker]$ sudo docker build -t ict/oe-
dev -f Dockerfile.dev .
   SSending build context to Docker daemon 2.048kB
   Step 1/2 : FROM openeuler/openeuler:24.03-lts-sp2
   22.03-lts-sp2: Pulling from openeuler/openeuler
   ... ...
   Step 2/2 : RUN dnf update -y && dnf install -y gcc
make cmake
   ---> Running in 5cc3a0770512
   ... ...
   Successfully built 0300598f1428
   Successfully tagged ict/oe-dev:latest
```

Upon successful creation of the **ict/openeuler24** image, run **sudo docker images** to inspect image details. This image serves as a template for creating multiple containers. Launch a container named **oe-dev** with the following command.

```
[ict@openEuler24 docker]$ sudo docker run -tid --name=oe-
dev -hostname=oe-dev \
   > -v /home/ict/my-utils:/my-utils ict/oe-dev
   a4d881bf004b3225a6795fdc269753911d5ca52d7652c23327b64b
f7f3512835
```

The container now runs successfully. The system hosting Docker, known as the host machine, maps its **/home/ict/my-utils** directory to the **/my-utils** directory of the container, enabling direct file access within the container. Monitor active containers using **sudo docker ps**.

Team members can replicate this development environment by building images from the same Dockerfile on their systems or sharing through image repositories, ensuring consistent development environments across the team.

(3) Development in containers

Access the container development environment by logging in with the following command.

```
[ict@openEuler24 ~]$ sudo docker exec -it oe-dev bash
   ... ...
   [root@oe-dev /]#
```

5.4 Portability Development and Docker Container Deployment

Upon successful root login to the container, execute **cmake** again to rebuild and test the project.

```
[root@oe-dev ~]# cd /my-utils/build/ && rm -rf &&
cmake ..
  --Configuring done
  --Generating done
  --Build files have been written to: /my-utils/build
[root@oedev build]# make && make test
... ...
Test project /my-utils/build
    Start 1: test_my-wc
1/1 Test #1: test_my-wc ....................... Passed
0.00 sec
    100% tests passed, 0 tests failed out of 1
    Total Test time (real) = 0.00 sec
```

The same Dockerfile enables rapid creation of identical development environments across Docker-enabled platforms—Linux, macOS, or Windows.

When environment modifications become necessary during development, create new images and containers by designing updated Dockerfiles based on the current image.

(4) Container-based application deployment

Container deployment offers superior efficiency and security, particularly for Linux-based network services. Containers encapsulate applications with their dependencies in isolated virtual environments on the host OS, protecting them from external interference. This isolation enhances stability and security while enabling swift deployment through simple container launches.

The container deployment process mirrors the development environment setup. Here is how to create a portable deployment environment using **my-nl** as an example.

my-nl requires minimal deployment—just copying a single executable to the container. Create **~/docker/Dockerfile.run** as follows:

```
FROM openeuler/openeuler:24.03-lts-sp2
COPY my-nl /usr/bin/
ENTRYPOINT ["/usr/bin/my-nl"]
```

This container executes **my-nl** automatically at startup. For complex applications, follow the development container pattern: install dependencies and deploy all software files to appropriate locations.

Create the deployment image on the target system with these commands:

```
[ict@openEuler24 docker]$ sudo docker build -t ict/oe-run -f Dockerfile.run .
Sending build context to Docker daemon 217.1kB
Step 1/3 : FROM openeuler/openeuler:24.03-lts-sp2
---> 52c91d8dab6f
Step 2/3 : COPY my-nl /usr/bin/
---> 2b19ef5fa93f
Step 3/3 : ENTRYPOINT ["/usr/bin/my-nl"]
... ...
Successfully built e7ed9dd9a256
Successfully tagged ict/oe-run:latest
```

Deploy by launching containers based on this new image. Test the containerized **my-nl** as follows:

```
[ict@openEuler24 ~]$ cat /etc/os-release | sudo docker run -i --rm oe-run
     1  NAME="openEuler"
     2  VERSION="24.03 (LTS-SP2)"
     3  ID="openEuler"
     4  VERSION_ID="24.03"
     5  PRETTY_NAME="openEuler 24.03 (LTS-SP2)"
     6  ANSI_COLOR="0;31"
```

This pipeline reads host machine files and feeds them to the standard input of the container. The container runs **my-nl** automatically, numbering lines and sending results to standard output.

The deployment image, viewable via **sudo docker images | grep ict/oe-run**, occupies just 200 MB. Even smaller base images work if they satisfy runtime requirements.

Alternatively, share deployment images through Docker repositories—local or remote. Target systems can then deploy instantly by downloading and running these images.

Docker container deployment for network services and complex applications delivers enhanced efficiency, security, and reduced infrastructure costs while ensuring cross-platform compatibility across Linux, macOS, and Windows.

5.4.4 openEuler Multi-Scenario Portability

openEuler adapts seamlessly to servers, cloud computing, and edge computing environments [7]. Its multi-scenario portability excels in these key areas:

- Hardware platform compatibility: openEuler runs across diverse hardware platforms and processor architectures—×86, Arm, MIPS—supporting Kunpeng, Phytium, and Loongson processors. This broad compatibility ensures optimal performance across varied computing environments.
- Distributed deployment capability: Through containerization technology, openEuler enables dynamic resource allocation and load balancing. Applications deploy flexibly across multiple nodes, maximizing resource utilization in cloud and edge computing scenarios.
- Customization: The open source nature of openEuler allows developers to optimize and tailor the system for specific use cases. This flexibility ensures the system meets precise requirements across diverse deployment scenarios.
- Community support: openEuler benefits from extensive technical expertise from the open source community. The community provides comprehensive tools and packages, streamlining the development of portable applications.
- Security: openEuler implements robust security mechanisms, including mandatory access control and encrypted communications. These features protect against threats and ensure data integrity across all deployment scenarios.

These combined attributes make openEuler highly adaptable, meeting the demands of diverse computing environments while maintaining security and performance.

5.4.5 Project 5-3: Cross-Platform Building of my-utils

Building on the openEuler container implementation of **my-nl**, this project challenges you to compile and deploy the enhanced **my-utils** from Project 5-2 on alternative Linux distributions or port it to Windows using standard C library functions.

Implement the development or deployment environment using VMs, cloud servers, or Docker containers. Choose from distributions like Ubuntu or CentOS for the target platform.

5.5 Learning in Open Source Communities

Learning programming through open source communities offers invaluable opportunities to study exemplary software projects, contribute to open source initiatives, and share developments rapidly with the global community.

Open source represents a software distribution model where source code remains publicly accessible, enabling users to use, copy, modify, and distribute it under specified licenses. This approach emerged from the free software movement, promoting collaborative software development and maintenance through community participation. Specific licenses govern the use and modification of open source software, safeguarding its fundamental principles of openness and accessibility [5].

The open source culture proved instrumental in the early adoption of UNIX. Following UNIX commercialization, the Free Software Foundation advanced the open source movement, which gained momentum through the development of the GNU project and Linux.

5.5.1 Linux and Open Source

The open source model operates on complete transparency, with all aspects visible in the source code.

Linux and open source maintain a symbiotic relationship. Linux exemplifies the power and benefits of open source at the OS level, while open source principles have driven the evolution and widespread adoption of Linux across enterprises and individual users. This collaborative approach has transcended Linux and open source software, emerging as a cornerstone of modern software development that propels industry innovation.

The open source ecosystem around Linux extends far beyond the kernel, encompassing distributions, desktop environments, and applications. Open source projects following these principles foster innovation through community collaboration, enabling swift issue resolution, vulnerability detection, and continuous improvement in both functionality and performance.

Linux serves as a foundation for building and running most open source projects, with many landmark initiatives closely integrated into its ecosystem. Developers benefit from exceptional software solutions such as glibc, the GNU C runtime library that forms the foundational API of Linux and sets standards for high-performance C code. Another example is gRPC, a high-performance Remote Procedure Call (RPC) framework from Google that utilizes HTTP/2 and Protocol Buffers, which has gained widespread adoption. These projects offer valuable development tools, architectural insights, and middleware components for integration, subject to licensing terms.

Novice developers gain access to well-architected, production-tested code through open source projects. The GNU Core Utilities (Coreutils) provide essential tools like **cat**, **nl**, and **wc** for file and data stream operations. The Linux kernel source code reveals sophisticated implementations of file systems, process management, and networking. Additionally, openEuler offers extensive shell scripting examples. These codebases serve as invaluable learning resources for beginners entering the field.

5.5.2 openEuler Community

openEuler stands as a freely available, open source Linux distribution that delivers a robust, secure, and scalable OS platform, engineered for modern ICT applications spanning cloud computing, big data, and AI.

The openEuler community functions as a global innovation hub, uniting developers and enterprises worldwide to advance next-generation OSs and ecosystems for the ICT era. Key contributors include industry leaders like Huawei and KylinSoft, which drive the development and adoption of the platform through collaborative efforts.

The community provides developers with comprehensive technical resources, enabling collaborative development, knowledge exchange, and technological advancement. Through active partnerships with other open source initiatives, openEuler facilitates cross-domain innovation and integration.

Readers interested in Linux and open source technologies can join the openEuler community to collaborate with global peers and contribute to shaping the future of open source software in the ICT landscape.

5.6 Summary

This chapter offers an in-depth analysis of the Linux development environment, encouraging practical exploration through hands-on experience.

Linux provides developers with a robust yet accessible development environment under POSIX standards. Users can work with consistent tools across platforms, process all text files—from source code to system configurations and logs—using uniform text stream methods, create portable automation scripts with streamlined syntax for POSIX-compatible systems, develop C/C++ applications using standardized and flexible build processes, and deploy portable development environments through Docker containerization.

openEuler maintains this development ecosystem while extending multi-scenario portability to emerging hardware architectures like Kunpeng for the ICT era. The openEuler community thrives as an innovation hub for emerging open-source software. Software development enthusiasts should participate in this global community to exchange knowledge and contribute to its growth.

While this chapter focuses on C/C++ development, Linux excels at supporting virtually all major programming languages, including Java and Python. Git and Docker represent essential native Linux tools that merit mastery, with detailed usage available in supplementary resources.

Reflection and Practice

1. Compare the strengths and limitations of Linux command-line text processing versus Windows-style desktop systems.

2. Master fundamental Vim operations.
3. Learn Git basics and apply them to source code management.
4. Examine shell script use cases and their programming paradigms versus the C language.
5. Develop **win2linux.sh** to strip carriage returns from Windows-edited text files.
6. Create a shell script for automated file backups by type.
7. Analyze the developmental distinctions between GCC and integrated development environments.
8. Implement a minimal **my-cat** utility in C on openEuler, featuring basic **cat** functionality, with CMake-based compilation, building, and testing.

Open Access This chapter is licensed under the terms of the Creative Commons Attribution-NonCommercial-NoDerivatives 4.0 International License (http://creativecommons.org/licenses/by-nc-nd/4.0/), which permits any noncommercial use, sharing, distribution and reproduction in any medium or format, as long as you give appropriate credit to the original author(s) and the source, provide a link to the Creative Commons license and indicate if you modified the licensed material. You do not have permission under this license to share adapted material derived from this chapter or parts of it.

The images or other third party material in this chapter are included in the chapter's Creative Commons license, unless indicated otherwise in a credit line to the material. If material is not included in the chapter's Creative Commons license and your intended use is not permitted by statutory regulation or exceeds the permitted use, you will need to obtain permission directly from the copyright holder.

Chapter 6
Embedded OS Development

Objectives

1. Understand embedded OS fundamentals.
2. Explore major embedded OSs.
3. Master Linux kernel tailoring and root file system development.
4. Comprehend the technical architecture of openEuler Embedded.

Modern breakthroughs in IoT, robotics, and AI have propelled embedded systems to the forefront of IT strategies. Early bare metal-based systems had limited hardware capabilities, designed primarily for simple tasks. These systems could only execute single-threaded programs, relying on a main loop and polling mechanisms, and lacked the reliability, concurrency, modularity, and scalability needed by modern workloads. This has sparked intense interest in advanced embedded systems and software technologies.

This chapter covers embedded OS fundamentals and mainstream options, Linux kernel customization and root file system development, and the technical architecture of openEuler Embedded.

6.1 Introduction to Embedded OSs

Breakthroughs in integrated circuits, wireless communications, and IoT have contributed to next-generation embedded systems, specifically in power and affordability. Embedded systems now run on efficient and reliable hardware, making it suitable for specific scenarios within distinct domains and with flexible hardware and software configurations.

Unlike general-purpose computers or servers, embedded systems target specific functions, running low computing resources and while meeting stringent requirements for power efficiency, functionality, reliability, cost-effectiveness, and compact design. Today's world teems with embedded systems, fueling everything from smartphones and wearables to smart appliances, autonomous vehicles, and drones in sectors like aerospace, mobile communications, healthcare, and autonomous driving.

An embedded OS manages hardware and software resources while coordinating concurrent activities in embedded devices. Though it shares core features with general-purpose OSs, it stands apart through its compact footprint, operational efficiency, and robust real-time performance [18].

In complex embedded systems, the OS proves indispensable. It amplifies system capabilities, streamlines development workflows, and delivers efficient, stable, and dependable performance across diverse applications in IoT and AI environments.

6.1.1 Software Architecture of Embedded Systems

The software architecture of embedded systems addresses specific hardware platforms and user requirements. As a vital component, it enables core system functionality. This architecture features solid-state storage requirements, premium code quality, high reliability, and robust real-time OS performance. The structure mirrors general computer software architecture with four distinct layers: driver, OS, middleware, and application, as illustrated in Fig. 6.1.

(1) Driver Layer
   This foundation layer interfaces directly with hardware, delivering drivers and low-level core support for the OS and applications. In embedded contexts, the board support package (BSP) handles system initialization after power-up, configuring essential hardware components like microprocessors, memory, interrupt controllers, DMA controllers, and timers. The layer encompasses three

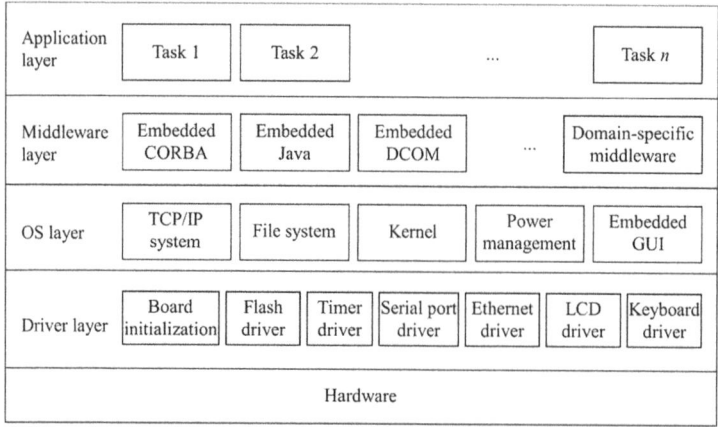

Fig. 6.1 Software architecture of embedded systems

program categories: board initialization, standard drivers, and application-specific drivers.

(2) OS Layer

The embedded OS delivers core functionality by managing resource virtualization and allocation, process scheduling, concurrent operation coordination, system administration tools, and proprietary application support. It ensures optimal system performance while maintaining security and reliability.

(3) Middleware Layer

Middleware facilitates application development through databases, network protocols, graphics support, and development tools. Key examples include MySQL, TCP/IP, and GUI frameworks.

(4) Application Layer

Embedded applications target specific domains to fulfill user requirements. Beyond meeting standard metrics for accuracy, security, and stability, these applications demand optimization to minimize resource usage and hardware costs.

Embedded system application development thrives across the ecosystem, with each application serving distinct purposes. Despite their compact nature, these systems demonstrate strong specialization. The rapid advancement of AI technology has expanded the role of embedded applications, particularly in scenarios requiring cloud-edge-device synergy.

6.1.2 Key Characteristics

Embedded OSs extend beyond general OSs. While retaining core functions like process scheduling, memory management, and interface control, they exhibit several distinctive features.

- Embedded systems excel in power efficiency, compact design, and specialized functionality. The embedded CPU integrates multiple PC card functions into a single chip, operating in purpose-built systems for specific user groups. This integration enables significant miniaturization of system design.
- System software resides in memory chips or microcontrollers, optimizing execution speed and reliability. The design demands efficiency in both hardware and software components, featuring streamlined systems and high-quality code. The OS integrates seamlessly with application software.
- These systems prioritize stability over user interaction. After initialization, embedded systems operate autonomously with minimal user intervention. This autonomy requires exceptional stability from the OS. Rather than providing direct operational commands, the system interfaces with user programs through system calls.
- Development relies on specialized tools and environments. Despite fluctuations in the broader technology sector, the embedded industry maintains robust growth,

achieving new benchmarks in practical application, system complexity, and operational efficiency.

6.1.3 Common Embedded OSs

Embedded OSs emerge from specific application needs, with each scenario demanding unique technical requirements. The embedded OS landscape encompasses over 40 distinct systems.

These systems fall into two main categories based on application:

- General-purpose embedded OSs: GNU/Linux, VxWorks, QNX, and Windows CE.NET
- Specialized embedded OSs: Android, iOS, Pocket PC, and Symbian

In control and communication domains where timing precision matters, real-time capability becomes essential. This capability ensures that system performance depends on both computational accuracy and result timing. System failure occurs when results fall outside specified time parameters. Every real-time application must execute tasks accurately within strict temporal constraints.

Based on real-time capabilities, these systems divide into:

- Non-real-time embedded OSs: target consumer electronics like mobile phones and set-top boxes. Examples include iOS, Android, and OpenHarmony.
- Real-time embedded OSs: serve control and communication sectors. Notable examples include μClinux, μC/OS-II, eCos, FreeRTOS, Mbed OS, RTX, VxWorks, QNX, NuttX, along with China-developed solutions like DJYOS, AliOS Things, Huawei LiteOS, RT-Thread, and SylixOS.

Let's examine several key general-purpose embedded OSs.

(1) VxWorks

VxWorks stands as a POSIX-compliant embedded RTOS, delivering hard real-time performance, high determinism, and reliability. It ensures predictable real-time responses and meets industry standards across aviation, defense, industrial, medical, automotive, consumer electronics, and networking sectors. Despite widespread adoption, it limits kernel customization and developer flexibility while carrying substantial licensing costs.

(2) QNX

QNX represents a distributed, embedded, scalable RTOS adhering to POSIX standards. This UNIX-like OS employs a microkernel architecture offering just four core services, resulting in an ultra-compact kernel (12 KB for QNX 4.0) and superior performance. While it provides extensive customization through comprehensive development tools and APIs, it demands advanced expertise, serves a limited user base, lacks community support for timely problem resolution, and requires significant licensing investment.

(3) Embedded Linux

Embedded Linux emerged as a revolutionary open-source, GPL-licensed system that has captured widespread attention in research and applications. This modified version of standard Linux preserves vast open-source resources while adapting to embedded system requirements. Though it lacks hard real-time capabilities, patches like PREEMPT_RT enable soft real-time features, making it ideal for applications with moderate timing demands.

(4) μClinux

μClinux (microcontroller Linux) offers a specialized embedded Linux solution. It maintains essential Linux features within a minimal kernel footprint. Designed specifically for processors without memory management units, it targets mid- to low-end embedded CPUs like STM32F103. However, it bypasses kernel preemption and provides basic real-time performance.

Given embedded compelling advantages of Linux in open-source accessibility and portability, we will explore its primary development methodologies.

6.2 Embedded Linux

Embedded Linux merges the Linux kernel and open-source components with embedded hardware platform portability to create a robust OS. Released under GPL and built upon UNIX design principles, it delivers exceptional stability, reliability, scalability, and portability. The system continues to gain traction in AI and IoT embedded applications, demonstrating significant growth potential [19].

Open-source innovations from the Linux community have spawned numerous successful embedded OSs, including Android for smartphones and openEuler Embedded for next-generation IoT deployments [20].

6.2.1 Embedded Linux Development Process

Embedded systems must meet stringent requirements for functionality, power efficiency, cost, and reliability due to their application-specific nature. Limited hardware and software resources typically prevent independent development capabilities, while post-release software updates and maintenance by users remain restricted. These constraints necessitate specialized development environments with dedicated tools for design, compilation, debugging, and testing, along with cross-development methodologies.

Embedded Linux development follows two primary approaches. The first leverages comprehensive distributions like Ubuntu, complete with root file systems and management mechanisms, serving complex applications such as the autonomous driving system of Tesla. The second starts from basics—the kernel and an empty root file system—ideal for simpler embedded scenarios. This fundamental approach forms the foundation of embedded Linux development, with its process outlined below.

(1) Setting up the Development Environment
Install a suitable GNU/Linux distribution on physical hardware or a VM. Configure network settings and install core development tools like Vim and CMake, along with platform-specific cross-compilation toolchains.
Configure tools for various system interfaces: Minicom for serial port communication and debugging output monitoring, NFS for file sharing between development and target systems, and JTAG tools for advanced system debugging.

(2) Building the bootloader
The bootloader initializes hardware, prepares the software environment, loads the OS kernel, and transfers control upon system startup. Due to diverse hardware configurations in embedded systems, no universal bootloader exists for all platforms. While U-Boot and vivi support many CPU architectures, they require customization for specific hardware setups.

(3) Porting the Linux kernel
The Linux kernel runs on virtually all CPU platforms. For new hardware platforms, developers can modify source code based on specifications. The flexibility of the kernel allows image sizes from hundreds of KB to tens of MB. Through careful tailoring and development, the kernel can be optimized for performance, stability, security, and cost efficiency.
Kernel customization involves configuring parameters and removing unnecessary features. Development focuses on creating new device drivers and kernel modules for specific hardware requirements.

(4) Building the root file system
Beyond the kernel, a complete OS requires multiple components: libc runtime library, editors, compilers, shell utilities, boot scripts, and configuration files. Tools like BusyBox, Buildroot, and Yocto facilitate root file system construction.
After establishing the base file system, add custom applications, and modify system configurations. Key configuration files in the **/etc** directory include **/etc/init.d/rc.S**, **/etc/profile**, and **/etc/fstab**, which control system startup behavior and file system mounting.

(5) Developing applications
Embedded systems exist to run specialized applications. Build these applications using cross-compilation tools, and deploy them to the target system. Complex applications integrate into the root file system, while simple ones can merge directly with the kernel.

(6) Verification and testing
All software components must be written to physical memory of the target system through appropriate peripheral interfaces. Conduct thorough testing of functionality, performance, and reliability before release.

6.2.2 Example 6.1: Embedded Development Environment Setup

This example demonstrates the setup of a basic embedded development environment, covering the installation of Linaro cross-compilation toolchain and QEMU emulator.

(1) Install basic compilation tools.
   Install essential development tools and dependencies for kernel and BusyBox compilation:

```
[ict@openEuler24 ~]$ sudo dnf install -y bc xz gcc gcc-c++ make cmake bison flex
   > ncurses-devel
```

(2) Install the cross-compilation toolchain.
   The Linaro toolchain serves as our example. Download packages from Linaro Releases based on specific cross-compilation requirements. The package name **gcc-linaro-7.5.0-2019.12-x86_64_aarch64-linux-gnu.tar.xz** indicates x86_64 for the development platform architecture and AArch64 for the target platform architecture.
   For openEuler 24.03 LTS, follow these steps:
   Download the Linaro package.

```
[ict@openEuler24 ~]$ wget http://releases.linaro.org/
components/toolchain/binaries/7.5-2019.12/arm-linux-gnueabi/
gcc-linaro-7.5.0-2019.12-x86_64_arm-linux-gnueabi.tar.xz
```

   Extract the package to designated directory.

```
[ict@openEuler24 ~]$ tar -xvf -C ~/
gcc-linaro-7.5.0-2019.12-x86_64_aarch64-
linux-gnu.tar.xz
```

   Add the Linaro directory to the Bash search path.

```
[ict@openEuler24 ~]$ export PATH=$HOME/
gcc-linaro-7.5.0-2019.12-x86_64_aarch64-
linux-gnu/bin\
   > :$PATH
```

Add the previous command to **~/.profile** for persistence across sessions.
Verify installation.

```
[ict@openEuler24 ~]$ aarch64-linux-gnu-gcc -v
```

(3) Install QEMU.

While QEMU can be installed directly via **dnf install -y qemu-system-aarch64**, source compilation offers customization options. For QEMU 5.0.0:
Install compilation dependencies.

```
[ict@openEuler24 ~]$ sudo dnf install -y bison flex glib2 glib2-devel libcap-ng-devel\
> libattr-devel pixman-devel SDL2-devel
```

Download and extract the QEMU source package.

```
[ict@openEuler24 ~]$ wget https://download.qemu.org/qemu-5.0.0.tar.xz
[ict@openEuler24 ~]$ tar -xvf qemu-5.0.0.tar.xz && cd qemu-5.0.0/
```

Configure, compile, and install QEMU.

```
# Configure arm64 emulation and virts support.
[ict@openEuler24 qemu-5.0.0]$ /configure --target-list=aarch64-softmmu,arm-softmmu,\
> aarch64-linux-user,arm-linux-user --enable-virtfs
# Build and install.
[ict@openEuler24 qemu-5.0.0]$ make -j8 && make install && make clean
```

Verify installation.

```
[ict@openEuler24 qemu-5.0.0]$ qemu-system-aarch64 --version
QEMU emulator version 5.0.0 (qemu-5.0.0-80.oe2203)
Copyright (c) 2003-2021 Fabrice Bellard and the QEMU Project developers
```

6.2　Embedded Linux

(4) Create a Docker environment.

Docker offers another approach to creating cross-compilation environments. While pre-built Linaro images exist, custom Dockerfile builds provide better flexibility and maintainability.

Build an image based on **openeuler/openeuler:20.03-lts-sp3** and include Linaro and QEMU. The Dockerfile content is as follows:

```
##
## openEuler for Embedded Linux System Development
##
FROM openeuler/openeuler:20.03-lts-sp3 as myesd
RUN dnf update -y && dnf install -y bc wget xz openssh-clients \
      gcc gcc-c++ make cmake bison flex ncurses-devel
## Temp image
FROM myesd as tools-builder
# linaro gcc
RUN wget http://releases.linaro.org/components/toolchain/binaries/7.5-2019.12/arm-linux-gnueabi/gcc-linaro-7.5.0-2019.12-x86_64_arm-linux-gnueabi.tar.xz
RUN tar -xf gcc-linaro-7.5.0-2019.12-x86_64_arm-linux-gnueabi.tar.xz -C /usr/local
# qemu-5.0.0
RUN dnf install -y glib2 glib2-devel pixman-devel libcap-ng-devel libattr-devel
#RUN wget
RUN wget https://download.qemu.org/qemu-5.0.0.tar.xz
RUN tar -xf qemu-5.0.0.tar.xz
RUN cd qemu-5.0.0 && ./configure --target-list=aarch64-softmmu,arm-softmmu,\
       x86_64-softmmu,\
     aarch64-linux-user,arm-linux-user --enable-virtfs --prefix=/usr/local/
       qemu-5.0.0 && \
    make -j4 && make install
## Final image
FROM myesd
MAINTAINER haojiash haojiash@qq.com
COPY--from=tools-builder/usr/local/gcc-linaro-7.5.0-2019.12-x86_64_arm-
       linux-gnueabi \
     /usr/local/gcc-linaro-7.5.0-2019.12-x86_64_arm-linux-gnueabi
```

```
    COPY --from=tools-builder /usr/local/qemu-5.0.0 /usr/
local/qemu-5.0.0
    ENV PATH="/usr/local/gcc-linaro-7.5.0-2019.12-x86_64_arm-
linux-gnueabi/bin:/usr/local/\
        qemu-5.0.0/bin:${PATH}"
    #ENTRYPOINT ["/usr/bin/bash", ""]\
```

Execute the following command in the Dockerfile directory to build the image:

```
[ict@openEuler24 ~]$ docker buildx build --platform linux/
amd64 -t
elsd-openeuler-amd64 .
```

The **--platform** option allows for creating x86_64 images on Arm platforms.

```
    [ict@openEuler24 ~]$ docker run -tid --platform=linux/
amd64 --name=elsd
--hostname=elsd \
    > -v ~/mnt:/mnt -p80:80 elsd-openeuler-amd64
```

Access the cross-compilation environment by logging in to the container. Share and maintain the Dockerfile to replicate the environment as needed.

6.3 Linux Kernel Customization and Development

Embedded systems require highly stable, secure, maintainable, and efficient software due to their specialized functions and hardware constraints. The Linux kernel, featuring a layered architecture and modular development mechanism, provides extensive customization options (Fig. 6.2), making it particularly suitable for embedded systems.

As the cornerstone of GNU/Linux, the Linux kernel manages hardware resources and provides unified abstract views and access interfaces [6]. It bridges hardware and software, controlling hardware devices while exposing interfaces to function libraries and applications through system calls. The kernel orchestrates application

6.3 Linux Kernel Customization and Development

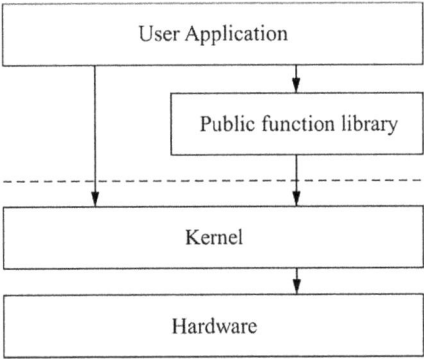

Fig. 6.2 Central role of the Linux kernel

scheduling, hardware resource allocation, and task execution, effectively separating applications from hardware platforms. This architecture enables superior system performance and versatile application development approaches. These advantages have facilitated its adoption across numerous hardware platforms, from routers and set-top boxes to smart watches and smartphones. With expanding hardware support and feature sets, the kernel source code has grown substantially, now surpassing 30 million lines.

> The massive codebase of the kernel ranks it among the most substantial and intricate open-source projects. From its modest beginning of under 88 files and 10,000 lines in version 0.0.1, it has grown tremendously. Developers can measure the current codebase using SLOCCount by running **sloccount.** in the kernel root directory.

Kernel customization involves removing unnecessary code from the standard source tree for specific embedded systems. This process yields multiple benefits: reduced kernel size, enhanced security, improved performance through faster boot times and lower memory consumption, and decreased vulnerability exposure. Configuration and compilation serve as the primary customization methods.

Kernel development focuses on creating system-specific components: hardware drivers, software drivers, and kernel-integrated applications. This work primarily involves driver module development and kernel-level software implementation.

Both customization and development require thorough knowledge of the Linux kernel architecture.

6.3.1 Introduction to the Linux Kernel

The Linux kernel architecture comprises five fundamental subsystems, each serving distinct core functions [15], as illustrated in Fig. 6.3.

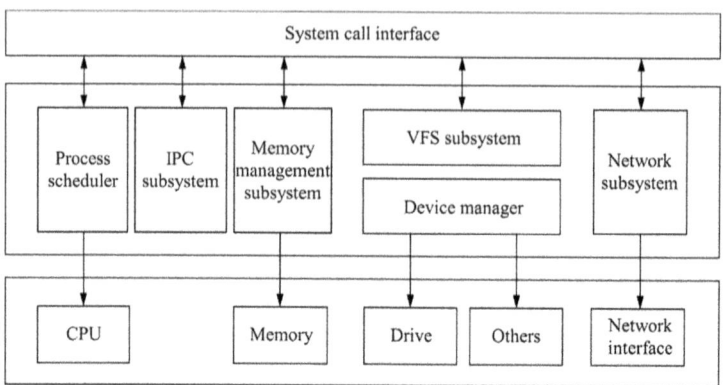

Fig. 6.3 Linux kernel architecture

- Process scheduler: manages CPU access allocation. It selects the most appropriate process for execution from the queue of runnable processes—those waiting solely for CPU time. Processes awaiting other resources are marked as non-runnable. The scheduler implements a straightforward priority-based algorithm for process selection.
- IPC subsystem: facilitates IPC without direct hardware management.
- Memory management subsystem: ensures secure memory sharing among multiple processes. It implements virtual memory, allowing programs to operate with combined code, data, and stack sizes beyond physical memory limits. The system retains actively used program blocks in memory while storing inactive ones on the drive, managing transfers as needed. This subsystem contains platform-agnostic components for process mapping and memory swapping, plus hardware-specific elements that interface with memory management units.
- VFS subsystem: provides a unified interface across diverse storage devices by abstracting hardware specifics. This subsystem handles numerous file systems—a key Linux feature—through two components: logical file systems (like ext2 and FAT) and device drivers for hardware controllers.
- Network subsystem: manages all network operations, including data transmission, reception, and routing, enabling communication with external devices and systems. It combines network protocol implementations with interface drivers.

The Linux kernel source code, available in the official repository, has reached version 6.5.6 as of early 2024, with an uncompressed size of 1.4 GB. The codebase consists of:

- Core kernel components encompassing the five main subsystems plus supporting functions like power management and system initialization
- Supplementary elements including self-contained libraries (which allow independent kernel compilation), firmware collections, and virtualization code (such as KVM)

6.3 Linux Kernel Customization and Development

- Support files covering build scripts, configuration settings, documentation, and licensing information

The Linux kernel source code maintains a hierarchical directory structure viewable with the **ls** command, as outlined in Table 6.1.

> Given the complexity of the Linux source code, navigating it effectively requires specialized tools. Consider using Linux Cross Referencer (LXR) or Source Insight on Windows for code exploration.

Kernel customization involves tailoring the source code by removing unnecessary components based on embedded system requirements. Kernel development extends this foundation by implementing new modules to meet specific system needs.

Table 6.1 Linux kernel source code directories

Directory/file	Description
include/	Kernel header files for module compilation
arch/	Architecture-specific code (Arm, AArch64, x86_64)
arch/mach	Board-specific hardware files
arch/include/asm	Architecture-specific assembly code
arch/boot/dts	Device tree specifications
init/	Boot initialization components
kernel/	Core functionality including process scheduler
mm/	Memory management subsystem
fs/	VFS subsystem
net/	Network subsystem (excluding network device drivers)
ipc/	IPC subsystem
block/	Block device drivers
sound/	Audio subsystem and drivers
drivers/	Device drivers (including network device drivers)
lib/	Kernel functions (such as CRC, FIFO, and MD5)
crypto/	Cryptographic functions
security/	Security modules including SELinux
virt/	Virtualization support (KVM)
firmware/	Third-party device firmware
samples/	Example implementations
tools/	Utilities for profiling and testing
Kconfig, Kbuild, Makefile, scripts/	Build system components
COPYING	License information
MAINTAINERS, CREDITS	Project contributors and maintainers
Documentation, README	Project documentation

6.3.2 Kernel Build Mechanism

The kernel build process enables kernel updates and customization across platforms, from desktop systems and servers to specialized embedded systems.

Linux kernel development relies on sophisticated configuration and compilation tools to facilitate module customization and feature implementation. With the codebase exceeding 30 million lines, the kernel demands efficient build management. The diverse deployment scenarios require flexible configuration options. To meet these challenges, developers created two core systems: Kbuild for building and Kconfig for configuration.

Kbuild, built on GNU Make, encompasses the top-level Makefile, architecture-specific Makefiles, Makefiles in subdirectories, and Makefiles in **scripts/**.

Kconfig manages kernel configurations through hierarchical Kconfig files and a root **.config** file. While Kconfig files define configuration symbols, **.config** specifies their values using three options:

- **Y**: Statically compiled into the kernel
- **N**: Excluded from building
- **M**: Built as loadable modules

The **.config** file serves as the central configuration repository, editable through both text editors and interactive interfaces (**make menuconfig** or **make xconfig**). Two methods exist to establish the initial **.config**:

- Import an existing configuration file, rename it to **.config**, and run **make oldconfig**.
- Generate a default configuration using **make defconfig**.

The build process combines the configuration data from **.config** with the build system to produce kernel images (such as **arch/x86/bzImage**). Available build targets can be viewed through **make help**.

The build environment requires a complete compilation toolchain. Working with different CPU architectures necessitates appropriate cross-compilation tools.

6.3.3 Example 6.2: Kernel Compilation and QEMU Emulation

This example demonstrates building an AArch64 architecture kernel of 'openEuler-22.09' using openEuler 24.03 LTS as development platform and validating it through QEMU emulation.

(1) Download openEuler 22.09 kernel source code.

Clone the **openEuler-22.09** branch from the openEuler repository with only the most recent commit:

```
ict@openEuler24 ~]$ git clone -b 'openEuler-22.09'
--single-branch --depth 1 \
   > https://gitee.com/openeuler/kernel.git kernel-22.09
```

6.3 Linux Kernel Customization and Development

(2) Configure the kernel.

The **kernel-22.09/arch/arm64/configs** directory contains various AArch64 configurations, including the baseline **openeuler_defconfig**.

Enter the **kernel-22.09** directory and generate the initial configuration:

```
[ict@openEuler24 kernel-22.09]$ make ARCH=arm64
openeuler_defconfig
```

This generates a **.config** file. Modify the configuration through the menu interface:

```
[ict@openEuler24 kernel-22.09]$ make ARCH=arm64
CROSS_COMPILE=aarch64-linux-gnu- menuconfig
```

(3) Compile the kernel.

Launch the build process with multi-threading:

```
[ict@openEuler22 kernel-24.09]$ make ARCH=arm64 CROSS_
COMPILE=aarch64-linux-gnu -j8
```

The **-j8** option enables eight parallel threads to accelerate compilation. Adjust this based on available CPU cores.

(4) Verify the build.

Check the generated **Image.gz** in the **arch/arm64/boot** directory:

```
[ict@openEuler24 ~]$ file ~/kernel-22.09/arch/arm64/boot
```

A missing file indicates compilation failure.

If the compilation fails, use **make clean**, **make mrproper**, or **make distclean** for cleanup, then restart the process.

Before deploying to AArch64 hardware, verify the **Image.gz** kernel file through QEMU emulation.

(5) Perform QEMU emulation.

QEMU provides hardware virtualization for testing. For **openeuler_defconfig** for the virt-4.0 platform, launch the emulation (Table 6.2):

```
[ict@openEuler24 ~]$ qemu-system-aarch64 -M virt-4.0 -cpu
cortex-a57 -m 1G \
    -kernel arch/arm64/boot/Image.gz -nographic
```

The emulation initially shows a kernel panic as expected, because the kernel lacks a root file system (Fig. 6.4).

The emulation initially shows a kernel panic as expected, because the kernel lacks a root file system. Exit QEMU by pressing **Ctrl+A** followed by **X**. For additional commands, press **Ctrl+A** then **H**.

Table 6.2 QEMU command options

Option	Function
-M	Device type selection
-cpu	CPU architecture specification
-m	Memory allocation
-kernel	Kernel image location
-nographic	Text-mode operation

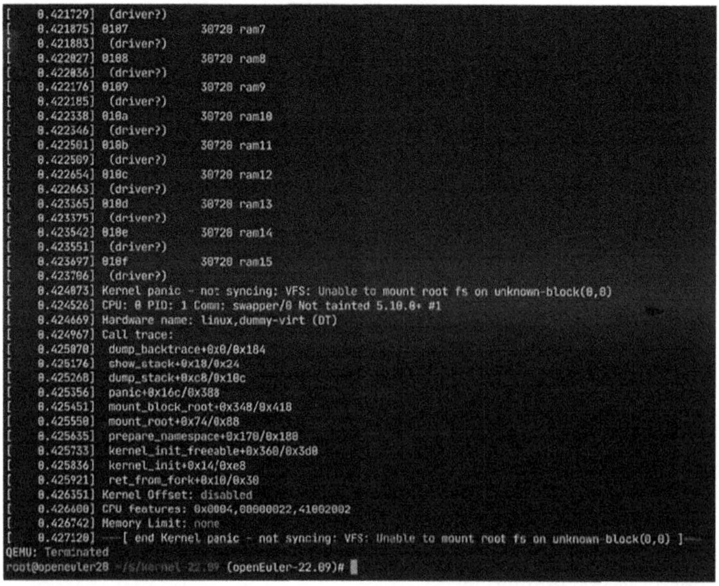

Fig. 6.4 QEMU kernel emulation

6.4 Root File System Development

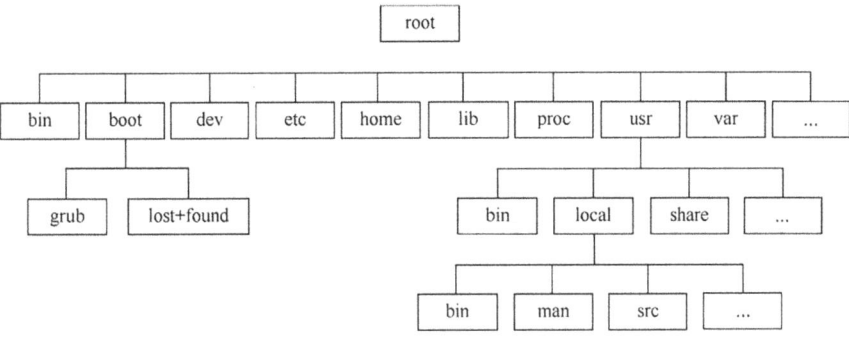

Fig. 6.5 Standard directory tree of a root file system

6.4 Root File System Development

The GNU/Linux root file system (rootfs) combines with the Linux kernel to create a complete OS.

As the first file system mounted during boot, the rootfs serves as the foundation for mounting additional file systems in its subdirectories. It encompasses essential components including system configurations, compilers, shared libraries, editors, system utilities, and shell environments, organized in a directory tree structure.

Figure 6.5 illustrates the standard directory tree of a root file system.

6.4.1 Introduction to BusyBox

BusyBox consolidates common system configurations and GNU tools into a single open-source project, featuring streamlined versions of roughly 400 essential commands to create a comprehensive environment for compact embedded systems. Bruce Perens developed BusyBox in 1996 for Debian installation disks, aiming to fit a bootable GNU/Linux system on a single floppy disk for installation and rescue purposes. The project now powers numerous embedded systems and Docker images.

BusyBox functions as a compact toolkit, earning its reputation as the "Swiss Army knife" of Linux. It packs common Linux utilities like **ls**, **cat**, **grep**, **find**, and **mount** alongside powerful tools such as **sed** and **awk**. With its built-in shell and PID 1-capable **init** command, BusyBox serves as a lightweight Coreutils alternative, particularly valuable in space-constrained embedded environments.

> The project achieves remarkable efficiency by implementing all command functionalities within a single executable under 1 MB. Through symbolic links, this executable provides multiple command interfaces, effectively simulating a full suite of utilities. By eliminating rarely used command options, BusyBox maintains minimal file size, driving its adoption across embedded systems, IoT devices, and cloud computing platforms.

BusyBox adopts a build process mirroring the Linux kernel, with three main phases: system configuration, compilation, and installation. Its configuration system precisely matches the Linux kernel menu interface, ensuring a familiar experience for developers.

6.4.2 Example 6.3: Root File System Compilation and QEMU Emulation

This example walks through building an AArch64 root file system on openEuler 24.03 LTS and validating it with QEMU emulation.

(1) Download BusyBox source code.

```
[ict@openEuler24 ~]$ cd ~ && wget https://busybox.net/downloads/busybox-1.35.0.tar.bz2
[ict@openEuler24 ~]$ tar -jxvf busybox-1.35.0.tar.bz2
```

(2) Configure and compile BusyBox.
   BusyBox features an interactive menu system for configuration, with space bar toggling options, as shown in Fig. 6.6.

```
[ict@openEuler24 ~]$ cd busybox-1.35.0/
# Use the default configuration.
[ict@openEuler24 ~]$ make ARCH=arm64 CROSS_COMPILE=aarch64-linux-gnu- defconfig
# Configure in the menu system.
[ict@openEuler24 ~]$ make ARCH=arm64 CROSS_COMPILE=aarch64-linux-gnu- menuconfig
```

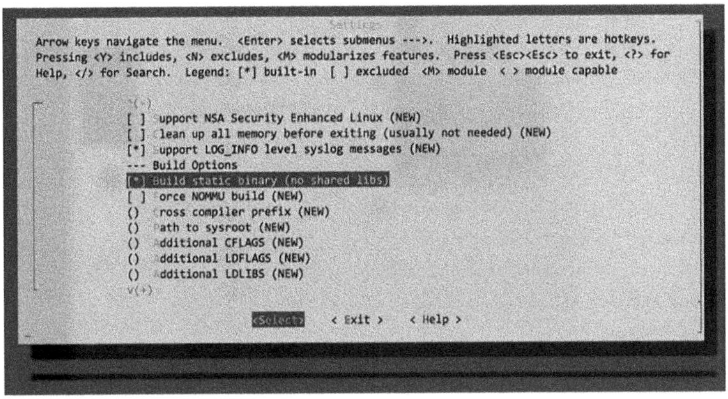

6.4 Root File System Development

Fig. 6.6 BusyBox configuration

Important: Enable **Settings > Build static binary (no shared libs)**.
Compile with 4 threads, installing the root file system to **busybox-1.35.0/_install**.

```
    # Set BusyBox compilation to static build.
    # Compile using 4 threads.
    [ict@openEuler24 ~]$ make ARCH=arm64
CROSS_COMPILE=aarch64-linux-gnu- -j4
    # Install compilation results to the target path.
    [ict@openEuler24 ~]$ make ARCH=arm64
CROSS_COMPILE=aarch64-linux-gnu- install
```

(3) Create the root file system.

```
    # Enter the QEMU emulation directory (create it first if
it does not exist).
    [ict@openEuler24 ~]$ cd ~/qemu/openEuler_embedded
    # Create the rootfs directory with home and lib
subdirectories.
```

```
[ict@openEuler24 ~]$ mkdir -p rootfs/{home,lib}
# Copy BusyBox-built root file system contents to rootfs.
[ict@openEuler24 ~]$ cp -af ~/busybox-1.35.0/_
install/* rootfs/
# Copy runtime libraries to rootfs/lib.
[ict@openEuler24 ~]$ cp -af ~/
gcc-linaro-7.5.0-2019.12-x86_64_aarch64-linux-gnu/\
> aarch64-linux-gnu/libc/lib/*.so* rootfs/lib/
# Strip dynamic libraries to reduce file size.
[ict@openEuler24 ~]$ aarch64-linux-gnu-strip
rootfs/lib/*
```

Create **rootfs/init** with this minimal startup script, which defines the entry point for application calls after boot. This simple file outputs a welcome message and calls the standard shell as the interactive interface:

```
#!/bin/sh
echo Welcome to mini_linux
exec /bin/sh +m
```

Add the execute permission:

```
[ict@openEuler24 ~]$ chmod +x rootfs/init
```

Package the file system into an image using **find**, **cpio**, and **gzip** connected by pipes:

```
[ict@openEuler24 ~]$ cd rootfs && find . -print0 |
cpio --null -ov --format=newc | \
> gzip -9 > ../rootfs.gz
```

(4) Perform QEMU emulation.
    Launch the complete embedded system by combining this root file system with the kernel from Example 6.2:

```
[ict@openEuler24 ~]$ qemu-system-aarch64 -M virt-4.0 -cpu
cortex-a57 -m 1G -kernel \
> ~/kernel-22.09/arch/arm64/boot/Image.gz -initrd \
> ~/qemu/openEuler_embedded/rootfs.gz -nographic
```

Figure 6.7 shows the resulting interface.

This demonstration covers essential BusyBox-based root file system customization and QEMU validation. While the system includes only basic tools, developers can add custom applications through cross-compilation to create application-specific embedded systems.

For more sophisticated needs, consider Buildroot for complex root file systems or Yocto for full distribution builds.

6.5 openEuler Embedded

openEuler Embedded represents a specialized version of openEuler designed for embedded scenarios. It pioneers next-generation embedded system software platforms and marks a notable advancement in GNU/Linux development [7].

The platform maintains code-level alignment with other openEuler versions regarding kernel and software package versions. It diverges primarily in embedded-specific aspects: kernel configurations, software package selections, feature patches, core capabilities, and build workflows.

Modern embedded systems operate in a dual-track environment. Advanced hardware now supports sophisticated OSs like Linux, while applications demand

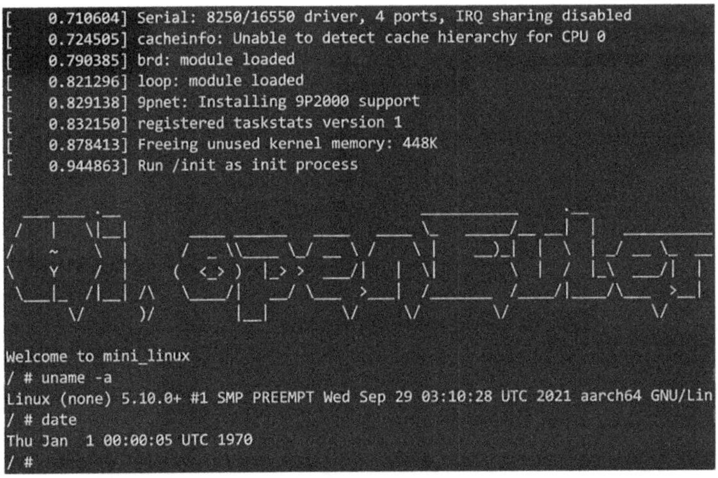

Fig. 6.7 Embedded OS emulation with the root file system

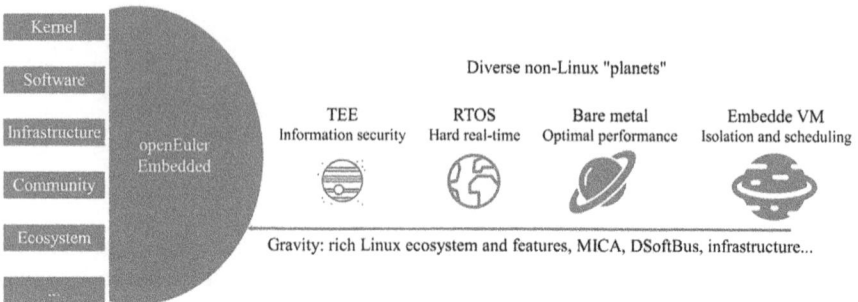

Fig. 6.8 openEuler Embedded ecosystem

increasingly complex features including connectivity, AI, and dynamic updates. These requirements typically necessitate robust OSs like Linux. This expansion has pushed Linux into previously unexpected domains, including sensors, industrial control, and aerospace. However, embedded systems face persistent constraints in resources, power consumption, real-time performance, reliability, and security—challenges undiminished by increasing system sophistication. The inherent complexity of Linux often struggles with these limitations, whereas lightweight alternatives like RTOS and bare metal implementations prove more effective.

openEuler Embedded addresses these challenges through a comprehensive Linux-centered software platform. Figure 6.8 illustrates its solar system architecture: Linux functions as the central star, delivering extensive ecosystem support and core capabilities. Surrounding runtime planets provide specialized functions—RTOS delivers hard real-time processing, the trusted execution environment (TEE) runtime ensures security, the bare metal runtime maximizes performance, and embedded VMs enable runtime isolation and scheduling. The platform leverages the Linux ecosystem, mixed-criticality systems, DSoftBus, and infrastructure to seamlessly integrate these runtime components into a cohesive system.

6.5.1 Technical Architecture and Key Features

The overall architecture of openEuler Embedded comprises several key components [21], as illustrated in Fig. 6.9.

(1) Hardware ecosystem

The platform primarily supports AArch64 and x86-64 architectures, with compatibility for hardware platforms including RK3568, Hi3093, Raspberry Pi 4 Model B, and x86-64 industrial computers. Initial support extends to AArch32 and RISC-V architectures through QEMU emulation, with ongoing ecosystem expansion.

6.5 openEuler Embedded

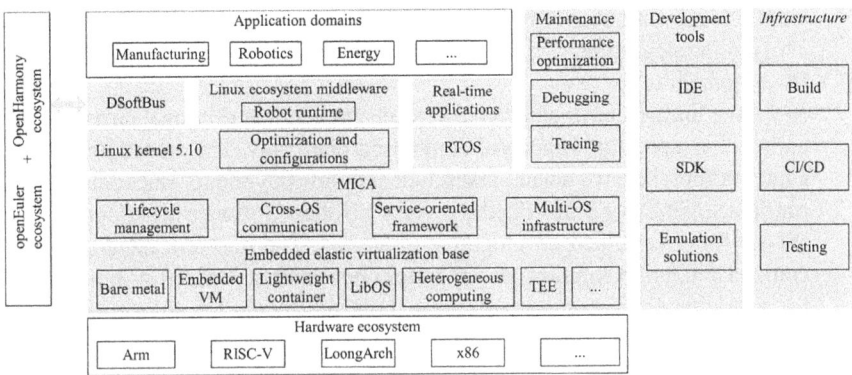

Fig. 6.9 openEuler Embedded architecture

(2) Embedded elastic virtualization base

This foundation enables concurrent operation of multiple OSs/runtimes on multicore SoCs through various implementations: bare metal, embedded VMs, lightweight containers, LibOS, heterogeneous computing, and TEE. Each implementation offers distinct advantages—bare metal maximizes performance, and embedded VMs enhance isolation and protection, while lightweight containers deliver superior flexibility and ease of use.

(3) MICA framework

Built atop the elastic base, the mixed criticality (MICA) framework is a unified framework that abstracts underlying implementation differences. This enables seamless mixed deployment of Linux with other OSs/runtimes, leveraging multicore capabilities to combine Linux versatility with RTOS specialization for flexible development and deployment.

(4) High-quality Linux kernel

The platform centers on Linux 5.10, aligned with other openEuler editions and supported for 6 years. Both kernel and package development maintain unified codebase progression across scenarios, currently encompassing over 250 packages with plans for expanded support.

(5) RTOS integration

To meet demands for reliability, real-time performance, and security, the platform integrates multiple RTOS options including Zephyr, RT-Thread, and UniProton, enabling flexible deployment combinations.

(6) DSoftBus

The openEuler and OpenHarmony communities have forged a strategic partnership to integrate DSoftBus into openEuler Embedded. This integration enables seamless device interconnection across both ecosystems. OpenHarmony excels in interactive capabilities for smart terminals, IoT devices, and industrial systems, while openEuler delivers high reliability and performance for servers, edge computing, cloud infrastructure, and embedded systems. Through DSoftBus and related technologies, this collaboration amplifies the strengths of both platforms, generating enhanced value through ecosystem integration.

(7) Development tools

Resource limitations in embedded systems prevent conventional development approaches common to general computing platforms. This constraint necessitates comprehensive development tool support. Beyond its embedded Linux runtime, openEuler Embedded provides a robust software development kit (SDK) for streamlined development processes. The platform integrates specialized emulation solutions designed for openEuler embedded systems. Plans for a graphical IDE complement these tools, advancing toward a comprehensive development ecosystem.

(8) Maintenance framework

To address the challenges of debugging and optimization in resource-constrained embedded environments, openEuler Embedded implements a comprehensive maintenance framework. The framework encompasses specialized Linux debugging tools, performance optimization utilities, and tracing mechanisms. This integrated approach enables developers to effectively maintain and troubleshoot embedded systems despite hardware limitations.

(9) Build infrastructure

openEuler Embedded implements the Yocto build system tailored for embedded platforms, distinct from the Open Build Service (OBS) infrastructure used in server deployments. Despite achieving code-level sharing for kernels and packages, the build processes for openEuler Embedded and server editions differ substantially. This divergence necessitates separate build configurations, preventing direct application of existing openEuler package build rules to embedded contexts. While openEuler Embedded now supports more than 250 packages, recreating build configurations for the entire package ecosystem under Yocto would be inefficient. To address this challenge, openEuler Embedded is partnering across platforms to develop a universal build system capable of serving all deployment scenarios.

(10) Software ecosystem

The ecosystem continues to evolve through partnerships focusing on industrial control, robotics, and energy applications. The lightweight robot runtime integration in version 23.03 marks a significant advancement in these capabilities.

6.5.2 Building with oebuild

oebuild emerges as an open-source initiative from the openEuler Embedded ecosystem, designed to streamline development processes for openEuler Embedded [22]. While the embedded Linux industry relies heavily on Yocto for customized builds, including openEuler Embedded, Yocto presents substantial complexity and setup overhead despite its flexibility. oebuild addresses these challenges by dramatically simplifying the build workflow.

> For detailed oebuild implementation examples, see the official openEuler website.

6.5.3 Example 6.4: Build and Emulation of openEuler Embedded with QEMU

openEuler Embedded supports embedded systems across diverse scenarios, offering highly flexible image sizes. This example demonstrates QEMU emulation with a minimal image.

The example utilizes two key files: kernel image **zImage** and root file system image **openeuler-image-qemu-aarch64-xxx.rootfs.cpio.gz**.

You can either build these image files through the oebuild system or download them directly from the openEuler community.

Run QEMU with the following command:

```
[ict@openEuler24 ~]$ qemu-system-aarch64 -M virt-4.0 -m 1G -cpu cortex-a57 -nographic \
> -kernel zImage \
> -initrd openeuler-image-qemu-aarch64-xxx.rootfs.cpio.gz
```

Upon successful QEMU execution and login, the system presents the openEuler Embedded shell.

6.5.4 Embedded ROS Runtime

The robotics field, particularly service robots, has experienced rapid growth in recent years. ROS, an open-source meta-OS for robots, has gained widespread adoption across multiple sectors. However, traditional ROS implementations face significant limitations, including heavy dependencies on desktop distributions like Ubuntu. The integration of ROS1 into unmanned systems across various domains revealed several operational challenges, leading to the development of ROS2 to address modern robotics requirements and evolving OS ecosystems.

The embedded ROS runtime in openEuler Embedded enhances usability, reduces entry barriers, and strengthens embedded runtime capabilities through real-time

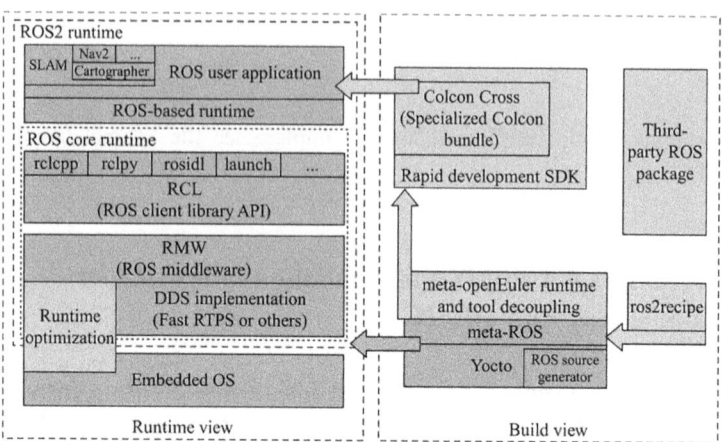

Fig. 6.10 ROS runtime architecture in openEuler Embedded

processing and system miniaturization. Figure 6.10 illustrates the ROS runtime architecture in openEuler Embedded, comprising runtime and build views, with the build view leveraging open-source meta-ROS.

The meta-openeuler layer handles dependency decoupling and embedded customization, focusing on onboard/runtime deployment separation for compilation, observation, and simulation tools. This layer manages rapid image integration and SDK generation.

The ros2recipe module converts third-party ROS source code to Yocto configuration files through a custom tool distinct from superflore of the ROS community, facilitating meta-openeuler image integration.

The rapid development SDK enables cross-compilation from third-party ROS source code to runtime applications.

The runtime optimization component interfaces with OS features, incorporating mixed-criticality deployment and RTOS bus capabilities to deliver real-time communication solutions for complex systems.

openEuler Embedded supports both standalone component building and integrated image building for ROS runtime components through oebuild. For qemu-ros building, execute:

```
[ict@openEuler24 ~]$ oebuild generate -p qemu-aarch64 -f
openeuler-ros -d
aarch64-qemu-ros
[ict@openEuler24 ~]$ oebuild bitbake
[ict@openEuler24 ~]$ bitbake openeuler-image-ros
```

6.5 openEuler Embedded

For Raspberry Pi building, use:

```
[ict@openEuler24 ~]$ oebuild generate -p raspberrypi4-64 -f
openeuler-ros -d
raspberrypi4-64-ros
   [ict@openEuler24 ~]$ oebuild bitbake
   [ict@openEuler24 ~]$ bitbake openeuler-image-ros
```

The built image can be verified through QEMU emulation.

6.5.5 Soft Real-Time Capabilities

Real-time performance forms the cornerstone of embedded systems, particularly in communication and control applications demanding rapid system response. The real-time domain encompasses two distinct categories: hard real-time and soft real-time.

- Hard real-time: These systems demand task completion by strict deadlines, where missed deadlines can trigger catastrophic failures. Autonomous vehicles exemplify this requirement—without hard real-time capabilities, even millisecond delays at high speeds could result in the vehicle traveling significant distances, potentially leading to severe accidents.
- Soft real-time: This approach implements real-time capabilities on a statistical basis. While quick response times remain important and delays should be minimized, the system does not enforce strict completion deadlines.

Linux real-time implementation follows two paths: internal kernel modification through the PREEMPT_RT patch and external implementation via a parallel real-time kernel (dual-kernel approach) exemplified by RTAI/Linux, now Xenomai. PREEMPT_RT excels through POSIX compliance and hardware independence, enabling straightforward application development and broad portability. While Xenomai boasts a lightweight kernel, it restricts standard C library usage, complicating development and limiting portability [20].

Performance testing reveals comparable worst-case latency metrics in user space for both approaches. PREEMPT_RT integration into the Linux mainline kernel brings significant advantages over Xenomai, including simplified development processes, extended product lifecycles, and streamlined maintenance requirements.

PREEMPT_RT implementation involves direct kernel source modification, activated by setting **CONFIG_PREEMPT_RT=y** during kernel compilation. The patch minimizes non-preemptible kernel sections, enabling prompt high-priority task preemption and reduced switching latency. It also optimizes locks, drivers, and various modules for enhanced responsiveness.

openEuler 24.03 LTS incorporates PREEMPT_RT patch support, delivering soft real-time capabilities. This enhancement, developed by the Industrial Control SIG with collaboration from Kernel, Embedded, and Yocto SIGs, now functions as an integral component in both openEuler 24.03 LTS Server and Embedded editions.

The process for creating soft real-time images follows the steps outlined below.

First, create a build configuration file in the oebuild working directory. Include the **-f openeuler-rt** option to enable soft real-time capabilities:

```
# AArch64
[ict@openEuler24 ~]$ oebuild generate -p qemu-aarch64 -f openeuler-rt -d
<build_arm64_rt>
# Raspberry Pi 4
[ict@openEuler24 ~]$ oebuild generate -p raspberrypi4-64 -f openeuler-rt -d
<build_rpi_rt>
# x86
[ict@openEuler24 ~]$ oebuild generate -p x86-64 -f openeuler-rt -d <build_x86_rt>
```

Next, navigate to the *<build>* directory and perform **openeuler-image** compilation:

```
[ict@openEuler24 ~]$ oebuild bitbake openeuler-image
```

To verify the successful activation of soft real-time features, check for the **PREEMPT_RT** identifier in the system information:

```
[ict@openEuler24 ~]$ uname -a
Linux openeuler ... SMP PREEMPT_RT Fri Tue 25 03:58:22 UTC 2025 aarch64 GNU/Linux
```

6.6 Summary

Embedded OSs are purpose-built for embedded systems, featuring high customization requirements and tight hardware-software integration. System porting is essential for specific hardware configurations, with modifications required even among products from the same brand and series. Tasks often necessitate significant system adjustments, and program compilation and deployment must integrate seamlessly with the system—a stark contrast to the straightforward software updates common in general-purpose computers.

This chapter explored fundamental concepts and variants of embedded OSs, emphasizing development methodologies for embedded Linux kernels and root file systems. It highlighted technical architecture and core features of openEuler Embedded as a next-generation embedded OS platform. Through practical examples using a cross-compilation environment on openEuler, it detailed Linux kernel development, root file system implementation, and oebuild construction techniques, including QEMU simulation verification examples.

The emergence of 5G technology and IoT applications drives the adoption of advanced embedded OS platforms like openEuler Embedded across AI-enabled embedded devices. This trend accelerates edge computing advancement and enables innovative ICT-based solutions.

Reflection and Practice

1. What distinguishes embedded OSs from general-purpose OSs?
2. Why has GNU/Linux become the dominant choice for embedded systems?
3. Set up an AArch64 cross-compilation environment on x86_64, and then configure, compile, and emulate a minimal kernel in QEMU. Document the process with screenshots, kernel size specifications, and custom characteristics.
4. Using the established cross-compilation environment, create a static build of a C-based Snake game, deploy it on a BusyBox root file system, and verify through QEMU emulation.
5. Deploy openEuler Embedded on a Raspberry Pi board and perform real-time testing for "openEuler Embedded for Raspi." Generate a comprehensive test report. For details, see openEuler community documents.

Open Access This chapter is licensed under the terms of the Creative Commons Attribution-NonCommercial-NoDerivatives 4.0 International License (http://creativecommons.org/licenses/by-nc-nd/4.0/), which permits any noncommercial use, sharing, distribution and reproduction in any medium or format, as long as you give appropriate credit to the original author(s) and the source, provide a link to the Creative Commons license and indicate if you modified the licensed material. You do not have permission under this license to share adapted material derived from this chapter or parts of it.

The images or other third party material in this chapter are included in the chapter's Creative Commons license, unless indicated otherwise in a credit line to the material. If material is not included in the chapter's Creative Commons license and your intended use is not permitted by statutory regulation or exceeds the permitted use, you will need to obtain permission directly from the copyright holder.

Chapter 7
Network Basics and Management

Objectives

1. Master the TCP/IP network model fundamentals.
2. Understand network management tool functions.
3. Apply network tools for basic network administration.

Our modern world is moving closer to pervasive networking and the Internet of Everything. TCP/IP networks represent the predominant networking paradigm, featuring a layered architecture that stands as a benchmark for industrial software design. Its smooth implementation on UNIX systems has played a pivotal role in Internet growth and catalyzed modern OSs to integrate extensive network connectivity features and management utilities.

This chapter explores the fundamentals and principles for TCP/IP networks, network management, and openEuler network management tools. This material is designed to improve your understanding of core networking concepts, openEuler network administration, and essential networking utilities. Our exploration also examines the approaches and implementation strategies to design and manage networks across PCs, embedded systems, and enterprise-grade servers.

7.1 TCP/IP Network Model

TCP/IP emerged in the 1970s through the work of two scientists for the Defense Advanced Research Projects Agency (DARPA): Vint Cerf and Bob Kahn, now recognized as the fathers of the Internet. The TCP/IP model features IP protocol which handles network layer addressing independently, enabling interconnectivity between networks running different underlying protocols [10]. A significant milestone occurred in 1981 when BSD implemented a high-performance TCP/IP protocol stack. This implementation led to TCP/IP becoming the standard protocol for ARPANET and an essential component of UNIX systems. By the early 1990s, the global TCP/IP-based Internet had taken shape. The proliferation of mobile computing and IoT has made TCP/IP networks ubiquitous in modern technology infrastructure.

TCP/IP encompasses multiple communication protocols that enable network interconnection and forms the Internet backbone. The vast scale of the Internet involves billions of devices exchanging massive amounts of data. Device communication requires multiple complex tasks: transmitting packets beyond local networks, routing them through extensive network infrastructure to reach destinations, and managing packet loss through detection and recovery mechanisms. Rather than creating a single, complex protocol to handle all these functions, the industry adopted a layered approach. Each protocol specializes in specific tasks, enabling focused development and optimization. This modular design allows different protocols to handle similar tasks, accommodating diverse requirements. The industry organized these protocols into layers based on their functions, creating the TCP/IP network model—a hierarchical framework where each layer handles distinct networking tasks [23]. Figure 7.1 illustrates this basic structure.

Host A and host B establish communication through the Internet. When an application on host A transmits data to host B, the data flows through multiple protocol layers following the solid arrows, with each layer processing it before it reaches the target program. Throughout this transmission journey, different layer protocols process the data while preserving its integrity by only adding or removing header

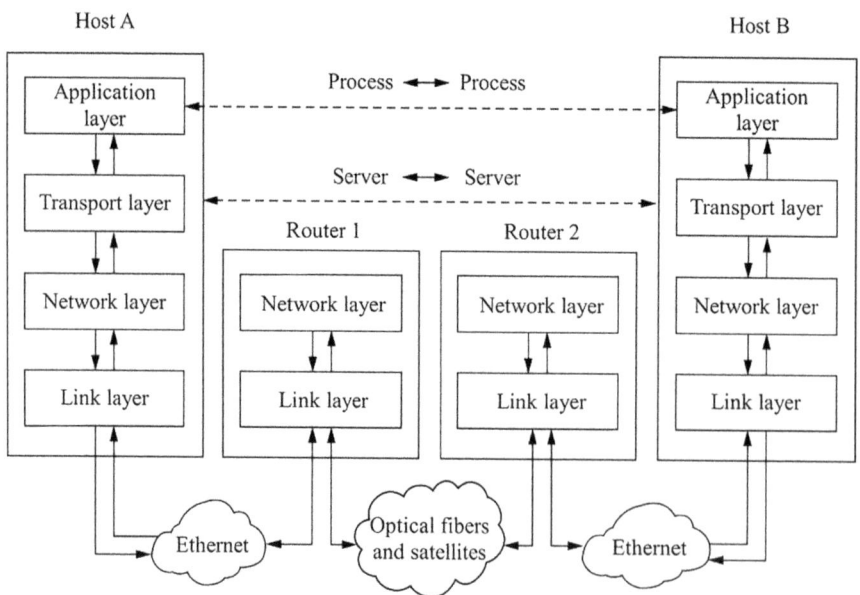

Fig. 7.1 Basic structure of the TCP/IP network model

information. For instance, when data exits an application on host A and moves through the transport layer, it grows in size as the transport layer header attaches. These additional headers enable network devices to perform essential functions like positioning and retransmission. Upon reaching host B, the protocol stack strips away these added headers, restoring the data to its original form.

This layered approach mirrors real-world systems like nationwide delivery networks. Consider a residential community as analogous to a computer—the local package pickup point functions like the transport layer protocol, focusing exclusively on distributing packages using phone numbers as identifiers and ensuring accurate delivery to recipients. The process of packaging items and attaching shipping labels reflects how network protocols append addressing information to data packets. The role of logistics companies, which handle bulk shipments between major warehouses before local distribution, parallels the function of the network layer: routing data to destinations based purely on addressing information, without concern for the final processing at the destination.

Attentive readers might observe that data packets traversing routers only pass through the network and link layers, rather than the complete network model stack. Routers function at the network layer and, similar to logistics companies, remain indifferent to packet contents, focusing solely on delivering packets to their designated addresses. This design eliminates the need for routers to process packets beyond the network and link layers.

Common Internet protocols operate across four distinct layers:

- Link layer: manages the physical transmission of data by encapsulating it into hardware-compatible frames for transmission through physical media like cables and optical fibers. It also handles frame extraction from received signals. These frames contain physical addressing information, such as media access control (MAC) addresses, for locating devices within local area networks (LANs). Ethernet represents a primary protocol at this layer.
- Network layer: orchestrates Internet routing and connectivity using IP addresses for device location. This layer implements unified addressing to integrate hosts across different link layer networks while abstracting underlying protocol differences. Devices use packet destination addresses to determine optimal routing paths. IP stands as the fundamental protocol at this layer.
- Transport layer: facilitates process-to-process communication between hosts, handling multiplexing and demultiplexing for concurrent applications. It ensures reliable, transparent data delivery through flow control, segmentation/reassembly, and error management mechanisms. TCP and UDP serve as key protocols, with TCP providing connection-oriented communication that tracks and retransmits lost segments.
- Application layer: encompasses protocols that serve specific network functions: HTTP for web access, FTP for file transfers, SMTP for email delivery, and Domain Name System (DNS) for domain resolution. These protocols interface directly with users and applications, resulting in extensive protocol diversity to meet varied requirements.

While application layer protocols vary by use case, TCP/IP protocols at the transport and network layers form the backbone of Internet communications. Understanding this TCP/IP-based network model proves essential for any network-related operations, as these protocols power the fundamental infrastructure of modern networking.

7.1.1 IP Addresses

In network terminology, computers are referred to as hosts, with each host requiring at least one IP address to establish its identity on the Internet.

Drawing a parallel to postal delivery networks, where package routing depends on detailed sender and receiver addresses, the Internet implements a similar positioning system. IP addresses, defined at the network layer, serve as the crucial identifiers in this system. Every device connecting to the Internet must configure an IP address according to protocol specifications. In technical terms, the Internet specifically refers to the IP-based network infrastructure.

IP addressing operates under two distinct, incompatible standards: IPv4 and IPv6. While IPv6 represents an evolution of IPv4, the extensive modifications rendered it incompatible with its predecessor.

IPv4 addresses utilize a 32-bit binary structure, occupying 4 bytes of storage. To enhance readability, these addresses appear in dotted decimal notation, such as 192.168.1.1. This format divides the address into four decimal numbers, each representing 8 bits with values from 0 to 255. The addressing scheme follows a hierarchical structure, much like postal addresses use country, state, and city designations. The 32-bit address splits into network and host portions. The network portion identifies the broader network segment, analogous to a neighborhood address, while the host portion pinpoints specific devices within that network, similar to individual building numbers.

The Internet Network Information Center (InterNIC) managed global IP address allocation until September 18, 1998, when Internet Corporation for Assigned Names and Numbers (ICANN) assumed this responsibility. InterNIC initially established a class-based addressing system, dividing addresses into classes A, B, and C based on network scale and requirements. Class A addresses dedicate 1 byte to the network portion, with the highest bit set to "0," and 3 bytes for hosts, spanning 1.0.0.0 to 127.255.255.255, supporting 126 networks. Class B addresses use 2 bytes for networks, beginning with "10," covering 128.0.0.0 to 191.255.255.255. While accommodating fewer hosts per network than class A, class B offers more network divisions. Class C addresses allocate 3 bytes to networks, starting with "110," ranging from 192.0.0.0 to 223.255.255.255. The IPv4 standard reserves class D and E addresses for special purposes and future deployment. Figure 7.2 illustrates this class-based addressing scheme.

7.1 TCP/IP Network Model

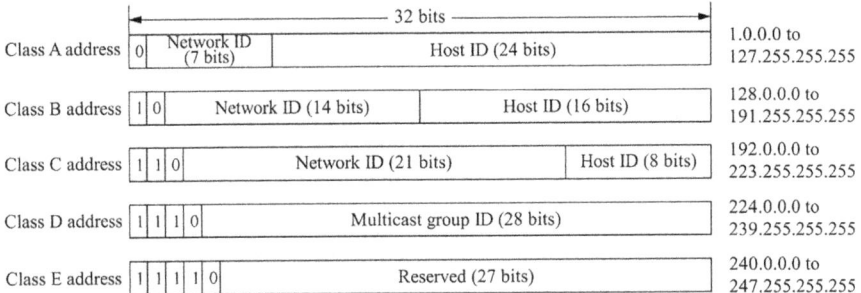

Fig. 7.2 Class-based address division

> 127.0.0.1 serves a unique purpose as the loopback address, enabling network application testing and communication without physical network connectivity. This address allows applications to send and receive packets locally, bypassing the physical network interface for efficient testing.

IPv4 addresses reveal network characteristics and relationships. For example, an address like 8.8.8.8 indicates membership in a class A network, sharing connectivity with all addresses from 8.0.0.0 to 8.255.255.255. IPv4 implements subnet masks to expedite network identification. The class A mask of 255.0.0.0, when applied through a bitwise AND operation with an IP address, extracts the network number. Routers utilize these network numbers to determine optimal packet forwarding paths.

The Internet explosion created unprecedented demand for IP addresses. With the finite IPv4 capacity of 4.29 billion addresses proving insufficient, the industry developed multiple mitigation strategies.

(1) NAT

Network Address Translation (NAT) connects physically proximate devices into a network with internal IP addresses, linking to the Internet through a dedicated NAT device. The NAT device holds the sole valid Internet IP address, while internal devices use only local addresses. NAT manages all Internet communications by binding its ports to internal device addresses and ports, forwarding Internet traffic to the corresponding internal destinations. This approach enables multiple devices to access the Internet with minimal IP addresses. IPv4 incorporates NAT support through three designated internal address ranges: 10.0.0.0 to 10.255.255.255, 172.16.0.0 to 172.31.255.255, and 192.168.0.0 to 192.168.255.255.

(2) CIDR

Classless Inter-Domain Routing (CIDR) implements flexible network segmentation rules for optimal address utilization. This system emerged when administrators recognized the limitations of class-based addressing, which left many class A addresses unused despite global address shortages. CIDR replaced fixed-length subnet masks with variable lengths to differentiate network and host portions. It employs "/x" notation to specify network ranges, where x denotes network bits. For instance, 8.145.1.0/24 encompasses all addresses starting with 8.145.1. While traditional class-based allocation would lock this range within Class A, CIDR enables its independent allocation and use.

(3) IPv6 addresses

The 32-bit limitation of IPv4 addresses inevitably restricts the total number of supported hosts, necessitating new standards for Internet expansion. IPv6 implements 128-bit addresses requiring 16 bytes of storage, using a distinct representation format. The address divides into eight colon-separated groups, each displaying 16 bits in hexadecimal format. For example, 2001:0db8:85a3:0000:0001:8a2e:0371:7334 represents a valid IPv6 address. The format allows omission of leading zeros, such as writing "0db8" as "db8," and "0001" as "1." Consecutive zero groups can compress into "::," appearing only once per address. Thus, 2000::1:2345:6789:abcd expands to 2000:0:0:0:1:2345:6789:abcd. IPv6 incorporates CIDR-style network segmentation by design but remains incompatible with IPv4, requiring hardware upgrades or replacement for IPv6 support.

These protocol advances occur exclusively at the network layer, leaving transport and link layer protocols unchanged. This architecture demonstrates the practical benefits of network layering for research, deployment, and management operations.

7.1.2 Ports

While IP addresses locate hosts on the Internet, ports identify specific network processes on these hosts.

A network access request requires more than just an IP address. Processes that initiate network requests are called clients, while those that respond to network requests are called servers. When data packets reach the target host, they must route to the appropriate server among multiple possible services, such as SSH and HTTP servers. Similarly, when response packets return to the source host, they must route to the specific requesting client among various applications like SSH terminals and web browsers.

To ensure successful packet transmission between clients and servers, an additional identifier beyond IP addresses becomes essential. Ports fulfill this role, existing in every network packet alongside IP addresses and data payloads. If IP addresses represent neighborhood addresses, ports function like phone numbers identifying specific package recipients. Just as phone numbers distinguish different deliveries to the same address, ports enable the transport layer protocols to differentiate communications between applications on network devices, providing both reliable and unreliable port-to-port data transmission. The transport layer streamlines network communication by managing packet routing and ensuring each data message reaches its intended application.

Ports use 16-bit binary numbers, ranging from 0 to 65535. Ports below 1024 are reserved for common network services, with specific ports designated for standard server applications. Servers utilize these fixed ports to ensure consistent service accessibility. For instance, DNS operates on port 53, SSH on port 22, HTTP on port 80, and Hypertext Transfer Protocol Secure (HTTPS) on port 443. In contrast, client applications use randomly assigned ports allocated by the OS during each execution.

Network services can operate on various ports, and a single port can host different services. This flexibility requires explicit protocol specification when accessing services on remote hosts. For example, accessing an HTTP service on localhost port 9090 requires uniform resource locator (URL) http://localhost:9090. Browsers default to HTTP when no protocol is specified.

> The openEuler community service URL omits the port number because it operates on the standard HTTPS port 443.

7.1.3 Sockets

Sockets represent a universal, cross-platform mechanism for inter-process communication, enabling processes on diverse systems to interact through a standardized programming interface. Originally developed by BSD (thus known as Berkeley sockets), this technology now serves as the foundation for network programming across Linux, VxWorks, and other UNIX-like OSs. Even Winsock of Windows builds upon the Berkeley socket architecture [24].

Initially designed for UNIX systems, sockets facilitate communication between processes with separate address spaces, functioning similarly to how telephones or letters enable distant communication. The socket architecture implements a layered design, offering a unified programming interface while maintaining flexible lower-level extensibility, creating an efficient abstraction model for TCP/IP network communication.

While the TCP/IP network model involves complex data exchange between hosts, sockets simplify this through an abstract programming model based on IP addresses and ports. This abstraction allows applications to integrate with networks seamlessly, handling data transmission and reception like basic file operations. Developers can focus on their application logic without managing the intricacies of TCP, UDP, or other protocols.

Figure 7.3 illustrates the basic socket communication flow, reducing network application development to essential steps. Network and transport layers handle packet routing and port management, allowing application layer programs to concentrate on data processing. The diagram shows a server providing network services

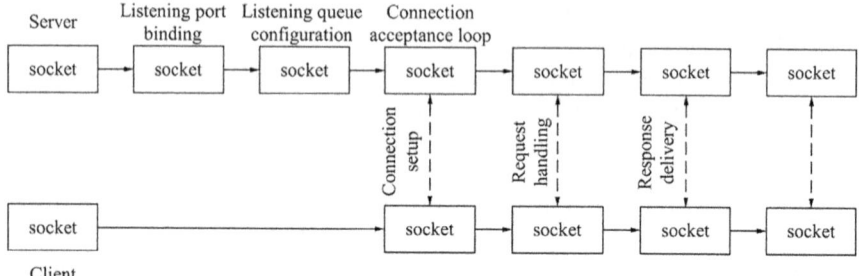

Fig. 7.3 Basic socket communication flow

(such as HTTP for web content or FTP for file sharing) through a fixed IP address and port, enabling clients to establish connections. Once connected, both parties exchange data freely.

In this system, transport layer ports function analogously to phone numbers in a delivery network. Just as delivery services use addresses and phone numbers to locate recipients, computer networks employ IP addresses and ports to identify application services. By creating an abstraction layer with these components, sockets transform complex network communications into straightforward interfaces, becoming the foundation for virtually all network software.

7.1.4 Socket API

The socket API, a component of the POSIX standards, employs an elegant design centered around key functions: **socket**, **bind**, **listen**, **connect**, **accept**, **send**, and **recv**. This standardized API enables network applications to operate seamlessly across various OSs.

For server applications to process port-specific data packets, developers must bind ports to applications and establish a listening queue. The connection process begins when a client application initiates contact through the **connect** interface. The server then verifies whether its application accepts the incoming connection. Upon acceptance, both parties exchange data through **send** and **recv** functions.

The core socket API includes these function prototypes:

```
#include <sys/types.h>
#include <sys/socket.h>
int socket(int domain, int type, int protocol);
int bind(int sockfd, const struct sockaddr *addr,
    socklen_t addrlen);
int connect(int sockfd, const struct sockaddr *addr,
```

7.1 TCP/IP Network Model

```
socklen_t addrlen);
   int listen(int sockfd, int backlog);
   int accept(int sockfd, struct sockaddr *addr, socklen_t
*addrlen);
   ssize_t send(int sockfd, const void *buf, size_t len,
int flags);
   ssize_t recv(int sockfd, void *buf, size_t len,
int flags);
```

Defined in **sys/socket.h**, these functions revolve around the socket file descriptor created by the **socket** function. This descriptor serves as the primary parameter for subsequent operations. For TCP/IPv4 communication, create a socket with:

```
int fd = socket(PF_INET, SOCK_STREAM, 0);
close(fd);
```

Here, **PF_INET** designates IPv4 protocol (use **PF_INET6** for IPv6), and **SOCK_STREAM** indicates TCP usage. The **close** function releases socket resources, preventing memory leaks.

Socket operations require configuration before data exchange. Server applications utilize **bind, listen,** and **accept** functions, while clients employ **connect**. This setup requires specifying server IP addresses and ports:

```
struct sockaddr_in address;
int addrlen = sizeof(address);
address.sin_family = AF_INET;
address.sin_addr.s_addr = INADDR_ANY;
address.sin_port = htons(8000);
```

In the code above, **AF_INET** in **sin_family** designates IPv4 for addressing. The **sin_addr** field determines the IP address configuration—setting **s_addr** to **INADDR_ANY** enables the server to listen on all available network interfaces, a typical server-side configuration. Client applications specify the target server IP address in **s_addr** instead. The **sin_port** field sets the port number, utilizing the **htons** function to handle byte-order conversion for cross-platform compatibility. These socket operations return 0 for successful execution and negative values for failures. Best practice dictates checking these return values to ensure proper operation. The following example demonstrates binding an address and port to an application:

```
    if (bind(server_fd, (struct sockaddr *)&address,
sizeof(address)) < 0){
        perror("bind failed");
        exit(EXIT_FAILURE);
    }
```

Servers initiate connection handling through **listen** and **accept** functions. The **accept** function blocks until client connection attempts arrive and then provides client address details through **addr** and **addr_len** parameters. Established connections enable data exchange via **send** and **recv** functions.

The socket implementation exemplifies the "everything is a file" philosophy of UNIX. The socket descriptor behaves like a file handle, supporting standard file operations such as read and write, demonstrating the elegant uniformity of UNIX design principles.

Since sockets operate as files in Linux, **lsof** can monitor open socket connections. During network application debugging or deployment, port conflicts frequently occur. When port 80 is occupied while launching an HTTP service, use this command to display all processes and their details currently using port 80:

```
    [ict@openEuler24 tmp]$ sudo lsof -i:80
        COMMAND    PID       USER FD  TYPE DEVICE SIZE/OFF
NODE NAME
        httpd     1012       root 4u  IPv6  15801      0t0  TCP
*:http (LISTEN)
        httpd     5715     apache 4u  IPv6  15801      0t0  TCP
*:http (LISTEN)
        httpd     5716     apache 4u  IPv6  15801      0t0  TCP
*:http (LISTEN)
        httpd     5717     apache 4u  IPv6  15801      0t0  TCP
*:http (LISTEN)
```

While this section covers socket network programming basics, practical development involves numerous additional considerations. Modern applications typically avoid direct socket programming in favor of established network middleware solutions to eliminate low-level network operations. Developers interested in this topic can explore additional documentation for comprehensive understanding.

7.2 Network Management Basics

Network connectivity is a critical component of modern computing systems. While network management can involve complex operations on servers, this section focuses on essential management tasks relevant to both small-to-medium servers and personal computers.

Basic TCP/IP network management encompasses IP address configuration, network connectivity setup, and routing configuration to enable network communications across applications[14].

7.2.1 Basic Concepts

In addition to understanding IP addresses covered in Sect. 7.1.1, network management requires knowledge of several other fundamental concepts.

(1) Subnet mask

   IP addresses are divided into network and host portions to enhance communication efficiency, address utilization, and management. A subnet mask indicates the number of leading binary bits that identify the network portion of an IP address. The subnet mask length determines the possible number of subnets and the host capacity within each subnet. Networks can be subdivided based on requirements by configuring appropriate subnet masks.

   Consider an IP address 192.168.0.65. With a subnet mask of 255.255.255.0 (24 leading 1s, written as 192.168.0.65/24), the network portion is 192.168.0.0, and the host portion is 65, accommodating 256 IP addresses. With a subnet mask of 255.255.255.192 (26 leading 1s, written as 192.168.0.65/26), the network portion becomes 192.168.0.64, and the host portion becomes 1, accommodating 64 IP addresses. This latter configuration splits the 192.168.0.0 network into four subnets: 192.168.0.0, 192.168.0.64, 192.168.0.128, and 192.168.0.192, each supporting up to 64 IP addresses.

   The IP address and subnet mask combination determines subnet membership. Hosts within the same subnet communicate through broadcast, while inter-subnet communication requires router intervention.

(2) Routing and gateway

   Routing finds network paths to other hosts, primarily managed by dedicated routers rather than server configurations. However, servers with multiple network exits may require specific routing setups for cost efficiency or security enhancement.

   Network computers access other hosts in two ways. First, within the same subnet, data packets travel via broadcast, where hosts with matching IP addresses process the packets. Second, accessing hosts in other networks involves more complexity due to different physical protocols or distance limitations. This requires a gateway—a network exit point for forwarding packets to external networks. Routing rules can assign different gateways to various networks for optimized transmission paths. Without specific routing rules, all external traffic routes through a default gateway.

Gateways serve as critical network infrastructure, typically implemented as dedicated routers that handle packet forwarding, protocol conversion, and route management efficiently. Routers connect different networks through multiple interfaces, directing packets based on IP addresses and subnet masks. In low-traffic environments, computers running Windows network sharing or Linux NAT services can function as basic gateways.

Network interface setup typically requires a default gateway configuration unless communication remains within a single network. Administrators can set this manually through network tools or configuration files, while Dynamic Host Configuration Protocol (DHCP) provides automatic gateway and IP address assignment. Default gateways often use the first or last network IP address (such as 192.168.1.1 and 192.168.1.254).

Multi-interface systems often need static routes—explicit routing rules managed through network tools. The complete path between hosts depends on intermediate routers and can be analyzed using **traceroute** or **tracepath** utilities.

The IP address 0.0.0.0 holds special significance in routing, representing any IP address.

(3) DNS

While IP addresses serve as essential network identifiers, their numerical format proves challenging for human users to remember and type correctly. This explains why the openEuler community website uses domain names instead of IP addresses, with DNS handling the conversion between them. DNS enables access to network hosts and services through user-friendly domain names, converting these names to IP addresses through a process called domain name resolution.

Internet connectivity requires proper DNS configuration, with DNS response times significantly impacting browsing experience. Popular free DNS servers include 8.8.8.8 and 114.114.114.114, though ISP-provided DNS servers often deliver faster resolution due to their proximity to users. DNS operates through local domain databases and hierarchical DNS servers. Organizations can deploy internal DNS servers to handle both Internet and private network name resolution.

On Linux systems, DNS addresses reside in the **/etc/resolv.conf** file.

OSs support local domain name to IP address mapping through hosts files: **/etc/hosts** on UNIX-like OSs and **C:\Windows\System32\drivers\etc\hosts** on Windows.

(4) DHCP

Manual IP address assignment and network configuration for multiple hosts creates administrative overhead. It can result in inefficient IP address utilization when hosts remain idle, while configuration errors may trigger IP address conflicts that disrupt network operations. DHCP, an application layer protocol, automates this process by dynamically assigning IP addresses and network parameters to hosts. Most local networks implement DHCP servers to manage address allocation across one or more subnets.

When DHCP-enabled devices connect to a network, they broadcast discovery requests. DHCP servers respond with configuration parameters, including IP address, subnet mask, default gateway, and DNS settings. The host then automatically applies this configuration to its network interface.

7.2.2 Host Names

Host names serve as identifiers for networked computer systems and are commonly used in three scenarios:

- Remote login shells display the local host name in command prompts to distinguish between network hosts. For instance, in the prompt **[ict@openEuler24 ~]$**, **openEuler24** represents the host name.
- Quick access to frequent network hosts becomes possible by adding static IP address and custom host name mappings to the **/etc/hosts** file.
- Network applications that require host identification benefit from host name to IP address mappings in the **/etc/hosts** file. This approach minimizes configuration changes when IP addresses change, such as when relocating database servers.

The local host name can be modified through two methods: the **hostname** utility or direct editing of the **/etc/hostname** file:

```
# Query the local host name.
[ict@openEuler24 ~]$ hostname
openEuler24
# Temporarily modify the local host name and query it.
The host name will be restored after reboot.
[ict@openEuler24 ~]$ sudo hostname openEuler24.03LTS && hostname
openEuler24.03LTS
# Modify the /etc/hostname file.
[ict@openEuler24 ~]$ sudo sh -c "echo 'openEuler24' > /etc/hostname" && hostname
openEuler24
```

Alternative tools include the **hostnamectl** command of systemd and **nmcli** of NetworkManager, which offer extended functionality for host name management.

To create aliases for other network hosts, modify the **/etc/hosts** file:

```
[ict@openEuler24 ~]$ cat /etc/hosts
127.0.0.1    localhost localhost.localdomain
127.0.0.1    localhost4 localhost4.localdomain4
::1          localhost6 localhost6.localdomain6
10.211.55.1        gw
10.211.55.128      mysql-svr
```

This configuration establishes multiple local host names and maps **gw** to 10.211.55.1 and **mysql-svr** to 10.211.55.128.

7.2.3 Network Interface Names

Linux uses two primary conventions for naming network interfaces.

Earlier OS versions (such as CentOS 6 and Ubuntu 15 or older) relied on the **biosdevname** convention. This method assigned sequential names like **eth0** and **eth1** based on device detection order during system startup. The unpredictable nature of this approach meant the second network interface card (NIC) might become **eth0**, the third **eth1**, and the first **eth2**. Network configurations could fail when adding or replacing NICs, making network administration challenging.

Modern systems including openEuler, RHEL, and CentOS 7 implement the Consistent Network Device Naming convention, generating names like **ens160** and **enp0s5**. This convention uses **dmidecode** to gather hardware data, ensuring unique, permanent interface names. openEuler employs **systemd-udevd** for interface naming, with configuration rules stored in **/lib/udev/rules.d/** (such as **60-net.rules**). This naming scheme offers several advantages:

Predictable interface names
Persistent naming despite hardware changes
Smooth hardware replacement without disrupting network settings

The system includes a special interface **lo** for loopback testing, permanently assigned to IP address 127.0.0.1.

Throughout this chapter, the examples demonstrate openEuler using **enp0s5** for Wide Area Network (WAN) connections and **enp0s6** for LAN connections.

7.3 Network Management

7.3.1 Tools

Linux network management relies on three primary toolsets: net-tools, iproute, and NetworkManager.

net-tools is a classic command-line toolkit featuring commonly referenced utilities like **ifconfig**, **netstat**, **arp**, and **route**. Though it evolved from the TCP/IP toolbox of BSD to become the core network management toolkit of Linux, development stopped in 2001. These independently developed tools lack consistency in usage and prove inadequate for modern network architectures like Wi-Fi and InfiniBand.

ChatGPT operates on InfiniBand architecture, a software-defined network solution engineered for large-scale data centers. InfiniBand delivers open-standard, high-bandwidth, low-latency, and reliable network interconnection for efficient data center infrastructure. Its groundbreaking implementation of Remote Direct Memory Access (RDMA) technology enables direct data access in remote host memory without multiple copies, eliminating data processing latency in network transmission.

iproute (iproute2) marks the next generation of TCP/IP network and traffic management tools for Linux. It features a more intuitive interface than net-tools and employs logical object abstractions for network resources like connections, IP addresses, routes, and tunnels, enabling consistent syntax across different network components. Since 2000, iproute has become the standard toolkit for many Linux distributions, with Arch Linux, CentOS 7/8, and RHEL 7+ adopting it as their default solution.

NetworkManager serves as a unified, systemd-based tool that automatically detects, configures, and connects to diverse networks. It streamlines modern networking tasks, particularly for wireless connections, through automatic NIC discovery and IP configuration. The system supports application switching between online and offline modes and provides three management interfaces: the **nmcli** command-line utility, the **nmtui** text-based menu, and the network-manager-applet GUI tool.

openEuler implements iproute and NetworkManager as its default network management solutions, which we will explore in the following sections.

(1) iproute

iproute is a lightweight network management utility for basic network diagnosis and administration. It supports modern networks like InfiniBand and works across Linux distributions. Note that like net-tools, changes made through iproute are temporary and reset after system restart. For persistent changes, configure settings in autostart scripts.

The package includes multiple commands, primarily **ip** and **ss**. The **ip** command handles network interface configuration, while **ss** displays network connection status. Additional tools include **tc** and **bridge**, with a total of 21 utilities available (verified using **rpm -ql iproute|grep sbin|wc**).

Table 7.1 compares basic iproute commands with their net-tools equivalents.

Table 7.1 iproute commands and their net-tools equivalents

iproute command	Net-tools command
ip address, ip link	ifconfig
ip route	route
ip neighbor	arp
ss	netstat

The **ip** command replaces traditional **ifconfig** for managing network interfaces, including activation, addressing, and routing. Its syntax follows:

```
ip [ OPTIONS ] OBJECT { COMMAND | help }
```

OBJECT specifies the target (**link**, **address**, or **route**), while *COMMAND* indicates the operation. **help** displays context-specific information. Common options include **-j** (JSON output for scripts), **-p** or **--pretty** (human-readable output), and **-d** (verbose output).

Example **ip** commands:

```
    [ict@openEuler24 ~]$ ip link                    # List
available network interfaces.
    [ict@openEuler24 ~]$ ip link help               # Display
link command help.
    [ict@openEuler24 ~]$ ip addr show dev lo    # Show lo
interface IP address.
    1: lo: <LOOPBACK,UP,LOWER_UP> mtu 65536 qdisc noqueue
state UNKNOWN group default qlen 1000
        link/loopback 00:00:00:00:00:00 brd
00:00:00:00:00:00
        inet 127.0.0.1/8 scope host lo
           valid_lft forever preferred_lft forever
        inet6 ::1/128 scope host
           valid_lft forever preferred_lft forever
    [ict@openEuler24 ~]$ ip -s link show lo         # Display
detailed lo interface stats.
    [ict@openEuler24 ~]$ ip route                   # Show the
routing table.
```

ip allows command abbreviations when unambiguous:

- **ip l** or **ip lin** for **ip link** (interface viewing)
- **ip a s** or **ip addr sh** for **ip address show** (IP address viewing)

- **ip r** or **ip ro** for **ip route** (gateway viewing)
  ss replaces **netstat** for monitoring network connections. Examples:

```
# Display all sockets.
[ict@openEuler24 ~]$ sudo ss -a
# Show socket statistics.
[ict@openEuler24 ~]$ sudo ss -s
# List TCP connections with process details.
[ict@openEuler24 ~]$ sudo ss -antp
```

While iproute excels at basic network management and diagnosis, Wi-Fi connections require additional tools like **wpa_supplicant** or **iwconfig**.

(2) NetworkManager

Early Linux distributions relied on a service named network for network management. Since RHEL 7, Red Hat has shifted to recommending NetworkManager over the traditional network service approach. Network configuration complexity increases with multiple interfaces, making the traditional method of creating separate configuration files, adding parameters, and restarting services both cumbersome and risky. This static management approach interrupts active connections during changes, potentially causing disruption in critical scenarios.

NetworkManager introduces a dynamic approach to network control and configuration. It unifies all network-related tasks under a single tool, eliminating the need for manual configuration file editing (while maintaining compatibility with traditional **ifcfg** files). Key advantages include:

- Comprehensive network support through three interfaces: NetworkManager handles Ethernet, Wi-Fi, VLAN, mobile broadband, and IP over InfiniBand networks. It offers a GUI that integrates with GNOME for intuitive control, a CLI (**nmcli**) ideal for scripting and automation, and support for dispatcher scripts that respond to network events automatically.
- Advanced configuration capabilities: For Wi-Fi setup, NetworkManager automatically scans and displays available networks, prompting for credentials and enabling automatic connections after reboot. It manages network aliases, IP addressing, routing, DNS, Virtual Private Network (VPN) connections, and various connection-specific settings with extensive customization options.
- D-Bus API integration: NetworkManager enables applications to monitor and control network settings and status, facilitating the development of network-aware software.

  Below we will explore network management using **nmcli**. The basic syntax follows:

```
nmcli OPTIONS OBJECT { COMMAND | help }
```

OBJECT accepts **general**, **device**, **connection**, **networking**, or **radio**. *COMMAND* varies by *OBJECT*, with **help** available for context-specific information. Common options include **-t** or **--terse** (colon-separated output for scripts), **-p** or **--pretty** (human-readable output), and **-h** or **--help** (help information).

The syntax mirrors **ip** from iproute, with both *OBJECT* and *COMMAND* supporting unique prefix abbreviations—even single letters suffice if unique.

However, as the tool evolves with new options, abbreviations may lose uniqueness. For script reliability and future compatibility, always use complete option names.

The following commands demonstrate general help and context-specific help for **general**:

device and **connection** stand out as primary objects. **device** manages physical interface parameters, while **connection** handles logical network settings. The separate handling of connections and devices enables network management by connection rather than interface, offering:

- Meaningful connection IDs through **con-name** (such as **wan-west**, **wan-south**, and **lan**) instead of hardware identifiers like **eth0** or **enp0s5**.
- Multiple connection profiles per device (such as **wifi-office**, **wifi-home**) in separate configuration files, allowing simple profile switching without configuration file edits.

```
[ict@openEuler24 ~]$ nmcli help
Usage: nmcli [OPTIONS] OBJECT { COMMAND | help }
OPTIONS
    -a, --ask                                    ask for
missing parameters
    -c, --colors auto|yes|no                     whether to
use colors in output
    -e, --escape yes|no                          escape
columns separators in values
    -f, --fields <field,...>|all|common          specify fields
to output
    -g, --get-values <field,...>|all|common      shortcut
for -m tabular -t -f
    -h, --help                                   print
this help
    -m, --mode tabular|multiline                 output mode
    -o, --overview
```

7.3 Network Management

```
overview mode
    -p, --pretty
pretty output
    -s, --show-secrets                            allow
displaying passwords
    -t, --terse
terse output
    -v, --version                                 show
program version
    -w, --wait <seconds>                          set
timeout waiting for finishing

operations
  OBJECT
  g[eneral]         NetworkManager's general status  and
operations
  n[etworking]      overall networking control
  r[adio]           NetworkManager radio switches
  c[onnection]      NetworkManager's connections
  d[evice]          devices managed by NetworkManager
  a[gent]           NetworkManager secret agent or
polkit agent
  m[onitor]         monitor NetworkManager changes
  [ict@openEuler24 ~]$ nmcli general help
  Usage: nmcli general { COMMAND | help }
  COMMAND := { status | hostname | permissions | logging |
reload }
      status
      hostname [<hostname>]
      permissions
      logging [level <log level>] [domains <log domains>]
```

Basic **nmcli** examples:

```
    [ict@openEuler24 ~]$ nmcli general          # Display
basic network status.
    [ict@openEuler24 ~]$ nmcli networking    # Show all
network configurations/status, or enable/disable networking.
    [ict@openEuler24 ~]$ nmcli device           # Show the
status of all network interfaces.
    [ict@openEuler24 ~]$ nmcli connection          # Show
```

```
the status of all network connections.
    [ict@openEuler24 ~]$ nmcli con help            # View
help information for connection.
    [ict@openEuler24 ~]$ nmcli c m help            # View
help information for modify.
    [ict@openEuler24 ~]$ sudo nmcli c m enp0s5 connection.id
wan  # Rename the connection to wan.
    [ict@openEuler24 ~]$ sudo nmcli dev connect enp0s6 #
Enable the network interface.
    # Create a LAN connection on enp0s6.
    [ict@openEuler24 ~]$ sudo nmcli c add con-name lan ifname
enp0s6 type ethernet
```

Two critical connection options are **type** and **id**. **type** defines the connection category (**ethernet**, **wifi**, **bluetooth**, **vlan**, **bridge**, **team**, or **infiniband**), while **id** identifies the connection—set via **con-name** during creation and visible in the **NAME** field of **nmcli conn** output (**UUID** serves as an alternative identifier).

7.3.2 Connection Configuration

Network connections support both dynamic and static configuration methods. Dynamic configuration utilizes DHCP, which NetworkManager employs by default to automatically configure network interfaces. This section emphasizes static configuration to enhance understanding of network connection settings and the usage of iproute and NetworkManager tools.

(1) Using iproute

iproute enables quick execution of essential network tasks including IP address management, interface control, and MAC address modification. Below are examples demonstrating these functions.

```
    # Assign multiple IP addresses for different network
services.
    [ict@openEuler24 ~]$ sudo ip addr add 172.16.0.253/24
dev enp0s6
    [ict@openEuler24 ~]$ sudo ip link set down enp0s6
# Disable a specified network interface.
    # Modify the MAC address of a network interface.
    [ict@openEuler24 ~]$ sudo ip link set dev enp0s6 address
00:1c:42:b0:72:13
```

7.3 Network Management

DNS configuration resides in **/etc/resolv.conf**, while default gateway setup follows the method in Sect. 7.3.4. Wireless connections require **wpa_supplicant** or similar tools to configure SSID and other network parameters.

(2) Using NetworkManager

NetworkManager offers three configuration tools, with **nmcli** being the most versatile for scripting purposes. The examples below illustrate common network configuration tasks using **nmcli**.

```
[ict@openEuler24 ~]$ sudo nmcli c m lan ipv4.address
172.16.0.9/24    # Modify the IP address.
[ict@openEuler24 ~]$ sudo nmcli c m lan +ipv4.addresses
172.16.0.10/24 # Add an IP address alias.
[ict@openEuler24 ~]$ sudo nmcli c m lan +ipv4.gateway
172.16.0.254 # Modify the default gateway.
[ict@openEuler24 ~]$ sudo nmcli c m lan ipv4.dns
172.16.0.53         # Modify the DNS server.
[ict@openEuler24 ~]$ sudo nmcli c m lan +ipv4.dns 8.8.8.8
# Add a DNS server.
[ict@openEuler24 ~]$ sudo nmcli c m lan ipv6.method
disabled           # Disable IPv6.
[ict@openEuler24 ~]$ sudo nmcli c m lan ipv4.method
manual # Change the default dynamic configuration to static
configuration.
[ict@openEuler24 ~]$ sudo nmcli c m lan connection.
autoconnect yes   # Enable the connection at startup.
[ict@openEuler24 ~]$ sudo nmcli c up id lan
# Activate the connection.
```

nmcli also handles Wi-Fi management directly. The following examples demonstrate Wi-Fi connection setup and management.

```
# Create two different connections.
[ict@openEuler24 ~]$ sudo nmcli con add con-name wifi-office
type wifi \
  > ssid "OFFICE" ifname wlp61s0
[ict@openEuler24 ~]$ sudo nmcli con add con-name wifi-home
type wifi \
  > ssid "HOME" ifname wlp61s0
# Set the Wi-Fi Protected Access 2 (WPA2) password to
"openeuler".
[ict@openEuler24 ~]$ sudo nmcli con modify wifi-office
wifi-sec.key-mgmt wpa-psk
```

```
[ict@openEuler24 ~]$ sudo nmcli con modify wifi-office
wifi-sec.psk openeuler
[ict@openEuler24 ~]$ sudo nmcli con modify wifi-home
wifi-sec.key-mgmt wpa-psk
[ict@openEuler24 ~]$ sudo nmcli con modify wifi-home
wifi-sec.psk openeuler
# Enable Wi-Fi.
[ict@openEuler24 ~]$ sudo nmcli radio wifi on
# Switch connection to the "OFFICE" network.
[ict@openEuler24 ~]$ sudo nmcli con up wifi-office
# Switch connection to the "HOME" network.
[ict@openEuler24 ~]$ sudo nmcli con up wifi-home
```

7.3.3 *ifcfg Files*

NetworkManager stores interface configuration files in **/etc/sysconfig/network-scripts/**, with file names starting with **ifcfg-** followed by the interface or connection name. The configuration file below shows the **lan** connection created through **nmcli** in Sect. 7.3.2, illustrating the file structure through comparison.

```
[ict@openEuler24 ~]$ cat /etc/sysconfig/network-scripts/
ifcfg-lan
    TYPE=Ethernet
    PROXY_METHOD=none
    BROWSER_ONLY=no
    BOOTPROTO=none
    DEFROUTE=yes
    IPV4_FAILURE_FATAL=no
    IPV6INIT=no
    NAME=lan
    UUID=4b26d360-5832-4839-82a5-2ab7cc069882
    DEVICE=enp0s6
    ONBOOT=yes
    IPADDR=172.16.0.9
    PREFIX=24
    IPADDR1=172.16.0.10
    PREFIX1=24
    GATEWAY=172.16.0.254
    DNS1=172.16.0.53
    DNS2=8.8.8.8
    IPV6_DISABLED=yes
```

While the system generates a default connection for each network interface, administrators can create multiple connections per interface. Each connection maps to a specific configuration file. NetworkManager and its three tools manage interfaces through these files to establish network connections. Though manual editing of these files is possible, using **nmcli** or similar tools ensures configuration accuracy and reliability.

7.3.4 Route Configuration

Both iproute and NetworkManager tools offer flexible routing rule management. Note that iproute cannot set the default gateway during IP address configuration. It requires separate route addition for this purpose.

```
# Set the default gateway to external router
192.168.0.254.
    [ict@openEuler24 ~]$ sudo ip route replace default via
192.168.0.254 dev enp0s5
# Add a routing rule to forward 172.16.0.0/24 traffic to an
internal router.
    [ict@openEuler24 ~]$ sudo ip route add 172.16.0.0/24 via
172.16.0.254 dev enp0s6
    [ict@openEuler24 ~]$ sudo ip route del 172.16.1.0/24   #
Delete the static route.
```

NetworkManager enables connection-specific routing rules configuration, as shown in the example.

```
    [ict@openEuler24 ~]$ sudo nmcli connection modify lan
+ipv4.routes \
    > "192.168.122.0/24 172.16.10.254"
```

Static routes can also be configured through **nmcli** editing mode, demonstrated briefly below.

```
    [ict@openEuler24 ~]$ sudo nmcli con edit type ethernet
con-name enp0s6
    ===| nmcli interactive connection editor |===
    Adding a new '802-3-ethernet' connection
    Type 'help' or '?' for available commands.
```

```
    Type 'describe [<setting>.<prop>]' for detailed property
description.
    You may edit the following settings: connection,
802-3-ethernet (ethernet),
    802-1x, ipv4, ipv6, dcb
    nmcli> set ipv4.routes 192.168.122.0/24 172.16.10.254
    nmcli>
    nmcli> save persistent
    Saving the connection with 'autoconnect=yes'. That might
result in an
    immediate activation of the connection.
    Do you still want to save?[yes] yes
    Connection 'enp0s5' (4b26d360-5832-4839-82a5-2ab
7cc069882) successfully
    saved.
    nmcli> quit
```

7.3.5 Network Diagnosis

(1) Connectivity Diagnosis

The **ping** tool tests network connectivity between local and target hosts to diagnose connection status.

After configuring and enabling a network interface, **ping** can verify gateway accessibility or connections to other local network hosts, confirming proper network configuration and physical connectivity. Pinging multiple known Internet hosts verifies Internet access. With confirmed local network functionality, **ping** can also check target host status, though some hosts may not respond due to firewall restrictions.

Example 1: TCP/IP protocol stack verification

localhost is the local machine with IP address 127.0.0.1 (loopback address). The command output below confirms proper TCP/IP protocol stack configuration and network functionality.

```
    [ict@openEuler24 ~]$ ping localhost
    PING localhost (127.0.0.1) 56(84) bytes of data.
    64 bytes from localhost (127.0.0.1): icmp_seq=1 ttl=64
time=0.087ms
    64 bytes from localhost (127.0.0.1): icmp_seq=2 ttl=64
time=0.104ms
    64 bytes from localhost (127.0.0.1): icmp_seq=3 ttl=64
time=0.079ms
```

7.3 Network Management

Example 2: Internet connectivity test
8.8.8.8 is a free public DNS server IP address. The command output below verifies proper network configuration and Internet access.

```
[ict@openEuler24 ~]$ ping 8.8.8.8
PING 8.8.8.8 (8.8.8.8) 56(84) bytes of data.
64 bytes from 8.8.8.8: icmp_seq=1 ttl=128 time=268ms
64 bytes from 8.8.8.8: icmp_seq=2 ttl=128 time=312ms
64 bytes from 8.8.8.8: icmp_seq=3 ttl=128 time=333ms
```

(2) Path Tracing

When remote hosts outside the LAN become inaccessible, **traceroute** helps determine whether the issue stems from the target host or an intermediary gateway, enabling swift problem identification and resolution.

traceroute maps the complete packet path to target hosts by sending small packets to routers and analyzing their responses. It utilizes packets with specially configured time-to-live (TTL) values to collect information about each router along the path through multiple sends. Though actual packet paths between identical source and destination points may vary slightly, they typically follow similar routes.

traceroute performs three tests per router by default, showing the domain name (when available) and IP address of each device, as well as individual test response times.

Example of **traceroute** in action:

```
[ict@openEuler24 ~]$ traceroute linux.org
traceroute: Warning: linux.org has multiple addresses;
using 104.26.14.72
traceroute to linux.org (104.26.14.72), 64 hops max, 52
byte packets
    1 192.168.1.1 (192.168.1.1) 4.732 ms 2.461 ms 2.939 ms
    2 113.54.152.1 (113.54.152.1) 3.066 ms 4.298 ms 4.220 ms
    3 10.253.0.53 (10.253.0.53) 6.022 ms 8.407 ms 7.844 ms
    4 202.115.0.9 (202.115.0.9) 5.131 ms 7.031 ms 4.772 ms
    5 * * *
    6 202.115.255.214 (202.115.255.214) 11.538 ms **
    ... ...(middle records omitted)
   17 172.71.212.2 (172.71.212.2) 80.780 ms
      172.71.216.2 (172.71.216.2) 80.594 ms 80.097 ms
   18 104.26.14.72 (104.26.14.72) 79.714 ms 79.668 ms
79.148 ms
```

The output displays numbered records called hops, each representing a router along the path. Three timestamps in milliseconds (ms) indicate response times for the test packets. Asterisks appear when responses fail, typically due to firewall restrictions or network delays from congestion or hardware limitations. DNS resolution of router host names adds latency; using the **-n** option bypasses this process for faster traces.

> **Traceroute** leverages TTL values by sending packets with increasing TTL counts to map each hop. It sets TTL to 1 for the first hop, 2 for the second, and continues this pattern. For hosts with multiple IP addresses, like in this example, traced paths may show variations between runs.

(3) Network Performance Testing

Network performance metrics include bandwidth, throughput, jitter, and packet loss rate—fundamentally measuring actual transmission speeds for large data volumes. Performance testing reveals network bottlenecks and enables targeted optimization. Basic speed tests involve transferring large files via **wget** or **scp** and calculating network speed from transfer duration. For comprehensive performance analysis, **iperf3** provides advanced testing capabilities.

iperf3 is a free, open-source cross-platform tool for IP network performance evaluation, measuring maximum TCP and UDP bandwidth capabilities. This versatile tool features extensive parameters and UDP testing options, delivering detailed metrics on bandwidth, latency jitter, and packet loss. Built on a client/server (C/S) architecture, **iperf3** runs concurrent tests between two hosts to evaluate network performance.

The command supports various options and parameters, accessible through **iperf3 --help**. The **-u** option enables UDP testing for bandwidth, jitter, and packet loss measurements, while **--get-server-output** captures server-side test results. Note: The iperf3 server port requires firewall allowlist configuration, or temporary firewall deactivation on the server host.

> For firewall configuration instructions, see Sect. 7.4.

7.3.6 Example 7.1: VLAN Creation

VLAN technology divides a physical LAN into multiple logical broadcast domains. This approach segments large networks into smaller, manageable units. VLANs enhance network performance and reduce congestion by isolating different traffic types, while strengthening security through restricted access to sensitive data.

7.3 Network Management

Each VLAN functions as a distinct broadcast domain. Hosts within a VLAN communicate directly but remain isolated from hosts in other VLANs. This containment of TCP/IP broadcast messages within VLAN boundaries optimizes transmission efficiency and security. Unlike network layer subnet divisions, VLANs operate at the link layer, providing more granular control over broadcast traffic. VLAN-enabled switches process packets based on VLAN tags, ensuring traffic remains within its designated VLAN. The IEEE 802.1Q protocol implements this by embedding a 4-byte VLAN tag in Ethernet frames.

The following steps detail VLAN creation using **nmcli**.

(1) Create a basic VLAN interface.

Create the **vlan10** interface using **enp0s6** as the parent interface, with a VLAN ID of 10 (VLAN ID r

```
[ict@openEuler24 ~]$ sudo nmcli con add type vlan con-
name vlan10 \
> dev enp0s6 vlan.id 10
```

ange: 0 to 4094).

(2) Configure an IP address.

Override the default DHCP configuration with static IP settings.

```
[ict@openEuler24 ~]$ sudo nmcli con mod vlan10 ipv4.
addresses '192.0.2.1/24' \
> ipv4.gateway '192.0.2.254' ipv4.dns '192.0.2.253' ipv4.
method manual
```

(3) Activate the connection.

```
[ict@openEuler24 ~]$ sudo nmcli con up vlan10
```

(4) Verify the setup.

```
[ict@openEuler24 ~]$ ip -d addr show vlan10
4: vlan10@enp1s0: <BROADCAST,MULTICAST,UP,LOWER_UP> mtu
1500 qdisc noqueue
    state UP group default qlen 1000
        link/ether 52:54:00:72:2f:6e brd ff:ff:ff:ff:ff:ff
promiscuity 0
```

```
            vlan protocol 802.1Q id 10 <REORDER_HDR> numtxqueues
1 numrxqueues 1
        gso_max_size 65536 gso_max_segs 65535
        inet 192.0.2.1/24 brd 192.0.2.255 scope global
noprefixroute vlan10
            valid_lft forever preferred_lft forever
        inet6 2001:db8:1::1/32 scope global noprefixroute
            valid_lft forever preferred_lft forever
        inet6 fe80::8dd7:9030:6f8e:89e6/64 scope link
noprefixroute
            valid_lft forever preferred_lft forever
```

Configure identical VLAN settings on another LAN host to test both intra-VLAN communication and interactions with external hosts.

7.4 Firewalls

Network firewalls protect against security risks from external networks, as illustrated in Fig. 7.4. Modern servers host multiple network services with varying access requirements: public services like DNS and news servers remain open to all users, internal services such as printer and file sharing stay restricted to local users, while certain services like private databases require controlled public exposure. Firewalls provide the specialized security controls needed to manage these diverse access requirements while ensuring both service availability and internal privacy.

Firewalls establish the initial security checkpoint for all incoming data packets, creating a protective barrier between internal and external networks. While various

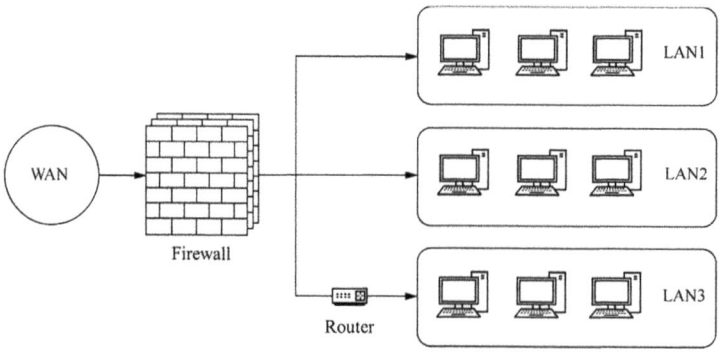

Fig. 7.4 Firewall

7.4 Firewalls

types exist—including packet filtering, application proxy, and stateful inspection firewalls—packet filtering firewalls operate at the network layer and excel at blocking unauthorized access and intrusion attempts. Their effectiveness and efficiency have led to widespread adoption [25]. This section explores packet filtering technology and two primary management tools.

Packet filtering firewalls (firewalls) inspect network layer traffic, evaluating both incoming and outgoing packets against predetermined rules. Only packets matching these rules gain passage, minimizing security risks from unauthorized access and attacks. System administrators define these rules using conditional logic: "if a packet header matches condition X, apply action Y." Headers contain crucial metadata: source and destination addresses, transport protocols (TCP, UDP, ICMP), and service types (HTTP, FTP, SMTP). When iptables identifies a match, it executes specified actions—ACCEPT, REJECT, or DROP. The kernel maintains these rules in dedicated filtering tables, where its packet filtering engine enforces them systematically.

The packet filtering engine debuted in BSD in 1992 as Berkeley Packet Filter (BPF), providing a raw link layer interface in UNIX-like OSs for handling raw packet transmission and reception. Linux 2.4 introduced netfilter, an innovative kernel-level packet filtering engine comprising filtering tables with rule sets for packet control. Firewall configuration primarily involves defining rules and managing them through dedicated tools that interface with the filtering engine for rule addition, modification, and removal.

Linux supports multiple firewall solutions, with iptables and firewalld emerging as the predominant choices. Both leverage netfilter and enjoy widespread adoption across Linux distributions. While systems often include both tools as system services, only one can operate as the active firewall manager. Administrators can control these services through systemctl commands for viewing status, activation, and deactivation. All firewall rule modifications in the following examples require root privileges.

7.4.1 iptables

iptables evolved from FreeBSD ipfirewall after its integration into the Linux kernel. Initially serving as a basic network layer packet inspection tool, it progressed through several iterations. The system evolved into ipchains during Linux kernel 2.x, enabling multiple concurrent rules. The final transformation to iptables introduced the "four tables and five chains" architecture with packet state monitoring, delivering advanced capabilities in packet filtering, redirection, NAT, and traffic management. This evolution established iptables as a cost-effective alternative to commercial firewall solutions.

The iptables framework comprises four tables and five chains. The tables—filter, nat, mangle, and raw—each serve distinct functions: packet filtering, NAT operations, packet modification, and connection tracking, respectively. The chains, including PREROUTING, INPUT, FORWARD, OUTPUT, and POSTROUTING, define packet traversal paths through the network stack. Each chain functions as a rule evaluation list, containing one or multiple rules. During packet processing, iptables evaluates rules sequentially within each chain. When a packet matches a rule, the specified action executes immediately. If no matches occur, iptables applies the chain default policy.

Figure 7.5 depicts the packet processing workflow when iptables handles server access requests. The diagram maps packets through a branched chain structure, with arrows indicating flow direction. Each processing point displays the module name and associated table in brackets, with individual modules representing distinct chains.

The iptables framework offers numerous rule configuration options. Below is a script demonstrating common rule operations. The example server contains two Ethernet interfaces: **eth0** for external connections and **eth1** for internal network access. The HTTP service runs on an internal host at 192.168.1.80. Comments precede each rule to explain its function. For comprehensive understanding, readers can consult additional documentation. By default, rules apply to the filter table unless explicitly specified.

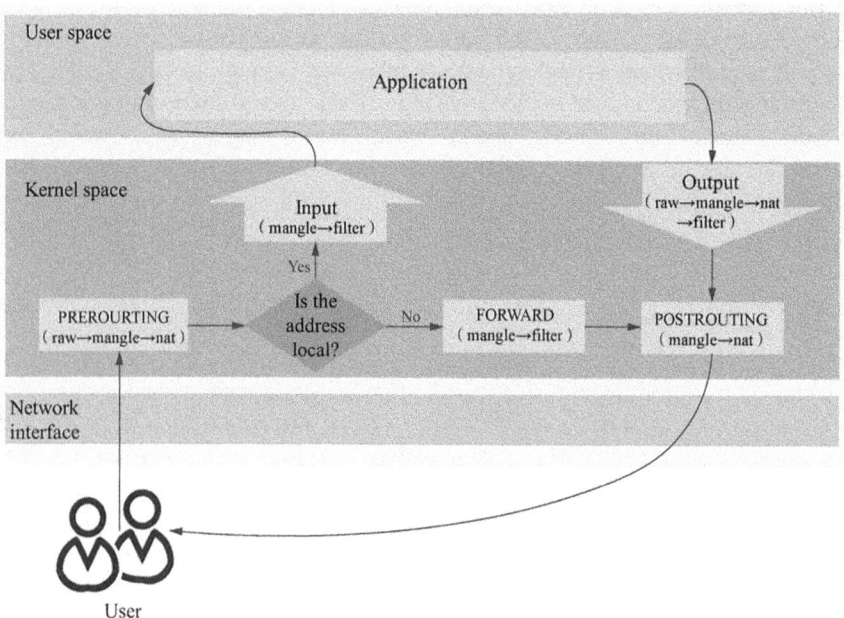

Fig. 7.5 Tables and chains of iptables

7.4 Firewalls

```
#!/bin/sh
# Clear all current rules.
iptables -F
# Forward port 80 traffic to the internal host (reverse proxy).
    iptables -t nat -A PREROUTING -i eth0 -p tcp --dport 80 -j DNAT --to 192.168.1.80:80
# Allow SSH access on port 22.
    iptables -A INPUT -i eth0 -p tcp --dport 22 -j ACCEPT
# Accept established connections while blocking new inbound connections.
    iptables -A INPUT -p tcp -m state --state ESTABLISHED,RELATED -j ACCEPT
# Drop all other incoming packets.
    iptables -A INPUT -j DROP
# Configure NAT for internal network routing.
    iptables -t nat -A POSTROUTING -s 192.168.1.0/28 -j MASQUERADE -o eth0
```

After implementing these rules, run **iptables-save > /etc/sysconfig/iptables** to persist the configuration for automatic application during system startup.

Modifying iptables rules on production servers risks network disruption and service interruption. As a static firewall management tool, iptables writes rules directly to the kernel for netfilter processing. Rule updates require policy refreshes, terminating active network sessions.

> The iptables framework faces criticism for its complex syntax and inefficient processing. Its successor, nftables, unifies multiple tools (iptables, ip6tables, arptables, ebtables) into a single, high-performance framework. CentOS 8 has adopted nftables as the default packet filtering solution, while openEuler provides all three options: iptables, nftables, and firewalld.

7.4.2 firewalld

firewalld, introduced with CentOS 7, serves as a dynamic firewall management daemon. This tool enables network zoning with defined security levels and connection parameters, offering flexible rule customization without service interruption. Its high-level abstraction interface streamlines firewall management through zone-based and service-based packet filtering. Many modern Linux distributions, including openEuler, implement firewalld as their primary firewall solution.

The architecture consists of two distinct layers: a core layer and a D-Bus layer (Fig. 7.6). The core layer manages configurations and various backends—iptables, ip6tables, ebtables, ipset, and module loaders. The D-Bus layer facilitates firewall configuration changes through standard interfaces used by tools like **firewall-cmd**, firewall-config, and firewall-applet. While **firewall-offline-cmd** exists for direct configuration file manipulation through I/O handlers of the core layer, its use during runtime is discouraged due to a 5-second delay in implementing permanent changes.

firewalld provides both command-line (**firewall-cmd**) and graphical (firewall-config) interfaces. Here is an overview of basic **firewall-cmd** operations:

(1) Basic management

These examples demonstrate essential rule configuration, enabling HTTP and SSH services while blocking other incoming traffic:

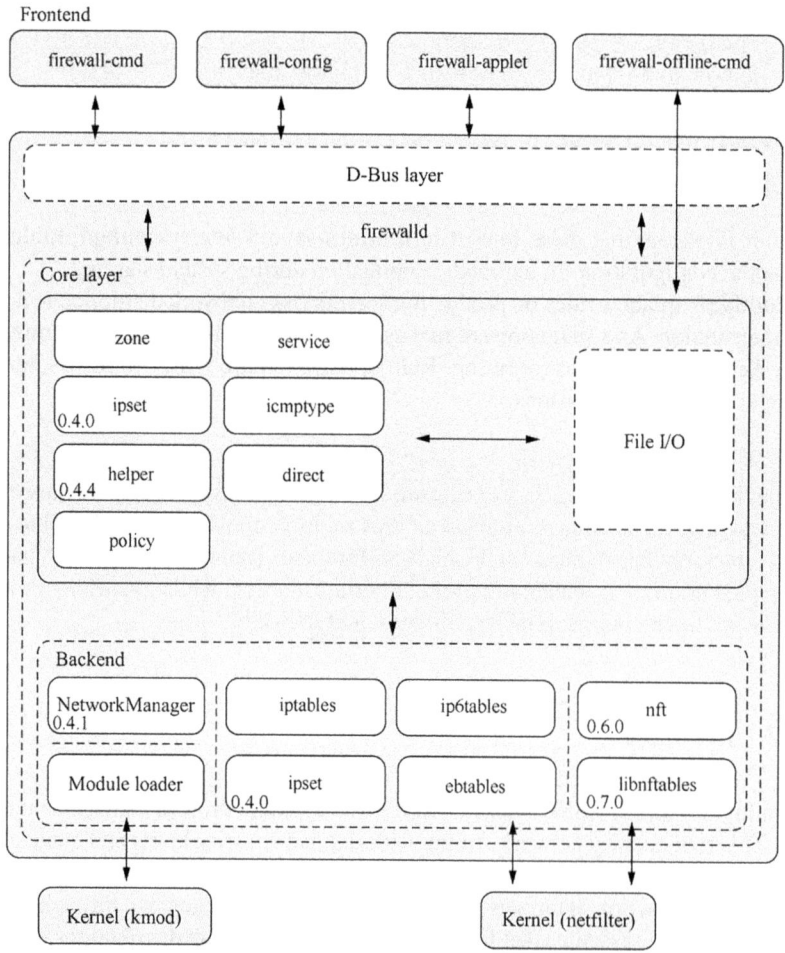

Fig. 7.6 firewalld architecture

```
# Enable HTTP service on port 80.
[root@openEuler24 ~]# firewall-cmd --add-port=80/tcp
# Enable SSH service on port 22 with 3-hour timeout.
[root@openEuler24 ~]# firewall-cmd --add-port=22/tcp --timeout=3h
# Remove port 8080 rules.
[root@openEuler24 ~]# firewall-cmd --remove-port=8080/tcp
# Block ICMP (ping) responses.
[root@openEuler24 ~]# firewall-cmd --add-rich-rule='rule protocol value=icmp drop'
# Configure NAT for internal network routing.
[root@openEuler24 ~]# firewall-cmd --add-masquerade
# Apply configuration changes.
[root@openEuler24 ~]# firewall-cmd --reload
```

Note that these commands affect the currently active default zone.

(2) Zone-based management

Zones represent predefined security rule sets corresponding to different trust levels. System administrators select appropriate zones based on network context, such as internal networks or public Internet connections.

Each zone implements comprehensive packet inspection for both incoming and outgoing traffic, applying its specific ruleset to determine access permissions. When no explicit rules match a packet, the **Target** parameter of the zone determines its fate. The **Target** parameter accepts four values:

- **default**: standard behavior (similar to **REJECT** but permits certain traffic like ICMP).
- **ACCEPT**: permits packet transmission.
- **REJECT**: blocks packets with rejection notification.
- **DROP**: silently discards packets without notification.

  firewalld includes nine built-in zones, configured through files in **/usr/lib/firewalld/zones/**. To view available zones:

```
[root@openEuler24 ~]# firewall-cmd --get-zones
```

Table 7.2 lists zones from the most to least trusted.

When examining in4coming packets, firewalld applies zone policies based on specific matching criteria:
- The source IP address of a packet can match source rules of only one zone. When a match occurs, policies of that zone are applied for inspection.
- Similarly, a network interface can belong to only one zone. When a packet arrives through an interface, policies of the corresponding zone are applied.

Table 7.2 Zone hierarchy

Zone	Description
trusted	Permits common services (ssh, mdns, samba-client, dhcpv6-client) from external sources plus return traffic
home	Permits common services (ssh, mdns, samba-client, dhcpv6-client) from external sources plus return traffic
internal	Mirrors the home zone settings with equivalent trust level
work	Permits common services (ssh, mdns, dhcpv6-client) from external sources plus return traffic
dmz	Restricts access to internal resources, permits SSH connections and related return traffic
external	Features NAT routing capabilities, permits SSH while restricting other external connections
public	Default zone with minimal trust, permits SSH and related return traffic
block	Actively rejects external connections while permitting outbound traffic
drop	Silently discards all incoming connections, allows only outbound traffic

- If no matches occur, policies of the default zone take effect.
  Each network interface or data source maps to a single zone. By default, all network interfaces are assigned to the public zone after installation.

```
# List default zone configuration details.
[root@openEuler24 ~]# firewall-cmd --list-all
# List configuration details for a specific zone.
[root@openEuler24 ~]# firewall-cmd --list-all --zone=public
# Check zone assignment for a network interface.
[root@openEuler24 ~]# firewall-cmd --get-zone-of-interface=enp0s5
```

Users can create custom zones and assign network interfaces or sources to them. Here is an example of creating a visitor zone that restricts traffic to HTTP and DNS based on router-assigned IP ranges:

```
    [root@openEuler24 ~]# firewall-cmd --new-zone=visitors -permanent
    [root@openEuler24 ~]# firewall-cmd --reload
    [root@openEuler24 ~]# firewall-cmd --zone=visitors --add-source=10.10.2.0/24
    [root@openEuler24 ~]# firewall-cmd --zone=visitors --add-service=http
    [root@openEuler24 ~]# firewall-cmd --zone=visitors --add-service=dns
    [root@openEuler24 ~]# firewall-cmd --runtime-to-permanent
    [root@openEuler24 ~]# firewall-cmd --reload
```

7.4 Firewalls

(3) Service-based operations

firewalld defines network services through service configurations that specify ports, protocols, and routing information. The system includes 183 predefined service templates in **/usr/lib/firewalld/services/**. Here is the SSH service configuration example:

```
<?xml version="1.0" encoding="utf-8"?>
<service>
  <short>SSH</short>
  <description>Secure Shell (SSH) is a protocol for
logging into and executing commands
    on remote machines. It provides secure encrypted
communications. If you plan on
    accessing your machine remotely via SSH over a
firewalled interface, enable this
    option. You need the openssh-server package installed
for this option to be useful.
  </description>
  <port protocol="tcp" port="22"/>
</service>
```

Custom service configurations should be stored in **/etc/firewalld/services/**, which takes priority over the default templates. To change the SSH port from 22 to 2222, copy **/usr/lib/firewalld/ssh.xml** to **/etc/firewalld/services/ssh.xml** and update the port number.

7.4.3 Example 7.2: firewalld Configuration

This example demonstrates basic firewall rule configuration using zones and services. The setup involves two ethernet interfaces: **enp0s5** for external network and **enp0s6** for internal network. The external interface operates under the **work** zone, permitting only HTTP access, while the internal interface uses the **internal** zone, allowing both HTTP and SSH services.

```
    # Set the default zone.
    [root@openEuler24 ~]# firewall-cmd --set-default-zone=work --permanent
    # Set the zone target.
    [root@openEuler24 ~]# firewall-cmd --zone=work --set-target=DROP
```

```
    # Assign network interfaces to specific zones (exclusive
zone assignment per interface).
    [root@openEuler24 ~]# firewall-cmd --zone=work --change-
interface=enp0s5
    [root@openEuler24 ~]# firewall-cmd --zone=internal --add-
interface=enp0s6
    # Enable HTTP access from the external network.
    [root@openEuler24 ~]# firewall-cmd --add-service=
http --zone=work
    # Disable SSH access from the external network.
    [root@openEuler24 ~]# firewall-cmd --remove-service=
ssh --zone=work
    # Enable SSH access from the internal network.
    [root@openEuler24 ~]# firewall-cmd --add-service=
ssh --zone=internal
    # Block ICMP messages to prevent ping responses.
    [root@openEuler24 ~]# firewall-cmd --add-rich-rule='rule
protocol value=icmp drop' --zone=work
    # Enable NAT for internal network routing.
    [root@openEuler24 ~]# firewall-cmd --add-
masquerade --zone=work
    # Apply the configuration.
    [root@openEuler24 ~]# firewall-cmd --reload
```

These firewalld rules remain active only during runtime. To persist these configurations across system reboots, either append **--permanent** to each command or execute the following after configuration:

```
    # Make runtime rules permanent.
    [root@openEuler24 ~]# firewall-cmd --runtime-to-permanent
```

The Linux firewall architecture exemplifies the UNIX philosophy of "provide mechanism, not policy." The netfilter engine implements filtering mechanisms in the kernel space, while tools like iptables and firewalld provide policy management in the user space.

iptables delivers granular control and extensive capabilities but requires significant expertise and operates statically. In contrast, firewalld offers dynamic management with an intuitive interface, better suited for general firewall administration. Administrators should select their firewall management tool based on network requirements and security needs to maintain effective network security controls.

7.5 Classic Network Tools

The UNIX philosophy of creating small, focused tools has spawned numerous compact yet powerful network utilities. These tools prove invaluable for both Linux software development and system administration. This section highlights several essential command-line utilities, offering a brief overview of their capabilities.

7.5.1 SSH

SSH server and client tools come standard with all UNIX-like OSs, with Windows joining the fold in 2018 by introducing native OpenSSH services and tools. SSH primarily enables remote host command execution, emerging as a crucial tool for system administrators and developers in the age of cloud computing and IoT [13]. This section outlines the fundamental SSH capabilities, including file transfer, port forwarding, and secure tunneling.

Early Internet communications relied on plain text transmission protocols like **telnet** for remote login and **rcp** for file copying. This approach left data vulnerable to interception at various network points, including LANs and routing paths, exposing sensitive information such as credentials and file contents. In 1995, Finnish researcher Tatu Ylonen developed the SSH protocol and released encryption tools for network communications, which rapidly gained popularity before becoming commercial software.

OpenSSH, developed under the OpenBSD project, stands as the predominant SSH implementation today and features as standard software across OSs. It creates secure tunnels between communicating parties, enabling protected remote communications across untrusted, open networks. The system implements multiple cryptographic algorithms and protocols to ensure data confidentiality and integrity, while facilitating public key authentication and key management.

openEuler integrates OpenSSH by default, functioning as both server and client. As a server, it accepts incoming connections from remote hosts, while as a client, it connects to other OpenSSH-enabled systems.

> openEuler supports remote access through various OpenSSH-compatible clients, including OpenSSH, PuTTY, MobaXterm, and Xshell.

SSH enables secure transmission for virtually any network service. Here are the key applications for client hosts:

- Remote login: Access remote systems for system maintenance and development tasks.

```
[ict@openEuler24 ~]$ ssh ict@localhost
```

Enter password for authentication to access the remote terminal. Enter **exit** to end the session.
- Remote commands: Execute commands directly on remote hosts with immediate output return.

```
[ict@openEuler24 ~]$ ssh ict@localhost who
```

- Remote copying: Transfer files or directories between local and remote hosts, or between two remote hosts using SCP.

```
[ict@openEuler24 ~]$ scp -r demo/ ict@localhost:/tmp/
```

- Remote editing: Edit remote files directly through compatible editors. Emacs users can access remote files via **//ssh:ict@openEuler24:/home/ict/foo.c**. Visual Studio Code users can install the Remote plugin to access and mount remote directories through the side bar.
- X11 forwarding: Display remote GUI applications locally through X11 forwarding.

```
[ict@MacbookAir ~]$ ssh -Y ict@openEuler24 xeyes
```

Note: Install xeyes on **openEuler24** in advance using **dnf install -y xeyes**.
- Port forwarding: Enable secure tunneling through SSH using various port mapping configurations. The **ssh -L** command maps local ports to remote destinations, while **ssh -R** establishes reverse tunnels. These capabilities support firewall traversal and reverse proxy access to internal networks.

7.5 Classic Network Tools

```
    # Forward local port 80 through the SSH tunnel to access
openEuler24 port 80,
    # circumventing firewall restrictions.
    [ict@MacbookAir ~]$ ssh -fNL 80:localhost:80 ict@
openEuler24
    # Create tunnel through openEuler24 to reach internal
host port 80.
    [ict@MacbookAir ~]$ ssh -fNL 80:192.168.2.2:80 ict@
openEuler24
    # Set up reverse proxy from openEuler24 to an
internal host.
    [ict@MacbookAir ~]$ ssh -fNR 80:192.168.2.2:80 ict@
openEuler24
```

- Remote mounting: Share remote directories locally through sshfs mounting.

```
    # Mount the remote /home/ict directory to local /mnt/ict.
    [ict@MacbookAir ~]$ sshfs ict@openEuler24:/home/ict/
/mnt/ict
```

OpenSSH enhances remote access security while maintaining convenience for clients. The local **~/.ssh/ssh_config** file stores remote host configurations including aliases, usernames, and ports to streamline connections. Public key authentication eliminates password prompts for SSH logins and commands. After generating keys with **ssh-keygen**, users can deploy them to remote hosts using **ssh-copy-id**. The following command provides an alternative method for key deployment:

```
    # Deploy the public key to openEuler24 for password-free
authentication.
    [ict@MacbookAir ~]$ cat ~/.ssh/id_rsa.pub | ssh ict@
openEuler24 'cat >> ~/.ssh/
authorized_keys'
```

OpenSSH also supports advanced features including X11 forwarding, port forwarding, and jump host configuration.

7.5.2 wget

Wget is a versatile command-line tool for automated file downloads from the Internet. This free software excels at downloading software packages, backing up data, and restoring backups from remote servers. It handles common protocols like HTTP and HTTPS, with built-in support for HTTP proxy connections.

The **wget** command offers extensive options with several key capabilities:

- Automated background operation: Downloads continue even after the user logs out, ideal for handling large data transfers.
- Recursive downloading: The tool traverses HTML page links sequentially to create local mirrors of remote web servers while maintaining the original directory structure.
- Resume capability: Interrupted downloads continue from the last stopping point instead of restarting.
- User-friendly interface: Users can operate wget through straightforward command-line parameters, with full script automation support.
  With its robust functionality and intuitive operation, Wget stands as an essential download utility for both system administrators and software developers.

7.5.3 cURL

cURL is a versatile command-line tool, derived from "client for URL," engineered for automated interaction with network services. It handles HTTP, HTTPS, FTP, and other network requests, processes response data, and executes specified actions. The tool excels at file downloads, form submissions, and API requests, offering extensive protocol support and granular control over data transmission parameters.

The command supports an impressive array of protocols, including DICT, FILE, FTP, FTPS, Gopher, HTTP, HTTPS, IMAP, LDAP, MQTT, POP3, RTMP, RTSP, SCP, SFTP, SMB, SMTP, Telnet, and TFTP. cURL shines at web request simulation through its customizable parameters. It integrates with SSL/TLS libraries, supports SOCKS proxy access, and implements Gzip compression for efficient data transfer.

Operating across multiple platforms, cURL extends beyond basic file transfer capabilities to provide advanced features:

- API testing and debugging: Enables comprehensive API testing through request simulation, response analysis, and status code verification. Developers can capture HTTP requests as **curl** commands to facilitate independent client-server debugging.
- Web crawling: Performs basic web crawling for public, structured data by emulating browser behaviors, handling authentication, and extracting specific content from web pages automatically.

7.5 Classic Network Tools

- Network monitoring: Tracks network performance by measuring response times and transfer speeds through HTTP requests, enabling effective performance analysis and troubleshooting.
- Task automation: Integrates seamlessly with command-line tools and scripts for automated workflows, such as fetching API data and processing it through shell scripts.

The following example illustrates segmented downloading and merging of a large file using **curl**, demonstrated with an openEuler installation ISO image.

First, retrieve the file header information using the **-I** option to determine the target file size of 773,849,088 bytes.

```
[ict@openEuler24 ~]$ curl -I https://mirrors.nyist.edu.
cn/openeuler/openEuler-24.03-LTS-SP2/ISO/x86_64/
openEuler-22.03-LTS-SP2-netinst-x86_64-dvd.iso
  HTTP/2 200
  server: nginx/1.25.3
  date: Thu, 27 Nov 2025 07:38:58 GMT
  content-type: application/octet-stream
  content-length: 1090519040
  last-modified: Thu, 26 Jun 2025 10:36:35 GMT
  etag: "685d22b3-41000000"
  accept-ranges: bytes
  strict-transport-security: max-age=63072000; preload
```

Next, download the file in three segments using parallel background processes.

```
[ict@openEuler24 ~]$ curl -r 0-200000000 -o dvd-part1
https://mirrors. ×××.cn/\ > openeuler/openEuler-24.03-
LTS-SP2/ISO/x86_64/openEuler-24.03-LTS-SP2-netinst-x86_64--
dvd.iso & [ict@openEuler24 ~]$ curl -r 200000001-600000000 -
o dvd-part2 https://mirrors. ×××.cn/\ > openeuler/
openEuler-24.03-LTS-SP2/ISO/x86_64/openEuler-24.03-LTS-SP2-netinst-
x86_64-dvd.iso & [ict@openEuler24 ~]$ curl -r 600000001--o
dvd-part3 https://mirrors. ×××.cn/openeuler/\ >
openEuler-24.03-LTS-SP2/ISO/x86_64/openEuler-24.03-LTS-SP2-netinst-
x86_64-dvd.iso &
```

Finally, concatenate the three segments to create the complete ISO file.

```
[ict@openEuler24 ~]$ cat dvd-part1 dvd-part2 dvd-part3
>dvd.iso
```

7.5.4 tcpdump

tcpdump, a powerful command-line packet capture utility, captures and analyzes network traffic traversing a system, encompassing all packets within the TCP/IP protocol suite. Network administrators rely on it for troubleshooting and security analysis, including intrusion detection. The tool excels at filtering traffic based on network layers, protocols, hosts, and ports, while incorporating logical operators (**and**, **or**, **not**) to eliminate irrelevant data.

As a command-line utility, **tcpdump** proves invaluable for packet collection on remote servers and headless devices, enabling post-capture analysis. It integrates seamlessly with task schedulers like cron for automated capture sessions.

The command below captures a single packet and renders its contents in ASCII format.

```
[ict@openEuler24 ~]$ sudo tcpdump -c 1 -A
dropped privs to tcpdump
tcpdump: verbose output suppressed, use -v[v]... for full protocol decode
listening on enp0s5, link-type EN10MB (Ethernet), snapshot length 262144 bytes
13:32:35.127281 IP openeuler24.03.shared.ssh > 10.211.55.2.61139: Flags [P.], seq 2340642970:2340643030, ack 4109906054, win 501, options [nop,nop,TS val 567481514
ecr 479656271], length 60
EJ.p..@.@...
.7.
.7........`...0......$.....
!......O%g.A. ..).n87.9.M..;j.i.......p...
w..H..{....H..'gr.......C
1 packet captured
8 packets received by filter
0 packets dropped by kernel
```

This command captures specific traffic on the **enp0s5** interface, filtering for packets with destination port 80 from source 192.168.0.7, saving the output to **ict.cap**.

```
[ict@openEuler24 ~]$ tcpdump tcp -i enp0s5 dest port 80 and src net 192.168.0.7
-w ./ict.cap
```

While packet analysis with **tcpdump** can be complex, converting captures to .cap format enables visual analysis through Wireshark, a cross-platform GUI tool available for Windows, Linux, and macOS.

7.5.5 netcat

netcat is a versatile network utility that excels at listening operations, file transfers, and security testing. The tool handles TCP and UDP network connections, functioning as a robust backend solution for applications and scripts. Its capabilities extend to establishing diverse connection types and include advanced features like port scanning, making it indispensable for network debugging and security analysis.

Originally released in 1995, netcat gained widespread adoption but lacked ongoing maintenance, with its v1.10 source code becoming increasingly scarce. This situation led the Nmap project to develop Ncat, a modern successor featuring SSL, IPv6, SOCKS and HTTP proxies, and connection brokering. The netcat ecosystem now includes multiple variants: socat, OpenBSD nc, Cryptcat, Netcat6, pnetcat, sbd, and GNU Netcat.

Ncat modernizes the original netcat concept, supporting both TCP and UDP communications while maintaining backward compatibility. It provides seamless network connectivity for applications and users, with comprehensive support for IPv4 and IPv6 protocols.

For systems without SSH access or user accounts, Ncat enables direct file transfers between hosts.

```
# Package /mnt/ict directory and listen on port 9999 for sending.
[ict@openEuler24 ~]$ tar -cvf - /mnt/ict | ncat -l 9999
# Connect to port 9999 to receive and extract the package to the current directory.
[ict@openEuler24 ~]$ ncat -v localhost 9999 | tar -xvf -
```

Similarly, Ncat facilitates remote shell access when SSH proves unavailable.

```
# Listen for connections and transmit echo results.
[ict@openEuler24 ~]$ ncat -l --exec "/bin/echo Hello openEuler!" &
[1] 45235
# Create a connection and receive remote application results.
[ict@openEuler24 ~]$ ncat localhost
Hello openEuler!
```

7.5.6 Nmap

Nmap (network mapper) is a powerful open-source tool for network discovery and security assessment. Engineered for rapid scanning of extensive networks, it performs equally well when examining individual hosts. Through innovative manipulation of raw IP packets, Nmap detects active hosts, identifies available services with their versions, determines OSs and their versions, and reveals the presence of packet filters or firewalls. While security professionals frequently deploy Nmap for auditing, system and network administrators rely on it for routine tasks like network inventory management, service upgrade planning, and uptime monitoring.

The tool supports flexible port scanning through the **-p** option, accepting specific ports, port lists, or ranges (such as **-p 80**, **-p 3389,22**, and **-p 1-65536**).

```
[ict@openEuler24 ~]$ nmap localhost -p-
Starting Nmap 7.94 at 2025-11-27 15:59 CST
Nmap scan report for localhost (127.0.0.1)
Host is up (0.000048s latency).
Not shown: 65532 closed tcp ports (conn-refused)
PORT      STATE SERVICE
22/tcp    open  ssh
80/tcp    open  http
9090/tcp  open  zeus-admin

Nmap done: 1 IP address (1 host up) scanned in 1.83 seconds
```

By default, Nmap displays only service names for scanned ports. Enhanced scanning options include **-sV** for service version detection and **-O** for OS identification.

```
[ict@openEuler24 ~]$ nmap localhost -p 80 -sV -O
TCP/IP fingerprinting (for OS scan) requires root privileges.
QUITTING!
[ict@openEuler24 tmp]$ sudo nmap localhost -p 80 -sV -O
Starting Nmap 7.94 at 2025-11-27 15:54 CST
Nmap scan report for localhost (127.0.0.1)
Host is up (0.00010s latency).

PORT STATE SERVICE VERSION
80/tcp open http nginx 1.21.5
```

```
    Warning: OSScan results may be unreliable because we
could not find at least 1 open
and
    1 closed port
    Device type: general purpose
    Running: Linux 2.6.X
    OS CPE: cpe:/o:linux:linux_kernel:2.6.32
    OS details: Linux 2.6.32
    Network Distance: 0 hops

    OS and Service detection performed. Please report any
incorrect results at
    https://nmap.org/×××/ .
    Nmap done: 1 IP address (1 host up) scanned in
7.79 seconds
```

7.6 Summary

This chapter explored the TCP/IP network model that powers the Internet, along with its core concepts. It also detailed the essential tools and methods for network management on openEuler. Readers should now possess the skills to establish network connections, transfer files, and troubleshoot basic network issues on both servers and embedded devices. Computer networking encompasses a vast domain, spanning from fundamental principles to network development and advanced management techniques—all areas meriting deeper study. While this chapter focused on common TCP/IP networks, numerous specialized networks serve specific industrial applications, including industrial control networks and Asynchronous Transfer Mode (ATM) networks. These advanced topics await further exploration by interested readers.

Reflection and Practice

1. What distinguishes TCP from UDP? What impacts occur when packets drop during UDP communication?
2. How do host names and domain names interact in the Internet ecosystem? What process resolves domain names to IP addresses?
3. Design and implement firewalld policies that align with your system requirements.
4. When applications like WhatsApp function normally but web browsers fail to load pages, what systematic approach would you take to diagnose the issue?
5. How would you investigate slow network performance? If you detect a device consuming excessive bandwidth, what methods would you use to identify it?

Open Access This chapter is licensed under the terms of the Creative Commons Attribution-NonCommercial-NoDerivatives 4.0 International License (http://creativecommons.org/licenses/by-nc-nd/4.0/), which permits any noncommercial use, sharing, distribution and reproduction in any medium or format, as long as you give appropriate credit to the original author(s) and the source, provide a link to the Creative Commons license and indicate if you modified the licensed material. You do not have permission under this license to share adapted material derived from this chapter or parts of it.

The images or other third party material in this chapter are included in the chapter's Creative Commons license, unless indicated otherwise in a credit line to the material. If material is not included in the chapter's Creative Commons license and your intended use is not permitted by statutory regulation or exceeds the permitted use, you will need to obtain permission directly from the copyright holder.

Chapter 8
Server OS Management

Objectives
1. Examine various common server OSs.
2. Master key administrative capabilities and techniques in openEuler server systems.
3. Understand the design principles that power management tools.

High-reliability server OSs are the foundation for many of our daily digital interactions. From browsing the Internet to online shopping and using ride-sharing services, these OSs are also the foundation for supercomputer systems. Modern server OSs now serve multiple purposes, such as internal operations, email systems, and data storage for small and medium businesses, development environments for version control and project management, and home file servers for personal media storage.

Improvements in computing power, connectivity, and storage costs have enabled server OSs to accommodate large-scale services. These systems require greater concurrency, stability, security, and maintainability compared to their desktop or embedded counterparts. This chapter explores the design principles behind mainstream server OSs, highlights the advantages of Linux servers, and examines openEuler capabilities. The topics covered, including user management, drive partitioning, package management, and task scheduling, benefit advanced users and developers working with desktop and embedded systems alike.

8.1 Typical Server OSs

Server OSs are sophisticated platforms that excel at managing large-scale computing resources. As the foundation of enterprise IT infrastructure, they deliver high-performance, stable services for applications ranging from search engines and e-commerce platforms to financial payment systems and online gaming services.

The evolution of server OSs parallels the growth of the internet, marked by continuous innovation and advancement. The landscape has changed dramatically over time, with formerly dominant systems like Solaris (commercial UNIX), FreeBSD (free UNIX), and Novell NetWare fading into history as new solutions emerge. These OSs demonstrate versatility, functioning effectively on both standard servers and high-performance PCs to support small and medium-scale applications.

The current server OS market primarily consists of two platforms: Windows Server and GNU/Linux distributions.

8.1.1 Windows Server

While most people are familiar with Windows as a desktop OS, Microsoft maintains a separate line of server-oriented Windows systems for enterprise use.

Introduced in 2003, Windows Server combines comprehensive networking capabilities with native GUI functionality to create a robust platform for network applications. The OS facilitates file and service sharing while offering administrators full control over network resources, data storage, and applications. It comes in three distinct editions for different service needs:

- Windows Server Standard: The most widespread edition, targeting small to medium enterprises. It delivers core server functions including file sharing, print services, web hosting, and application serving. Hardware support extends to two physical processors, 24 logical processors, and 64 GB of memory. Its balanced pricing makes it suitable for most standard deployments.
- Windows Server Datacenter: Built for enterprise-scale operations and data centers, this edition extends Standard features with enhanced hardware support and advanced capabilities. It includes sophisticated networking tools, automated deployment options, and comprehensive update management. This edition excels in high-load environments requiring extensive data processing.
- Windows Server Essentials: A streamlined solution for small businesses, featuring core server functions with simplified management tools. Its straightforward setup process and maintenance requirements, combined with competitive pricing, make it ideal for organizations with basic server needs and limited IT resources.

Windows Server stands out as a comprehensive, turnkey solution. Its Windows-like interface ensures quick adoption, with straightforward installation and configuration processes that minimize training requirements. Remote management becomes intuitive through the built-in remote desktop client, providing direct visual access to the server interface. The platform leverages extensive development resources and a robust developer ecosystem to enable swift, cost-effective application deployment.

The system excels in web development through technologies like Active Server Pages (ASP), enabling rapid creation of script-enhanced web pages with efficient server-side processing. The industry-standard .NET Framework deploys seamlessly on Windows Server, while available premium support services reduce technical barriers for organizations.

Despite significant improvements in stability and maintainability through ongoing development, Windows Server faces challenges in security, scalability, concurrency, and maintenance efficiency.

Cost remains a consideration, with substantial licensing fees for both the core system and essential middleware components like database software.

8.1.2 Popular Linux Distributions for Servers

While Linux holds a modest share of the desktop computing market, it dominates the server landscape with explosive growth, emerging as the de facto standard for servers and supercomputers. Current market analysis shows Linux commanding approximately 75% of the server market, with even Microsoft embracing Linux for cloud service delivery. Notably, since 2017, Linux powers all entries in the TOP500 list of supercomputers.

This prevalence stems from the core strengths of Linux: openness, security, stability, and adaptability. Enterprise deployments benefit from superior performance and reliability while achieving substantial cost savings. System administrators particularly value the robust CLI and scripting capabilities, which enable extensive automation and streamline maintenance procedures.

Three Linux distributions stand out as leaders in the server space.

(1) RHEL

RHEL stands as the premier enterprise Linux OS globally, backed by certifications from hundreds of cloud providers and thousands of hardware and software vendors. RHEL excels in stability, reliability, and performance while leveraging open-source flexibility and community innovation to deliver a robust platform for hybrid cloud deployments. The 2022 release of RHEL 9 focuses on hybrid cloud requirements, enabling fluid deployment across edge computing and cloud environments. This version seamlessly operates as a guest system on KVM, VMware hypervisors, physical servers, cloud platforms, or as containers built from Red Hat UBI.

RHEL licensing requires either a paid subscription or trial registration, granting access to technical support, system updates, and upgrades within specified time frames to maintain system integrity and reliability.

(2) CentOS and CentOS Stream

Since 2004, CentOS has served as the free community alternative to RHEL, attracting users through its open-source framework, zero-cost model, and robust stability. This distribution became particularly popular among organizations with Linux expertise seeking enterprise-grade capabilities without RHEL licensing costs.

A significant shift occurred in December 2020 when Red Hat announced the transition to CentOS Stream, with support ending for CentOS 8 and 7 in December 2021 and June 2024, respectively. CentOS Stream adopts a rolling-release model as the upstream development platform of RHEL, fundamentally changing its role from a stable RHEL clone to a preview channel—a change that fails to meet enterprise requirements for stability and security.

(3) Ubuntu Server

Ubuntu Server represents a Debian-derived distribution that powers diverse computing environments from personal devices to cloud infrastructure and IoT systems. This free platform delivers enterprise-grade reliability, scalability, and security through consistent updates. The distribution follows a dual-release strategy: regular releases every 6 months and long-term support (LTS) versions maintaining security patches for 5 years. Ubuntu Server 20.04 LTS exemplifies stability and security in Linux distributions, proving optimal for production environments spanning public clouds, data centers, and edge computing scenarios.

8.1.3 The Rise of openEuler

Server OSs represent critical infrastructure software targeted for independent development during China's 14th Five-Year Plan. The discontinuation of CentOS has catalyzed a migration wave, creating opportunities for open-source alternatives like openEuler. Major Chinese tech companies—Alibaba Cloud, Huawei, KylinSoft, and UnionTech—continue advancing core technologies. The openEuler community leads efforts to build an ecosystem founded on indigenous technology. China-developed solutions including openEuler, UnionTech OS Server, and NeoKylin Linux Advanced Server OS now fill the security gap left by CentOS.

openEuler emerges as an open-source, enterprise-grade Linux platform delivering robust security, scalability, and performance. The OS leverages Kunpeng processors and container virtualization to serve diverse computing environments from edge to cloud, establishing a modern software foundation for digital infrastructure. Key attributes include:

– High performance: Advanced multi-core acceleration and virtualization capabilities deliver exceptional system performance for demanding workloads.
– High reliability: Robust technical assurance backed by compliance with critical industry standards including the Single UNIX Specification Version 3 (UNIX 03), Linux Standard Base (LSB), IPv6 Ready, and GB 18030.

- High security: Recognized among top-tier secure OSs through certification by Chinese security standards (GB/T 20272—2006) and German BSI PP (CC EAL4+), ensuring maximum system protection.

Public data reveals openEuler's exceptional growth since its open-source debut on December 31, 2019. The platform has emerged as one of China's most vibrant open-source communities, drawing more than 10,000 contributors and 300 partners while establishing nearly 100 SIGs—a growth trajectory that stands out globally.

Following its transfer to the OpenAtom Foundation in 2021, openEuler gained significant momentum. The platform now serves critical national industries and leads the transition to Chinese server OSs. Dozens of global vendors offer openEuler-based commercial distributions. Installation numbers reached 6.1 million by December 2023, with IDC projecting a 36.8% share of China's server OS market for the year.

This open-source journey has propelled openEuler to dominance in China's server OS landscape. The platform excels across technological innovation, ecosystem development, community engagement, and commercial deployment, fostering sustainable industry growth. As the first Chinese base software to achieve market leadership, openEuler marks a pivotal milestone in the nation's software industry and establishes a dependable foundation for Digital China.

> The subsequent sections will explore server OS management functions and methodologies using openEuler as the reference platform.

8.2 Users and User Groups

User and user group management forms a cornerstone of multi-user OSs and stands essential for server operations. This feature proves valuable even in personal computing environments, where multiple user accounts enhance system security. The text-based approach to user management exemplifies the elegant simplicity of UNIX philosophy.

Linux implements user and user group functionality for two critical purposes:

- Resource allocation and protection at the user level, preventing unauthorized access, alterations, or removal of user data
- Program execution under specific user and group contexts, ensuring appropriate resource access while protecting processes from external interference

Linux delivers a streamlined yet powerful mechanism for managing users and groups. This framework enables precise control over system resources while simplifying administrative tasks such as creating, modifying, and removing user accounts and group memberships.

8.2.1 User Management

Linux systems implement three distinct user categories: **root**, common, and virtual users. The **root** user, or superuser, wields unrestricted system control and requires prudent handling. Common users operate with limited permissions, accessing only their home directories and authorized files. Virtual users, like **sshd**, **nginx**, and **mysql**, serve solely for file permission management without system login capabilities.

System services operate under virtual user identities to enhance security. For instance, MySQL runs as the **mysql** user, while Apache operates as the **apache** user. This practice mitigates root-level security risks while safeguarding resources from unauthorized access.

Linux features a streamlined user and group management framework, enabling straightforward account administration. All these operations demand root privileges.

(1) Adding users

Creating a user establishes essential elements including the UID, username, group membership, home directory, and shell path. The **useradd** utility handles this process, requiring root privileges.

The command follows this syntax, where *username* specifies the new username, and *options* define custom configurations. Without specified options, the system applies default settings. Run **useradd --help** to view comprehensive usage instructions.

```
useradd [options] username
```

Run the following command as **root** to create the **openEuler** user:

```
[root@openEuler24 ~]# useradd openEuler
```

Verify the new user with the **id** command:

```
[root@openEuler24 ~]# id openEuler
uid=1000(openEuler) gid=1000(openEuler)
groups=1000(openEuler)
```

The system prevents new user logins until a password is assigned. To set a user password, execute the **passwd** command with root privileges:

```
[root@openEuler24 ~]# passwd openEuler
```

8.2 Users and User Groups

Passwords must fulfill these requirements:

- Have a minimum length of eight characters.
- Must contain at least three of the following: uppercase letters, lowercase letters, digits, and special characters.
- Must differ from the username.
- Must avoid dictionary words.
  Upon successful password configuration, the **openEuler** user becomes fully operational for system access.

(2) Modifying users
    The root user possesses full authority to modify any user, while common users can only adjust their own settings. Modifiable attributes include passwords, login shells, home directories, and user validity periods.
    The **usermod** utility provides comprehensive user modification capabilities. It can alter login shells from the default Bash to tcsh or set **nologin** to restrict user login. For instance, to modify both the group membership and login shell of the **openEuler** user:

```
[root@openEuler24 ~]# usermod -g wheel -s /sbin/nologin
openEuler
```

(3) Deleting users
    Root privileges are required to remove inactive users using the **userdel** utility. Detailed removal options are accessible via **userdel --help**.
    Unlike Windows and other OSs that store authentication data in binary format, UNIX-like OSs maintain user information in text files. Each entry occupies a single line with colon-separated fields. Example entries from **/etc/passwd**:

```
root:x:0:0:root:/root:/bin/bash
bin:x:1:1:bin:/bin:/sbin/nologin
daemon:x:2:2:daemon:/sbin:/sbin/nologin
ict:x:1002:1002::/home/ict:/bin/bash
nginx:x:986:986:Nginx web server:/var/lib/nginx:/sbin/nologin
```

While binary storage might appear more space-efficient, the compact nature of user data makes compression benefits negligible. Text storage offers superior advantages: accessibility through standard text editors and compatibility with command-line utilities like **grep** for searching and filtering.
Table 8.1 lists files related to user management.

Table 8.1 User management files

File	Description	Remarks
/etc/passwd	User information	Uses **x** to indicate passwords, which are actually stored in **/etc/shadow**
/etc/shadow	Encrypted user information	Contains actual password entries
/etc/group	Group definitions	Maintains group memberships
/etc/default/useradd	Default user parameters	
/etc/login.defs	System-wide settings	
/etc/skel	Template configurations	

8.2.2 User Group Management

Linux assigns each user to at least one group for efficient resource management and access control. By default, when creating a user without group specification, the system generates a new group matching the username.

Group management encompasses three primary operations: creation, modification, and deletion. These tasks require root privileges and utilize distinct command-line utilities.

The **groupadd** command creates new groups using this syntax, with details available through **groupadd --help**:

```
groupadd [options] groupname
```

options configure specific parameters, defaulting to system settings when omitted. For example:

```
[root@host ~] groupadd groupexample
```

Group modifications utilize **groupmod** for adjusting names and GIDs, while **groupdel** handles group removal. Comprehensive documentation is available through exists through their respective help options.

Linux provides additional group management tools:

- **gpasswd** manages group membership.
- **newgrp** enables users to switch their active group context during sessions.

These utilities enhance group administration flexibility, particularly for users with multiple group affiliations.

Table 8.2 lists files related to user group management.

Table 8.2 User group management files

File	Description
/etc/group	User group information
/etc/gshadow	Encrypted user group information

8.2.3 Example 8.1: Batch User Creation

Creating multiple users individually becomes impractical at scale, especially when you provision users for large groups like development teams or student classes. Linux shell scripting offers an elegant solution through pipes and redirection, enabling automated batch user creation—a task that proves cumbersome in typical GUI environments.

```
#!/bin/sh
USER_LIST="test_user1
test_user2
test_user3"
echo "$USER_LIST" | while read name; do
    useradd $name
    echo "12345678" | passwd --stdin $name &> /dev/null
    #userdel "$name"
done
```

The script streamlines user creation by processing a list of usernames from **USER_LIST**. It automates both user generation via **useradd** and password configuration via **passwd**, setting **12345678** as the default password for each user. This automation eliminates manual input requirements, executing the entire process unattended.

8.3 Drives and Logical Volumes

Storage management challenges, particularly insufficient file system space, emerge regularly in system operations. Both developers and system administrators must master the skills of efficient drive utilization and file system management. Drives function as the fundamental storage medium for file systems and constitute critical system resources. OSs implement partition-based management of these drives to accommodate diverse file system requirements. To enhance storage flexibility, OSs introduce logical volumes (LVs)—an abstract storage framework that consolidates multiple physical drives into unified logical devices. This approach enables dynamic operations like file system expansion and reduction.

The LV implementation demonstrates key software engineering principles, particularly abstract encapsulation and layered architecture design.

8.3.1 Drive Partitions

Physical drives come in two primary forms: HDDs and SSDs. These drives connect through various interfaces including M.2, SATA, and SAS. Partitioning segments a drive into distinct logical storage units called partitions, each functioning as an independent section.

Linux partitions follow the standardized naming format **/dev/**xxyN, which consists of three components:

- *xx* indicates the device type: **hd** represents legacy IDE drives, while **sd** designates modern storage devices including SATA, SCSI, USB drives, and SSDs.
- *y* identifies the device sequence, using **a** or **0** for the first device, **b** or **1** for the second, continuing in this pattern.
- *N* represents the partition number, starting with **1** for the first partition and incrementing sequentially.

> In the Linux file system hierarchy, partitions appear as files within the **/dev** directory. This design extends to entire physical drives, allowing direct file-based access. The **dd** utility leverages this architecture for direct drive operations, enabling tasks like backup and replication.

- Partition management offers practical benefits for both organization and functionality. A typical configuration might distribute space across multiple partitions—allocating separate areas for Windows and Linux systems, applications, and user data. This structure allows each partition to utilize an appropriate file system format based on specific requirements.

The security advantages of partitioning prove equally significant. By isolating system and user data in separate partitions, the scheme creates natural boundaries that contain potential damage from drive failures, user errors, or system maintenance. For example, reinstalling an OS affects only its designated partition, preserving data and configurations stored elsewhere on the drive.

8.3.2 MBR and GPT

Drive partitioning divides a drive into multiple sections by modifying the partition table information. Two primary partitioning schemes exist: the legacy MBR and the modern GPT.

MBR, short for Master Boot Record, supports drives up to 2 TB and remains prevalent in 32-bit systems. Located in the initial boot sector, MBR contains both bootloader code and partition information within 512 bytes. The bootloader initiates the OS, while the partition table uses 64 bytes to define up to 4 primary partitions, allocating 16 bytes per partition. Additional partitions require creating an extended partition to house multiple logical partitions.

GPT stands for GUID Partition Table, where GUID is an acronym for Globally Unique Identifier. GPT represents the evolution of partitioning technology, working in tandem with Unified Extensible Firmware Interface (UEFI) as they replace MBR and Basic Input/Output System (BIOS), respectively. GPT assigns each partition a GUID, enhancing portability compared to traditional partition numbers and streamlining file system management. GPT eliminates size constraints, supporting volumes up to 18 EB and accommodating 128 primary partitions, thus removing the need for extended or logical partitions.

Users can implement their chosen partitioning scheme through tools like **fdisk** based on hardware specifications and system requirements. During OS installation, the installer typically creates and formats partitions automatically unless custom preferences are specified. Each partition can receive a distinct file system through formatting tools like **mkfs**, becoming accessible once mounted to the root file system via **mount** commands.

8.3.3 *Example 8.2: Partition Creation and Mounting*

This example illustrates the complete workflow of creating partitions on a drive, formatting, and mounting file systems.

The **fdisk** utility requires root privileges and operates in interactive mode. Upon executing **fdisk /dev/sdb**, an interactive interface launches where **m** displays help documentation, **p** shows current drive parameters and partition details, and **q** exits the tool.

For identical partitioning across multiple drives, scripts offer an efficient alternative to manual operations. The example script below combines redirection and here document techniques. Redirection suppresses output messages, while the here document automates command input until reaching **CMDS_END**, which triggers **fdisk** to exit.

The script partitions **/dev/sdb** into three segments: 12 GB, 4 GB, and the remaining space, with the middle partition configured as the Linux swap partition. The command sequence works as follows: **g** initializes the GPT partition scheme; **n** generates a new partition; blank lines accept default parameters including partition number and starting sector; **+12G** allocates 12 GB from the default starting point. The second partition follows a similar pattern, with **t** and **19** designating it as the swap partition. The third partition, created without size specification, automatically claims all remaining space. The **p** command verifies the partition table, and **w** commits changes to the drive—a crucial final step for the changes to take effect.

```
[root@openEuler24 ~]# fdisk /dev/sdb >/dev/null <<
CMDS_END
  g
  n


  +12G
  n


  +4G
  t
  19
  n



  p
  w
CMDS_END
```

Scripts eliminate the need for manual input when performing identical partitioning across multiple drives, dramatically enhancing operational efficiency. Note that line breaks simulate pressing **Enter** and must be preserved. Be aware that **fdisk** behavior may vary across Linux distributions, potentially requiring command adjustments.

The following example demonstrates creating an ext4 file system on partition /**dev/sdb1** and mounting it to the /**mnt** directory.

```
[root@openEuler24 ~]# mkfs -t ext4 /dev/sdb1
[root@openEuler24 ~]# mount /dev/sdb1 /mnt/
```

This mount point persists only until system restart. For permanent mounting across reboots, register the file system in /**etc/fstab**.

/**etc/fstab** stores static file system configurations that enable automatic mounting during system startup. Add these lines to the file using any text editor:

```
/dev/sdb1 /mnt ext4 defaults 0 0
```

This entry contains:

- **sdb1**: device partition identifier
- **mnt**: mount point location
- **ext4**: file system format

8.3 Drives and Logical Volumes

- **defaults**: standard mount options
- First **0**: backup flag (**1** enables automatic backup and **0** disables it)
- Second **0**: boot-time scan flag (**1** enables boot-time scanning and **0** disables it)

Exercise caution when editing **fstab**, as incorrect entries can prevent system login. The **mount** utility includes validation features: the **--fake** or **-f** option tests the configuration without actual mounting, while **-v** provides detailed output for error detection.

After modifying **/etc/fstab**, run **mount -afv** to validate the configuration. If no errors appear, reboot the system for automatic mounting to take effect.

Using partition device names in the first column of **fstab** presents a risk: if the drive device name changes (for instance, switching from **/dev/sdb** to **/dev/sdc** when connecting to a different interface), mount operations will fail. Universally Unique IDentifiers (UUIDs) offers a more reliable alternative. Each UUID consists of 32 hexadecimal characters split into 5 sections by hyphens, guaranteeing uniqueness. GUID represents an implementation of the UUID standard.

The **blkid** utility reveals UUID and file system information for partitions. For example, to inspect **/dev/sdb3**:

```
[root@openEuler24 ~]# blkid /dev/sdb3
```

With a UUID output of **8f61dc87-472b-4a8d-b289-238e66a73f56**, the corresponding **fstab** entry becomes:

```
UUID=8f61dc87-472b-4a8d-b289-238e66a73f56 /mnt ext4
defaults 0 0
```

Linux distributions featuring GNOME desktop environments provide GUI tools for drive management tasks. These interfaces automatically detect and mount removable drives upon connection.

To unmount file systems, use the **umount** command with either device names or mount points. While it supports options like **-f** for forced unmounting, the operation often encounters resistance:

```
[ict@openEuler24 ~]$ sudo umount /boot
umount: /boot: target is busy.
```

This typically occurs when processes access files within the target file system, including cases where the current working directory resides there. Use **lsof** to identify these processes:

```
[ict@openEuler24 ~]$ lsof /boot
   COMMAND    PID USER     FD       TYPE DEVICE SIZE/OFF  NODE NAME
      bash  44170  ict    cwd        DIR    8,2     4096     2 /boot
      lsof  44737  ict    cwd        DIR    8,2     4096     2 /boot
      lsof  44738  ict    cwd        DIR    8,2     4096     2 /boot
```

After identifying the processes, either terminate them gracefully or use **kill** to force termination, enabling successful unmounting.

8.3.4 LVs

Traditional drive partitioning with separate file systems offers efficient storage utilization but lacks flexibility in capacity management. When partitions reach capacity limits, conventional solutions involve either adding new drives or replacing existing ones with larger alternatives. These approaches prove problematic: new drives cannot expand existing file systems, while drive replacement requires service interruption for unmounting and data migration—an untenable situation for production environments. Linux addresses these limitations through Logical Volume Management (LVM).

LVM implements an abstraction layer between physical storage and file systems, masking the underlying partition structure and delivering enhanced management flexibility. Unlike traditional systems where file systems directly access physical partitions, LVM establishes an intermediary layer of LVs. These volumes manage physical drive operations while presenting a unified interface to file systems. This architecture enables seamless capacity expansion by incorporating additional physical drives into existing LVs without service disruption. By replacing static physical partitions with dynamically adjustable LVs, LVM removes physical size constraints and enables file systems to span multiple drives. Figure 8.1 depicts the LVM storage architecture and implementation workflow in Linux.

To clarify LVM architecture, let's explore its four core components:

Physical extent (PE): The fundamental building block of LVM, representing a 4 MB storage segment on the physical drive.

Physical volume (PV): The primary storage unit, comprising multiple PEs. PVs can span entire drives or partitions, with creation involving PE block allocation across the storage medium.

8.3 Drives and Logical Volumes

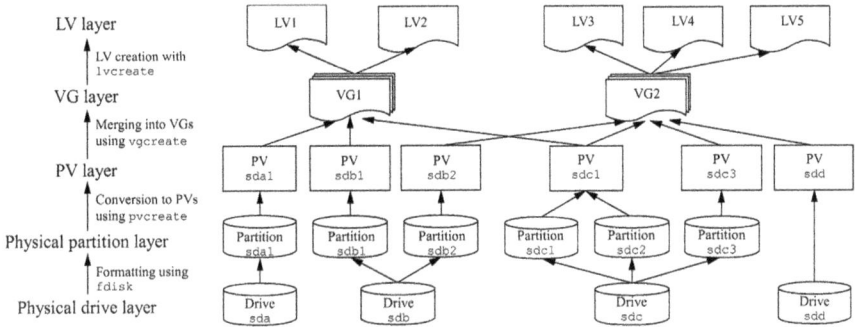

Fig. 8.1 LVM storage architecture and implementation workflow

Volume group (VG): An aggregation of multiple pvs that pools PE blocks from various sources. This creates an abstraction layer that masks physical drive complexities by establishing a unified PE repository.

LV: The manageable storage entity created within VGs. Users can establish multiple LVs, each allocating specific PE quantities from the VG. These volumes support various file systems and become accessible upon mounting.

LVs surpass traditional partitions through dynamic space management capabilities. This flexibility enables storage expansion from multiple drives or space reclamation, facilitating seamless file system growth or reduction.

> While LVs parallel traditional drive partitions in function, they transcend the limitations of physical partitioning. Unlike drive partitions that demand contiguous space on a single drive, LVs can incorporate PE blocks from multiple physical drives, enabling dynamic storage expansion.

8.3.5 Example 8.3: LV Creation and Mounting

This example demonstrates the management of LVs using LVM within openEuler, covering creation and utilization. All operations require root privileges.

LV Creation

openEuler includes LVM packages by default, verified by the **rpm -ql lvm2** command, which lists all installed files such as configuration files in the **/etc/lvm** directory and various tools in the **/usr/sbin/** directory.

Creating an LV involves these three steps:

(1) Create PVs.
PVs can be established directly on a drive or its partition using **pvcreate**.
For instance, to create PVs on **/dev/sdb** and **/dev/sdc2**:

```
[root@openEuler24 ~]# pvcreate /dev/sdb /dev/sdc2
```

Detailed information about these PVs—including their names, associated VGs, sizes, block sizes, total, available, and allocated block counts, and UUIDs—is accessible via **pvdisplay** or **pvs**. Modify PV attributes with **pvchange** and delete PVs using **pvremove**.

(2) Create a VG.
A VG is created by adding previously formed PVs to it and assigning it a name. **vgcreate** is the tool for this task.
For example, to create a VG named **vg1** and incorporate the **/dev/sdb** PV:

```
[root@openEuler24 ~]# vgcreate vg1 /dev/sdb
```

You can view information about this VG with **vgdisplay** or **vgs**. Expand the VG by adding new PVs with **vgextend**.
For example, to extend **vg1** by adding **/dev/sdc2**:

```
[root@openEuler24 ~]# vgextend vg1 /dev/sdc2
```

Modify VG attributes with **vgchange,** reduce the VG size by removing PVs using **vgreduce**, and delete the VG with **vgremove**.

(3) Create an LV.
LVs are created within the VG storage pool on the physical layer using the **lvcreate** tool. Here is an example of creating a 200 MB LV named **lv1** within **vg1**.

```
[root@openEuler24 ~]# lvcreate -L 200M -n lv1 vg1
```

You can examine LV details, such as space size, read/write status, and snapshot information, with the **lvdisplay** command. The device file for the new LV is **/dev/vg1/lv1**.

Now, the LV is ready, and its device file can serve to establish a new file system. Use the **lvremove** tool to delete an LV, but beware—deleting the LV with an unmounted file system leads to data loss. Exercise caution.

8.3 Drives and Logical Volumes

LV Utilization

LVs facilitate file system creation. The process resembles that of creating a file system on a drive partition, differing only in the device file used—the one of the LV.

For example, to create an ext4 file system on **lv1**:

```
[root@openEuler24 ~]# mkfs.ext4 /dev/vg1/lv1
```

Mount the file system on an LV using the same techniques applied to drive partitions. In theory, you can dynamically resize the file system on an LV without compromising or losing data. To ensure data safety, approach such operations with care on volumes storing critical data.

Expanding a file system involves two steps: first, expand the LV storage space, and then expand the file system capacity.

Use the **lvextend** tool to increase the storage space of an LV. This operation does not disrupt application access to the volume.

For instance, to add 2 GB of space to **lv1**:

```
[root@openEuler24 ~]#   lvextend -L +20G /dev/vg1/lv1
[root@openEuler24 ~]#   lvs
```

The tool for increasing the capacity of an ext4 file system is **resize2fs**, while **xfs_growfs** is used for expanding an XFS file system. Other file systems require different tools for capacity expansion.

Below is an example of adding 20 GB to the file system on **/dev/vg1/lv1**.

```
[root@openEuler24 ~]#   resize2fs /dev/vg1/lv1
[root@openEuler24 ~]#   df -h
```

Shrinking a file system follows a two-step process: first, reduce the file system capacity, and then decrease the LV storage space. This sequence is the opposite of expanding a file system. Use **lvreduce** to shrink the storage space of an LV, an operation that may erase data on the volume, requiring careful confirmation beforehand. The tools for shrinking and expanding file system capacities are identical.

Beyond dynamic space adjustments, LVs offer snapshot capabilities, allowing data rollback to a prior state for recovery. A snapshot captures data of an LV at a specific moment, akin to photographing it. Subsequent data alterations move the original data to the snapshot area, leaving unchanged areas to be shared between the snapshot and the file system. These capabilities surpass those of traditional drive partitions.

LVM establishes an abstract logical layer above physical drive partitions, creating a storage pool from multiple drives. This pool supports the creation of multiple LVs with adjustable space, enhancing drive management flexibility significantly. When facing storage shortages, you can add physical drives to the pool rather than unmounting and transferring file systems. This allows for seamless expansion of LV space across drives and real-time expansion of the file system on an LV.

8.4 Software Packages

Applications extend OS functionality, making software management mechanisms crucial for system performance, security, maintenance, and user experience. While smartphone users enjoy one-tap installation and removal of apps through digital stores, the process remains more complex on PCs and servers.

Package management tools emerged from BSD to streamline software maintenance, reflecting the UNIX philosophy of creating efficient tools for specific tasks.

Most OSs, including Windows, UNIX, and Linux, require application files to reside in specific file system locations before execution. Without package managers, users face multiple manual steps for program installation.

Windows systems prior to Windows 10 exemplified this challenge through a multi-step installation process:

- Locating official software sources or using third-party software centers
- Downloading installation packages manually
- Extracting or executing installers
- Following installation wizards and cleaning up temporary files

This inefficient approach introduced security vulnerabilities and consumed excessive time. Microsoft addressed these issues in May 2020 at the Microsoft Build conference by launching WinGet, the official Windows package manager. Alternatively, the open-source Scoop offers robust command-line package management for Windows, enabling streamlined software operations through PowerShell or Command Prompt with single-line commands for installation, removal, and updates.

UNIX-like OSs face additional complexity due to their file permission system. These true multi-user environments must track ownership and access rights for every file. Software installation requires meticulous file placement in appropriate directories, permission configuration, and ownership assignment. For complex applications with extensive file structures, manual management becomes impractical.

Software maintenance adds further challenges. Applications must support clean uninstallation and seamless upgrades. The upgrade process typically involves removing older versions while preserving configuration files, installing new versions, and restoring these configurations. Unlike Windows systems, which often struggle with dependency management during these operations, UNIX-like OSs needed a robust solution.

Package management emerged as the answer to these software lifecycle challenges. FreeBSD pioneered effective package management in the 1980s, with GNU/

8.4 Software Packages

Linux soon developing its own solutions. Though package managers existed for decades as command-line tools for software lifecycle management, the concept gained widespread recognition through mobile platforms, beginning with the Apple App Store in 2007 and the subsequent Android Market.

Package managers deliver comprehensive functionality across different OSs. Their core features encompass package searching, automated downloading, verification, installation, and cleanup processes. A crucial capability involves automatically resolving and installing dependencies during software installation, enhancing both security and user experience.

OSs implement diverse package management solutions. macOS offers dual approaches with the command-line Homebrew and graphical App Store. FreeBSD relies on pkg for .tgz packages, while Debian-based systems use Advanced Packaging Tool (APT) for .deb packages. RHEL, CentOS, and openEuler primarily utilize DNF for .rpm packages. Though Linux distributions generally stick to one package management system, proficiency with multiple package managers proves valuable in heterogeneous environments where workstations and servers run different distributions.

Package managers primarily handle binary packages, which contain precompiled executables for efficient installation. Alternatively, systems can utilize source packages, requiring local compilation before installation. This approach enables customization and optimized runtime performance.

Package management operations demand root privileges. Taking openEuler as our example, we will examine three primary package management methods: RPM, DNF, and source package management.

8.4.1 Package Management with RPM

RPM, initially created by Red Hat, evolved from Red Hat Package Manager to RPM Package Manager as it gained widespread adoption across Linux distributions and even non-Linux systems [14].

This package management system delivers comprehensive functionality with broad Linux distribution compatibility. Its robust database tracks installed packages and versions, handles package operations (installation, upgrades, removal), and supports binary RPM package compilation from source code. Binary packages follow a structured naming convention: *name-version-release.arch*.**rpm**, indicating the software name, version number, release number, and processor architecture.

The **rpm** command offers extensive management capabilities through various options. Table 8.3 outlines key options, with comprehensive documentation available via **rpm --help**.

Example of local RPM package installation:

```
[root@openEuler24 ~]# rpm -hvi /tmp/downloads/
samba-4.17.5-8.oe2203sp2.aarch64.rpm
```

Table 8.3 Common rpm options

Option	Description	Option	Description
-i	Installs RPM packages	-V	Queries installed package versions
-h	Displays progress with hash marks	-p	Queries/verifies package files
-v	Shows detailed installation progress	-ql	Lists package contents
-U	Upgrades specified packages	-qi	Shows package description
-q	Queries package installation status or contents	-qf	Identifies package ownership of files
-qa	Lists all installed packages	-Va	Verifies all packages for missing files

Despite its capabilities, RPM has significant drawbacks. It lacks automatic dependency resolution during installation, requires careful handling of package dependencies during removal, and demands manual package discovery and downloading.

Yellowdog Updater Modified (YUM) emerged as a Python-based frontend for RPM, offering automated package downloads from repositories and dependency resolution. While it improved upon RPM management, YUM struggled with performance issues, memory inefficiency, slow dependency processing, and poor user experience.

These persistent challenges led to the development of Dandified YUM (DNF) as a modern replacement.

8.4.2 Package Management with DNF

Many Linux distributions, including openEuler, now use DNF as their primary package management tool. As the next-generation RPM package manager, DNF stands among the most robust package management solutions available. Built on C libraries like libsolv and hawkey, it resolves many limitations of YUM, delivering substantial improvements in memory efficiency, dependency resolution, and operational speed.

DNF streamlines package management by automating repository downloads, handling dependencies during installation and removal operations, managing package groups, and maintaining software currency. It maintains **yum** command compatibility while providing extensive APIs for extensions and plugins.

Table 8.4 outlines essential DNF operations for package management. Beyond these core functions, DNF offers advanced features like history tracking and automatic dependency cleanup, with comprehensive documentation accessible through **dnf --help**.

DNF enhances package management through group operations. Package groups bundle related software serving common purposes, such as system utilities, development tools, or scientific computing packages. DNF efficiently handles group installations and removals, with comprehensive documentation available through **dnf group --help**.

8.4 Software Packages

Table 8.4 Common dnf commands

Command	Description
dnf search *string*	Search packages by name, abbreviation, or description keywords to locate desired software, particularly useful for finding Nginx-related packages
dnf info *string*	Display detailed package information
dnf install *string*	Install and update packages with automatic dependency resolution
dnf list *string* | installed	Display information for specific or all installed packages
dnf remove *string*	Execute package removal with intelligent dependency analysis, automatically removing unused dependent packages
dnf update *string*	Update packages and dependencies system-wide or selectively by package/group name, ensuring all dependencies remain current

View available package groups with **dnf group list**:

```
[root@openEuler24 ~]# dnf group list
Last metadata expiration check: 22:49:03 ago on Sun Nov 12 03:28:40 2025.
Available Environment Groups:
   Minimal Install
   Server
   Virtualization Host
Available Groups:
   Container Management
   Development Tools
   Headless Management
   Legacy UNIX Compatibility
   Network Servers
   Scientific Support
   Security Tools
   System Tools
   Smart Card Support
```

Examine required and optional packages within the "Development Tools" group using:

```
dnf group info 'Development Tools'
```

Group management commands follow a simple syntax. Install "Development Tools" with either:

```
[root@openEuler24 ~]# dnf group install "Development Tools"
```

Or:

```
[root@openEuler24 ~]# dnf group install development
```

For removal, replace **install** with **remove**. Update groups using **dnf group update**. DNF stores its configuration through two primary methods:
1. The **/etc/dnf/dnf.conf** file containing:
   Global settings in the "main" section
   Repository configurations in the "repository" section
2. Repository files in **/etc/yum.repos.d** supporting both network URLs and local paths. For example, create a local repository from a locally mounted openEuler ISO:

```
    [ict@openEuler24 ~]$ sudo sh -c 'mkdir /var/repo && mount -o loop \
    > openEuler-24.03-LTS-SP2-x86_64-dvd.iso /var/repo/'
    [ict@openEuler24 ~]$ file /var/repo/RPM-GPG-KEY-openEuler
    /var/repo/RPM-GPG-KEY-openEuler: PGP public key block Public-Key (old)
```

Configure a local repository by creating **openEuler24.03-local.repo** containing the following content in **/etc/yum.repos.d**:

```
[OS]
name=openEuler 24.03-LTS -OS
baseurl=file:///var/repo/
enabled=1
metadata_expire=-1
gpgcheck=1
gpgkey=file:///var/repo/RPM-GPG-KEY-openEuler
[everything]
name=openEuler 24.03-LTS -Everything
baseurl=file:///var/repo/
enabled=1
metadata_expire=-1
gpgcheck=1
gpgkey=file:///var/repo/RPM-GPG-KEY-openEuler
```

Customize repository configurations based on network conditions and system requirements. View configured repositories using:

```
[root@openEuler24 ~]# dnf repolist
[root@openEuler24 ~]# dnf update
```

8.4.3 Source Package Management

Source packages provide a versatile and flexible software management approach, primarily serving professional developers and high-performance production environments.

While package managers like DNF offer simple and efficient software installation for most users, their reliance on binary packages can present several limitations:

- Outdated versions or unsuitable compilation parameters
- Lack of package support for current systems
- Missing features in binary packages
- Need for performance optimization through custom compilation

For open-source software, these limitations can be overcome by installing from source packages. The installation process typically follows these steps:

- Download and extract source package, verifying integrity.
- Check **README** and **INSTALL** documentation for instructions.
- Generate a Makefile using the **./configure** script.
- Compile source code with the **make** command.
- Install software using **make install**.

> The installation process places compiled binaries in designated directories. By default, files install to **/usr/local/**, with configuration files in **/usr/local/etc** or **/usr/local/***/etc**.

openEuler users can reference Example 6.1, which details the complete source installation process for QEMU 5.0.0.

Most OSs follow similar source package management procedures for local compilation and installation. The Ports system of FreeBSD stands out as an elegant solution. This Makefile-based system uses text descriptions to automate the entire process—from downloading and patching to compilation and installation. While Ports enables automated installation with optimized parameters and pre-prepared patches, it requires significant local resources and longer processing times.

> Ports demonstrates sophisticated software management through source packages and Makefiles. The system showcases Makefile capabilities—a single make world command in the source tree root compiles the entire OS.

Source packages excel in portability and customization, letting users compile software optimized for their systems from a single source distribution. However, this approach has limitations: not all software offers source packages, and the compilation process often involves complex configurations and dependencies that may challenge non-developers.

8.5 System Services

OSs run certain applications in a distinctive way—they automatically launch in the background at startup, terminate during shutdown, and deliver continuous services to users both locally and over networks. These applications, known as system services, are managed differently across various OSs.

Windows Task Manager displays multiple system services, including input method and printer services. Some services activate automatically but can be stopped manually when unnecessary, while others remain inactive until manually started.

In Linux, system services (called daemons) operate in the background independently of the shell. These include NetworkManager for system network management (covered in Chap. 7), firewall services for network security, and other services like SSH, task scheduling, system logging, and security auditing that we will explore later. As vital extensions of OS functionality, these services must balance efficient operation with straightforward management, requiring effective implementation mechanisms.

Modern Linux distributions implement systemd (meaning "system daemon") as their service mechanism. This system improves upon traditional SysVinit by eliminating its inherent limitations and accelerating service startup [14]. Major distributions including Ubuntu, Debian, Fedora Linux, CentOS, and openEuler now use systemd as their default initialization system.

systemd exemplifies the UNIX design philosophy of "provide mechanism, not policy."

8.5.1 systemd

In early Linux service management based on SysVinit, init was the first process created after kernel initialization, typically assigned PID 1. The kernel launched it using a hardcoded file name, and any failure to start init triggered a kernel panic. After initializing itself, init started additional system services by executing configuration scripts from the **/etc/init.d** directory. Administrators could start or stop these system services using the service tool. As the direct or indirect "ancestor" of all other processes, init automatically adopted orphaned processes and ran continuously as a daemon until system shutdown. However, the init mechanism had drawbacks: services started sequentially, leading to lengthy boot times, and service scripts were complicated to create.

systemd emerged as a modern replacement for traditional SysVinit. It introduces on-demand daemon startup policies, system state snapshots, and restoration and implements precise service dependency management. With enhanced parallel processing capabilities, it delivers robust service management and monitoring. systemd features on-demand task activation triggered by specific events (such as USB device connections) or port activity, launching services only when needed. This approach reduces initial process load during startup and enables true parallel service launching. System services live in separate service files within the **/etc/systemd/system/** directory and are controlled through the **systemctl** tool for operations like starting, stopping, or restarting, streamlining service administration and improving efficiency.

systemd manages various system resources as units, introducing a unified configuration format that replaces multiple legacy formats used for services, scheduled tasks, device mounting, and network configuration. Each resource type uses a specific file extension: .service files control system services, .mount files handle file system mounting, and .socket files manage message-triggered services for system or network events. systemd also replaces traditional runlevels with targets, providing enhanced flexibility in system state management.

The shift from SysVinit to systemd represents a fundamental change in Linux system management philosophy. While SysVinit comprised lightweight, elegant services with complex but transparent configuration, systemd emerged as a comprehensive system offering simplified configuration but significantly expanded functionality. This transformation has divided the Linux community—proponents value its powerful features and operational simplicity, while critics argue it deviates from core UNIX design principles.

8.5.2 systemctl

The **systemctl** command serves as the management interface of systemd, requiring root privileges for system service administration. Use **systemctl status** to view all active system services.

Adding system services is straightforward with systemd-compatible software. During installation, service configuration files automatically appear in **/usr/lib/systemd/system/**. For example, installing httpd via **dnf** creates **/usr/lib/systemd/system/httpd.service**. Enable httpd as a system service with:

```
[ict@openEuler24 ~]$ sudo dnf install -y httpd
[ict@openEuler24 ~]$ systemctl enable httpd
Created symlink /etc/systemd/system/multi-user.target.wants/httpd.service → /usr/lib/
    systemd/system/httpd.service.
```

This process creates a symbolic link in **/etc/systemd/system**, the primary directory systemd monitors for service configurations. This symbolic linking pattern appears frequently across Linux systems.

Enabled services start automatically at boot. To start a service immediately:

```
[ict@openEuler24 ~]$ systemctl start httpd
```

Check service status with:

```
[ict@openEuler24 ~]$ systemctl status httpd
```

Stop a running service with:

```
[ict@openEuler24 ~]$ systemctl stop httpd
```

Apply configuration changes to running services by restarting them:

```
[ict@openEuler24 ~]$ systemctl restart httpd
```

This command starts the service if it is not already running.
Disable a service with:

```
[ict@openEuler24 ~]$ systemctl disable httpd
```

systemctl also manages system operations like shutdown, restart, and hibernation, plus additional service management features. Access complete documentation with **systemctl --help**.

8.5.3 .service Files

systemd uses .service files for service configuration, which can be modified with any text editor for simple and flexible management.

8.5 System Services

Windows requires registry modifications or the **sc** tool to create services, with limited configuration options:

```
sc create TestService binpath= "D:\Test\TestService.exe"
start= auto displayname=
"TestService"
```

UNIX-like OSs offer greater flexibility through text-based configuration files. While early Linux used SysVinit with complex service scripts managed by the **service** command, systemd simplifies this process using **systemctl** with more straightforward configuration syntax.

Each .service file contains three main sections: **[Unit]**, **[Service]**, and **[Install]**. Here is how they work, using httpd as an example:

```
[ict@openEuler24 ~]$ cat /usr/lib/systemd/system/httpd.service
  [Unit]
  Description=The Apache HTTP Server
  Wants=httpd-init.service
  After=network.target remote-fs.target nss-lookup.target httpd-init.service
  Documentation=man:httpd.service(8)
  [Service]
  Type=notify
  Environment=LANG=C
  ExecStart=/usr/sbin/httpd $OPTIONS -DFOREGROUND
  ExecStartPost=/usr/bin/sleep 0.1
  ExecReload=/usr/sbin/httpd $OPTIONS -k graceful
  # Send SIGWINCH for graceful stop
  KillSignal=SIGWINCH
  KillMode=mixed
  PrivateTmp=true
  [Install]
  WantedBy=multi-user.target
```

(1) **[Unit]**

This section provides basic service information through fields like:

- **Description**: brief service summary
- **Documentation**: help document location
- **After/Before**: service start order
- **Wants/Require**: service dependencies

(2) **[Service]**

This section controls service execution with fields including:

- **Type**: startup behavior
- **ExecPre**: pre-start commands
- **ExecStart**: start commands
- **ExecReload**: restart commands
- **KillMode**: service termination method

(3) **[Install]**

This section manages boot-time configuration, primarily through the **WantedBy** field, which specifies the target (group) of the service. For instance, **WantedBy=multi-user.target** places the service in the multi-user **target** group. When services are enabled with **systemctl enable**, symbolic links appear in **/etc/systemd/system/multi-user.target.wants/**.

Creating systemd services requires only a basic .service file, making it accessible for users to implement their own services.

8.5.4 SSH Service

SSH service, essential for secure remote sessions including login and management, is one of the most vital Linux system services. openEuler includes pre-installed OpenSSH server with **/usr/sbin/sshd** as its daemon process.

The OpenSSH server uses **/etc/ssh/sshd_config** for configuration, offering extensive security controls including root login restrictions, X11 forwarding options, and user access management.

```
# Disable root remote login.
PermitRootLogin no
# Prohibit empty passwords.
PermitEmptyPasswords no
# Allow specific users (allowlist).
AllowUsers ict
# Deny specific users (blocklist).
DenyUsers tom
# Disconnect after 300s timeout.
ClientAliveInterval 300
# X11 forwarding is risky and can be disabled if unnecessary.
X11Forwarding no
```

To apply configuration changes, restart the service with **systemctl restart sshd**.

Linux provides additional login security through **/etc/hosts.deny** (blocklist) and **/etc/hosts.allow** (allowlist). Further access control policies can be set in **/etc/ssh/sshd_config**.

As the root process (PID 1), systemd serves as the cornerstone of Linux system management. It handles complex background operations while maintaining a simple interface for service management. This approach separates service implementation from system management, letting users focus on service functionality, while systemd handles the underlying complexity.

8.5.5 Example 8.4: LAMP Stack Installation

The LAMP stack—Linux, Apache, MySQL, and PHP—remains one of the most popular web hosting solutions. This combination provides core services for website deployment: OS, HTTP server, database server, and dynamic web page processing.

This example shows LAMP installation on openEuler with two key differences: openEuler replaces traditional Linux distributions, and MariaDB serves as the database instead of MySQL, offering similar functionality with more permissive licensing.

(1) Install the packages.
   Install the required packages: httpd (Apache), mariadb-server (MariaDB), php, and php-mysqlnd (for PHP-database connectivity):

```
[ict@openEuler24 ~]$ sudo dnf install -y httpd mariadb-server php php-mysqlnd
```

(2) Enable system services.

```
    [ict@openEuler24 ~]$ sudo systemctl enable mariadb
    Created symlink /etc/systemd/system/mysql.service → /usr/lib/systemd/system/
mariadb.service.
    Created symlink /etc/systemd/system/mysqld.service → /usr/lib/systemd/system/
mariadb.service.
    Created symlink /etc/systemd/system/multi-user.target.wants/mariadb.service →
/usr/lib/
        systemd/system/mariadb.service.
    [ict@openEuler24 ~]$ sudo systemctl restart httpd mariadb
```

(3) Verify service status.

```
[ict@openEuler24 ~]$ sudo systemctl status httpd mariadb
```

DNF handles package dependencies automatically, streamlining the installation process. These basic steps establish a robust LAMP environment on openEuler. Example 8.6 will explore building a full-featured website using this stack.

(4) Test Apache.

Verify that port 80 is open on the firewall, then access Apache using a browser from another computer through the server IP address (e.g., http://10.211.55.26/). The Apache test page (Fig. 8.2) indicates successful installation.

8.6 Scheduled Tasks

While system services run continuously in the background, certain applications require execution at specific times or intervals, terminating after completing each task. Common examples include regular data backups on production servers or scheduled system maintenance like reboots. To automate these repetitive operations and minimize human intervention, UNIX-like OSs implement task scheduling capabilities.

Linux provides two scheduling utilities: **at** for one-time tasks and **crontab** for recurring operations. Notably, the task scheduler daemons themselves run as background system services. This separation of scheduling functionality into dedicated tools exemplifies the successful modular approach of UNIX design philosophy.

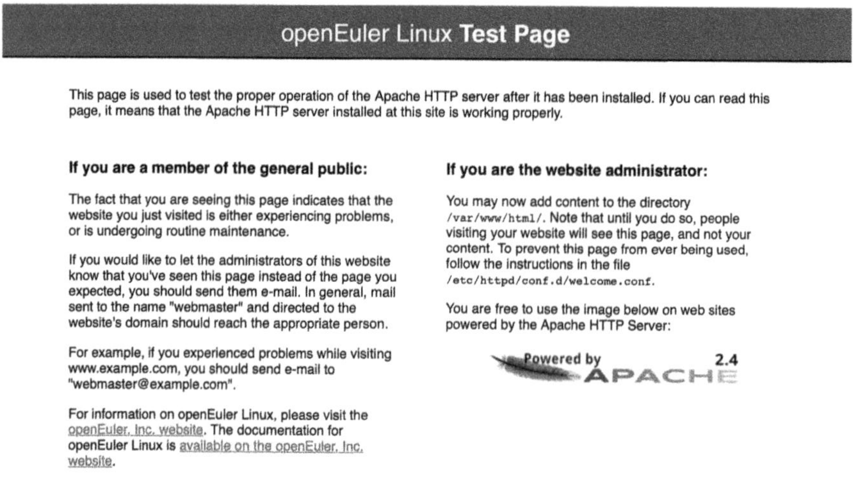

Fig. 8.2 Apache test page

8.6.1 One-Time Tasks

The **at** command provides a flexible system for scheduling one-time tasks by specifying when they should run.

Time can be specified in several formats. The basic format is *hh:mm* (hour:minute)—if this time has already passed, the task runs the next day. You can use 12-hour format with AM/PM indicators. Dates can follow the time specification in formats like *month day*, *mm/dd/yy*, or *dd.mm.yy*. Simple terms like **today** or **tomorrow** are also accepted. The command recognizes common time references like **midnight**, **noon**, and **teatime** (4 PM).

For tasks that need to run soon, relative timing offers a convenient alternative to absolute timing. The format is **now** + *count time-units*, where *count* specifies the number of minutes, hours, days, or weeks from the current time.

Linux implements a simple permission system for **at** through two files: **/etc/at.deny** (blocklist) and **/etc/at.allow** (allowlist). The system follows these rules:

- If the allowlist exists, only listed users can schedule tasks.
- If only the blocklist exists, all users except those listed can schedule tasks.
- If neither file exists, only **root** can schedule tasks.

Typically, systems only use the blocklist, allowing most users to schedule tasks. The **root** user always has scheduling privileges regardless of these files.

Here is an example of creating a one-time task that creates an empty file in **/tmp** after 1 minute:

```
[root@openEuler24 ~]# at now+1minutes
warning: commands will be executed using /bin/sh
at> touch /tmp/at_test.txt
at> <EOT>
job 1 at Fri Nov 15 00:00:00 2025
```

Note: Press **Ctrl+D** to end the input (shown as EOT above). If **at** is not available, install it with **dnf install at** and start the service with **systemctl start atd**.

8.6.2 Periodic Tasks

The cron service, which starts automatically with the system, manages periodic tasks that users can schedule using the **crontab** command.

cron is one of the most useful tools in UNIX-like OSs. Running continuously in the background, it monitors system-level periodic tasks in the **/etc/crontab** file and **/etc/cron.*** directories, as well as user-level tasks in **/var/spool/cron/crontabs**. To prevent errors that could cause task failures or unnecessary system load, never edit these configuration files directly—always use the **crontab** tool to manage periodic tasks.

The **crontab** tool offers a straightforward way to add, modify, or delete periodic tasks. Enter the task editor by running **crontab -e**. Each line defines one task with six fields—five for timing and one for the command:

```
    *  *  *  *  *  command
    |  |  |  |  |
    |  |  |  |  .---- command to execute (system command
or script)
    |  |  |  .------- day of week (0-6) (Sunday=0 or 7) or
sun,mon,tue,wed,thu,fri,sat
    |  |  .---------- month (1-12) or jan, feb, mar, apr, ...
    |  .------------- day of month (1-31)
    .---------------- hour (0-23)
    .---------------- minute (0-59)
```

crontab provides four operators for specifying multiple values in time fields:

- Asterisk ("*"): represents all possible values (such as every hour and every month).
- Comma (","): lists specific values (**0, 15, 30, 45** in the minute field runs a task every 15 minutes).
- Hyphen ("-"): defines a range (**1–5** means 1, 2, 3, 4, and 5).
- Slash ("/"): sets an interval (***/2** in the hour field runs a task every second hour).

The command field accepts simple system commands, complex commands (with pipes and redirections), and custom scripts.

The examples below illustrate how to set up periodic tasks.

Schedule the nginx service to restart every two hours from midnight to 8 AM on Saturdays:

```
59 0-8/2 * * 6 nginx restart
```

Configure a backup script to run at midnight on the 1st and 15th of each month, silencing all output:

```
0 0 1,15 * * /home/openEuler/bin/backup.sh > /dev/null 2>&1
```

Use **crontab -l** to list your tasks and **crontab -r** to remove them all. The cron service implements access control through **/etc/cron.deny** and **/etc/cron.allow** files, following similar rules to the **at** command.

> "Do one thing and do it well"—both **at** and **crontab** exemplify this fundamental UNIX design philosophy.

8.7 System Security

In our interconnected world, network services are fundamental to both business operations and daily life. While external network threats pose significant risks, the security of server OSs is paramount. For large-scale network services, security incidents such as service disruptions or data breaches can result in severe disruptions and potentially catastrophic losses. Both server operational reliability and data protection ultimately depend on the security of the underlying OS.

This section examines basic security measures for GNU/Linux OSs, using openEuler as the reference platform. System security encompasses two key components: the built-in security mechanisms of the OS and the security measures implemented by administrators. While modern OSs provide robust security features by default, the focus for server administrators should be on implementing appropriate security measures and best practices.

8.7.1 Root Privileges

The **root** user holds the highest level of system privileges, enabling nearly unlimited access to system resources. These elevated permissions, known as root privileges, grant complete control over server operations. This level of access makes root privileges a primary target for cybersecurity attacks.

Operating with root privileges presents significant security risks. These include potential password compromises, accidental modification or deletion of critical system files, execution of malicious Trojan programs, and unintended privilege escalation. For these reasons, logging in as **root** is discouraged even on personal computers unless absolutely necessary.

> UNIX-like OSs intentionally exclude the current directory from search paths (the shell **$PATH** environment variable) as a security measure. This prevents malicious programs sharing names with system tools from gaining root privileges through accidental execution.

When root privileges are required, **sudo** offers a safer alternative by providing temporary privilege escalation. **sudo** enables authorized regular users to execute specific commands with root privileges.

For example, an authorized user can execute:

```
[ict@openEuler24 ~]$ sudo dnf update
```

Authorization is managed through the **/etc/sudoers** file, which specifies users, groups, and their permitted commands. **sudo** configurations can precisely control what authorized users can and cannot do. The simplest implementation uses the default configuration of **sudo** by adding users to either the **wheel** or **admin** group.

An alternative to **sudo** is the **su** (switch user) command, which enables switching between users. Authorized users can elevate to root privileges, while the **root** user can switch to regular users. Detailed usage instructions are available through **su --help**.

Security-conscious servers typically disable SSH remote login for the **root** user. Administrators instead log in as regular users and use temporary privilege escalation methods to perform root-level tasks.

Root privileges can be restricted for critical system files to prevent accidental modifications. The **chattr** tool manages special file attributes, allowing restrictions like append-only or read-only status that apply even to **root** users. These special attributes can be viewed using **lsattr**.

8.7.2 Special File Permissions

This section covers two types of special file permissions in Linux: temporary privilege elevation and granular file access control [14].

Linux implements special permissions for certain commands and directories. For instance, the **passwd** command enables all users to change their passwords and write to **/etc/shadow**, despite regular users lacking direct read-write access to this file. Similarly, the **/tmp** directory allows any application to write temporary files while preventing access to files created by other users.

The permission bits for **passwd** and **/tmp** demonstrate these special attributes:

```
[ict@openEuler24 ~]$ ls -ld /usr/bin/passwd /tmp
drwxrwxrwt 17 root root 4096 Nov 15 17:28 /tmp
-rwsr-xr-x 1 root root 63744 Feb 7 2025 /usr/bin/passwd
```

Linux supports three special permissions:

- SUID (setuid): Marked by **s** in the user execution bit, SUID lets programs run with privileges of the program file owner instead of those of the executing user. This enables regular users to run specific programs requiring elevated permissions.
- SGID (setgid): Marked by **s** in the group execution bit, SGID lets programs run with privileges of the program file owner group instead of those of the executing user's group. This is particularly useful for shared directories requiring group-based access control.
- SBIT (sticky bit): Marked by **t** in the execution bit, SBIT protects shared directories by restricting file deletion. In directories with SBIT, only the file owner and **root** can delete files, preventing unauthorized removal of other users' files.

The SUID permission on the **passwd** command, combined with root ownership, enables regular users to modify system password files. Similarly, the SBIT permission on **/tmp** protects users' temporary files from unauthorized access or deletion.

System administrators must exercise caution when assigning special permissions through **chmod**. Routine audits using **find** help identify files with unexpected privilege assignments. This command locates root-owned files with SUID permission, suppressing error output:

```
[ict@openEuler24 ~]$ find / -perm -u=s -type f 2>/dev/null
```

Special permissions provide targeted privilege elevation for specific resources, offering a more secure alternative to system-wide root access through **su** or **sudo**. However, their application is limited to specific files like **passwd** and **/tmp**, constraining their broader security benefits.

Linux Access Control List (ACL) enables granular file access management, addressing limitations of traditional permissions. Large organizations, particularly those using NFS or Samba for file sharing, benefit from the ability of ACL to handle complex access requirements.

ACL extends beyond standard permissions of the user, group, and others by allowing specific permission assignments for individual users and groups. Users can configure ACL on their files and directories, granting read, write, or execute permissions to multiple named users and groups.

Managing ACL involves two primary commands:

getfacl: views ACL permissions.

setfacl: modifies ACL permissions.

Here is an example of managing ACL permissions, granting read-write access to user **guest** on **some_file**, viewing ACL permissions on the file, and removing access for **guest**:

```
[ict@openEuler24 ~]$ setfacl -m u:guest:rw ~/some_file
[ict@openEuler24 ~]$ getfacl ~/some_file
[ict@openEuler24 ~]$ setfacl -x u:guest ~/some_file
```

Implementation of ACLs requires enabling ACL mount attributes and activating relevant system services.

8.7.3 SELinux

As demonstrated in Sects. 8.7.1 and 8.7.2, root privileges allow nearly unlimited access to system resources, creating significant security vulnerabilities. The traditional permission management system of Linux uses discretionary access control (DAC), where resource access depends solely on user permissions. To effectively restrict root privileges, a more robust permission management mechanism became necessary.

Security-Enhanced Linux (SELinux) serves as a powerful Linux security subsystem that enforces the principle of least privilege by limiting service processes to only essential resources. SELinux implements mandatory access control (MAC) at the kernel level, shifting the focus from users to processes. Under MAC, resource access requires both appropriate user permissions and process-level authorization for specific resource types. This means even root-level processes can only access their designated resources. If a root-running program has security vulnerabilities, the potential damage remains contained within its permitted resource boundaries.

The SELinux configuration file at **/etc/selinux/config** takes effect after system reboot and contains two primary settings: operational state and type.

```
# This file controls the state of SELinux on the system.
# SELINUX= can take one of these three values:
#         enforcing -SELinux security policy is enforced.
#         permissive -SELinux prints warnings instead of enforcing.
#         disabled -No SELinux policy is loaded.
SELINUX=enforcing
# SELINUXTYPE= can take one of these two values:
#         targeted -Targeted processes are protected,
#         mls -Multi Level Security protection.
SELINUXTYPE=targeted
```

SELinux operates in one of three modes:

- disabled: deactivates SELinux completely, reverting to standard DAC security.
- permissive: logs policy violations without enforcing restrictions.
- enforcing: actively enforces security policies by blocking unauthorized operations.

8.7 System Security

SELinux defaults to enforcing mode, offering stronger access control and security protection than standard Linux, though its complexity makes configuration and management challenging. Users often encounter difficulties accessing certain files or applications with SELinux enabled. Its strict predefined policies can also complicate integration with various programs and services, leading many to disable it or switch to permissive mode.

```
[openEuler@host ~]# sed -i 's/SELINUX=enforcing/SELINUX=disabled/' /etc/selinux/config
[openEuler@host ~]# setenforce 0
```

These commands demonstrate how to disable SELinux completely and switch it to permissive mode temporarily. In permissive mode, while policy violations are not blocked, they are logged in **/var/log/audit/audit.log** for review.

Rather than abandoning security features of SELinux, a better approach is mastering and properly implementing the semanage tool to strengthen system security effectively.

> macOS implements an alternative approach to root privilege restriction. System files with special attributes remain protected from modification or deletion, even with root access, during normal operation. Such changes require a system reboot in "recovery mode." While this effectively protects desktop systems from both accidental damage and malware, the requirement to reboot for system maintenance makes it impractical for servers requiring continuous operation.
> FreeBSD jail provides comprehensive virtualization of file system access, users, network subsystems, and other resources, containing processes within minimal virtual environments. By virtualizing **root** users within jail environments, it maintains effective security control. Similarly, Docker on Linux offers containerization technology that enhances host system security by isolating potentially vulnerable applications within containers.

8.7.4 Logging System

OSs use logs to record crucial information about system operations, which is essential for performance optimization, troubleshooting, security auditing, and other server management tasks. UNIX-like OSs feature a sophisticated logging architecture with flexible, user-friendly solutions that perfect the logging functionality. This design merits in-depth study by embedded system users and application developers. This section explains Linux logs, their location, usage, and the underlying design principles.

Logging plays a vital role in system security. With numerous background services running remotely and systems operating unattended for extended periods, timely awareness of server events becomes crucial for security. Critical events include drive space reaching capacity, failed login attempts (particularly for root access), sustained connection request floods, or sequential probing of multiple service ports. Regular log review (log inspection) provides the best insight into system status.

The **dmesg** command stands as the primary tool for viewing kernel-level logs. It retrieves log information from the kernel ring buffer, capturing system boot details, hardware detection, driver loading, and runtime errors. This information offers deep visibility into system operations, facilitating problem diagnosis and system debugging. While **dmesg** does not read log files directly, users can redirect its output to files or filter specific messages using tools like **grep**.

Beyond kernel logging, systems maintain broader system-level and application-level logs in various log files, requiring robust and flexible logging tools for effective management.

Linux implements three core logging services: journald, rsyslog, and logrotate. These services capture and store all critical system information—from kernel events and background services to user operations—in structured log files. This comprehensive logging system serves two key purposes: it provides essential data for security analysis while offering developers a standardized programming interface to integrate application-specific logging within the unified logging framework of the system.

(1) journald

journald, a systemd component, revolutionizes system logging by implementing binary-format storage to address traditional syslog vulnerabilities like log forgery and format inconsistency. Through its **journalctl** command, it presents logs from diverse system services in a standardized format, streamlining analysis and processing workflows.

The service captures comprehensive logging data from system startup, encompassing kernel messages (via **printk**), system service output (stdout/stderr), and user process logs (via syslog). Its versatile **journalctl** command supports sophisticated log viewing with filters for boot logs, system logs, user logs, time ranges, grep pattern matching, and multiple output formats. Details about the command are available through **journalctl -h**.

```
[ict@openEuler24 ~]$ journalctl -g 'passwd'
   Nov 18 16:12:41 sshd[39618]: Failed publickey for root
from 10.211.55.2 port 61859
ssh2: RSA S>
   Nov 18 16:12:44 sshd[39618]: Accepted password for root
```

8.7 System Security

```
from 10.211.55.2 port 61859
ssh2
   Nov 18 16:12:44 sshd[39618]: pam_unix(sshd:session):
session opened for user
root(uid=0) by (u>
   Nov 18 17:53:31 sshd[39618]: pam_unix(sshd:session):
session closed for user root
   Nov 18 17:53:39 sshd[39988]: Accepted key RSA SHA256:hGHK
3gU7ggO0bzOTBltPT7wzECsEq04XE4/
1UEIYN>
   Nov 18 17:53:39 sshd[39988]: Accepted publickey for ict
from 10.211.55.2 port 61184 ssh2: RSA >
   Nov 18 17:53:39 sshd[39988]: pam_unix(sshd:session):
session opened for user
ict(uid=1002) by
   Nov 17 21:26:54 sudo[24391]: openEuler : TTY=tty1 ; PWD=/
home/openEuler ; USER=root ; COMMAND=>
   Nov 17 22:39:48 passwd[28998]: pam_
unix(passwd:chauthtok): password changed for ict
```

However, journald operates with two key constraints: a 4 GB default storage limit (with log rotation) and non-persistent logs that clear on system reboot. These limitations stem from its storage location in **/run/log/journal**, which resides in kernel-mapped memory space on a temporary file system.

At its core, journald functions as an efficient log collection service, optimized to capture logging requests from system processes while maintaining minimal performance impact. It delegates permanent storage and advanced analysis functions to the rsyslog service.

(2) rsyslog

rsyslog, "the rocket-fast system for log processing," serves as a high-performance log management system that handles formatting, forwarding, and storage of log data. Its architecture emphasizes speed, security, and modularity, featuring customizable output formats, precise timestamps, queuing capabilities, and comprehensive message filtering.

The flexible architecture of rsyslog, illustrated in Fig. 8.3, scales effectively from small deployments to enterprise environments. It implements a multi-stage processing pipeline where logs flow through specialized input modules, preprocessing stages, a main queue, filtering systems, parallel execution queues, and finally output modules. The system supports diverse input sources (files, kmsg logs, kernel logs, systemd journal, TCP/UDP) and output destinations (files, pipes, systemd journal, TCP/UDP, MySQL), with extensibility for additional formats.

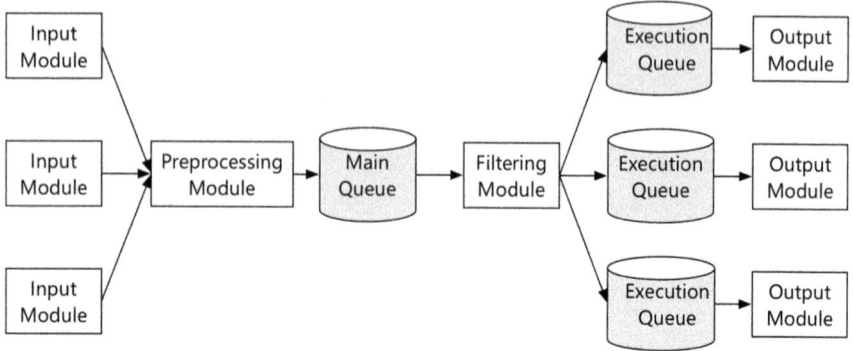

Fig. 8.3 rsyslog architecture

Configuration occurs through **/etc/rsyslog.conf** in three major sections:

- **GLOBAL**: defines core settings including working directory and timestamp formats.
- **MODULES**: specifies input modules like imuxsock for **logger** commands and imjournal for systemd journal access.
- **RULES**: establishes log routing using selector-target pairs.

The selector syntax "facility.priority" determines log handling based on source (facility) and severity (priority). Facilities include **authpriv, cron, kern, mail, user,** and **local**, while priorities include **debug, info, notice, warn, error, crit, alert,** and **emerg** in ascending severity. Multiple facilities can be combined with commas, and **none** suppresses logging for specified facilities:

```
*.info;mail.none;authpriv.none;cron.none
/var/log/messages
   cron.*                                      /var/log/cron
```

Targets can include files, log server addresses, pipes, usernames, or databases. While local file storage remains the most common approach, enterprise systems often forward high-volume transaction logs to dedicated database servers for efficient storage and processing.

Here is an example of application logging to journald using a simple C program that sends a message through the **syslog** function:

```
#include <syslog.h>
int main(int argc, char *argv[]) {
        syslog(LOG_NOTICE, "Hello, open Euler!");
        return 0;
}
```

8.7 System Security

Once compiled and executed, the message can be viewed through **journalctl**. Based on rsyslog default rules, the message also appears in **/var/log/messages**:

```
[ict@openEuler24 ~]$ gcc -o log_test log_test.c && ./log_test && journalctl -rlhead -n3
Nov 18 18:05:09 openEuler24.03 log_test[40151]: Hello,openEuler!
Nov 18 18:01:01 openEuler24.03 CROND[40099]: (root) CMDEND (run-parts /etc/cron.hourly)
Nov 18 18:01:01 openEuler24.03 run-parts[40109]: (/etc/cron.hourly) finished 0anacron
```

For environments lacking native logging support, such as certain embedded systems, developers can implement alternative logging frameworks like Log4c or EasyLogger to maintain detailed logs for troubleshooting and debugging.

Running as a system service, rsyslog automatically processes and forwards logs to various files and directories under **/var/log** based on its configuration settings. Table 8.5 lists the common log locations in openEuler.

As systems run continuously, log files grow rapidly, creating two main challenges: slower log analysis due to large file sizes, and excessive drive space consumption that may impact system operation. While older logs often provide little value, managing log retention and storage becomes crucial. The logrotate utility effectively addresses these common logging challenges through automated log management.

(3) logrotate

logrotate manages log file growth by archiving older records while creating fresh log files, enabling efficient storage management within defined constraints.

logrotate operates as a scheduled task through cron, with its script located at **/etc/cron.daily/logrotate**. Log rotation happens automatically in the background at set intervals. While the main configuration resides in **/etc/logrotate.conf**, additional rotation rules can be defined in the **/etc/logrotate.d** directory. Table 8.6 lists the key configuration parameters.

The firewalld package includes its own rotation configuration, which rotates logs weekly, ignores missing file warnings, uses copy-truncate mode, maintains

Table 8.5 Common log locations in openEuler

Log file/directory	Description
audit	Audit daemon logs, including SELinux audit logs
auth.log	System authorization information, including user logins and authentication mechanisms
boot.log	System boot logs, covering service startups, and daemon status changes
btmp	Failed login attempts (binary file, viewable with **lastb**)
cron	Scheduled task logs, including detailed cron job execution records
daemon.log	System background daemon logs
dnf.log	Package management logs, including installation and cleanup operations
lastlog	Most recent login information for all users (binary file, viewable with **lastlog**)
maillog	Mail server operation logs
message	Primary system log containing boot information, errors, and critical events from security-related services (mail, cron, daemon, kern, and auth)
secure	Authentication and access logs, including all sshd activities and failed login attempts
utmp	Current user session information (binary file, viewable with **w** or **who**)
wtmp	Historical login records including system events (binary file, viewable with **last**)

Table 8.6 Primary logrotate configuration parameters

Parameter	Description
Rotate *n*	Number of log files to retain (0 disables backup)
Daily	Daily rotation schedule
Weekly	Weekly rotation schedule
Monthly	Monthly rotation schedule
Compress	Compression for old logs
Create	Definition of new log file permissions, owner, and group (e.g., **create 0640 root adm**)

4 weeks of backups, and only rotates files exceeding 1 MB. Here is the complete configuration:

```
[ict@openEuler24 ~]$ cat /etc/logrotate.d/firewalld
/var/log/firewalld {
    weekly
    missingok
    rotate 4
    copytruncate
    minsize 1M
}
```

8.7 System Security

> Consider this: How does logrotate clear current log files during rotation while ensuring continuous log output from running programs?

logrotate exemplifies excellent UNIX-like OS design and comes pre-installed on Linux distributions. This streamlined service elegantly handles common logging challenges through automated file rotation, simplifying log cleanup and storage management.

The Linux logging ecosystem combines three specialized services: journald for log collection, rsyslog for filtering and forwarding, and logrotate for rotation storage. Each service focuses on its specific role while working harmoniously together.

System administrators rely on comprehensive logging to monitor system health effectively. While mastering rsyslog and logrotate requires initial effort, the combination offers powerful automation for log management tasks like compression, cleanup, and email notifications. These time-tested services maintain consistency across Linux distributions and have remained stable for decades.

From a design perspective, the separation of log rotation from rsyslog exemplifies thoughtful system architecture. Instead of expanding the scope of rsyslog, developers maintained its focus on efficient log filtering and forwarding to multiple destinations. Since local storage remains optional, avoiding additional complexity in rsyslog proved wise. The creation of a dedicated log rotation service addresses a universal logging challenge while embodying the UNIX philosophy of "do one thing and do it well." This architecture also emphasizes the importance of proper logging practices for application developers, enabling better troubleshooting and optimization through traceable operational records.

8.7.5 Security Auditing

While Linux provides extensive logging capabilities for system status and critical user operations, it lacks built-in tracking for routine user activities such as modifications to business-critical files or shared directories. The security auditing system (Audit) bridges this gap.

The Audit subsystem forms an essential component of Linux security architecture. It systematically collects and logs security-relevant events based on custom requirements. Unlike rsyslog, which only captures predefined logs from system services and applications, the Audit subsystem operates at kernel level, monitoring diverse system activities including system calls, file operations, and program executions. Users can define specific audit rules, enabling the subsystem to automatically track and log events of interest, thereby strengthening system security management.

In openEuler, the audit functionality runs by default as the auditd service, managed through the **auditctl** utility. Temporary audit rules follow the syntax

auditctl -w *path* **-p** *permission* **-k** *key*, where *path* specifies the target file or directory, *permission* combines r, w, x, a (read, write, execute, modify), and *key* serves as an identifier linking logs to their source rules.

Consider this example tracking changes to **/etc/rsyslog.conf**:

```
# Add an audit rule.
[root@openEuler24 ~]# auditctl -w /etc/rsyslog.conf -p wa -k change_rsyslog
# View current audit rules.
[root@openEuler24 ~]# auditctl -l -w /etc/rsyslog.conf -p wa -k change_rsyslog
# Modify the timestamp of the target file.
[root@openEuler24 ~]# touch /etc/rsyslog.conf
# View audit logs.
[root@openEuler24 ~]# grep change_rsyslog /var/log/audit/audit.log |tail -n1
type=SYSCALL msg=audit(1700338339.646:3790):
arch=c00000b7 syscall=56 success=yes exit=3
    a0=ffffffffffffff9c a1=ffffdb68e8a1 a2=941 a3=1b6 items=2 ppid=48049 pid=48131 auid=1002
    uid=0 gid=0 euid=0 suid=0 fsuid=0 egid=0 sgid=0 fsgid=0 tty=pts0 ses=62 comm="touch"
    exe="/usr/bin/touch"
subj=unconfined_u:unconfined_r:unconfined_t:s0-s0:c0.c1023
    key="change_rsyslog"ARCH=aarch64 SYSCALL=openat AUID="ict" UID="root" GID="root"
    EUID="root" SUID="root" FSUID="root" EGID="root" SGID="root" FSGID="root"
```

The Audit system provides lightweight security monitoring focused on event tracking rather than enforcement. Unlike MAC of SELinux, Audit simply records system events for analysis, enabling administrators to implement appropriate security measures based on the audit trail.

8.8 System Administration and Maintenance Examples

8.8.1 Example 8.5: System Management with Cockpit

Cockpit is an open-source web-based management and monitoring platform for Linux (see Fig. 8.4). Through its intuitive web interface, it delivers comprehensive system administration capabilities, streamlining routine management tasks and providing

8.8 System Administration and Maintenance Examples

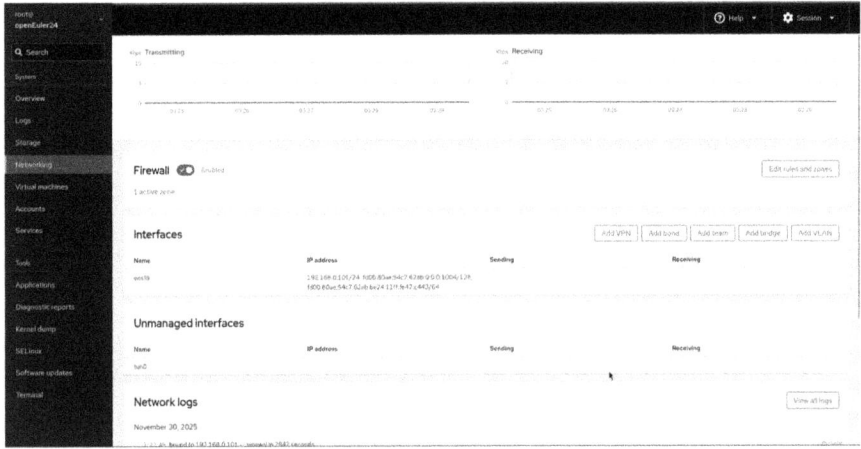

Fig. 8.4 Cockpit management interface

administrators with a powerful control center. Both CentOS 8 and RHEL 8 feature Cockpit as their standard server management solution. Key capabilities include:

- Comprehensive management of users, system services, networking, storage, firewalls, logs, and virtualization
- System monitoring features covering storage metrics, network status, and Docker container oversight
- Batch operations for multiple services, supporting automation and bulk processing
- Browser-based shell access
- Intuitive dashboard interface

The following example shows the installation of Cockpit and necessary firewall configuration. Once the installation is complete, access the Cockpit interface by navigating to **http://**$IP\_address$**:9090** in your web browser, replacing $IP\_address$ with the IP address of your openEuler host.

```
[root@openEuler24 ~]# dnf install -y cockpit
# To install optional GUI desktop plugins, run:
# dnf install -y cockpit-docker cockpit-machines cockpit-dashboard cockpit-storaged
# Start the Cockpit service and enable auto-start.
[root@openEuler24 ~]# systemctl enable --now cockpit.socket
# Configure the firewall and add the Cockpit service for remote access.
[root@openEuler24 ~]# firewall-cmd --permanent --zone=public --add-service=cockpit
# Reload rules.
[root@openEuler24 ~]# firewall-cmd --reload
```

8.8.2 Example 8.6: WordPress Blog Setup

WordPress is a free, open-source content management system (CMS) distinguished by its robust functionality, extensive extensibility, and minimal setup costs. It leads the global CMS market, with studies indicating that 40% of all websites run on WordPress, and this percentage continues to rise.

This guide builds on the LAMP stack installed in Example 8.4 to deploy WordPress. Through several straightforward steps, you can establish yourself as a WordPress site administrator.

> Note: Verify that HTTP service is enabled on the openEuler firewall and confirm your actual IP address to substitute for 10.211.55.26 used below.

(1) Set up the database.
Set the MariaDB administrator password to **654321**.

```
[ict@openEuler24 ~]$ sudo mysqladmin -uroot password '654321'
```

Connect to the local MariaDB database through the MySQL client, accessing it with administrator credentials and the configured password.

```
   [ict@openEuler24 ~]$ mysql -uroot -p
   Enter password:
   Welcome to the MariaDB monitor.  Commands end with ; or \g.
   Your MariaDB connection id is 45
   Server version: 10.5.16-MariaDB MariaDB Server
   Copyright (c) 2000, 2018, Oracle, MariaDB Corporation Ab and others.
   Type 'help;' or '\h' for help. Type '\c' to clear the current input statement.
   MariaDB [(none)]>
```

Create a **wordpress** database. For security best practices, create a dedicated **wordpress** user instead of using the administrator user for WordPress operations.

8.8 System Administration and Maintenance Examples

```
MariaDB [(none)]> create database wordpress;
Query OK, 1 row affected (0.001 sec)
MariaDB [(none)]> create user wordpress;
Query OK, 0 rows affected (0.001 sec)
MariaDB [(none)]>
```

Configure full database privileges for the **wordpress** user on the **wordpress** database, using **123456** as the password.

```
MariaDB [(none)]> GRANT ALL PRIVILEGES ON wordpress.* TO 'wordpress'@'localhost'
    -> identified by '123456';
Query OK, 0 rows affected (0.002 sec)
MariaDB [(none)]> quit
Bye
```

(2) Install WordPress.

Download and extract the latest WordPress package into the web content directory of Apache.

```
[ict@openEuler24 ~]$ wget https://cn.wordpress.org/latest-zh_CN.zip
[ict@openEuler24 ~]$ sudo unzip latest-zh_CN.zip -d /var/www/html/
```

Set appropriate ownership and permissions for the **wordpress** directory contents, as the HTTP service operates under the **apache** user.

```
[ict@openEuler24 ~]$ sudo chown -R apache:apache /var/www/html/wordpress/
[ict@openEuler24 ~]$ sudo chmod -R 755 /var/www/html/wordpress/
```

(3) Configure database connection.

Before proceeding, disable SELinux temporarily, as the configuration file cannot be created automatically otherwise.

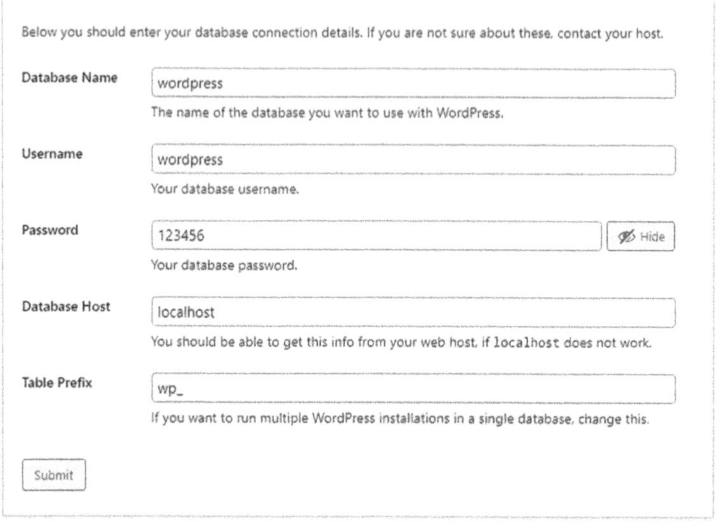

Fig. 8.5 WordPress configuration page

```
[ict@openEuler24 ~]$ sudo setenforce 0
```

Using a GUI web browser with access to the specified IP address, navigate to **http://10.211.55.26/wordpress/wp-admin/install.php** to access the database connection configuration page.

Read the instructions and click **Let's go!** to access the configuration page (see Fig. 8.5). Enter **wordpress** as the database name, and use username **wordpress** and password **123456** that were created in Step (1). Click **Submit**.

If you see **Run the installation** on the page after submission, the configuration file has been created successfully. Click the button to proceed to Step (4).

If you encounter any errors, such as configuration file creation failure or incorrect database connection details, review the error messages carefully and either re-enter the correct database information or create the configuration file manually.

Create the database configuration file at **/var/www/html/wordpress/wp-config.php** in the wordpress directory with the following content (comments are optional):

```
<?php
/** The name of the database for WordPress */
define( 'DB_NAME', 'wordpress' );
/** Database username */
```

8.8 System Administration and Maintenance Examples

```
define( 'DB_USER', 'wordpress' );
/** Database password */
define( 'DB_PASSWORD', '123456' );
/** Database hostname */
define( 'DB_HOST', '127.0.0.1' );
$table_prefix = 'wp_';
require_once ABSPATH . 'wp-settings.php';
?>
```

(4) Install WordPress.

On the installation page, enter your site title, administrator username, password, and email address. Make sure to save the password as you'll need it for future administrative access, as shown in Fig. 8.6.

Click **Install WordPress** at the bottom left to complete the installation. A success page will confirm the installation is complete.

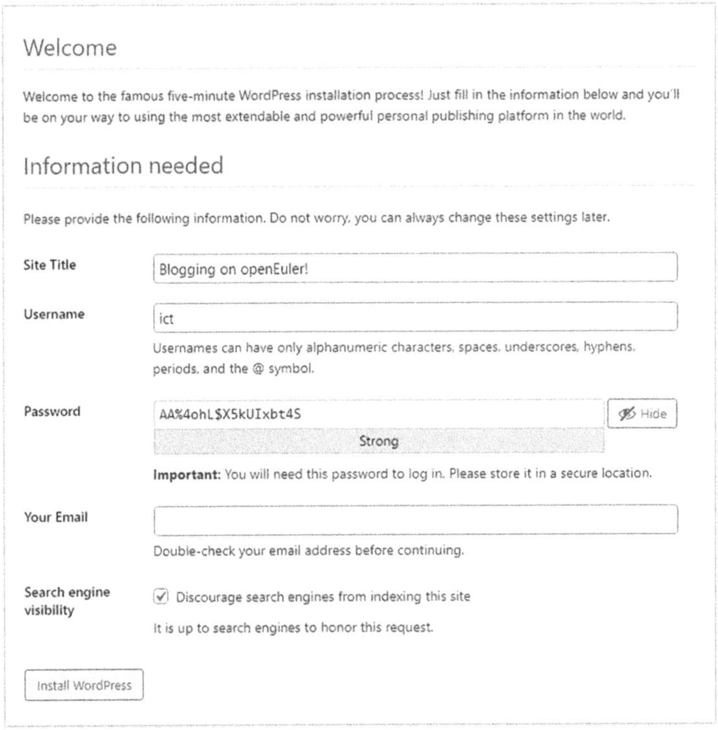

Fig. 8.6 WordPress installation page

```
Use the following command to re-enable SELinux or restore it
to its previous state:
[ict@openEuler24 ~]$ sudo setenforce 1
```

(5) Manage WordPress.

Click **Log In** in the lower left corner to access the login page. Enter the administrator credentials created in step (4), then click **Log In** to enter the administration dashboard, as shown in Fig. 8.7.

Customize the WordPress site appearance and create content based on your preferences.

(6) Access the WordPress site.

You now have access to this powerful CMS platform that delivers high-performance content management capabilities for both individuals and organizations.

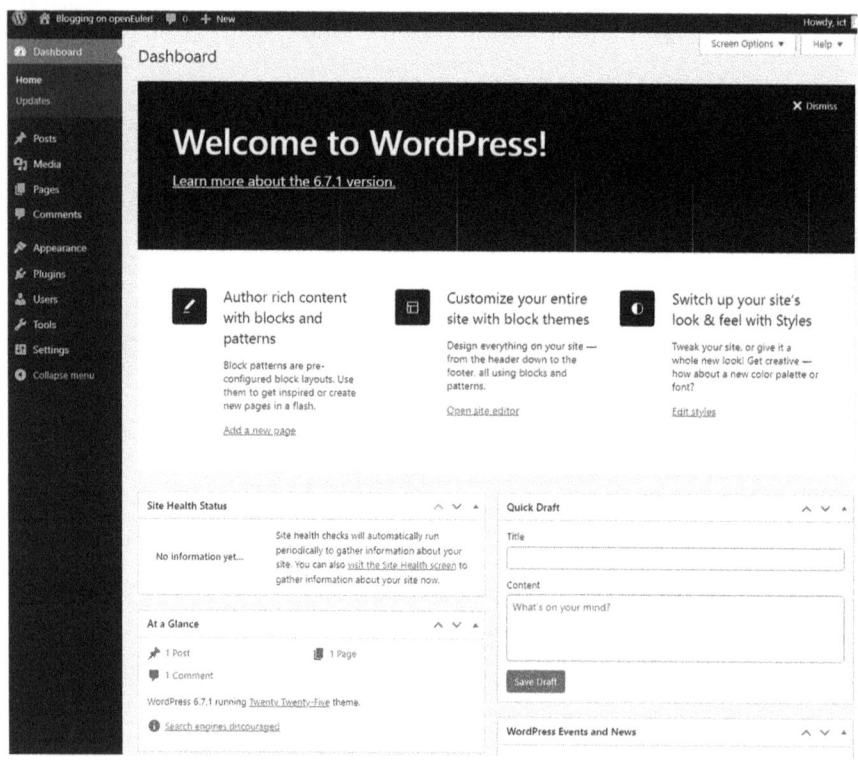

Fig. 8.7 WordPress administration dashboard

To enable domain name access, add DNS records on your domain server or temporary domain entries in the local hosts file of the accessing machine. To enhance site security, consider implementing these best practices:

- Schedule regular off-site **wordpress** database backups using cron jobs.
- Implement security auditing for database operations and the **wordpress** directory.
- Set up log rotation and perform regular inspection.
- Deploy Nginx as a reverse proxy to protect against external attacks while enabling advanced features like load balancing and rapid failover to backup sites.

8.9 Summary

This chapter introduces the core features of three typical server OSs, emphasizing practical aspects for both production and development servers. It covers key areas including user roles, storage management, applications, system services, task scheduling, and security. The chapter includes hands-on examples using the LAMP stack and WordPress, making it relevant for production server administrators, small server users, and advanced embedded systems developers.

Readers will gain a solid understanding of server OS design principles, particularly multi-user and multi-tasking capabilities, along with shell scripting automation in command-line environments. This knowledge enables practical application of various GNU/Linux distributions like openEuler in both academic and professional settings.

The chapter also explored the logging system design, demonstrating UNIX philosophy in action— knowledge crucial for both system administration and software development.

Reflection and Practice

1. Consider the unique nature of password files: users can change their own passwords but cannot modify others' passwords or directly edit the file. How does Linux implement this functionality?
2. What are the key differences between MBR and GPT partitioning, and how should one choose between them?
3. Create LVs using virtual drives and practice expanding and shrinking file systems using these volumes.
4. Develop a small program and create a .service file to run it as a system service, and then verify its operation.
5. Familiarize yourself with **at** and **crontab** by creating periodic backup tasks for the **wordpress** database and verify their correct execution.
6. Configure rotation for Apache logs and observe the results.
7. Deploy Nginx in a Docker container and implement WordPress reverse proxy services using a single host.

Open Access This chapter is licensed under the terms of the Creative Commons Attribution-NonCommercial-NoDerivatives 4.0 International License (http://creativecommons.org/licenses/by-nc-nd/4.0/), which permits any noncommercial use, sharing, distribution and reproduction in any medium or format, as long as you give appropriate credit to the original author(s) and the source, provide a link to the Creative Commons license and indicate if you modified the licensed material. You do not have permission under this license to share adapted material derived from this chapter or parts of it.

The images or other third party material in this chapter are included in the chapter's Creative Commons license, unless indicated otherwise in a credit line to the material. If material is not included in the chapter's Creative Commons license and your intended use is not permitted by statutory regulation or exceeds the permitted use, you will need to obtain permission directly from the copyright holder.

Chapter 9
Open-Source Innovation Within openEuler

Objectives

1. Learn about openEuler's key innovations in kernel, fundamental capabilities, scenario enablement, and toolchains.
2. Explore typical industry applications of openEuler.

openEuler is an open-source OS and free Linux distribution that offers a range of excellent tools developed in collaboration with our global developer ecosystem. The open and innovative platform always welcomes new ideas, approaches, and software or architecture solutions. Since its launch, openEuler has become an influential open-source community and is the benchmark in China.

Specifically, openEuler has also made positive innovations in AI for OS and OS for AI. In the era of intelligence, operating systems need to constantly evolve towards AI. On the one hand, AI is empowered throughout the entire process of operating system development, deployment, and operation to make the operating system more intelligent; On the other hand, in addition to supporting all mainstream general-purpose computing architectures such as ARM, x86, RISC-V, the operating system must also support mainstream AI processors such as NVIDIA and Ascend. OpenEuler has taken the lead in innovating in these two areas and evolving towards AI native operating systems.

This chapter explores major innovations of the openEuler community in kernel development, situation enablement, and toolchains, highlighting contributions from enterprises, universities, research institutes, and individuals. It also describes openEuler in key industry sectors, positioning it as an OS for digital infrastructure and fostering an open-source community to encourage readers to participate in its ongoing innovation.

9.1 Kernel

The openEuler community continuously contributes to the Linux kernel in areas including processor architecture, ACPI, memory management, file systems, multimedia, kernel documentation, quality improvements through bug fixes, and code refactoring [7].

openEuler inherits the competitive advantages of community versions and innovative features released in the openEuler community.

- Simultaneous multithreading (SMT) expeller free of priority inversion: This feature resolves the priority inversion problem in the SMT expeller feature and reduces the impact of offline tasks on the quality of service (QoS) of online tasks.
- CPU QoS priority-based load balancing: CPU QoS isolation is enhanced in online and offline hybrid deployments, and QoS load balancing across CPUs is supported to further reduce QoS interference from offline services.
- Tidal affinity scheduling: The system dynamically adjusts CPU affinity based on the service load. When the service load is light, the system uses preferred CPUs to enhance resource locality. When the service load is heavy, the system adds new CPU cores to improve the QoS.
- Kernel Same-page Merging (KSM) at the process or container level: Before this feature was introduced, user-mode programs needed to explicitly call the madvise function to specify the memory address range involved in memory deduplication. However, some programs written in non-C languages cannot call madvise. openEuler supports the following functions, which enable KSM for programs without explicitly calling madvise.
- Enhanced Data Access MONitoring (DAMON): This feature enables online, proactive, and lightweight monitoring and reclamation of memory resources when the memory load is light. You can customize a policy to initiate the most appropriate operation on the memory areas based on the monitoring result.
- Enhanced uswap: Memory pages can be swapped out to the backend storage in user mode, which saves memory resources.
- Intel Emerald Rapids (EMR): It is Intel's next-generation CPU platform built on the Intel 7 process. With Intel EMR, openEuler boosts hardware performance and delivers new hardware features such as Trust Domain Extensions (TDX). The support for Intel EMR is critical to fully unleashing the performance of users' mission-critical applications and computing platforms on openEuler.
- ACPI for AArch64 MPAM 2.0: Memory System Resource Partitioning and Monitoring (MPAM) is an extension feature of Armv8.4. It resolves system-wide or application-specific performance deterioration due to contention for shared resources (cache, DMC, and interconnects) in server systems that run diverse types of services concurrently.

9.1 Kernel

9.1.1 SMT Expeller Free of Priority Inversion

In cloud scenarios where online and offline services are deployed together to improve resource utilization, prioritizing the QoS of online services is a difficult challenge. When SMT is enabled, offline and online tasks running on the same CPU may interfere with each other. The SMT expeller for a hybrid deployment can prevent offline tasks from causing IPC interference to online tasks. Any change made by the SMT expeller to the Completely Fair Scheduler (CFS) task policy may cause priority inversion. The SMT expeller free of priority inversion feature prevents critical resources from being occupied by expelled offline tasks.

Assume that CPU A and CPU B are associated for SMT. Assign an online task to CPU A and an offline task to CPU B. The online task on CPU A occupies 100% of CPU A's resources for a long time. The offline task on CPU B is expelled and is not executed, and critical resources cannot be released. In this case, if a high-priority task waits for the critical resources occupied by the offline task, the task priority is reversed. The system checks how long the offline task has been throttled to check whether the system is at risk of priority inversion. If such a risk exists, the system stops throttling the offline task until the critical resources in the kernel are released.

The kernel provides two user-configurable interfaces:

(1) /proc/sys/kernel/qos_overload_detect_period_ms

It defines the duration (in milliseconds) before priority inversion triggers for non-offline tasks occupying the CPU. The range is 100–100,000, defaulting to 5000.

– A value too small triggers excessive priority inversions, disrupting online tasks with false alerts.
– A value too large extends system lag during priority inversion.

(2) **/proc/sys/kernel/qos_offline_wait_interval_ms**

It sets sleep duration (in milliseconds) for offline tasks returning to user mode during overload. The range is 100–1000, defaulting to 100.

– A value too large creates CPU idle periods when online tasks stop, reducing CPU utilization.
– A value too small disrupts online tasks through frequent offline task wake-ups.

To implement SMT expeller free of priority inversion in a hybrid deployment scenario, enable the **CONFIG_QOS_SCHED_SMT_EXPELLER** option.

9.1.2 CPU QoS Priority-Based Load Balancing

Task priorities are not differentiated in first-in first-out (FIFO) task migration queues between CPUs. Therefore, the QoS of high-priority tasks is not ensured in cross-CPU migration preemption. For example, CPU-sensitive tasks may not be scheduled preferentially. In scenarios where online and offline containers are deployed together, CFS load balancing requires a priority-based queuing model to implement QoS load balancing between high and low priorities. Such a model must schedule and execute online services more quickly than offline services, minimize the QoS interference from offline tasks, and make full use of CPUs.

Online and offline tasks managed by the CFS are assigned to task queues of different priorities. During multi-CPU load balancing, high-priority tasks are preferentially selected from the task queue to ensure that they are preferentially scheduled. Low-priority tasks are throttled during migration to reduce QoS interference and performance overhead caused by context switches and wakeup preemption of low-priority tasks.

The kernel provides the **/proc/sys/kernel/sched_prio_load_balance_enabled** interface to control CPU QoS priority-based load balancing. The value can be 0 (default) or 1.

To implement CPU QoS priority-based load balancing in a hybrid deployment scenario, enable the **CONFIG_QOS_SCHED_PRIO_LB** option.

9.1.3 Tidal Affinity

Multi-core servers allow you to deploy multiple types of services on the same server. A hybrid deployment improves CPU utilization but also aggravates conflicts of resources such as cache. Each service can use more CPU resources to meet the QoS. However, CPU utilization deteriorates due to problems such as more frequent migration between CPUs, idle switchovers, and cross-NUMA memory access.

Tidal affinity technology detects service load changes and dynamically allocates CPU resources to services. Specifically, when the service load is light, fewer CPU resources are allocated to the services, so as to reduce CPU migration, idle switchovers, and cache misses while meeting QoS requirements, improving CPU utilization, and increasing the energy efficiency ratio. When the service load is high, more CPU resources are allocated to improve the QoS and increase the CPU usage.

Core binding improves service performance for online-online and online-offline hybrid service deployments. When CPUs fail to be bound accurately due to dynamic load changes, tidal affinity is an effective solution to improve performance and reduce power consumption.

9.2 Fundamental Capabilities

The openEuler community has driven significant open-source innovation in core OS capabilities. These advances cover lightweight container engines, virtualization platforms, high-performance service management, kernel live patching, security, and reliability. This section highlights key innovative projects in these areas [7].

9.2.1 Lightweight Container Engine

A container is an isolated environment that streamlines application packaging and distribution. Compared with virtualization technologies, containers accelerate distribution and reduce overhead, effectively improving development and deployment efficiencies. As the Docker container engine, Kubernetes container orchestration and scheduling, and cloud-native deployments have become more widespread, the container ecosystem is developing rapidly.

However, evolving user needs present new challenges for container technology. Users increasingly demand faster startup and deployment times while minimizing resource usage. The emergence of IoT and edge computing has also introduced additional technical requirements for container platforms.

The openEuler container engine, iSulad, features a unified architecture design optimized for ICT environments. Despite its lightweight nature, iSulad delivers powerful functionality, serving as a flexible, stable, and secure foundation across diverse use cases.

iSulad provides commands similar to those of Docker, for greater usability. It supports the Container Runtime Interface (CRI) in the northbound direction and can connect to Kubernetes. You can use iSulad as the container base to orchestrate and schedule containers through Kubernetes. It also supports the Open Container Initiative (OCI) Runtime Specification in the southbound direction and is compatible with multiple container runtime environments, such as runc, LXC, kata, and Kuasar. Figure 9.1 illustrates the architecture of iSulad.

iSulad delivers four core services: container, image, volume, and network management. The container service controls container lifecycles, while the image service handles container image operations. Following the OCI Image Specification, iSulad supports industry-standard image formats alongside the external root file system for system containers and embedded formats for embedded systems. The volume service manages container data storage, while the network service integrates with Container Network Interface (CNI)-compliant plugins to enable container networking.

As a versatile container engine, iSulad supports three container types: common, system, and secure containers.

- Common containers: Traditional application containers that provide standard containerization features.
- System containers: Enhanced containers that build upon functionality of common containers. They integrate systemd management services and support dynamic management of drives, network interfaces, routes, and volumes during runtime. These containers excel in compute-intensive, high-performance, and high-concurrency environments, making them ideal for demanding applications and cloud services.
- Secure containers: A hybrid solution combining virtualization and container technologies. Unlike common containers that share the host kernel, secure containers maintain isolation through a virtualization layer. Each secure container

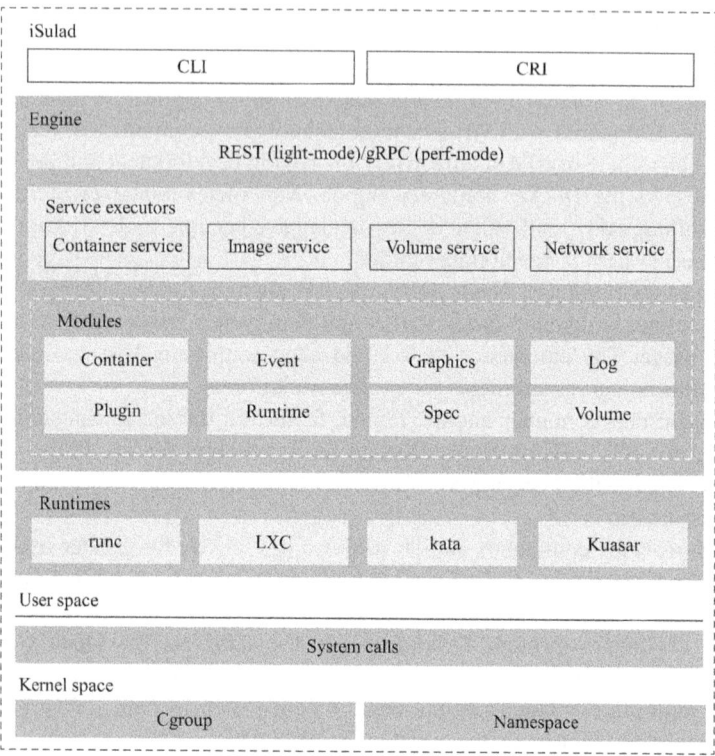

Fig. 9.1 iSulad architecture

operates with its own kernel in a lightweight virtual machine environment, ensuring complete separation between containers on the same host.

Compared with Docker, iSulad features faster container startup and lower resource overhead. That is because iSulad is developed using C/C++ and has lower running overhead than in other languages. iSulad optimizes the call chain at the code layer. iSulad calls functions directly through the link library, whereas Docker call fork and exec functions on binary files for multiple times. The shorter call length enables iSulad to start containers faster, and what's more, the C language is a system programming language that allows iSulad to fully play its role on embedded and edge devices. In contrast, Docker is developed using Go and has a narrower application scope.

According to tests, iSulad brings only 30% of the memory overhead incurred by Docker, and in Arm and x86 environments, iSulad can start 100 containers concurrently in less than half of the time Docker takes. These advantages enable iSulad users to start up containers faster and reduce resource consumption, minimizing the impact on containerized applications.

iSulad has been widely used in cloud computing, ICT, embedded, and edge scenarios, empowering banking, finance, communications, and cloud services. The openEuler community has been developing the iSulad+Kuasar+StratoVirt solution for a more effective full-stack secure container solution.

9.2 Fundamental Capabilities

9.2.2 Virtualization

As the QEMU virtualization software has been gradually evolving, the code scale of its core open-source components is becoming increasing large, among which there is a large amount of outdated code. In recent years, CVE security vulnerabilities frequently occur, and problems such as poor security, code redundancy, and low efficiency are awaiting handling. A practicable solution is the rust-vmm architecture, which is developed using the memory-safe programming language Rust. General-purpose virtualization technologies for all scenarios (data centers, terminals, and edge devices) are the future trend, due to their security, light weight, and performance advantages. StratoVirt emerges as a next-generation virtualization technology designed for openEuler.

StratoVirt is an open-source lightweight virtualization technology based on Kernel-based Virtual Machine (KVM). It reduces memory consumption and accelerates VM startup while maintaining the isolation and security capabilities of traditional virtualization technologies. StratoVirt can be applied in serverless scenarios such as microservices or function computing and retains virtualization interfaces and designs for quickly importing more features to supplement general virtualization capabilities.

Figure 9.2 depicts the core architecture of StratoVirt, divided into three layers from top to bottom.

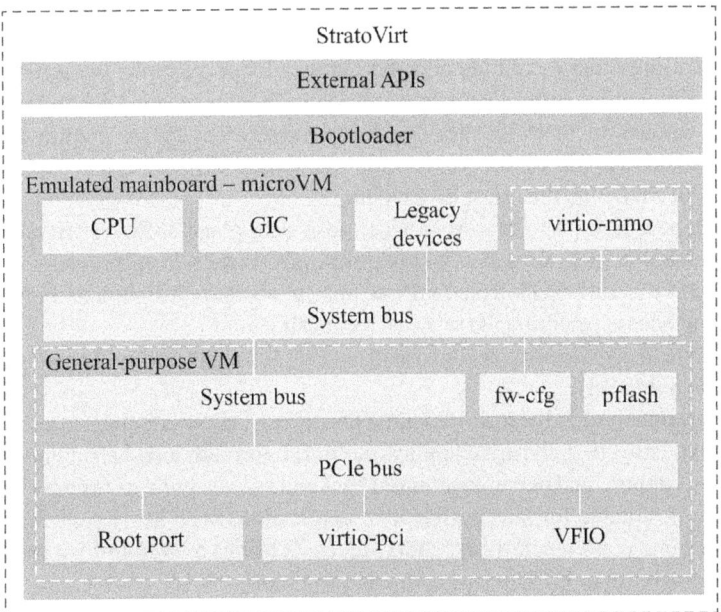

Fig. 9.2 StratoVirt core architecture

- External APIs: StratoVirt uses the QEMU Machine Protocol (QMP) to communicate with external systems, is compatible with OCI, and supports interconnection with libvirt.
- Bootloader: In lightweight scenarios, StratoVirt uses a simple bootloader to load kernel images, much faster than the traditional BIOS+GRUB boot method. In general-purpose virtualization scenarios, StratoVirt supports UEFI boot.
- Emulated mainboard – microVM: To improve performance and reduce the attack surface, StratoVirt minimizes the emulation of user-mode devices. With the emulation capability, KVM-based devices and paravirtualization devices are available, such as generic interrupt controller (GIC) and virtio-mmio devices.
- General-purpose VMs: StratoVirt provides an ACPI table to implement UEFI boot. virtio-pci and Virtual Function I/O (VFIO) passthrough devices can be added to further improve the VM I/O performance.

StratoVirt, iSula, and Kubernetes combine to form a complete container solution, which processes serverless loads efficiently.

9.2.3 High-Performance Service Management

The boom of AI and live streaming applications has seen data centers expand to connect to more cluster services and manage soaring volumes of data. It is a big challenge to efficiently implement traffic governance between microservices in a data center. Service meshes are one of next-generation microservice technologies that separate traffic governance from services and offload it to the mesh infrastructure, implementing application-unaware traffic governance. However, their proxy architecture introduces extra latency and overhead. For example, the service mesh software Istio increases the single-hop service access latency by 2 ms to 3 ms, making Istio unable to meet the Service Level Agreement (SLA) requirements of latency-sensitive applications. Application-unaware, high-performance traffic governance is a challenge that must be tackled.

Kmesh is a high-performance service mesh data plane software. Based on the programmable kernel, Kmesh offloads traffic governance from proxies to the OS and shortens the traffic path from multiple hops to one hop. It significantly improves application access performance in a service mesh.

The Kmesh architecture is illustrated in Fig. 9.3, and its key components are detailed in Table 9.1.

Kmesh connects to Dynamic Resource Discovery (xDS)-compliant mesh control planes (like Istio) to orchestrate application traffic through load balancing policies, L7 routing support, and percentage-based backend service policies for gray releases.

Kmesh is suitable for latency-sensitive applications such as e-commerce, cloud gaming, online conferencing, and short videos. It brings a fivefold forwarding performance increase in HTTP tests, compared to Istio.

9.2 Fundamental Capabilities

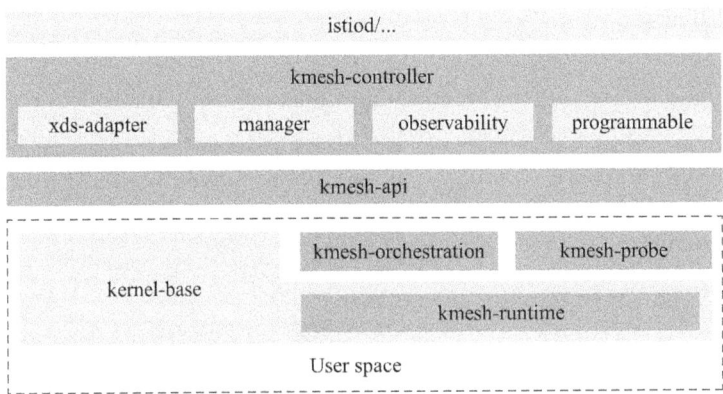

Fig. 9.3 Kmesh architecture

Table 9.1 Kmesh key components

Component	Description
kmesh-controller	Kmesh management program, which is responsible for Kmesh lifecycle management, xDS protocol interconnection, and O&M monitoring
kmesh-api	API layer provided by Kmesh for external systems, including orchestration APIs converted by xDS and O&M monitoring channels
kmesh-runtime	Runtime that supports L3–L7 traffic orchestration implemented in the kernel
kmesh-orchestration	L3–L7 traffic orchestration implemented based on eBPF, such as routing, gray, and load balancing
kmesh-probe	O&M monitoring probe, which provides end-to-end monitoring capabilities

9.2.4 Kernel Live Upgrade

The Linux kernel's ongoing open-source development continuously introduces new features. This constant code expansion often leads to security vulnerabilities and other issues requiring immediate remediation. Two primary approaches exist for fixing vulnerabilities: hot patching and live migration.

Hot patching shows limitations with significant changes such as kAPI modifications, inline functions, or major logical alterations. Additionally, maintaining numerous hot patches becomes increasingly complex. While live migration works well for VMs, it involves substantial migration overhead. Kernel live upgrade emerged as an enhanced solution, enabling seamless kernel updates without disruption.

openEuler implements kernel live upgrade through rapid kernel restart and program hot migration, achieving process state preservation and recovery with second-level end-to-end latency. This feature typically applies in scenarios where:

– Kernel restart is required for vulnerability patches or version updates
– Applications running on the kernel can quickly restore their state post-restart

openEuler provides nvwa, a user-space utility that automates the kernel live upgrade process. The following section explains the installation and usage of this kernel live upgrade tool.

(1) Install nvwa.

```
[ict@openEuler24 ~]$ sudo dnf install -y nvwa
[ict@openEuler24 ~]$ sudo nvwa --help
```

nvwa operates as a background systemd service. Enable this service after installation.

```
[ict@openEuler24 ~]$ sudo systemctl enable nvwa
[ict@openEuler24 ~]$ sudo systemctl status nvwa
```

nvwa uses two configuration files: **/etc/nvwa/nvwa-restore.yaml** and **/etc/nvwa/nvwa-server.yaml**.

(2) Configure **nvwa-restore.yaml**.

This configuration file defines the state preservation and restoration procedures during kernel live upgrade. Table 9.2 lists the main configuration items. Configuration example:

```
pids:
  -14109
services:
  -redis
restore_net: false
enable_quick_kexec: true
enable_pin_memory: true
```

Table 9.2 Main configuration items in nvwa-restore.yaml

Item	Description
pids	Lists process IDs to preserve and restore during upgrade. Processes under nvwa management automatically restore after nvwa service startup
services	Defines services to preserve and restore during upgrade. While nvwa handles process states directly, it requires systemd for service operations. Service names must match systemd naming conventions. For nvwa-managed services, automatic restoration depends on systemd service enablement. Currently, only **notify** and **oneshot** service types are supported
restore_net	Controls network configuration preservation and restoration. Incorrect settings may cause post-restoration network failures. This feature is disabled by default
enable_quick_kexec	Toggles the quick kexec feature for faster kernel restart. **quickkexec = 128 M** in kernel command-line is required, where 128 represents allocated memory size for loading the kernel and initramfs during upgrade. Allocation must exceed the combined kernel and initramfs size. This feature is disabled by default
enable_pin_memory	Controls the memory pinning feature for faster process state preservation and restoration

9.2 Fundamental Capabilities

(3) Configure **nvwa-server.yaml**.
This configuration file defines the temporary data paths used during kernel live upgrade operations. Table 9.3 lists the main configuration items.
Configuration example:

```
criu_dir: /var/nvwa/running/
criu_exe: /usr/sbin/criu
kexec_exe: /usr/sbin/kexec
systemd_etc: /etc/systemd/system/
log_dir: /etc/nvwa/log/
```

(4) Start the nvwa service.
Restart the nvwa service after configuration changes.

```
[ict@openEuler24 ~]$ sudo systemctl restart nvwa
```

(5) Perform kernel live upgrade.
nvwa looks for kernel images and ramfs in the **/boot** directory during upgrades. File names must follow these formats: **vmlinuz-**<*kernel-version*> for kernels and **initramfs-**<*kernel-version*>**.img** for rootfs.

```
# Clear previous state information before kernel live upgrade.
[ict@openEuler24 ~]$ sudo nvwm init
# Perform kernel live upgrade.
[ict@openEuler24 ~]$ sudo nvwm update
```

Be aware that kernel live upgrades may fail, resulting in stopped processes or services. nvwa currently supports only the AArch64 architecture.

Table 9.3 Main configuration items in nvwa-server.yaml

Item	Description
criu_dir	Directory path for storing state preservation data. This may require substantial drive space
criu_exe	Path to the **criu** executable. Modify only when debugging **criu**
kexec_exe	Path to the **kexec** executable. Modify only when debugging **kexec**
systemd_etc	Directory path for systemd configuration overrides. This path is defined by systemd and rarely requires modification
log_dir	Directory path for nvwa log files

9.2.5 Security and Reliability

openEuler has launched multiple innovative projects addressing system security and reliability, with key initiatives including secCrypto, secGear, and sysMaster.

(1) secCrypto

SM algorithms are being increasingly adopted in the industry. However, most open-source software in openEuler's repository that uses cryptographic algorithms does not support SM algorithms. As a result, openEuler and its upper-layer applications cannot utilize SM algorithms natively to ensure service security. In addition, the current SM algorithm implementations still bring performance loss, which need to be optimized to fully realize the potential of hardware and software collaboration.

openEuler provides support for cryptographic services such as Chinese cryptographic algorithm libraries, certificates, and secure transmission protocols. Key security features that use cryptographic algorithms, including OS user authentication, drive encryption, and integrity protection, are enhanced SM algorithms. Figure 9.4 shows the secCrypto planning overview.

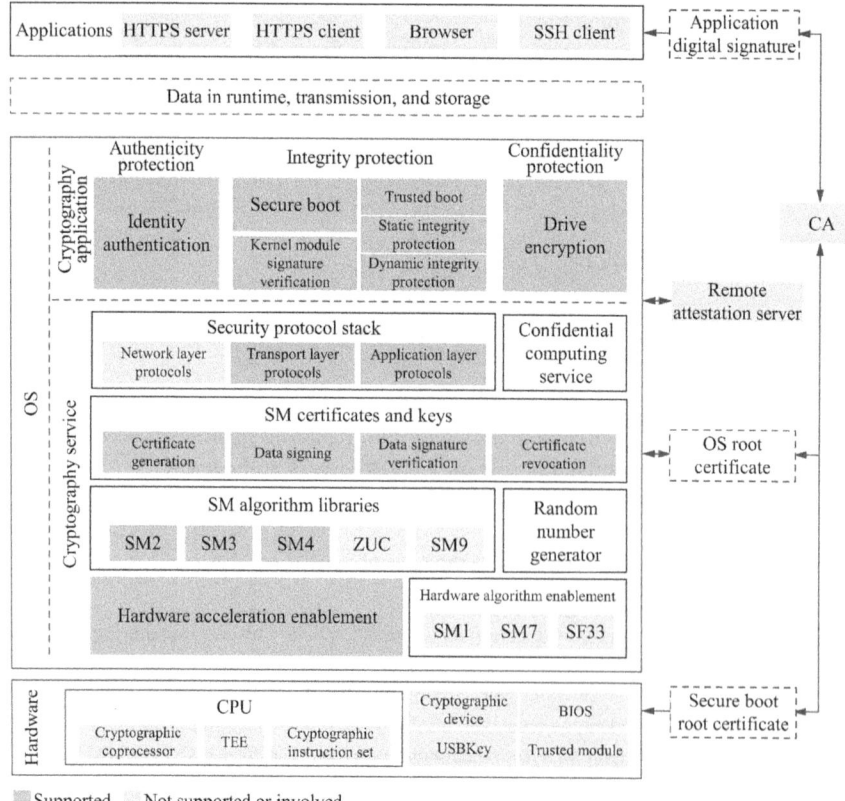

Fig. 9.4 secCrypto planning overview

9.2 Fundamental Capabilities

Currently, the following SM features are supported by openEuler:

- User-mode algorithm libraries, such as OpenSSL and Libgcrypt, support SM2, SM3, and SM4.
- OpenSSH supports SM2, SM3, and SM4.
- OpenSSL supports the Transport Layer Cryptography Protocol (TLCP) stack of the SM standards.
- SM3 and SM4 are supported for drive encryption (dm-crypt and cryptsetup).
- SM3 is supported for password encryption in user identity authentication (pam, libuser, and shadow).
- SM3 is supported for data digest in Advanced Intrusion Detection Environment (AIDE).
- SM2, SM3, and SM4 are supported in the kernel cryptographic framework (crypto), allowing algorithm performance optimization using instruction sets such as AVX, CE, and NEON.
- The SM3 data digest algorithm and SM2 certificate are supported in Integrity Measurement Architecture and Extended Verification Module (IMA/EVM) of the kernel.
- The SM2 certificate is supported in kernel module signing and module signature verification.
- SM4-CBC and SM4-GCM algorithms are supported in Kernel Transport Layer Security (KTLS).
- OS secure boot (shim and GRUB) supports signature verification of SM certificates.
- SM3 and SM4 are supported in the Kunpeng Accelerator Engine (KAE).
The SM algorithm stack of openEuler is mainly used in server and cloud scenarios, supporting SM2, SM3, and SM4 in both kernel and user modes. openEuler, now has been reconstructed for SM algorithms, serving as the information system foundation to enable SM algorithms for various industries and help them meet the cryptography assessment.

(2) secGear

The rapid development of confidential computing technologies allows chip vendors to launch their own confidential computing solutions, but it poses the following problems for security application developers:

- Ecosystem isolation: To deploy a confidential computing application on a different platform, secondary development is necessary based on the SDK of the target platform.
- Difficult development: Some platforms provide only awkward bottom-layer interfaces, which come at a high cost in terms of learning and development.
- Low performance: A confidential computing application is designed to run in both the rich execution environment (REE) and TEE. However, frequent context switches between these two environments can significantly degrade performance.

secGear is a security application development kit (SADK) that delivers confidential computing for the computing industry. It is a unified development framework that masks the differences between TEEs and SDKs. It provides development tools and common security components to help security application developers focus on services and improve development efficiency (Fig. 9.5).

secGear features the following benefits:
- Architecture compatibility: It masks differences between different SDK APIs to share the same set of source code across multiple architectures.
- Easy development: The development tools and common security components allow users to focus on services, significantly improving development efficiency.
- High performance: The switchless feature improves the interaction performance between the REE and TEE by more than tenfold in typical scenarios such as frequent interactions between the REE and TEE and big data interaction.

secGear is widely used in scenarios such as databases, hardware security module alternatives, AI model and data protection, and big data. It helps customers in industries such as finance and telecom quickly port services to confidential computing environments and protect data runtime security.

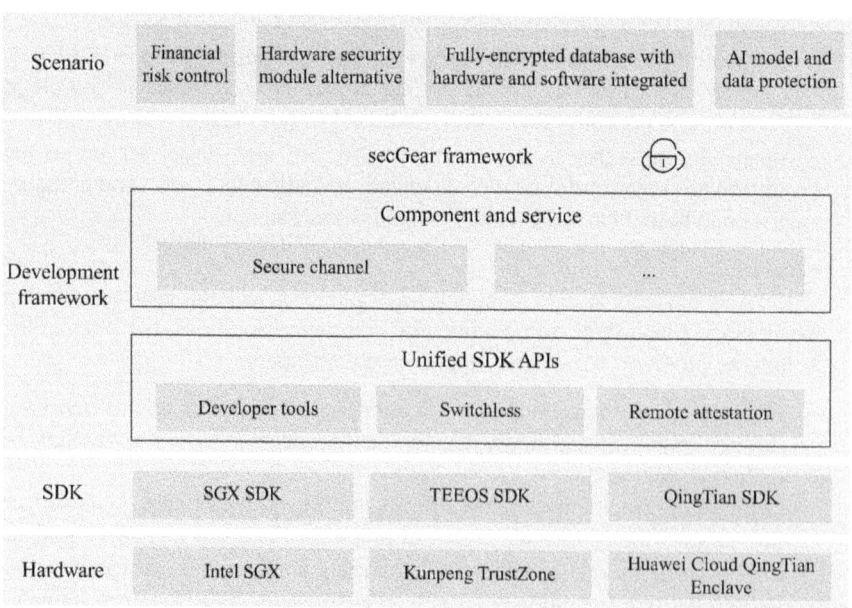

Fig. 9.5 secGear architecture

9.2 Fundamental Capabilities

(3) sysMaster

In Linux, PID 1, traditionally the init process, is the parent of all user-mode processes. The init process is the first process that is created when the system is started. It starts and manages all other processes and ends them when the system is shut down. In modern Linux distributions, init is usually replaced by the systemd process. However, the concept of PID 1 (whose minimum functions include system startup and zombie process recycling) still exists.

PID 1 is a key system process and is responsible for system initialization and runtime service management. It faces the following challenges:

- Poor reliability: The function problem of PID 1 has a bigger impact. When PID 1 is faulty, the OS must be restarted to rectify the fault.
- High complexity: systemd becomes the de facto standard for PID 1, introducing many new concepts, tools, and extended components that depend on each other. It is difficult to tailor the components based on actual application scenarios.

sysMaster is a collection of ultra-lightweight and highly reliable service management programs. It provides an innovative implementation of PID 1 to replace the conventional init process. Written in Rust, sysMaster is equipped with fault monitoring, second-level self-recovery, and quick startup capabilities, which help improve OS reliability and service availability. sysMaster manages processes, containers, and VMs centrally and provides fault monitoring and self-healing mechanisms to help deal with Linux initialization and service management challenges. All these features make sysMaster the ideal choice for server, cloud computing, and embedded scenarios.

sysMaster divides the functions of traditional PID 1 into a $1 + 1 + N$ architecture based on application scenarios. As shown in Fig. 9.6, sysMaster consists of three components.

- sysmaster-init, which is a new implementation of PID 1, features simplified functions, minimalist codebase, and ultimate reliability. It is applicable to embedded systems with functions such as system initialization, zombie process recycling, and keep-alive monitoring.
- sysmaster-core undertakes the core service management functions and incorporates the reliability framework to enable live updates and quick self-recovery in the event of crashes, ensuring 24/7 service availability.
- sysmaster-extends offers a collection of components (such as devMaster for device management and busMaster for bus communication) that deliver key system functions, which are coupled in traditional PID 1. You can choose the components to use as required.

Featuring a simple component architecture, sysMaster improves the scalability and adaptability of the overall system architecture while reducing development and maintenance costs. sysMaster provides the following advantages:

- Live updates and self-recovery in seconds in the event of crashes
- Faster startup speed with lower memory overhead

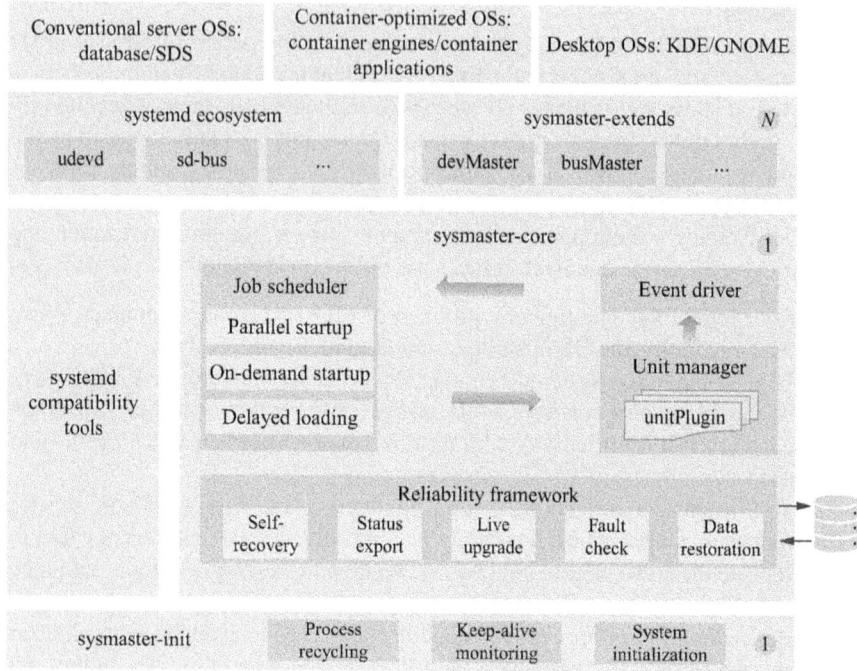

Fig. 9.6 sysMaster architecture

- Plugin-based service types that can be dynamically loaded as required
- Migration tools that provide seamless migration from systemd to sysMaster
- Unified interfaces that work with the iSulad container engine and QEMU for management of container and virtualization instances

In the future, sysMaster will extend to more scenarios and have its architecture and performance further optimized for higher scalability and adaptability. In addition, new features and components will be developed to meet the requirements of container, virtualization, and edge computing scenarios. These features will make sysMaster a powerful, efficient, and user-friendly system management framework.

sysMaster can be used in containers, virtualization, servers, and edge devices to deliver a reliable and lightweight experience.

9.3 Scenario Enablement

Scenario enablement stands as a cornerstone of openEuler's innovation. It supports a diverse range of devices, covers various application scenarios, and interfaces with other OSs such as OpenHarmony, achieving ecosystem interoperability through shared capabilities. With a unified OS architecture supporting all mainstream computing architectures, openEuler is one of the best open-source OSs for diverse computing powers.

It introduces the concept of the versatile-scenario OS, which achieves flexible version build and service composition through a full-stack atomization decoupling and Lego-style architecture, making it ideal for servers, cloud computing, edge computing, and embedded systems. The white paper provides a comprehensive overview of openEuler's architecture and its capabilities in supporting various digital infrastructure scenarios [1]. openEuler spans the kernel, middleware, and applications across diverse technical domains. This section highlights several key innovative projects.

9.3.1 Server

The key server innovations of openEuler include DPUDirect, eNFS, and WayCa Scheduler.

(1) DPUDirect

In data centers and cloud environments, Moore's Law has reached its limits. As general-purpose CPU performance growth slows while network I/O speeds surge, a "scissors effect" has emerged where processors can no longer handle the processing demands of network, drive, and other I/O operations effectively. Traditional data centers face a growing "data center tax"—the CPU resources consumed by I/O and the management plane. AWS and Google Cloud report this tax can exceed 30% of data center computing power, sometimes significantly more.

The data processing unit (DPU) addresses this challenge by offloading these tasks from host CPUs to dedicated processors that handle management plane, network, storage, and security functions. This approach improves efficiency and reduces costs. Major cloud providers including AWS, Alibaba Cloud, and Huawei Cloud now use custom processors for management and data plane offloading, enabling them to sell their entire data center computing capacity to customers.

openEuler's DPUDirect creates a seamless collaborative environment between hosts and DPUs. This OS-level framework enables transparent workload offloading and migration between HOST and DPU systems, as illustrated in Fig. 9.7. DPUDirect supports process-level offloading without requiring modifications to management plane processes, maintaining their ability to manage host-side operations after migration. The feature requires minimal code adaptation while preserving software compatibility and scalability, dramatically reducing implementation costs and operational complexity in environments with DPUs.

DPUDirect allows you to combine the following collaboration mechanisms to achieve seamless offloading in various scenarios.

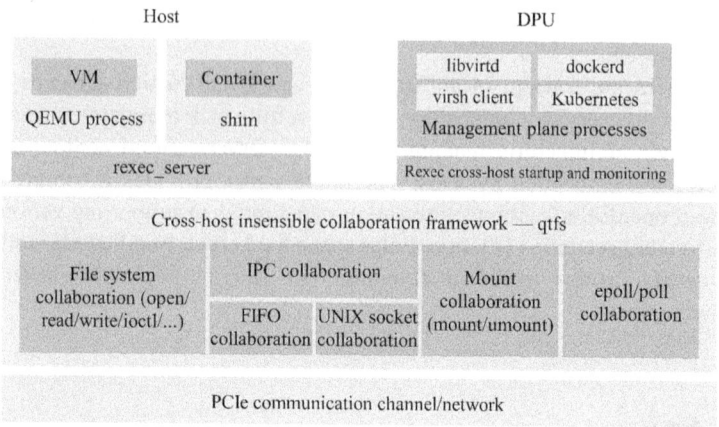

Fig. 9.7 DPUDirect architecture

- File system collaboration supports cross-host file system access and provides a consistent file system view for host and DPU processes. It also supports special file systems such as **proc**, **sys**, and **dev**.
- IPC collaboration enables unaware communication between hosts and DPU processes. It supports FIFO and Unix domain sockets for cross-host communication.
- Mounting collaboration performs the mounting operation in a specific directory on the host, which can adapt to the container image overlay scenario. The offloaded management-plane process can construct a working directory for the service process on the host, providing a unified cross-node file system view.
- epoll collaboration supports epoll operations for cross-host access of remote common files and FIFO files and supports read and write blocking operations.
- Process collaboration uses the rexec tool to remotely start executable files. The rexec tool takes over the input and output streams of the remotely started processes and monitor the status to ensure the lifecycle consistency of the processes at both ends.

By combining these mechanisms, policies can be tailored for different scenarios to fulfill the service requirements of the management-plane processes, eliminating the need to split and reconstruct too many services.

DPUDirect facilitates the complete offloading of the container management plane such as kubelet and dockerd, as well as the virtualization management plane libvirtd. It eliminates the need of splitting over 10,000 lines of code, thereby reducing the workload of adapting and maintaining by almost 20-fold. Furthermore, the service logic of the management plane remains unaltered, ensuring service software compatibility and evolution.

9.3 Scenario Enablement

(2) eNFS

With the emergence of diverse application scenarios, data importance is increasing, and various industries are putting forward higher requirements for the reliability and performance of network-attached storage (NAS). However, traditional NFS only specifies one server IP address for a single mount point, which poses several challenges.

- When a network interface card (NIC) or link is faulty, the mount point becomes inaccessible, suspending service I/Os and compromising reliability.
- The performance of a mount point is limited by the performance of a physical link, which poses challenges for the performance of important services.
- NAS is often deployed in the public zone, and accessing it from the host requires crossing three layers of networking. If one end is faulty, the IP address cannot detect the fault. File systems are manually mounted on the application layer, and active-active links cannot be automatically switched over.

The eNFS protocol is a driver module running in the openEuler OS kernel, consisting of the mounting parameter management module at the NFS protocol layer and the multipathing management module at the transport layer. eNFS specifies multiple local and server IP addresses to establish multiple TCP/RDMA links for different IP addresses, achieving functions such as multi-path link setup, fault recovery and failover, and load balancing. Figure 9.8 shows the distributed file system of eNFS.

Compared to native NFS, eNFS boasts three key innovations.

- It enables second-level failover in the event of software or hardware faults on I/O paths. It also ensures multiple links between the client and server for each single NFS mount point to support I/O transmission over those links, achieving cross-controller and cross-site reliability. All configurations are

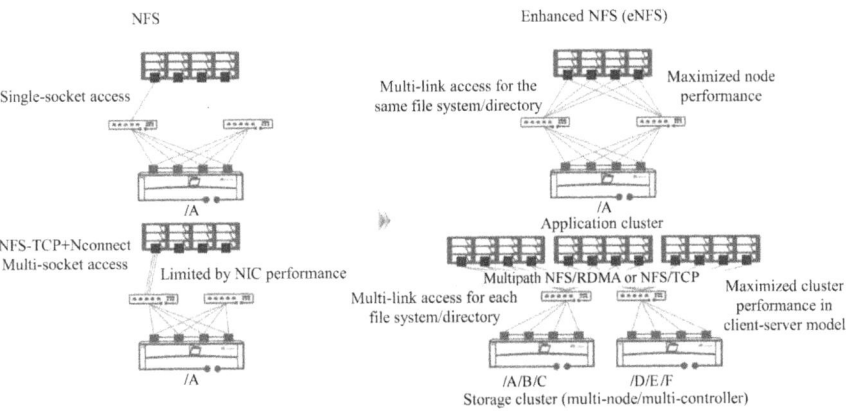

Fig. 9.8 Distributed file system of eNFS

recorded in one file, making it easy to deploy HPC applications on different hosts by simply modifying the configuration file.
- Multi-link aggregation, covering NIC ports, NICs, and nodes, significantly improves host access performance.
- eNFS offers active-active path failover on a three-layer network. It enables cross-site active-active failover in the event of storage faults or host-side I/O timeouts, effectively resolving cross-engine failures and host unawareness issues.

eNFS provides high-performance data sharing capabilities beyond local file systems and also solutions to faults between the client and server, ensuring service continuity and replacing native NFS.

(3) WayCa Scheduler

The number of server cores is on the rise, and the cache and interconnection structures are becoming increasingly complex. Server designs differ greatly from vendor to vendor. Although Linux is a general-purpose OS and supports hardware from various vendors, it does not fully support the newly introduced hardware topology of Kunpeng. This presents a challenge in fully utilizing the Kunpeng hardware performance on the existing software platform.

By optimizing the firmware topology description, hardware topology establishment, and topology information export in the Linux kernel, as well as the kernel scheduling algorithm, WayCa Scheduler enables applications to fully utilize components such as the CPUs, cache, memory, and I/O peripherals. This feature improves system hardware utilization and memory bandwidth, while reducing memory, cache, and peripheral access latency, thereby significantly improving application performance on Kunpeng servers (Fig. 9.9).

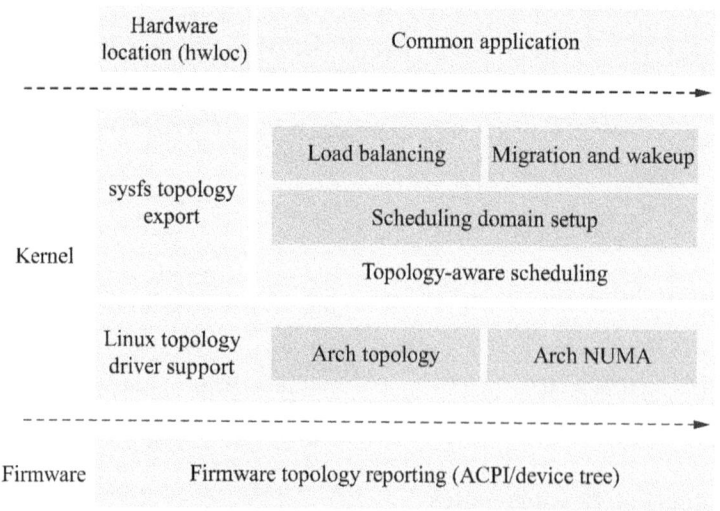

Fig. 9.9 WayCa scheduler architecture

WayCa Scheduler offers several features, including topology discovery and export, scheduling support and optimization, and user-mode topology support.

- The Linux ACPI and topology driver can enumerate and create hardware topologies for CPUs, cache, NUMA, and devices, and search for hardware topology information through kernel interfaces such as **sysfs**.
- Cluster and NUMA scheduling domains are established based on the hardware topology, and the scheduler supports load balancing and migration based on hardware clusters and NUMA nodes. This fully utilizes L3 cache and memory resources, reducing system latency and improving throughput.
- Furthermore, WayCa Scheduler provides user-mode topology support, which allows for optimization based on specific service characteristics and requirements. For example, specific CPU or device binding policies can be implemented. To meet the requirements of these applications, **hwloc** is adapted to provide hardware topology information for applications.

WayCa Scheduler has been integrated into the openEuler kernel and its related user-mode tools. This integration enables hardware topology awareness and optimizes scheduling for applications on the Kunpeng server and openEuler OS, for example, general-purpose databases, thereby improving system performance. In certain application scenarios, such as HPC applications, tools like **hwloc** can be utilized to obtain topology information that meets the optimization policy requirements, further improving the application performance.

9.3.2 Cloud

openEuler's cloud computing innovations primarily feature Rubik for mixed container deployment, KubeOS container OS, and NestOS cloud OS.

(1) Rubik

The expenditure on global cloud infrastructure services is enormous. However, the average CPU usage of user clusters in data centers is low, ranging from only 10% to 20%. This results in significant resource waste and additional O&M costs, which have become a critical issue for enterprises seeking to improve computing efficiency. Therefore, improving data center resource utilization has become an urgent matter that needs to be addressed. One solution is to deploy online and offline jobs together, utilizing idle online cluster resources to meet the computing requirements of offline jobs. This approach has become a research hotspot in academia and industry.

Rubik, openEuler's hybrid container deployment engine, features an architecture illustrated in Fig. 9.10. It combines adaptive single-node computing optimization with QoS assurance to maximize resource utilization without compromising critical workload performance. Named after the Rubik's Cube, the engine represents openEuler's systematic approach to server management.

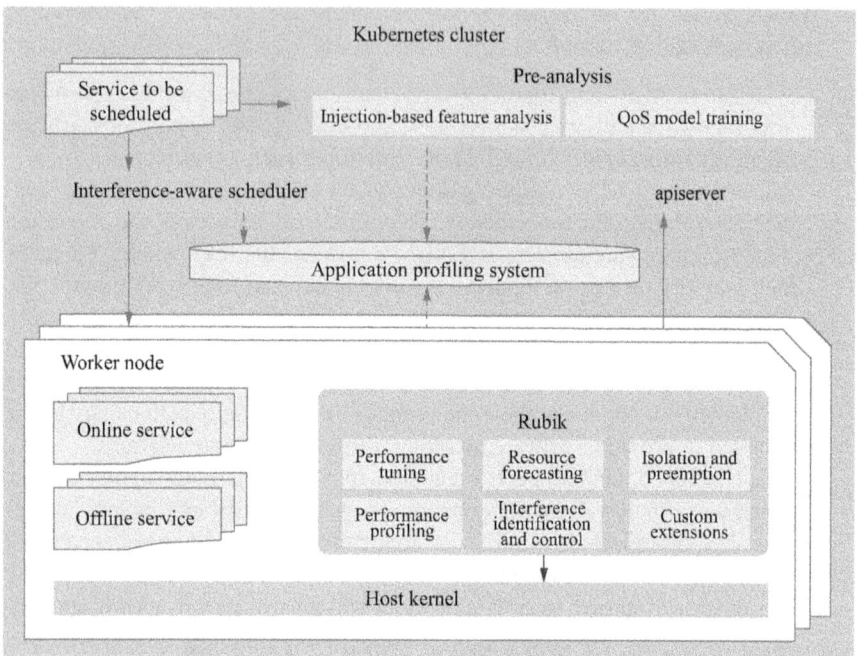

Fig. 9.10 Rubik architecture

Major Rubik features include:

- Compatibility with the native Kubernetes system: Capabilities are extended based on extended APIs of native Kubernetes.
- Compatibility with the openEuler system: Enhanced features (such as hierarchical kernel resource isolation) provided by openEuler are automatically enabled. For other Linux distributions, only restricted management capabilities are provided because some kernel features are missing.
- Interference identification and control during system running: Real-time interference identification and control capabilities are provided for mission-critical services.
- Adaptive dynamic optimization: The performance of mission-critical services is optimized to ensure efficient and stable operation, and the ratio of resources for online and offline services is dynamically adjusted to reduce QoS violations of mission-critical services.
- Custom extensions: Advanced users can develop custom extensions for specific service scenarios.
  Rubik is widely used in hybrid deployment of cloud service containers, covering hybrid deployment of web services, databases, big data, and AI. It helps customers in industries such as Internet and communications achieve a data center resource utilization rate of over 50%.

9.3 Scenario Enablement

(2) KubeOS

In cloud-native scenarios, containers and Kubernetes are widely used. However, the management of OSs is affected.

- With applications being containerized, new challenges arise for OSs. Traditional OSs are too heavy and no longer fully applicable.
- Containers and OSs are maintained and managed separately, which results in redundant management functions and difficult scheduling.
- Siloed package management causes problems such as scattered and inconsistent container OS versions in the cluster. This requires a unified container OS management mechanism.

To address these issues, openEuler launched KubeOS, an OS O&M solution that uses Kubernetes to manage containers and OSs in a unified manner (Fig. 9.11).

Major KubeOS features include:

- Unified management: KubeOS connects the OS to the cluster as a component, uses Kubernetes to manage the OS and service containers, and manages the OSs of all nodes.
- Collaborative scheduling: It can detect the cluster status before the OS changes to implement collaborative scheduling of service containers and OSs.

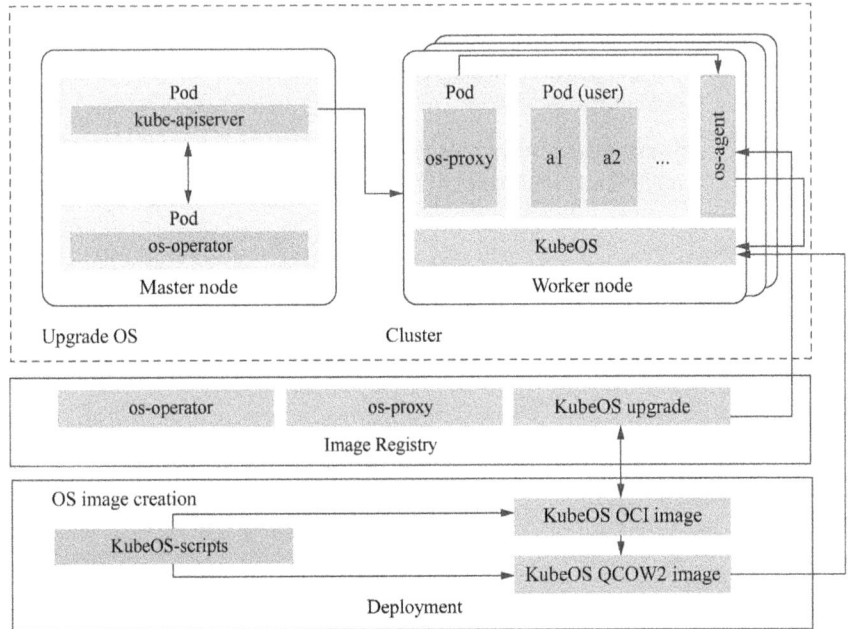

Fig. 9.11 KubeOS architecture

- API O&M: Kubernetes-native declarative APIs are used to manage and maintain OSs in a standard manner.
- Atomic management: Based on the Kubernetes ecosystem, the atomic upgrade and rollback of the OS are implemented to ensure consistency between cluster nodes.
- Lightweight security: Only components required for container running are included, reducing the attack surface and vulnerabilities, overheads, and reboot time of the OS. The rootfs is read-only to protect the system from attacks and malicious tampering.

KubeOS is mainly used as a cloud-native infrastructure, providing a basic operating environment for cloud services, helping cloud vendors and customers in the telecom industry solve OS O&M problems in cloud-native scenarios.

(3) NestOS

Various runtimes and management software have been emerging as containers and Kubernetes are widely adopted in cloud native scenarios. Technologies such as container and orchestration further decouple service rollout and O&M from the underlying environment. Without a unified O&M stack, O&M platforms need to be built repeatedly.

NestOS is a cloud OS incubated in the openEuler community. It runs rpm-ostree and Ignition technologies over a dual rootfs and atomic update design and uses nestos-assembler for quick integration and build. NestOS is compatible with platforms such as Kubernetes and OpenStack, reducing container overheads and providing extensive cluster components in large-scale containerized environments. Figure 9.12 shows the NestOS architecture.

Major NestOS features include:

- Out-of-the-box design: Integrates popular container engines such as iSulad, Docker, and Podman to provide lightweight and tailored OSs for the cloud.

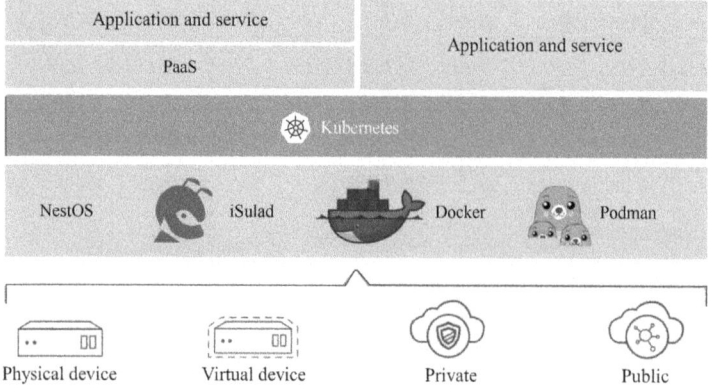

Fig. 9.12 NestOS architecture

9.3 Scenario Enablement

- Easy configuration: Uses the Ignition feature to install and configure a large number of cluster nodes with a single configuration.
- Secure management: Runs rpm-ostree to manage software packages and works with the openEuler software package source to ensure secure, stable atomic updates.
- Hitless node updating: Uses Zincati to provide automatic node updates and reboot without interrupting services.
- Dual rootfs: Executes dual rootfs for active/standby failovers, to ensure integrity and security during system running.

NestOS aims to meet the demands of containerized cloud applications, to solve problems such as inconsistent and repetitive O&M operations of stacks and platforms. These problems are typically caused by the decoupling of containers and underlying environments when using container and container orchestration technologies for rollout and O&M, but NestOS resolves this to ensure consistency between services and the base OS.

9.3.3 Embedded

openEuler's embedded system innovations feature projects like MICA, UniProton, and ZVM.

(1) MICA

Deploying both Linux and RTOS on embedded systems poses three key challenges when addressing requirements for security, real-time performance, and extensive functionality:

- Deployment of multiple OSs requires collaboration on the same multi-core (homogeneous or heterogeneous) SoC to implement system functions.
- System isolation to prevent impact of failures, such as a crash or fault, to OSs that have high security, reliability, and real-time requirements.
- Improved resource scheduling and utilization to ensure full use of hardware resources.

MICA is a multi-core SoC framework that supports mixed-criticality deployment of real-time and non-real-time OSs or secure and non-secure OSs based on hardware-assisted virtualization, TEE, and heterogeneous architectures. It utilizes the characteristics of each OS to meet the multi-objective constraints of embedded systems, such as security, real-time response, and extensive functions. The MICA architecture is illustrated in Fig. 9.13.

The MICA project is positioned for mid-range and high-end embedded systems in manufacturing, energy, and robotics fields. It currently supports OpenAMP and Jailhouse and is in development to work with ZVM and Rust-Shyper.

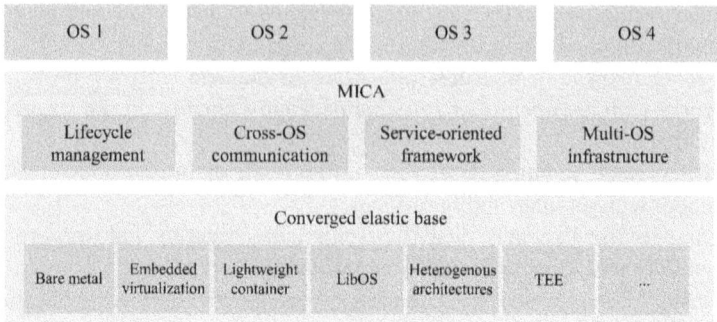

Fig. 9.13 MICA architecture

(2) UniProton

Industrial control systems require low deterministic latency from Oss, which is not possible with Linux due to the large size and complex functions. Small embedded systems like UniProton feature a lightweight kernel, optimized performance, and custom functions that combine to achieve ultra-low latency.

UniProton is a hard RTOS that delivers ultra-low latency in microseconds and mixed-criticality deployment. It can be deployed together with general-purpose OSs such as openEuler Embedded and supports microcontroller units (MCUs) and multi-core CPUs in industrial control systems. UniProton has the following features:

- Low Latency

  - Deterministic latency: maximum scheduling latency meeting service requirements
  - Ultimate performance: task scheduling and interrupt latency in microseconds
  - Lightweight: running in an environment with only tens of KB of memory

- Universality

  - POSIX-compliant APIs
  - Compatible with multiple instruction set architectures (ISAs) such as x86, AArch64, and Cortex-M, and chips such as Intel and Raspberry Pi
  - Multi-core processors delivering efficient low-latency, multi-core computing

- Usability

  - Customized functions
  - Maintenance and testing, including **cpup** and exception takeover
  - Mixed-criticality deployments using Linux and RTOS capabilities

9.3 Scenario Enablement

- Extensive Middleware
  - Unified and standard driver development framework that improves driver development efficiency
  - Various network protocol stacks and standard NICs
  - Industrial middleware that works with mainstream protocols and standards and bus communication capabilities such as EtherCAT

  Huawei is an experienced vendor specializing in hard real-time scenarios in the CT field who, in June 2022, released UniProton as an open-source software to the openEuler community, where the software has been developed by the Embedded SIG. Thanks to its low deterministic latency, UniProton has been widely used in manufacturing, healthcare, energy, electric power, aerospace, and other industries that perform industrial production and robotic control.

(3) ZVM

Embedded real-time virtualization allows multiple OSs to run on a single hardware platform at the same time while maintaining deterministic and time-critical performance. It equips typical embedded systems with hardware integration, system isolation, and brilliant flexibility, reliability, security, and scalability. There are several challenges when developing embedded real-time virtualization software. Questions include: how to ensure isolation and security between different guest OSs, especially those with different levels of criticality and credibility; how to share or allocate I/O devices among different guest OSs that require device emulation or passthrough; and how to deliver consistent latency and throughput when the RTOS is running as a guest OS.

Zephyr-based Virtual Machine (ZVM) is an embedded real-time VM. Developed on the Zephyr RTOS and hardware-assisted virtualization, it supports hybrid deployment and mixed-criticality scheduling of multiple runtimes, including Linux, RTOSs, and bare metal programs. ZVM uses architecture-level hardware-assisted virtualization and virtualization host extension (VHE). It implements guest OS isolation, device allocation, and interrupt handling, ensuring system security and real-time performance.

ZVM provides benefits in security isolation, device management, and system performance.

- Security isolation: The virtualization technology runs applications of different privileges, isolating guest OSs, especially those with different criticality levels, for security purposes. Further, virtual address spaces (VASs) and virtual devices are allocated to guest OSs to isolate VMs and ensure system security.
- Device management: Management programs that support device emulation and passthrough are used to share or allocate I/O devices between guest OSs. Devices that need to be exclusively occupied by the interrupt controller are allocated in full virtualization mode. Non-exclusive devices such as the

Universal Asynchronous Receiver/Transmitter (UART) are allocated in device passthrough mode.
- System performance: AArch64 virtualization extensions reduce the context overhead for processors, hardware-based twostage address translation reduces performance overhead for memory, and hardware-based interrupt injection reduces the context overhead and interrupt latency.

9.3.4 Edge

openEuler's key innovations in edge computing comprise DSoftBus and openEuler Edge.

(1) DSoftBus

Collaboration between edge devices includes the discovery, connection, networking, and transmission phases, though interconnection between edge devices has the following difficulties:

- Different types of devices: There is no unified solution to cover various hardware capabilities and supported connection modes, such as Wi-Fi, Bluetooth, and near field communication (NFC).
- Unstable and slow networking: It is difficult to automatically create and allocate network management roles between edge devices and maintain network stability after devices exit, power off, or experience a fault.
- Poor transmission: Data transmission performance cannot be guaranteed between edges and devices, especially for devices that have certain restrictions on power consumption.
- Difficult API adaptation: There are no unified APIs that mask differences in underlying hardware and networking, to allow one service process to be reused by different edge devices.

To develop a digital infrastructure OS and improve collaboration between devices and edges, openEuler marks an industry feat by applying DSoftBus technology to the server, edge, and embedded. DSoftBus provides a unified platform to enable collaboration and communication for distributed devices, achieving fast device discovery and efficient data transmission.

DSoftBus consists of four basic modules: discovery, networking, connection, and transmission, as shown in Fig. 9.14. For southbound devices, DSoftBus supports Wi-Fi, wired network, and Bluetooth connection, whereas for northbound distributed applications, it provides unified APIs that mask the underlying communication mechanism. DSoftBus depends on peripheral modules such as device authentication, inter-process communication (IPC), log, and system parameters (SNs). In embedded environments, such modules can be tailored or replaced to provide basic functions of DSoftBus, meet actual service scenarios, and extend DSoftBus capabilities.

9.3 Scenario Enablement

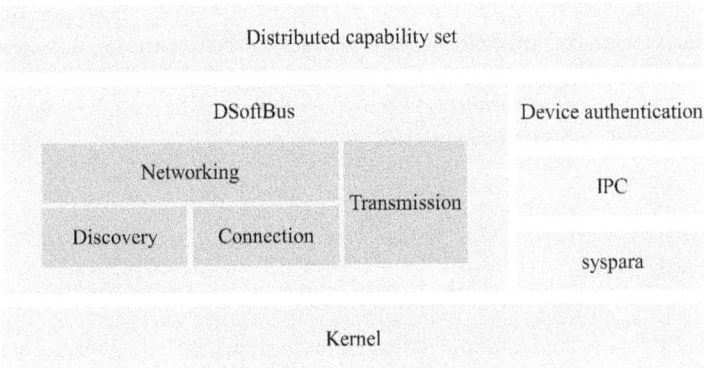

Fig. 9.14 Relationship between DSoftBus and external modules

DSoftBus is best suited for device discovery and interconnection between openEuler edge servers and common and OpenHarmony embedded devices. It provides unified APIs and protocol standards to enable self-connection, self-networking, and plug-and-play of multi-vendor, multi-type devices, implementing the peripheral access needed in industrial production lines and campus management.

(2) openEuler Edge

Edge computing is one of the top 10 technology trends and, as such, is dominating current and future business models. Consider how emerging fields like smart city, autonomous driving, and industrial Internet applications are generating huge data volumes that cannot be processed by centralized cloud computing. For example, IDC forecasts that in 2025, 48.6 ZB of data will be generated in China alone. There is a demand for high-speed, low-latency, and cost-efficient edge computing solutions.

openEuler Edge positioned as an edge computing edition for edge-cloud collaboration. It uses KubeEdge that delivers basic capabilities such as unified management and provisioning for edge and cloud applications, to streamline AI deployments and service collaboration for edge-cloud service discovery and traffic forwarding and offer enhanced data collaboration to improve southbound capabilities. KubeEdge is equipped with the following features:

- Edge-cloud management collaboration allows users to provision applications and manage southbound peripherals across edge and cloud.
- Improve service discovery and routing by deploying EdgeMesh Agent and EdgeMesh Server at the edge and on the cloud, respectively.
- Optimized southbound edge services using Device Mapper, which provides the peripheral profile and parsing mechanisms to help manage and control southbound peripherals and service streams. The southbound edge services are compatible with the EdgeX Foundry open-source ecosystem.

- Edge data services, including on-demand persistence of messages, data, and media streams, and data analysis and export operations.

  openEuler Edge supports diverse edge-cloud collaboration scenarios across sectors like energy, transportation, manufacturing, finance, healthcare, campuses, and autonomous systems.

9.4 Toolchains

openEuler has pioneered multiple toolchain innovations, including testing and environment setup tools for developers, high-performance compilers, and smart management tools for O&M teams. Let's examine some key innovative projects in this section.

9.4.1 GCC for openEuler

GCC is fundamental to the OS as it is the default compiler of the Linux kernel and the de facto standard of cross-platform compilers. Any change made to GCC may heavily impact upper-layer applications. Therefore, GCC developers must familiarize themselves with the knowledge needed, such as compilation principles while improving feature security and robustness.

The GCC for openEuler compiler is developed based on the open-source GCC. It has optimizations on C, C++, and Fortran languages and delivers enhanced features such as automatic feedback-directed optimization (FDO), memory optimization, and automatic vectorization, boosting performance for database and other applications. The compiler also features a plugin framework that enables general-purpose plugin functionality and optimizations for various computing power and microarchitectures. GCC for openEuler is compatible with a wide range of hardware platforms such as Kunpeng, Phytium, and Loongson, fully unleashing the computing power of these hardware platforms (Fig. 9.15).

GCC for openEuler has made major breakthroughs in the following aspects:

- Basic performance: Improves computing performance in general scenarios and also applies to multi-architecture computing.
- Compilation optimization: Integrates industry-leading FDO technologies to implement multi-modal FDO throughout the process, improving key applications such as databases in cloud-native applications.
- Chip enablement: Supports multi-architecture computing instruction sets and leverages computing advantages based on hardware systems such as memory to improve scenario-specific performance such as HPC.
- Plugin framework: Offers one set of plugins that is compatible with different compilation frameworks, streamlining the GCC and LLVM ecosystems.

9.4 Toolchains

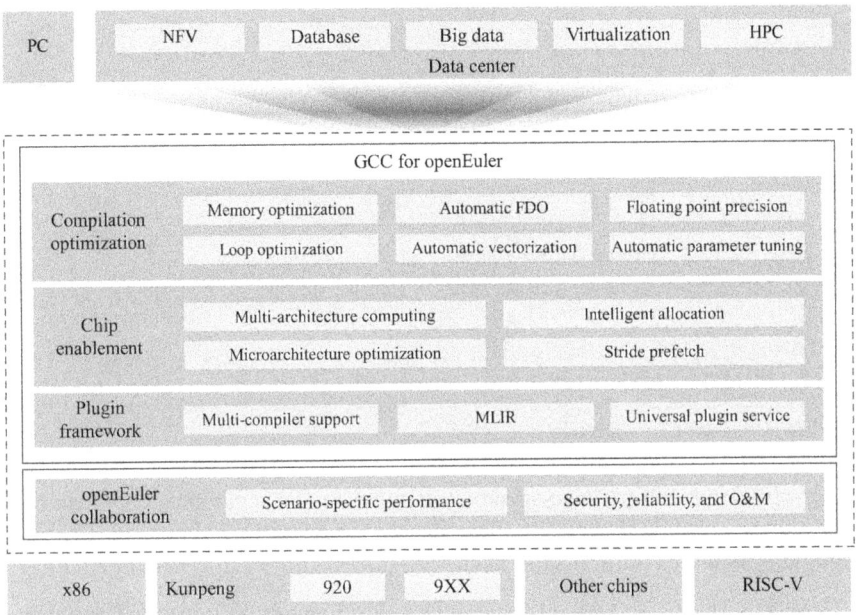

Fig. 9.15 GCC for openEuler architecture

GCC for openEuler is developed based on the open-source GCC. It is widely used in Linux environments such as openEuler and is perfect for databases, virtualization, and HPC. On the Arm platform, GCC for openEuler delivers 1.2 times higher basic performance of SPEC CPU 2017 than the open-source GCC, boosting the performance of the MySQL database by more than 15%.

9.4.2 Compass-CI

The increasing complexity of Linux poses a significant challenge for open-source developers due to the limited resources. With the numerous Linux distributions available, developers are looking at ways to quickly introduce, test, and verify the open-source software. Facing diverse application scenarios, limited resources can lead to numerous problems during subsequent use, which require further modifications. Reproducing these issues is challenging, resulting in considerable costs for preparing the environment and making rapid issue localization impractical.

Compass-CI is an integrated open-source CI platform that combines build and test systems, debug access, test analysis, comparison, and fault localization tools. It offers developers comprehensive services for upstream open-source projects hosted on GitHub, Gitee, and GitLab, including testing, system access, fault diagnosis, and historical data analysis. The platform automates pull request (PR) testing through

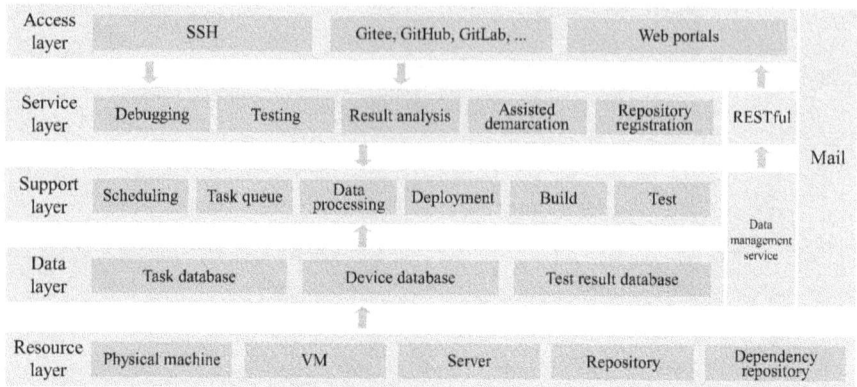

Fig. 9.16 Compass-CI architecture

build verification and package-specific test suites to create an open, complete task execution framework. Figure 9.16 illustrates the Compass-CI architecture. The platform delivers these core services:

- Testing services: To support local device development, Compass-CI automatically retrieves the code submitted to GitHub for testing and provides feedback on the test results.
- Debugging environment: Supports logging in to the debugging environment via SSH if issues are detected during testing.
- Test result analysis: Analyzes historical test results and provides web and CLI for developers, helping users identify factors that affect the outcomes.
- Assisted location: Automatically identifies error messages and triggers tests based on Git tree, pinpointing the changes that introduced the problematic modules.

Compass-CI actively tests thousands of open-source software projects to expose issues related to chips and OSs and automatically locates faults in real-time. Feedback is then sent to software developers, who can perform troubleshooting to ensure software quality. Compass-CI provides an excellent development experience for community developers, and contributes to a thriving open-source software ecosystem.

9.4.3 EulerLauncher

Mainstream desktops must ensure convenient and stable resources, such as VMs and containers, to deliver an excellent experience, especially for individuals and university students who have limited development resources. Common VM management platforms have many limitations. Many premium solutions require costly licenses, while free alternatives have significant drawbacks. VirtualBox users must download large ISO files and perform complete OS installations. Windows Subsystem for Linux (WSL) lacks openEuler kernel support, and most VM management software remains incompatible with Apple Silicon processors.

EulerLauncher is a developer toolkit developed by openEuler's technical operation and infrastructure teams that integrates virtualization technologies, such as LXD, Hyper-V, and virtualization framework, of mainstream desktops. It provides development resources such as VMs and container images for unified provisioning and management, delivering a consistent experience across Windows, macOS, and Linux. It simplifies the building of openEuler development environment on mainstream desktops.

EulerLauncher supports the x86_64 and AArch64 hardware architectures, including Apple silicon chips. It also supports virtual hardware acceleration capabilities for different platforms and provides high-performance development resources. EulerLauncher allows users to use community VMs, containers, daily build images, and other custom images to meet development requirements. Container images will be supported soon.

EulerLauncher simplifies openEuler development environment setup across Windows, macOS, and Linux desktops. It streamlines access to development tools and reduces complexity in configuring dependencies for community contributions.

9.4.4 A-Ops

In recent years, the implementation of cloud-native, serverless, and other technologies has made cloud infrastructure O&M increasingly challenging. Specifically, the characteristics of subhealth problems, such as intermittent emergence, short duration, multiple problem types, and wide involvement, have brought great challenges to cloud infrastructure troubleshooting. The subhealth fault diagnosis in Linux poses even higher requirements for capabilities such as observability, massive data management, and generalization of AI algorithms. In openEuler, the existing O&M methods fail to detect and locate subhealth problems promptly due to insufficient capabilities, including online continuous monitoring, refined observation from the application perspective, and AI automatic analysis based on full-stack observation data. The difficulties in diagnosing subhealth faults are as follows:

- Full-stack nonintrusive observation
- Continuous, refined, and low-resource consumption monitoring
- Adaptive exception detection and visualized fault deduction for various scenarios
- Patch management and application without affecting services

A-Ops is an OS-oriented O&M platform that provides intelligent O&M solutions covering data collection, health check, fault diagnosis, and fault rectification. The A-Ops project includes the following sub-projects: fault detection (gala), fault location (X-diagnosis), and defect rectification (Apollo) (Fig. 9.17).

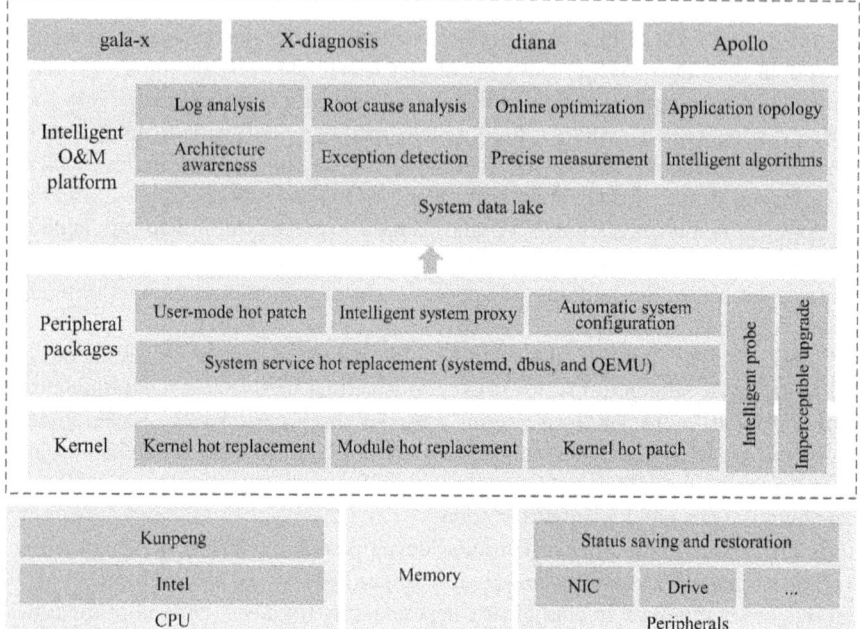

Fig. 9.17 A-Ops architecture

(1) gala

gala utilizes a nonintrusive observation technology based on the eBPF + Java agent and provides intelligent assistance to diagnose subhealth faults, such as performance jitter, increased error rate, and slow system response. gala has the following features:

- Online application performance jitter diagnosis: Online performance diagnosis for database applications, to identify issues including network issues (packet loss, retransmission, latency, and TCP zero window), I/O issues (slow drives and I/O performance deterioration), scheduling issues (high system CPU usage and deadlock), and memory issues (out of memory and leakage).
- System performance diagnosis: TCP and I/O performance jitter diagnosis in common scenarios.
- System risk inspection: Second-level inspection on kernel protocol stack packet loss, virtualization network packet loss, TCP exceptions, I/O latency, system call exceptions, resource leakage, Java virtual machine (JVM) exceptions, application remote procedure call (RPC) exceptions (including error rates and latency of eight common protocols), and hardware faults (uncorrectable errors and drive media errors).

9.4 Toolchains

- Full-stack I/O monitoring: Full-stack I/O monitoring for the SDS scenario, covering the process I/O and block layer I/O of the guest OS, virtual storage layer frontend I/O, and SDS backend I/O.
- Refined performance profiling: Online real-time continuous collection of performance statistics, including CPU performance, memory usage, resource usage, and system calls in high precision (collected every 10 ms) and multiple dimensions (covering system, process, container, and Pod) to generate flame and timeline graphs.
- Full-stack monitoring and diagnosis of Kubernetes Pods: Real-time topology of Pod cluster service flow, Pod performance monitoring, DNS monitoring, and SQL monitoring from the perspective of Kubernetes.

(2) X-diagnosis

X-diagnosis is an O&M suite for Linux, providing a fault location toolkit, system exception inspection, and enhanced ftrace functions.

- Various fault location tools: Locates faults related to the network, I/O, CPU scheduling, file system, and memory, such as, ICMP, TCP, and UDP packet loss and exceptions, read-only system files, and slow I/O.
- Abundant inspection items for system problems: Inspects network, CPU scheduling, drives, services, configurations, and system resources to detect exceptions such as incorrect DNS configurations, high CPU usage, full drive space, time changes, and excessive processes. Inspection results can be output to logs and interfaces.
- eftrace and ntrace for system debugging and analysis: eftrace is an enhanced version of ftrace that supports automatic calculation of structure offsets, making ftrace more accessible. ntrace can quickly output key parameters of the kprobe protocol stack function to assist in locating protocol stack process problems. What's more, the parameters can be filtered by IP address, port, and protocol.

(3) Apollo

The Apollo project is an intelligent patch management framework. It provides real-time inspection of CVEs and bugs and cold and hot patching, in order to implement automatic discovery and zero-interruption fixing.

- Patch service: Cold and hot patch subscription allows patches to be acquired online.
- Intelligent patch inspection: Supports CVE/bug inspection and notification based on single-node systems and clusters, hybrid management of cold and hot patches, and one-click repair and rollback, significantly reducing patch management costs.
- ragdoll: More than 50% of OS faults are caused by incorrect configurations. ragdoll can monitor system configurations to detect real-time configuration changes and quickly locate incorrect configurations.
- Configuration baseline: Configuration file types, including user-defined configuration files, can be added to the cluster baseline through plugins.

– Configuration source tracing: Automatically detects system configuration file changes in the backend and notifies the administrator of the changes through alarms and emails.
 – Configuration location: Quickly locates the cause of configuration file changes by monitoring file operations through eBPF.

A-Ops is applicable to openEuler and other Linux distributions in database, software-defined storage (SDS), virtualization, and cloud-native scenarios. A-Ops provides full-stack monitoring capabilities for users in industries such as finance, telecom, and Internet to diagnose subhealth faults, and promptly checks configuration errors caused by manual operations in cluster scenarios. In addition, A-Ops manages cold and hot patches in a unified manner to simplify patch management and directly provides hot patches for high-severity kernel CVEs to prevent the system from being restarted when dealing with the emergent kernel issues.

9.4.5 A-Tune

The development of hardware and software applications over the past few decades has coincided with a larger, more comprehensive Linux kernel. In openEuler, the sysctl command is used to configure kernel parameters and has over 1000 parameters (verified through **sysctl -a | wc -l**). A typical IT system covers the CPU, accelerator, NIC, compiler, OS, middleware framework, and upper-layer applications and uses 7000 parameters, most of which are default settings, which cannot tap into the full system performance.

Parameter tuning faces the following difficulties:

 – A large number of parameters that depend on each other.
 – Various types of upper-layer application systems require varying tuning of parameters.
 – Complex and diversified loads require the parameters to vary accordingly.

A-Tune is an AI-powered OS performance tuning engine, whose architecture is illustrated in Fig. 9.18. It uses AI technologies to enable the OS to learn services statuses, simplify IT system tuning, and deliver excellent performance.

A-Tune is in a client/server (C/S) architecture. **atune-adm** on the client is a command-line tool that communicates with the atuned daemon on the server through the gRPC protocol. atuned contains a frontend gRPC service layer (implemented in Go) and a backend service layer, the former of which manages optimization configurations and data and provides tuning services for external systems, including intelligent decision-making (Analysis) and automated tuning (Tuning). By contrast, the backend service layer is an HTTP service layer executed by Python that consists of the Model Plugin Interface (MPI)/Configurator Plugin Interface (CPI) and AI engine. The MPI/CPI discovers system configurations, and the AI engine provides machine learning capabilities for the upper layer, including

9.4 Toolchains

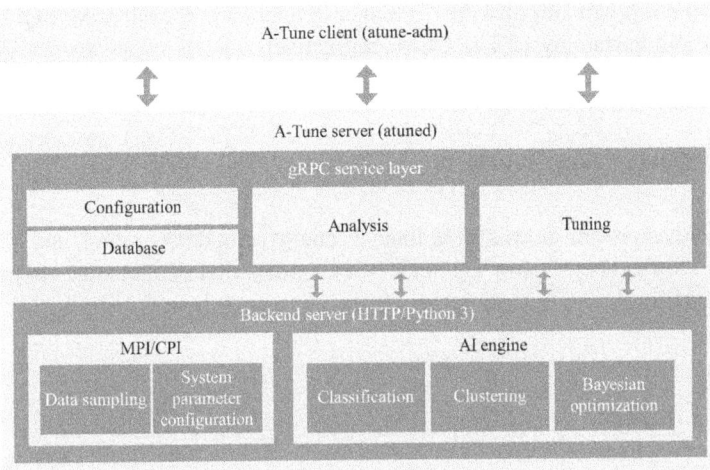

Fig. 9.18 A-Tune architecture

classification and clustering for model identification and Bayesian optimization for parameter search.

A-Tune delivers intelligent decision-making and automated tuning.

Intelligent decision-making is to sample system data and identify the corresponding loads using the clustering and classification algorithms of the AI engine, obtain the types of service loads, extract optimization configurations from the database, and select the optimal parameter values to fit each service load.

- Automatically selects key features and removes redundant ones for precise user profiling.
- Two-layer classification model accurately identifies service loads using the classification algorithm.
- Load awareness proactively identifies application load changes and implements adaptive tuning.

Automated tuning takes the configuration parameters and performance metrics of a system or application as its basis and iteratively refines them using the parameter search algorithm of the AI engine. This can obtain parameter configurations that deliver optimal performance.

- Automatically tunes core parameters to reduce search space and improve training efficiency.
- Allows users to select the optimal tuning algorithm based on the application scenario, parameter type, and performance requirements.
- Adds load features and optimal parameters to the knowledge base to improve future tuning operations.

A-Tune is widely used in Linux environments that handle big data, databases, middleware, and HPC workloads. Commonly used in industries such as finance and telecom, the software improves performance of applications such as MySQL, Redis, and BES middleware by 12% to 140%, respectively.

9.5 Industry Applications

openEuler has proven successful in finance, energy, cloud computing, and scientific research sectors [26]. Below are select case studies that demonstrate its practical implementation.

9.5.1 Finance

(1) A bank's distributed system for the core credit card service
A bank implemented a distributed system for the credit card core service powered by openEuler and Kunpeng. The system handles over 100 million daily transactions, achieving peak transaction rates beyond 6000 transactions per second (TPS).

The credit card system leads the industry across four core metrics, including customer volume and credit scale. Given the bank's extensive customer base, diverse user profiles, and complex operations, the system demands exceptional consistency and stability. Furthermore, the IT infrastructure must deliver elastic scalability and agile deployment while maintaining maximum availability and reliability. Like other financial institutions, The bank faces the challenge of securing critical infrastructure while balancing security requirements with digital transformation needs.

The bank deployed Kylin Advanced Server Operating System V10 with extensive optimization. They modernized their legacy infrastructure (x86+RHEL+Oracle) using GaussDB for data management and TaiShan 200 servers for computing power. This enabled seamless data migration from mainframe to distributed systems and established dual-track operations across Arm and x86 platforms. The architecture supports a microservice-based agile framework at the application layer and a distributed processing platform for high-volume data operations.

Key advantages include:

- Modernized credit card processing through Kunpeng processors and Kylin Advanced Server Operating System V10
- Reduced deployment costs, rapid business responsiveness, enhanced scalability, improved processing efficiency, and superior fault tolerance

- Comprehensive security through Kylin Advanced Server Operating System V10's native security framework, protecting kernel, service, and application layers

(2) A bank's core banking system modernization project
   As a leader in financial industry innovation, the bank addressed market requirements for enhanced security and technological independence by migrating its core service systems to a China-developed platform. The new full-stack platform needed to satisfy rigorous core banking requirements for performance, security, and functionality.
   The modernization project deployed Huawei Kunpeng servers for computing infrastructure and Kylin Advanced Server Operating System V10 for the OS. Built on Huawei's FusionCompute virtualization platform, the upgrade delivered these key advantages:

   - Complete technology stack independence: Deployed secure, innovative self-developed products to power headquarters-level core banking operations.
   - Enhanced security: Leveraged Kylin Advanced Server Operating System V10's broad compatibility with mainstream virtualization platforms, middleware, and databases, reducing network security infrastructure costs.

(3) A company's distributed core platform for securities trading
   The innovative distributed core platform for securities trading optimizes low-latency scenarios through deep integration between openEuler and Archforce Message Interconnection (AMI), a leading distributed low-latency messaging middleware. This integration maximizes end-to-end performance and delivers superior business outcomes.
   Built on openEuler+Kunpeng infrastructure and the Archforce Trading Platform (ATP), this solution serves Chinese securities companies by providing rapid, comprehensive exchange connectivity. The platform features high-throughput, minimal latency, loose coupling, high availability, scalability, and an open architecture with intuitive interfaces. The ATP leverages Kunpeng BoostKit alongside openEuler and BiSheng JDK to deliver high-performance, low-latency trading services.
   Key advantages include:

   - Performance optimization through openEuler and BiSheng JDK integration
   - Microsecond-level order processing for thousands of transactions using ultra-low latency computing and high-throughput capabilities of Kunpeng hardware, with 66% improved I/O bandwidth
   - Support for demanding low-latency and high-availability requirements from futures companies and banks, strengthening Chinese financial infrastructure through innovative distributed trading technology

9.5.2 Energy

(1) Power distribution automation system

The master station of the next-generation distribution automation system integrates large-scale operations and maintenance capabilities. It streamlines operational control and maintenance management while monitoring power distribution networks, reducing implementation costs and enhancing operational efficiency.

Built on Kylinsec Server OS V3 (openEuler-based) and Kunpeng architecture, the system meets Level 4 security requirements of GB/T 20272-2019 standards and incorporates trusted computing measurement. The platform centers on distribution network analysis modeling and operational data, delivering unified applications for control and maintenance while ensuring comprehensive network monitoring and state management.

Key advantages:

- IEC 61968 and IEC 61970 compliance enables seamless data exchange with the energy management system (EMS), production management system (PMS), and other systems.
- Comprehensive equipment monitoring creates closed-loop management across all distribution and dispatch operations.
- Advanced management capabilities span network control, maintenance, condition monitoring, and defect analysis, supporting strategic network planning with data-driven insights.

(2) D5000 smart grid dispatch control system

The OS migration initiative launched in 2009, prioritizing reliability, efficiency, and security. Kylinsec OS was chosen to run the dispatching system, offering enhanced security and accessibility. After completing the x86 platform migration, the project expanded to Huawei Kunpeng servers in 2019 using Kylinsec OS (powered by openEuler), modernizing the core dispatch infrastructure.

Key advantages:

- Successful migration from legacy systems to Kylinsec OS
- Optimized business operations on Kunpeng hardware with Kylin Security OS
- Thorough technical validation supporting future comprehensive D5000 infrastructure migration

9.5.3 Cloud Computing

(1) CTyun

CTyunOS, developed in response to OS industry trends and business requirements, is a proprietary openEuler-based OS. This platform advances the company's cloud and digital transformation strategy while driving digital economy growth. CTyunOS delivers cloud-optimized performance through enhanced core components—from CPU scheduling to process management. The system offers high performance, reliability, security, and scalability, enabling unified scheduling across varied workloads and computing architectures.

(2) Edge computing cloud service platform

The platform delivers cloud infrastructure for next-generation 5G applications in graphics computing, AI, HPC, and industry Internet, featuring supercomputing performance, minimal latency, and high-volume data transfer. While currently operating on CentOS and Ubuntu, the rapid business growth demands immediate solutions for OS reliability and maintenance challenges.

The openEuler community delivered customized servers and innovative FusionOS. This integrated hardware-software solution enhances platform reliability, maintenance, and performance. Using the one-stop migration platform, they streamlined the transition of both OS and service operations.

9.5.4 Scientific Research

A university developed an industrial robot OS on openEuler, delivering a turnkey robotics software platform.

The robot OS provides essential software infrastructure, meeting core requirements for real-time performance, security, and AI capabilities in robotics. The university's breakthrough in open architecture design focused on intelligent industrial robotics. Their research encompassed real-time kernels, communication protocols, motion control, and development tools, creating a comprehensive plug-and-play robotics platform. Figure 9.19 illustrates the OS architecture.

Key system advantages include:

- Based on the kernel of openEuler 24.03 LTS, supporting x86 with future Arm platform compatibility
- Real-time kernel performance with continuous operation, 10 μs maximum interrupt latency, supporting 1 ms EtherCAT communication cycles
- openEuler-based open embedded control architecture powers six-axis industrial robot arms with excellent extensibility and ease of use
- Proven reliability through successful industrial deployments

9.6 Summary

This chapter reviewed the core principles of the openEuler community, highlighting its innovative open-source projects in kernel development, fundamental capabilities, scenario enablement, and toolchains. It demonstrated successful implementations across finance, energy, cloud computing, and scientific research sectors,

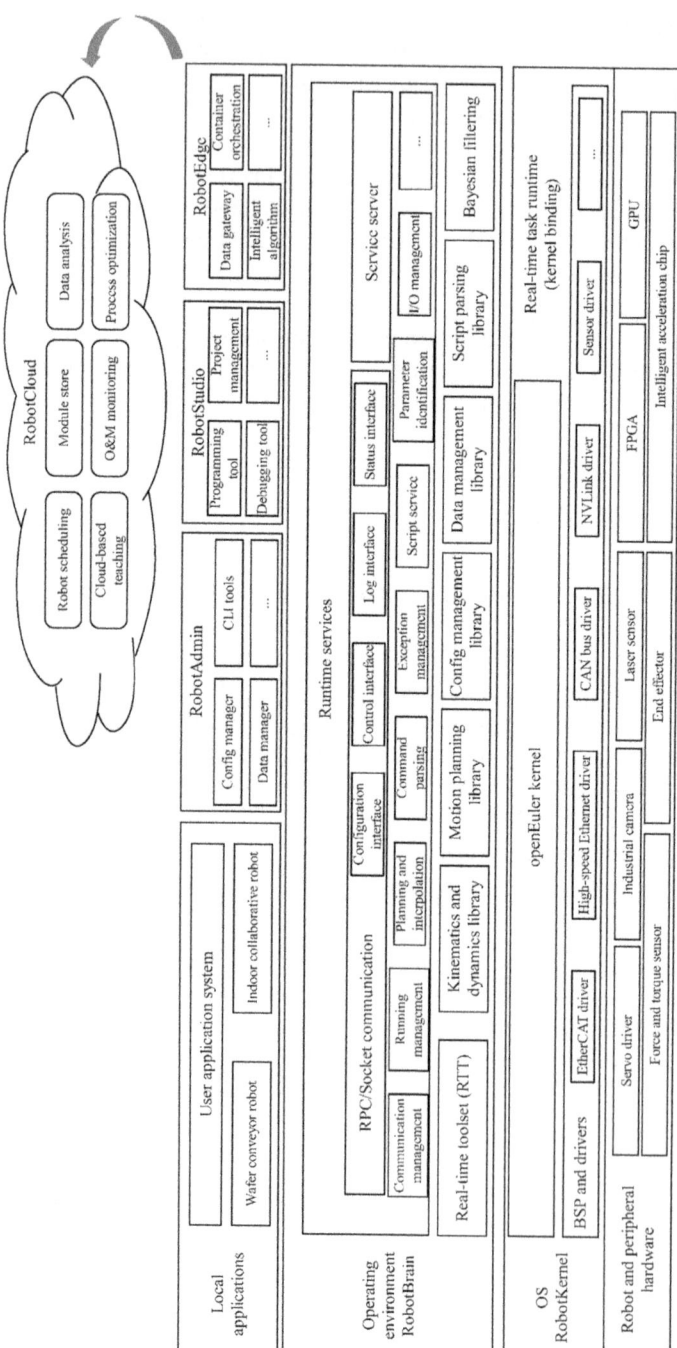

Fig. 9.19 Architecture of the robot basic software platform

9.6 Summary

showcasing the community's innovation strength, development momentum, and growth potential.

The chapter provides deeper insights into openEuler's significant contributions to the GNU/Linux community, particularly its value in addressing diverse computing needs across cloud, edge, and endpoint scenarios in the ICT era. As a China-initiated open-source community, openEuler's rapid growth has fostered a comprehensive upstream and downstream ecosystem, steadily expanding its global influence.

openEuler also offers migration tools like x2openEuler for enterprise application upgrades. These solutions address OS compatibility, assessment, adaptation, and implementation, enabling seamless and efficient system transitions. With continued community support, openEuler shows promise for wider industry adoption and sustained growth.

Reflection and Practice

1. Examine openEuler kernel source code to understand its kernel innovations.
2. Deploy network services using iSulad containers following community documentation.
3. Test kernel live upgrade in an openEuler VM.
4. Explore A-Tune optimization capabilities on Raspberry Pi.
5. Develop an openEuler upgrade strategy for typical use cases in your industry.

Open Access This chapter is licensed under the terms of the Creative Commons Attribution-NonCommercial-NoDerivatives 4.0 International License (http://creativecommons.org/licenses/by-nc-nd/4.0/), which permits any noncommercial use, sharing, distribution and reproduction in any medium or format, as long as you give appropriate credit to the original author(s) and the source, provide a link to the Creative Commons license and indicate if you modified the licensed material. You do not have permission under this license to share adapted material derived from this chapter or parts of it.

The images or other third party material in this chapter are included in the chapter's Creative Commons license, unless indicated otherwise in a credit line to the material. If material is not included in the chapter's Creative Commons license and your intended use is not permitted by statutory regulation or exceeds the permitted use, you will need to obtain permission directly from the copyright holder.

References

1. **Bryant** RE, O'Hallaron DR. *Computer systems: A programmer's perspective (3rd ed.)*. Pearson, 2015.
2. **Zhang YF et al.** *Integrating Artificial Intelligence into Operating Systems: A Survey on Techniques, Applications, and Future Directions*. Preprint at https://arxiv.org/abs/2407.14567.
3. **Kernighan BW.** *UNIX: A History and a Memoir* [M]. Independently published, 2019
4. **Tanenbaum AS, Bos H.** *Modern Operating Systems* (4th ed.) [M]. Beijing: China Machine Press, 2015.
5. **Raymond ES.** *The Cathedral & the Bazaar: Musings on Linux and Open Source by an Accidental Revolutionary [M]. O'Reilly Media*, 2015.
6. **Bovet DP, Cesati M.** *Understanding the Linux Kernel* (3rd ed.) [M]. Sebastopol: O'Reilly Media, 2005.
7. **openEuler Community.** *openEuler Open Source Community Technical White Paper* [R/OL]. https://www.openeuler.openatom.cn/en/showcase/technical-white-paper/. openEuler Community, 2024.
8. **Bach MJ.** *The Design of the UNIX Operating System* [M]. Prentice Hall, 1986.
9. **Silberschatz A, Galvin PB, Gagne G.** *Operating System Concepts* (10th ed.) [M]. Wiley, 2021.
10. **Stevens WR, Rago SA.** *Advanced Programming in the UNIX Environment* (3rd ed.) [M]. Addison-Wesley, 2013.
11. **Raymond ES.** *The Art of Unix Programming* [M]. Boston: Addison-Wesley, 2003.
12. **Robbins A.** *Bash Pocket Reference* (2nd ed.) [M]. O'Reilly Media, 2016.
13. **Barrett DJ, Silverman RE, Byernes RG.** *SSH, The Secure Shell: The Definitive Guide* (2nd ed.) [M]. O'Reilly Media, 2005.
14. **Nemeth E, Snyder G, Hein TR, et al.** *UNIX and Linux System Administration Handbook* (5th ed.) [M]. Addison-Wesley, 2017.
15. **Love R.** *Linux Kernel Development* (3rd ed) [M]. Addison-Wesley, 2010.
16. **Huawei Technologies Co., Ltd.** *Technical Analysis of Huawei openEuler Operating System* [M]. Beijing: Publishing House of Electronics Industry, 2024.
17. **Matloff N, Salzman PJ.** *The Linux Programming Interface: A Linux and UNIX System Programming Handbook* [M]. San Francisco: No Starch Press, 2010.
18. **Stallings W.** *Operating Systems: Internals and Design Principles (9th ed)* [M]. Pearson, 2017.
19. **Yaghmour K.** *Building Embedded Linux System Development* (2nd ed.) [M]. Sebastopol: O'Reilly Media, 2003.
20. **Huawei Technologies Co., Ltd.** *openEuler Real-Time Kernel Optimization Guide* [M]. Beijing: Publishing House of Electronics Industry, 2024.
21. **Huawei Technologies Co., Ltd.** *openEuler Industry Solutions White Paper* [M]. Beijing: Publishing House of Electronics Industry, 2024.

22. **openEuler Community.** *openEuler Developer Tools Technical Guide* [R/OL]. openEuler Community, 2024.
23. **Kozierok CM.** *The TCP/IP Guide: A Comprehensive, Illustrated Internet Protocols Reference* [M]. No Starch Press, 2005.
24. **Stevens W R, Fenner B, Rudoff AM.** *UNIX Network Programming, Vol. 1: The Sockets Networking API* (3rd ed.) [M]. Addison-Wesley, 2003.
25. **Liebeault L, Puriton M.** *Linux Firewalls: Attack Detection and Response with iptables, psad, and fwsnort* [M]. No Starch Press, 2007.
26. **Chen HB, Zeng QF, Xiong W.** *openEuler Core Technologies and Industry Applications* [M]. Beijing: Publishing House of Electronics Industry, 2023.

GPSR Compliance

The European Union's (EU) General Product Safety Regulation (GPSR) is a set of rules that requires consumer products to be safe and our obligations to ensure this.

If you have any concerns about our products, you can contact us on

ProductSafety@springernature.com

In case Publisher is established outside the EU, the EU authorized representative is:

Springer Nature Customer Service Center GmbH
Europaplatz 3
69115 Heidelberg, Germany